Media Education Assessment Handbook

LEA'S COMMUNICATION SERIES
Jennings Bryant/Dolf Zillmann, General Editors

Selected titles include:

Blanchard/Christ • Media Education and the Liberal Arts: A Blueprint for the New Professionalism

Christ • Assessing Communication Education: A Handbook for Media, Speech, and Theatre Educators

Dennis/Wartella • American Communication Research: The Remembered History

DeWerth-Pallmeyer • The Audience in the News

Gershon • The Transnational Media Corporation: Global Messages and Free Market Competition

Vorderer/Wulff/Friedrichsen • Suspense: Conceptualizations, Theoretical Analyses, and Empirical Explorations

For a complete list of other titles in LEA's Communication Series, please contact Lawrence Erlbaum Associates, Publishers.

Media Education Assessment Handbook

edited by
William G. Christ
Trinity University

 LAWRENCE ERLBAUM ASSOCIATES, PUBLISHERS
1997   Mahwah, New Jersey

Lawrence Erlbaum Associates, Inc., Publishers
10 Industrial Avenue
Mahwah, New Jersey 07430

Cover design by Jessica LaPlaca

Library of Congress Cataloging-in-Publication Data

Media education assessment handbook / edited by William G.
Christ.
        p.   cm.
    Includes bibliographical references and indexes.
    ISBN 0-8058-2185-6
    1. Mass   media—Study   and   teaching
(Higher)—Evaluation.   I.   Christ, William G.
    P91.3.M386   1996
    302.23'071'1—dc20   96-32296
                                         CIP

Books published by Lawrence Erlbaum Associates are printed
on acid-free paper and their bindings are chosen for strength
and durability.

Printed in the United States of America
10 9 8 7 6 5 4 3 2 1

This book is dedicated to
Bob and Marie Christ
Jack and Judy Robinson
and to the memory of
Helen and John Sloan

CONTENTS

PREFACE

Calls for assessment in higher education will continue to grow as state legislatures, regional accrediting bodies, parents, students, and administrators question colleges and universities about what they are teaching and what their students are learning. This book is conceived as an action handbook to be used by media faculty and administrators who are faced with developing assessment programs. What makes this book special is that it addresses not only how programs and courses should be assessed, but what should be assessed. It provides usable and useful information for addressing the assessment challenges facing diverse and complex media programs.

There are two parts to the book. Part I defines media education, provides case studies for three types of media programs, and establishes assessment strategies for distance learning. Christ's first chapter identifies how media education has been traditionally defined in terms of knowledge, skills, attitudes, and values. He makes a case for educators deciding on what should be assessed before determining how programs should be assessed. Christ, McCall, Rakow, and Blanchard discuss three different types of integrated communication/media programs and how these programs have developed assessment strategies based on their unique missions and objectives. Orlik and Donald present information on telecommunications (broadcasting) programs and show in one case how to develop an assessment strategy with limited resources and in another how to use portfolio assessment to transform a program for the better. VanSlyke Turk discusses assessment within a College of Journalism and Mass Communication and shows how the process of assessment has been important for developing agreed upon outcomes. Finally, Krendl, Warren, and Reid lay out how media is used in distance learning and suggest how distance learning programs should be evaluated.

In Part II of the book, the chapters emphasize media knowledge and skills assessment. Several chapters deal with material usually taught in "free-standing" courses like media writing, ethics, and reporting and editing. Others concentrate on cross-course functional areas like media literacy, critical thinking, and information gathering; areas of study like production and management; or, programs of study like public relations and advertising.

In the first chapter in this section, Wulff explains Alverno College's multi-year project to define what is meant by and what should be taught in terms of media literacy. Ruminski and Hanks explain how the key construct, "critical thinking," can be conceptualized and assessed in media programs. They argue that the term is widely used in the mission statements and objectives of media education programs but rarely measured. Finn, using research done in English writing assessment, acknowledges the difficulty in assessing media writing, but crafts specific assessment suggestions. Rubin and Rubin define information gathering in the Information Age and present key knowledge and skills areas that should be assessed. Haefner defines the study of ethics and recommends assessment procedures. Williams and Medoff conceptualize production broadly and argue for an assessment strategy that goes beyond measuring technical proficiency. Sherman identifies the problems with defining management within a media curriculum but provides definitions and an assessment instrument for management functions. Dickson addresses the formidable task of assessing reporting and editing and demonstrates how objectives and goals and measurement strategies can be successfully linked. Finally, Kruckeberg and Applegate take on public relations and advertising, respectively. Both chapters give overviews of the areas and suggest assessment strategies.

As was written before (Christ, 1994), "assessment is an integral part of what we do as teachers, researchers, and administrators. It can be formal or informal, systematic or haphazard, harmful or rewarding. At its best, assessment can have a transforming effect on education. At its worst, it can be used as an instrument to punish people and programs" (p. x).

At the very least, the hope is that this book will challenge media educators to reexamine what they are teaching in many key areas as they work to build stronger programs and develop better courses and educational experiences for their students.

ACKNOWLEDGMENTS

A book like this is truly a collaborative effort. First, there were those, like professors Sherwyn Morreale (University of Colorado-Colorado Springs), Willard Rowland, Jr. (University of Colorado-Boulder), and Margaret Haefner (Northern Illinois University), who suggested the need for more specific information on media education assessment. Their concerns helped spur interest in developing the framework for this book.

Second, there are the chapter authors. I would like to publicly acknowledge the hard work of the authors involved in this project. Working long distance with many different authors is not always easy, but these authors made my job a pleasure.

And, finally, there are the behind the scenes people. From Lawrence Erlbaum, I would like to thank Kathleen O'Malley who took this project as it was just beginning and saw it through with grace. I would also like to thank Teresa Horton, a terrific production/copy editor. And, finally, I would like to thank Joe Petrowski who handled the business side of the project and Hollis Heimbouch who believed enough in the book to do the initial signing.

From the Speech Communication Association, I would like to again thank Sherwyn Morreale, Chair of the Committee on Assessment and Testing, who shepherded the SCA review of the manuscript through her committee. Dr. Morreale continues to be a strong voice and advocate for communication assessment and a staunch believer in SCA's role in disseminating assessment information. I would like to thank Ted Spencer, SCA Publications Manager, for his support in this co-publication venture and the SCA reviewers, some whose names I do not know, who gave their time to this worthwhile project.

From Trinity University, I would like to thank my department and the administration for their support. Trinity is an intellectually stimulating place where educational issues dealing with teaching, courses, and curriculum are vigorously debated. A special thank you goes to Scott Sowards and James Bynum for their computer help and to Tiffany Wiescamp and Delia Rios for their secretarial support.

On a more personal note, I would like to thank the World Wide Web, Rick Bloomstrom, Mary Bloomstrom, Craig Childs, Ruth MacArthur, Steve Glass, Claudia Glass, Art Severance, Cathie Severance, John and Debbie Robinson, J. T. and Chris Robinson, Rob and Ginny Christ, Tom and Robin Christ, Nathan and Jonathan Christ, and, my true friend, Judith Anne Christ. Thank you one and all.

William G. Christ
San Antonio, Texas

I Programmatic Assessment

1

Defining Media Education

William G. Christ
Trinity University

Before media education programs develop assessment strategies, they would profit from reflecting on what they should be assessing. This chapter highlights five interrelated areas (skills, attitudes, affect, values, and knowledge) in terms of outcomes. An instrument (matrix) for assessing media programs is included.

INTRODUCTION

Assessing media education is a formidable task because both *assessment* and *media education* involve complex and controversial issues. Assessment, which can take place at the individual student, class, sequence, program, department or unit, and university levels, is questioned in terms of reliability, validity, relevance, and cost (for an overview of assessment see Banta, 1993; Rosenbaum, 1994). Media education, which has been challenged at a number of schools, finds faculty and administrators in the midst of soul-searching about how to clearly articulate its missions and purposes to a broader audience (see, e.g., Blanchard & Christ, 1993; Sholle & Denski, 1994).

Although a number of strategies for assessing media education have been identified including portfolios, capstone courses, exit exams, internships, exit interviews, advisory boards, and faculty and course evaluations (see Christ, 1994), the focus of this chapter is not on strategies but rather on *what* should be assessed. Before assessment strategies are implemented, there needs to be agreement about "the what" of media education. (Much of this chapter was first presented in Christ & McCall, 1994.)

Departments are under increasing national, state, and institutional pressure to get assessment procedures carried out quickly. But there is an obvious danger in rushing to implement assessment strategies before establishing what is essential in media education. In communication education in general, "the what" of assessment is often discussed in terms of skills, attitudes, affect, values, and knowledge (see Hay, 1994; Morreale, 1994). People assess students to determine what they know, think, feel, value, and can do. Here, it is suggested that one of the places to start with defining what students should learn from their media education is by identifying outcomes (Christ & Blanchard, 1994). Outcomes can be assessed in a variety of ways, but first they need to be developed and clearly articulated.

SKILLS

All successful courses teach skills. Whether media educators should teach skills or content, applied or theory courses deflects curricular debate from where it should be focused. Instead of being concerned with distracting dichotomies, media educators should be discussing how we can broaden our students' understanding through a variety of experiences including courses, symposia, practica, and internships. We should be debating which skills and content will help our students reach the *educational outcomes* of our universities and programs. Teaching television production, for example, without theory is as short-sighted as teaching mass media theory without demonstrating its importance and application to people's lives as citizens, consumers, and practitioners (see chap. 11).

Two broad, overlapping areas have developed in media education that have implications for skills assessment. The first can be categorized under the broad heading of *critical viewing skills*, visual or media literacy. The second can be categorized under *communication competencies*.

Media Literacy

Brown (1991), as part of his analysis of national and international media literacy or critical viewing skills projects, suggested 20 assessment criteria for judging the projects. Many of his criteria are useful as starting points for assessing media education programs in higher education (see pp. 50-53). Although skills criteria are presented here, it is important to note that the dichotomy between theory and skills is blurred in the media literacy projects where programs are expected to address the "development of cognitive and affective as well as behavioral skills and values—in a holistic setting" (Brown, 1991, p. 44). To have critical thinking skills requires theory. To understand theory requires critical thinking skills. Under "Cognition: Reasoning Skills," Brown (1991) listed two criteria (several of Brown's criteria are presented under the "attitudes . . . " and "knowledge" sections later in this chapter):

> Projects should train participants in the process of selective discrimination, analytical observation, and reasoned assessment based on factual data judged according to meaningful criteria. (p. 52)

> The process should begin with analysis and end with synthesis, merging learned factual data with receivers' experience of TV and their own value-system; it should stress inductive (heuristic, a posteriori) exploration from

which principles are drawn out, along with the deductive (a priori) process. (p. 52)

Stated more expansively, both criteria would do well as outcomes for liberal education in general. In fact, at their best, the outcomes of media education should be similar to the outcomes of a liberal education in general (see chap. 2). Media education programs should be in the business of working toward the liberal education of their students (see Blanchard & Christ, 1993; McCall, 1987). If, as Gerbner suggested, "liberal education today is the liberation of the individual from the necessity of drifting with the swift cultural tides of our time and the preparation for such self-direction as may be necessary and possible" (*Planning for curricular change*, 1987, p. 40), then media education outcomes need to reflect this.

After comparing the Association of American Colleges (AAC) outcomes (Association of American Colleges, 1985) and the Carnegie Foundation (Boyer, 1987) outcomes with a synthesized list of professional education outcomes, the Michigan Professional Preparation Network Report (*Strengthening the ties*, 1988) concluded that, although there are important differences, "one cannot fail to notice that the goals of professional program educators overlap with those traditionally espoused by liberal arts educators" (p. 26). (For an analysis of these three reports see Blanchard & Christ, 1993.) Of the 10 outcomes they cite, the critical thinking competency is one that closely reflects the two skills articulated by Brown.

Critical thinking is described as an ability "to examine issues rationally, logically, and coherently" (*Strengthening the ties,* 1988, p. 23)–a universally recognized and desired liberal outcome. Professional graduates seek to possess "a repertoire of thinking strategies that will enable them to acquire, evaluate, and synthesize information and knowledge" (p. 23). Professionals also are taught "to develop analytical skills to make decisions in both familiar and unfamiliar circumstances" (p. 23). This competence has also been identified as a key component of the "National Education Goals: 5.5" (U.S. Department of Education, 1991). All classes should have critical thinking as a major outcome (see chap. 7). However, it is particularly possible to demonstrate the "process of selective discrimination, analytical observation, and reasoned assessment based on factual data" (Brown, 1991, p. 52) in reporting and editing, media research, and audience and textual analysis classes, to name a few.

Brown's two criteria acknowledge the *process* of education. They suggest that developing critical viewing skills takes time and that there are stages that students go through when learning critical thinking. Stating that "the process should begin with analysis and end with synthesis, merging learned factual data with receivers' experience" suggests that information is important, but not an end in itself. This criterion suggests that media education programs need to take into account not only teaching styles and curricular concerns, but learning styles (see Grow, 1991; Potter, 1994) and students' development. If one goal of media education is to educate our students to become "self-directed" (Grow, 1991), then we need to be aware of where our students are and what it will take to meet different student needs. It suggests different methods may be called for to reach different kinds of students and even that different students should be assessed in different ways.   (Under Section 504 of the Rehabilitation Act of 1973 [nondiscrimination on the basis of handicap] and the Individuals with Disabilities Act [IDEA] students can *demand* modified programs for their disabilities. The act, which applies to students through age 21, suggests that although *what* gets assessed may be the same across students, *how* it is assessed or the method that information is presented may need to be modified depending on the students' disabilities.)

As a result of teaching critical thinking skills, "individual and institutional efforts strive not only to guide adults and children to better, more reasonable, more responsive and active analysis and reaction to media experience, but also at times to influence the media managers and governmental bodies responsible for overseeing them" (Brown, 1991, p. 13). This suggests that those with critical thinking skills have the ability as citizens and practitioners to challenge the status quo.

Competency

Whereas media literacy suggests a critical thinking or evaluation function as its main objective or outcome, the competency movement suggests an ability to perform specific communication skills as a *fundamental outcome*. This is not to say that competency should be limited to skills. For example, McCroskey (1984) wrote, "Communication competence requires not only the ability to perform adequately certain communication behaviors, it also requires an understanding of those behaviors and the cognitive ability to make choices among behaviors" (p. 264). However, where the critical viewing skills perspective stresses analysis, synthesis, and evaluation from an "audience" or "receivership" point of view (see Ploghoft & Anderson, 1981,1982), the competency literature tends to stress a "use," "behavioral," or "practitioner" orientation. Although it is possible to identify numerous media education competencies, the discussions in the Oregon Reports (*Planning for curricular change*, 1984, 1987) and the Michigan Professional Preparation Network Report (*Strengthening the ties*, 1988) are instructive. Under its "Elements of a Model Curriculum" heading, the Oregon Report (*Planning for curricular change*, 1987) suggested five kinds of communication competencies:

1. General literacy–competence in the use of the language.
2. Visual literacy–understanding of visual grammar and phenomena in mass communication.
3. Computer literacy–especially a general knowledge and "hands-on" skills in computer applications in journalism/mass communication fields.
4. Information gathering–ability to systematically gather and use information for various sources pertinent to mass communication.
5. Media writing capability–ability to produce media messages in two or more areas (news, advertising, etc.). (p. 51)

Notice these are broad-based competencies. They do not say information gathering for newspapers or information gathering for television. Information gathering is as important for the newspaper writer as it is for the academic writer; as important for the television and film student and Internet user as it is for the history student. Computer literacy is as vital to the public relations, advertising, or integrated marketing practitioner as it is to the PhD student. Visual literacy is as important to the magazine designer as it is to the conscientious citizen who is trying to understand if the graphs presented in the media accurately reflect the facts (see Tufte, 1983, 1990).

To these competencies of the Oregon Report, we add the competency of "production literacy or competence." Although perhaps implied by the Oregon Report in its visual literacy category, or later in its "professional modules" section, an argument for production competency needs to be made more explicitly. Using McCroskey's (1984, p. 264) communication competency statement as a model: "Production competency requires not only the ability to perform adequately certain production behaviors, it also requires an understanding of those behaviors and the cognitive ability to make choices among behaviors." If people learn by doing, then people should learn about the persuasive force of television, for example, by doing television production (see Christ, 1975; Lawson, 1983; Williams, 1992). It makes explicit what might be considered implicit in the Oregon Report, that knowing how to tell stories with and through various media is an important outcome for media education (see Gerbner, 1984).

We would expect these competencies to be taught in a variety of ways. For some programs, visual literacy might be a function of one or more courses that stress the interpretation of media messages. For others, the computer literacy competency might be "farmed out" to a computer science department or taught through a self-paced, instructional computer program. Information gathering might be a separate course that looks at all the different methods and techniques now being used by people, including reporters, to access and use information (see chap. 9). Media writing might take the form of one all-encompassing core course, or be presented in two or more courses under different sequences (see chap. 8). And, finally, general literacy, which is an ongoing process, could be assessed through portfolios that require students to keep and reflect on past essays, tests, and term reports (see chaps. 3 & 6).

The Michigan Professional Preparation Network Report (*Strengthening the ties*, 1988) suggested a number of competencies that either overlap with or expand on the Oregon Report communication competencies:

Communication competence is the ability to "read, write, speak, and listen and use these processes effectively to acquire, develop, and convey ideas and information" (p. 23). These skills, which are highly valued by most professional curricula, are also fundamental to desired liberal outcomes of "informed citizenship and continued personal growth" (p. 23). It has been identified as a key component of the "National Education Goals: 5.5" (U.S. Department of Education, 1991). We would expect this competency to be an outcome of most courses and be accentuated in classes like writing, production, research, and design.

Contextual competence is "an understanding of the societal context (environment)" (p. 23) in which one is living and working. The liberally educated person needs "to comprehend the complex interdependence between the profession and society" (p. 23). Likewise, "the ability to make judgments in light of historic, social, economic, scientific, and political realities is demanded of the professional as well as the citizen" (p. 23). Although presented as a competence, this also would apply to several of the knowledge areas that are presented later. Classes that would stress this outcome would include those that discuss the economic, technological, legal, philosophical, and ethical aspects, critical and cultural studies, mass media and society, and international and intercultural communication.

Adaptive competence is anticipating, adapting to, and promoting "changes important to a profession's societal purpose and professional's role. A liberally educated person has an enhanced capacity to adapt to and anticipate changes in society" (p. 24). This would be an appropriate outcome for classes in management, technological, legal and historical aspects, and communication theory.

These competencies, when stated as outcomes and if agreed on, give a focus for course and curricular development and assessment.

ATTITUDES, AFFECT, AND VALUES

The media literacy and competency literature implies or directly addresses attitudes, affect, and values.

Media Literacy

Brown (1991) wrote that "media education–just as education in general–ought not limit itself to one form of critical assessment of mass media. In fact, criteria themselves–including ethical concepts–are to be questioned and analyzed" (p. 47). In other words, an outcome of media education should be a critical attitude toward media and the criteria presented by media and its critics. Sholle and Denski (1994, p. 157) have suggested that this critical attitude should also apply to media education itself where students are invited to be part of debates over "pedagogy."

A second, more implied, outcome is that students should *feel* comfortable evaluating media and be respected for who they are and what they think. Media education programs "must respect the individuality of the person, including their distinctive upbringing by family, so they are not merely indoctrinated with others' opinions and conclusions" (Brown, 1991, p. 51). Brown (1991) went so far as to suggest that "values presented should not be narrowly instructional nor exclusively moralistic in a single tradition. But the project <<education>> ought not be valueless; it should relate to broad humanistic heritage and Judeo-Christian ethic"(p. 51). The importance of Brown's comments is that they counter the perception that assessment takes away both academic and student individuality and freedom. Assessment should not become a monolithic, bureaucratic, lock-step educational process where the joy, spontaneity, creativity, and diversity of experiences is turned into a series of pat worksheets, exercises, or tests that never connect with people's lives, concerns, and felt needs. Rather, assessment should be set up to *guarantee* flexibility, integration, and humanness. By stressing outcomes, and valuing people and the process of education, a liberal education can be achieved in a variety of ways.

Competency

The Michigan Professional Preparation Network Report (*Strengthening the ties,* 1988) identified six competencies/outcomes that can be included in the area of attitudes, affect, and values: aesthetic sensibility, professional identity, professional ethics, leadership capacity, scholarly concern for improvement, and motivation of continued learning.

Aesthetic sensibility is similar to the visual literacy category of the Oregon Report, but a sensibility goes beyond a skills level of knowing how images and sound are put together in the creation of video, audio, or film. It implies attitudes, values, and the ability to articulate an emotional response to media. It is "an enhanced aesthetic awareness of arts and human behavior for both personal enrichment and application in the enhancement of the profession" (*Strengthening the ties,* 1988, p. 23). We would expect this outcome in classes that deal with historical, philosophical, and ethical aspects, production, internships, and media criticism.

Professional identity requires the identifying, understanding, and critiquing of a profession's values, ethos, and expectations. It is an important function of professional programs. Whether or not we want students to identify with practitioners in the "real world" (i.e., be assessed as if they were reporters or writers for a local newscast) depends on a program's mission. As has been suggested, assessment and the criteria of assessment, including how we measure achievement, needs to be understood, debated, and critiqued as carefully as we expect our students to critique other kinds of information. That being said, the question remains: How can media educators develop and assess programs "for improving the knowledge, skills, and values of the profession" (*Strengthening the ties,* 1988, p. 24)? Professional identity "both parallels and supplements the liberal education goal of developing a sense of personal identity" (*Strengthening the ties,* 1988, p. 24). Class areas where this outcome would be especially appropriate would include management, practica, internships, ethics, and media philosophy and theory courses.

Professional ethics is an important outcome of media education. In her chapter on public speaking, Morreale (1994) suggested that students, "will be able to demonstrate a defined personal set of ethics and values, in regard to communication competency, that takes responsibility for self, other(s), and relationship(s) and outcome(s) in communication interaction(s)" (p. 234). Here, the suggestion is that "the graduate understands and accepts the ethics of the profession as standards that guide professional behavior. Liberally educated individuals are expected to have developed value systems and ethical standards that guide their behavior" (*Strengthening the ties,* 1988, p. 24). The thrust of this outcome should not be to accept the professional ethics at face value, but rather to see if and how they are applied and to understand and grapple with the relationship between personal and professional ethics. Class areas for this outcome would include media philosophy, ethics, and internships.

Leadership capacity is an attitude or approach to or potential for leadership that should be developed in our media education programs. It is exhibiting "the capacity to contribute as a productive member of the profession and assuming appropriate leadership roles. . . . Not only does leadership imply both functional and status obligations, it requires the intelligent, humane application of knowledge and skills" (*Strengthening the ties*, 1988, p. 25). Class areas would include management, internships, organizational and small group communication.

Scholarly concern for improvement is not often discussed at the undergraduate level. It is, in fact, central to what undergraduates should be doing, for "the heart of the intellectual process is attention to a spirit of inquiry, critical analysis or logical thinking" (*Strengthening the ties*, 1988, p. 25). Students should recognize "the need to increase knowledge and to advance the profession" (*Strengthening the ties*, 1988, p. 25). What it means, of course, to "advance the profession" is, and should be, open to spirited debate. All classes can work toward this outcome although it is typically formalized in communication theory, studies, and research courses.

Motivation of continued learning is perhaps the most important attitudinal outcome for students. The exploring and expanding of "personal, civic and professional knowledge and skills throughout a lifetime" (*Strengthening the ties*, 1988, p. 25) are both appropriate liberal and professional outcomes. As Bell (1968, p. 8) suggested, "All knowledge . . . is liberal (that is, it enlarges and liberates the mind) when it is committed to continuing inquiry." This, like several of the other outcomes, might be considered more a function of how a course is taught rather than what information is in the course itself.

KNOWLEDGE

As a developing field, the approach to and scope of mass communication is still being debated (see Ball-Rokeach, 1985; Beniger, 1993; Benson, 1985, Berger & Chaffee, 1988; Blanchard & Christ, 1993; Davis & Jasinski, 1993; Delia, 1987; Dervin & Voigt, 1984; Gumpertz & Cathart, 1982; Hawkins, Wiemann, & Pingree, 1988; Lang & Lang, 1993; Levy & Gurevitch, 1993; Lowenstein & Merrill, 1990; Newcomb, 1993; Rogers & Chaffee, 1983; Rosengren, 1993; Rowland, 1993; Shepherd, 1993; Wiemann, Hawkins, & Pingree, 1988). Even with this diversity of opinion, it has been suggested that there are approaches to or areas of knowledge that the educated media student should understand.

Media Literacy

As we wrote earlier, Brown (1991) suggested that critical viewing skills must educate "participants in the process of selective discrimination, analytical observation, and reasoned assessment based on factual data judged according to meaningful criteria" (p. 52) and that "the process should begin with analysis and end with synthesis, merging learned factual data with receivers' experience of TV and their own value-system; it should stress inductive (heuristic, a posteriori) exploration from which principles are drawn out, along with the deductive (a priori) process" (p. 52). In order to do this, he wrote that participants should learn about the "social context and impact" (p. 50) of television, and "social, political, aesthetic, and ethical perspectives, including 'administrative' analysis (functional, utilitarian, experimental, behavioral–atomistic) and 'critical' analysis (judgmental, value-oriented, sociopolitical, cultural, interpretive–holistic)" (p. 50).

In other words, understanding or knowledge comes from both information (e.g., social, political, aesthetic, etc.), and how that information is analyzed (e.g., administrative and critical). This idea is very important, because there are times when the assessment of knowledge becomes simply tests of facts. The use of exit exams by some media programs has demonstrated the problem of simply testing for facts (see Eastman, 1994). What is important is being able to understand facts within a variety of contexts and in terms of their multiple interpretations.

Understanding this connection between facts and interpretation informs this discussion about knowledge and brings us back to the issue of what areas of knowledge should be analyzed.

Areas

The Oregon Report (*Planning for curricular change*, 1987, pp. 51-52) suggested eight conceptual knowledge areas for media education. Using Brown's (1991) argument, each of these areas should be analyzed from both an administrative and critical perspective. Because the administrative approach "(functional, utilitarian, experimental, behavioral–atomistic)" has been more common in textbooks than the critical approach "(judgmental, value-oriented, sociopolitical, cultural, interpretive–holistic)" (Brown, 1991, p. 50), suggestions about what might be included in the critical approach will be added to each knowledge area.

"1. Mass communication and society–a conceptual map of the literature and documented experience that explains the relationship of media to society and to individuals in society" (*Planning for curricular change*, 1987, p. 52). From a critical or cultural studies approach, this might include discussions of communication industries, messages and content, and audiences and publics (see Rowland, 1993). Dennis and DeFleur (1991) suggested a creative way of reaching the general student with this course:

> They suggested key topical essays that make linkages between the media and other key disciplines. They suggested, for example, "Noam Chomsky and Why is He Saying Such Awful Things About the Media" to illustrate media ethics from a linguistic viewpoint. Or, "How children Learn to Buy" to discuss advertising from a consumer behavior, sociological, and psychological perspective. Or, "The Novel as Quantitative Research" to emphasize mass communication research from an English and American literature orientation. (Blanchard & Christ, 1993, p. 106)

"2. The history of mass communication–an overview both in conceptual and chronological terms of the history and traditions of mass communication, its institutions, people, enterprises" with a strongly suggested "link between this study and intellectual, cultural and economic history" (*Planning for curricular change*, 1987, p. 52). From a critical perspective this might include "exposure to the diverse work on the rise and characteristics of electronic culture by Harold Adams Innis (1950, 1951), Walter Ong (1967), or Joshua Meyrowitz (1985)" (Rowland, 1993, p. 214).

"3. The economics of mass communication–an examination of the economic basis of communication activity in the United States and internationally; . . . should be tied to instruction in economic history and microeconomics as well as political economy" (*Planning for curricular change*, 1987, p. 52). From a critical perspective, Rowland (1993) suggested that "none should have failed to consider the critiques of conventional marketplace communication economies and the analysis of the global culture and information industries represented by Dallas Smythe (1957, 1982) or Nicholas Garnham (1990), or of media ownership patterns of Ben Bagdikian (1990)" (p. 214).

"4. The philosophy and ethics of mass communication–a cultural review of the values on which modern mass communication is based, its aims and objectives. Theories of ethics and standards of professional practice are to be included. A tie with university courses in philosophy and ethics is essential." (*Planning for curricular change*, 1987, p. 83). From a critical perspective this would include "critiques of the mythology of technology as value-free and politically neutral in Clifford Christians (1989) or Arnold Pacey (1983)" (Rowland, 1993, p. 214).

"5. The legal and regulatory aspects of mass communication–the system of freedom of expression under which media operate. The communication law regime of the United States in a comparative context; regulatory patterns as they affect the media; and a 'survival kit' for the communicator who needs self-protection" (*Planning for curricular change*, 1987, p. 52). Here, Rowland (1993) suggested that students "should know Robert Horwitz's (1989) interpretation of the contradictions in telecommunications deregulation and Daniel Schiller's (1982) and Jeremy Tunstall's (1986) analyses of the interactions among the government, broadcast, telephone, and computer industries, and the implications of such sources. . ." (pp. 214-215).

"6. The technology of mass communication–the relationship of mass communication to developments in communication technology; communication concerns. A contemporary portrait of new technology and its meaning for society and individuals" (*Planning for curricular change*, 1987, p. 52). As Rowland (1993) wrote:

> Telecommunications must never become the simple creature of the technologies it studies and the institutions that promote it. It is incumbent upon telecommunications to foster a critical social understanding of the changing information technologies, to understand not only their promises but also their limitations and vulnerabilities, and to apply that same

interpretive disciplines on the parallel problems in telecommunications policy. (p. 215)

If nothing else, media programs should be studying and teaching the impact of communication technology on such issues as culture (Meehan, 1986; Thomas & Evans, 1990), texts (Banks & Tankel, 1990; Barker, 1985), politics (Armstrong, 1988; Gandy & Simmons, 1986; Lull, 1991), community (Larson & Oravec, 1987), family (Lull, 1988), privacy (Diebold, 1973; Donner, 1981), and identity (Rakow, 1988).

"7. Communication theory–an advanced examination of the various theories of mass communication and the differing scholarly traditions from which they evolve. Scholarly methods and connections to other fields that study media and communication should be emphasized" (*Planning for curricular change*, 1987, p. 52). Brown (1991) suggested four areas for study:

- Media effects on audiences (impact mediation).
- Uses and gratifications (goal attainment; interaction with media).
- Cultural understanding (symbol-systems reflecting society).
- Visual literacy (media techniques, grammar, syntax) (p. 52).

The strength of Brown's recommendation is its call for a broad approach to media study that challenges the inclination of some to indoctrinate students and presents only one viewpoint or form of analysis.

Although not discussed in the Oregon Report, it might be particularly useful, especially at the graduate level, to study two other areas. First, it would be important to discuss the history of the field of communication study itself in order to understand how theories, perspectives, and orientations have affected the study of the discipline (see Delia, 1987). Second, as Sholle and Denski (1994) suggested, there needs to be a debate over teaching and curriculum. Too many PhD students end up with strong research skills (Boyer's [1990] scholarship of discovery) without ever grappling with the scholarships of teaching, integration, or application.

"8. International communication systems– . . . the need for international understanding, including the literature of international mass communication, development communication and comparative mass communication should be included" (*Planning for curricular change*, 1987, p. 52). Again, from a critical perspective, Rowland (1993) suggested that students "should all have some clear understanding of the arguments wrapped up in the debates about dependency and the New World Information order (International Commission, 1980; Roach, 1987) and how Anthony Smith (1980) approached the problems of technological convergence and global information policies" (p. 215).

Within each competency area or attitude or knowledge area there will be disagreement about how and what should be taught. This is only right. The position taken here is that from a pedagogical, practical, academic, and practitioner point of view that a broad-based, integrative, cross-media approach is the best (see Blanchard & Christ, 1993; McCall, 1990, 1991). Starting with these knowledge areas as a way of determining *what* knowledge should be taught in media education programs is prudent and defensible.

WHERE TO START?

As faculty develop their mission statements and anticipated outcomes, we would suggest that they inventory their strengths and weaknesses and focus on what is taught in their core courses.

Outcomes Inventory

As was suggested in the beginning of the chapter, there are many strategies for assessing media education. Before a strategy is implemented, units may find the chart in the Appendix helpful for identifying strengths and weaknesses of their programs (see Arnold, 1994). Filling out the chart can also suggest program imbalances. Units with limited resources may decide to emphasize their strengths based on their own mission and anticipated outcomes. A cautionary note needs to be raised, however, for those units who are not making efforts to position themselves centrally within their universities. Programs that see themselves as serving their majors in what we would consider a limited fashion (e.g., stressing practitioner competencies at the expense of conceptual knowledge areas) need to broaden their appeal and reach out to the general student (see Blanchard & Christ, 1993).

Core Courses

In 1985, Blanchard and Christ asked, "Most of us would argue that our discipline is basic. But can we explain what is basic about our discipline?" (pp. 28-29). Is it skills? Attitudes? Affect? Values? Knowledge? As has been suggested, skills, attitudes, affect, values, and knowledge are, if not taught, at least learned in most classes. Whether the teaching is purposeful and explicit is another matter (see chap. 2).

One place to look for what is basic in the discipline is in core courses. It might seem more doable to start with a program's skills courses, even if they are outside the core, because these tend to be behavioral and might be considered easier to evaluate. Although skills are an important part of what we do, concentrating on them first, unless they are part of the core, can give the wrong impression about what we are about. As Rosenbaum (1994) argued, "The temptation to stress skills at the expense of broader, more comprehensive objectives should be resisted. Assessment should not force us to compromise our expansive visions for the field and our students" (p. 26). Core courses are good places to start when developing outcomes because programs can define what they feel is basic about media studies through their core courses and thus send a clear signal to colleagues about who and what we are.

Although many programs offer core courses, there does not appear to be overwhelming agreement about what these core courses should be. In a survey conducted for the Broadcast Education Association's Courses and Curricula

Division, Warner and Liu (1990) noted that more than half of the 128 schools that responded to the survey offered "between two and six core courses" (p. 7). They continued with the observation that "there was great diversity in the number of required core courses and no pattern in the data was discerned" (p. 7) although 35% of the schools required Introduction to Media.

If it is true that core courses are supposed to introduce students to the field and provide them with an overview of the discipline, then we might expect that all eight conceptual knowledge areas mentioned by the Oregon Report should be addressed in the core. If not only specific content areas are important, but the approaches used to study this content are important as well, then articulating the outcomes for core courses will require faculty to consider whether content is presented in the context of an administrative, critical, or integrative approach. Assessment of course content, where the administrative approach is implemented, will necessarily be different from the assessment of course content with a critical or integrated approach. Our recommendation is clearly in favor of an integrated approach in the core.

SUMMARY

At its worst, assessment can be used as an excuse to punish programs and people. At its best, it can be a powerful aid in our attempts to develop a coherent and complete quality education. Although there are different strategies for assessing media education, the bottom line is that ultimately we need to decide *what* it is we are trying to assess. As you move through the book, you discover a variety of methods and ideas being tried or suggested. Chapters 2, 3, and 4 explain outcome assessment strategies for three different kinds of programs: integrated, telecommunications, and journalism and mass communication programs. Chapter 5 looks at how media have been used for distance learning and how it can be assessed. Chapters 6 through 15 discuss assessment in 10 different knowledge and skills areas. It is our hope that the ideas presented here will help facilitate needed dialogue about the complex, challenging, and changing world of media education and media education assessment.

APPENDIX: ASSESSMENT INVENTORY FORM
FOR MEDIA EDUCATION PROGRAMS:

What Is Being Assessed?	Where In Program?	How Assessed?	How Can We Improve?
Skills			
Critical Thinking (reasoning skills)			
General Literacy and Communication Competence			
Visual Literacy			
Computer Literacy			
Information Gathering			
Media Writing Capability			
Production Competency			
Contextual Competency			
Adaptive Competency			
Attitudes, Affect, and Values			
Aesthetic Sensibility			
Professional Identity			
Professional Ethics			
Leadership Capacity			
Scholarly Concern for Improvement			
Motivation of Continued Learning			

What Is Being Assessed?	Where In Program?	How Assessed?	How Can We Improve?
Knowledge areas			
Mass Communication and Society Administrative and Critical Analysis			
Historical Aspects Administrative and Critical Analysis			
Economic Aspects Administrative and Critical Analysis			
Philosophical and Ethical Aspects Administrative and Critical Analysis			
Legal and Regulatory Aspects Administrative and Critical Analysis			
Technological Aspects Administrative and Critical Analysis			
Communication Theory Administrative and Critical Analysis			
International Communication Systems Administrative and Critical Analysis			

REFERENCES

Armstrong, R. (1988). *The next hurrah: The communication revolution in American politics.* New York: Murrow.

Arnold, J. (1994). Using accreditation for assessment. In W. G. Christ (Ed.), *Assessing communication education: A handbook for media, speech, and theatre educators* (pp. 333-349). Hillsdale, NJ: Lawrence Erlbaum Associates.

Association of American Colleges (AAC). (1985, February). *Integrity in the college curriculum: A report to the academic community.* Washington, DC: Author.

Bagdikian, B. (1990). *The media monopoly* (3rd ed.). Boston: Beacon Press.

Ball-Rokeach, S. (1985, October). *Convention speaker questions communication theory, structure* (Keynote speech, convention of the Association for Education in Journalism and Mass Communication). *AEJMC News,* pp. 1, 4-5.

Banks, J., & Tankel, J. D. (1990). Science fiction: Technology in prime time television. *Critical Studies in Mass Communication, 7*(1), 24-36.

Banta, T. W., & Associates (1993). *Making a difference. Outcomes of a decade of assessment in higher education.* San Francisco: Jossey-Bass.

Barker, D. (1985). Television production techniques as communication. *Critical Studies in Mass Communication, 2*(3), 234-246.

Bell, D. (1968). *The reforming of general education: The Columbia College experience in its national setting.* New York: Columbia University Press.

Beniger, J. R. (1993). Communication—embrace the subject, not the field. *Journal of Communication, 43*(3), 18-25.

Benson, T. W. (1985). *Speech communication in the 20th century.* Carbondale: Southern Illinois University Press.

Berger, C. R., & Chaffee, S. H. (1988). On bridging the communication gap. *Human Communication Research, 15*(2), 311-318.

Blanchard, R. O., & Christ, W. G. (1985). In search of the unit core: Commonalities in curricula. *Journalism Educator, 40*(3), 28-33.

Blanchard, R. O., & Christ, W. G. (1993). *Media education and the liberal arts: A blueprint for the New Professionalism.* Hillsdale, NJ: Lawrence Erlbaum Associates.

Boyer, E. L. (1990). *Scholarship reconsidered: Priorities of the professorate.* New York: The Carnegie Foundation for the Advancement of Teaching.

Boyer, E. L. (1987). *College: The undergraduate experience in America.* The Carnegie Foundation for the Advancement of Teaching. New York: Harper & Row.

Brown, J. A. (1991). *Television "critical viewing skills" education: Major media literacy projects in the United States and selected countries.* Hillsdale, NJ: Lawrence Erlbaum Associates.

Christ, W. G. (1975). *The role of television production in a liberal arts education.* Unpublished master's thesis, University of Wisconsin at Madison.

Christ, W. G. (Ed.). (1994). *Assessing communication education: A handbook for media, speech, and theatre educators.* Hillsdale, NJ: Lawrence Erlbaum Associates.

Christ, W. G., & Blanchard, R. O. (1994). Mission statements, outcomes, and the New Liberal Arts. In W. G. Christ (Ed.), *Assessing communication education: A handbook for media, speech, and theatre educators* (pp. 31-55). Hillsdale, NJ: Lawrence Erlbaum Associates.

Christ, W. G., & McCall, J. (1994). Assessing "the what" of media education. In S. Morreale & M. Brooks (Eds.), *1994 SCA Summer Conference Proceedings and*

Prepared Remarks (pp. 477-493). Annandale, VA: Speech Communication Association.

Christians, C. (1989). A theory of normative technology. In E. F. Byrne & J. C. Pitt (Eds.), *Technological transformation: Contextual and conceptual implications* (pp. 123-140). Dordrecht, The Netherlands: Kluwer Academic.

Davis, D. K., & Jasinski, J. (1993). Beyond the culture wars: An agenda for research on communication. *Journal of Communication, 43*(3), 141-149.

Delia, J. G. (1987). Communication research: A history. In C. R. Berger & S. H. Chaffee (Eds.), *Handbook of communication science* (pp. 20-98). Newbury Park, CA: Sage.

Dennis, E. E., & DeFleur, M. L. (1991). A linchpin concept: Media studies and the rest of the curriculum. *Journalism Educator, 46*(2), 78-80.

Dervin, B., & Voigt, M. J. (Eds.). (1984). *Progress in the communication sciences.* Norwood, NJ: Ablex.

Diebold, J. (1973). *The world of the computer.* New York: Random House.

Donner, F. J. (1981). *The age of surveillance: The aims and methods of America's political intelligence system.* New York: Vintage.

Eastman, S. (1994). Exit exams and the media major. In W. G. Christ (Ed.), *Assessing communication education: A handbook for media, speech, and theatre educators* (pp. 351-382). Hillsdale, NJ: Lawrence Erlbaum Associates.

Gandy, O. H., & Simmons, C. E. (1986). Technology, privacy and the democratic process. *Critical Studies in Mass Communication, 3*(2), 155-168.

Garnham, N. (1990). *Capitalism and communication: Global culture and the economics of information.* London: Sage.

Gerbner, G. (1984). Defining the field of communication. *ACA Bulletin, (48)*, 10-11.

Grow, G. (1991). Higher-order skills for professional practice and self-direction. *Journalism Educator, 45*(4), 56-65.

Gumpertz, G., & Cathart, E. (Eds.). (1982). *Inter/media: Interpersonal communication in a media world.* New York: Oxford University Press.

Hawkins, R. P., Wiemann, J. M., & Pingree, S. (Eds.). (1988). *Advancing communication science: Merging mass and interpersonal processes.* Newbury Park, CA: Sage.

Hay, E. A. (1994). Interpersonal communication. In W. G. Christ (Ed.), *Assessing communication education: A handbook for media, speech, and theatre educators* (pp. 237-256). Hillsdale, NJ: Lawrence Erlbaum Associates.

Horwitz, R. B. (1989). *The irony of regulatory reform: The deregulation of American telecommunications.* New York: Oxford University Press.

Innis, H. A. (1950). *Empire and communications.* Oxford, England: Clarendon.

Innis, H. A. (1951). *The bias of communication.* Toronto: University of Toronto Press.

International Commission for the Study of Communication Problems. (1980). *Many voices, one world: Communication and society, today and tomorrow: Toward a new, more just and more efficient world information and communication order.* London: K. Page.

Lang, K., & Lang, G. E. (1993). Perspectives on communication. *Journal of Communication, 43*(3), 92-99.

Larson, C. U., & Oravec, C. (1987). "A prairie home companion" and the fabrication of community. *Critical Studies in Mass Communication, 4*(3), 221-244.

Lawson, R. G. (1983). Liberal arts and television production training: The University of Wisconsin Program. *Feedback, 25*(1), 6-10.

Levy, M. R., & Gurevitch, M. (Eds.). (1993). The future of the field I. *Journal of Communication, 43*(3).

Lowenstein, R. L., & Merrill, J. (1990). *Macromedia.* New York: Longman.

Lull, J. (1988). The family and television in world cultures. In J. Lull (Ed.), *World families watch television* (pp. 9-21). London: Routledge.

Lull, J. (1991). *China turned on (television, reform, and resistance).* London: Routledge.

McCall, J. M. (1987). Liberal arts focus provides training for media centers. *Journalism Educator, 41*(2), 13, 15-18.

McCall, J. M. (1990). Beyond the Roper report. *Feedback, 31*(3), 9-10.

McCall, J. M. (1991, April). *Mass communication education belongs to the university.* Paper presented at the annual conference of the Broadcast Education Association, Las Vegas, NV.

McCroskey, J. C. (1984). Communication competence: The elusive construct. In R. N. Bostrom (Ed.), *Competence in communication: A multidisciplinary approach* (pp. 259-268), Beverly Hills, CA: Sage.

Meehan, E. R. (1986). Conceptualizing culture as commodity: The problem of television. *Critical Studies in Mass Communication, 3*(4), 448-457.

Meyrowitz, J. (1985). *No sense of place.* New York: Oxford University Press.

Morreale, S. P. (1994). Public speaking. In W. G. Christ (Ed.), *Assessing communication education: A handbook for media, speech, and theatre educators* (pp. 219-236). Hillsdale, NJ: Lawrence Erlbaum Associates.

Newcomb, H. (1993). Target practice: A Batesonian "Field" guide for communication studies, *Journal of Communication, 43*(3), 127-132.

Ong, W. J. (1967). *Presence of the word.* New Haven, CT: Yale University Press.

Pacey, A. (1983). *The culture of technology.* Cambridge, MA: MIT Press.

Planning for curricular change in journalism education (2nd ed.) (1987). (Project on the Future of Journalism and Mass Communication Education). Eugene, OR: The Oregon Report.

Ploghoft, M. E., & Anderson, J. A. (Eds.). (1981). *Education for the television age.* Athens, OH: Cooperative Center for Social Science Education.

Ploghoft, M. E., & Anderson, J. A. (1982). *Teaching critical television viewing skills: An integrated approach.* Springfield, IL: Thomas.

Potter, W. J. (1994). In W. G. Christ (Ed.), *Assessing communication education: A handbook for media, speech, and theatre educators* (pp. 89-112). Hillsdale, NJ: Lawrence Erlbaum Associates.

Rakow, L. F. (1988). Gendered technology, gendered practice. *Critical Studies in Mass Communication, 5*(1), 57-70.

Roach, C. (1987). The U.S. position on the New World Information and Communication Order. *Journal of Communication, 37*(4), 36-51.

Rogers, E. M., & Chaffee, S. H. (1983). Communication as an academic discipline: A dialogue. Journal of Communication, 33(3), 23-25.

Rosenbaum, J. (1994). Assessment: An overview. In W. G. Christ (Ed.), *Assessing communication education: A handbook for media, speech, and theatre educators* (pp. 3-29). Hillsdale, NJ: Lawrence Erlbaum Associates.

Rosengren, K. E. (1993). From field to frog ponds. *Journal of Communication, 43*(3), 6-17.

Rowland, W. D., Jr. (1993). The traditions of communication research and their implications for telecommunications study. *Journal of Communication, 43*(3), 207-217.

Schiller, D. (1982). Telematics and government. Norwood, NJ: Ablex.

Shepherd, G. (1993). Building a discipline of communication. *Journal of Communication, 43*(3), 83-91.

Sholle, D., & Denski, S. (1994). *Media education and the (re)production of culture.* Westport, CT: Bergin & Garvey.

Smith, A. (1980). *The geopolitics of information: How western culture dominates the world.* Boston: Faber & Faber.

Smythe, D. W. (1957). *The structure and policy of electronic communication.* Urbana: University of Illinois Press.

Smythe, D. W. (1982). Radio: Deregulation and the relation of the private and public specters. *Journal of Communication, 32*(1), 192-200.

Strengthening the ties that bind: ntegrating undergraduate liberal and professional study (Report of the Professional Preparation Network). (1988). Ann Arbor: The Regents of the University of Michigan.

Thomas, S., & Evans, W. (Eds.). (1990). *Communication and culture: Language, performance, technology and media.* Norwood, NJ: Ablex.

Tufte, E. R. (1983). *The visual display of quantitative information.* Cheshire, CT: Graphics Press.

Tufte, E. R. (1990). *Envisioning information.* Cheshire, CT: Graphics Press.

Tunstall, J. (1986). *Communication deregulation: The unleashing of America's communication.* Oxford, England: Basil Blackwell.

U.S. Department of Education. (1991). *America 2000: An education strategy.* Washington, DC: Author.

Warner, C., & Liu, Y. (1990). Broadcast curriculum profile (A freeze-frame look at what BEA members offer students). *Feedback, 31*(3), 6-7.

Wiemann, J. M., Hawkins, R. P., & Pingree, S. (1988). Fragmentation in the field— and the movement toward integration in communication science. *Human Communication Research, 15*(2), 304-310.

Williams, S. (1992, February). *Innovative techniques for moving toward conceptually based television production courses.* Paper presented at the spring meeting of the Texas Association of Broadcast Educators, Dallas.

2

Integrated Communication Programs

William G. Christ
Trinity University
Jeffrey M. McCall
DePauw University
Lana Rakow
University of North Dakota
Robert O. Blanchard
Trinity University

Assessing media education is seen as beginning with a strong vision that emphasizes the mission and outcomes of a program. This chapter presents three case studies of integrated communication programs. The first is Trinity University's Department of Communication, which has integrated media subspecialties. DePauw University's Department of Communication Arts and Sciences integrates speech, theatre, and media courses. The University of North Dakota's School of Communication integrates its courses around three key issues: community, information, and technology.

INTRODUCTION

Picture a scenario where a campus visitor asks a university dean or president, "Where is the study of communication conducted on your campus"? How many different places might this visitor be sent? On all too many campuses, sadly, this visitor would have to be sent in several directions. The person might be sent to the department of rhetoric, or interpersonal communication, or theatre, or maybe to a school of mass communication (which might have separate departments of broadcasting, journalism, film, advertising, etc.). In order to give the visitor a proper direction, we might need to ask whether he or she is interested in how to produce or analyze public messages; in what channels are the messages delivered; or, are the messages analyzed in an artistic or social scientific framework? The point becomes clear. The study of communication is fragmented on many campuses and virtually every facet has been stuck into a department structure all its own.   This trend could reflect increasing sophistication and specialization. But more likely to administrators, colleagues in other fields, and even external publics, this untidy nature of the communication discipline is viewed negatively. They see a discipline with no vision, cohesion, or common purpose.

THE CASE FOR INTEGRATED COMMUNICATION STUDY

Regardless of the historical reasons for having the communication discipline fragmented in different geographic and political worlds of a university, a case should now be made to integrate the discipline (see Blanchard & Christ, 1993; McCall, 1994a; Rakow, 1995; Wartella, 1994). An integrated communication program allows for the study and performance of human messages across a variety of contexts grappling with central issues. Thus, an integrated program can comfortably include subdivisions within the discipline such as traditional speech communication and rhetoric, interpersonal and organizational communication, mass media study, and others.

This chapter is divided into three main sections. The first section describes the program and assessment procedures at Trinity University where the department has integrated mass media subspecialties. The second describes the Department of Communication Arts and Sciences at DePauw University where speech, media, and theatre are integrated under one major. The third explains the University of North Dakota's School of Communication, which has integrated its program around three key issues: community, information, and technology. Each section shows how student and programmatic assessment can and should be linked to the underlying philosophy of a program.

TRINITY UNIVERSITY'S
DEPARTMENT OF COMMUNICATION

Due to state, regional, national, and/or professional accreditation requirements, most programs have been going through periodic assessment for years. What makes systematic assessment more urgent now is the implicit or explicit linkage of assessment to funding levels and other resources. Academic units are routinely expected to justify their programs in terms that administrators can defend and parents and legislatures can understand.

Christ and Blanchard (1994, p. 32) argued that, "Program assessment . . . should begin with a determination of 'where are we and where are we going?'" At Trinity, "where we are" can be seen partly as an outgrowth of the faculty trying to address the question, "Most of us would argue that our discipline is basic. But can we explain what is basic about our discipline?" (Blanchard & Christ, 1985, pp. 28-29). This question, due to retrenchment, cutbacks, and calls for accountability over the last 10 years, has had particular relevance for media communication programs.

At Trinity, where we are now has been the product of a long, interesting, sometimes contentious, intellectual and pragmatic curricular journey, as faculty members fought for their ideas about what was important and central to media education (see Blanchard & Christ, 1993; Christ & McCall, 1994). Presently, the department's curriculum is organized around three levels of courses. The first level is core courses that are required of all majors. The second level of courses is within three functional areas: theory and studies, production and writing, and management. Majors are required to take one course in each area under the guidance of their advisor. The third level of courses is electives. These are open to the major to develop as much specialization as needed or wanted in a particular area. Besides the three levels of classes, students are required to take 18 hours in a coherent "minor" outside the major.

As the department developed and implemented its mission and anticipated outcomes, the core courses became the main battlefield for clashing viewpoints. If core courses are truly core to the discipline and represented the intellectual frame that oriented students to the field, then they should be the most important courses a department can offer. To understand how Trinity University's Department of Communication assesses its program begins with understanding the Department's core.

Core

There are three interrelated decisions a unit works through when developing a core. The first is to decide whether or not to have a core (cf. Moore, 1990; Quenzel, 1990). The second is to agree on the kind of core (e.g., universal or sequence; practitioner or studies). The third is to agree on the courses, experiences, and outcomes of the core. (Much of this material on the core can be found in Blanchard & Christ, 1993.)

Should Programs Have Core Courses?   Core courses are one way a department puts its resources where its philosophy is, of demonstrating what is basic, what is fundamental about the discipline (see Blanchard & Christ, 1990; Brock, 1996; Dates, 1990; Finney, 1990; Fletcher, 1990; McCall, 1990). In a survey conducted by an Association for Education in Journalism and Mass Communication Curriculum Task Force, Dickson (1995, p. 43) reported that "the larger the institution, the fewer hours in the JMC core." Warner and Liu (1990) noted, in a Broadcast Education Association survey, "More than half of the 128 schools offer between two and six core courses. This situation is especially the case with large schools (67.3% required between two and six core courses). There was great diversity in the number of required core courses and no pattern in the data was discerned" (p. 7). They found that 35% of the schools required Introduction to Media whereas over 25% required Media Law & Regulation and Introduction to Broadcasting.

If the goal of media education is to provide students with an integrated perspective, a foundation from which to understand media's impact from a variety of viewpoints, then an argument can be made for a *universal* core, a core required of all communication students. Universal cores are not the norm. Programs that have core courses tend to have sequence core courses that are required of all students in a particular sequence, but not universal cores that are required of all students in the major (Blanchard & Christ, 1993). And, even when programs require courses of all their majors, they may not be integrative in the sense meant here because the majors are limited to only one area of mass communication like, for example, telecommunications.

In 1982, Trinity University had four sequences (journalism, broadcast journalism, radio production, and television production) with three courses in a universal core: Introduction to Mass Media, Communications Law, and a Senior Research Seminar. When the sequences were eliminated in favor of a broader, more foundational approach in 1984, a fourth course was added: Aesthetics of Sight, Sound, and Motion. A year later a fifth course, Media Writing, was added to the core. The department was committed to teaching all five courses from a broad, cross-media perspective that broke down the barriers between the traditional, sequential print and electronic media focuses.

In 1990, the department eliminated the Senior Research Seminar from the core and replaced it with a U.S. Media Systems class that had been developed for the General Education program of the university. The Senior Research Seminar had not "been working," and it was felt that the new course would better prepare students for the changes taking place in the industries that many of them wanted to enter. During this time a debate developed over keeping Communication Law in the core. Some on the faculty felt that Communication Law represented a "journalism" perspective and that a broader communication perspective would not dictate that *all* students take the course. Those in favor of Communication Law won the argument.

A Practitioner Versus Studies Core. Writing is a strong part of most journalism programs. Few would argue against the importance of writing. However, having writing be important and requiring a core writing course are two different things. Writing classes are labor intensive and requiring them in a core is a major commitment of any program. Although for several years a writing course was required in the department's core, it was eventually eliminated for two philosophical and two practical reasons.

Philosophically, there were those who argued that writing should be a vital part of all college courses and need not be required in a core. Second, it was argued that a broad media writing course ended up stressing format over content and gave students the wrong "message" about writing. Practically, it was suggested that the university already had two required writing courses and that a third "filter" course on the Departmental level was not necessary. Finally, it was argued that eliminating writing would release faculty to teach more studies/theory classes.

Based on the mission of the university and the department and the strong background of the students who enrolled, the department, in 1991, changed from the five core courses to three as it moved closer to a "studies" perspective. Both media writing and communication law were eliminated as required core courses and the aesthetics course was reworked as a message theory class (see Christ & Williams, 1993). Writing, production, and management courses were still offered in the department but were not required as part of the core.

This change, the elimination of media writing and communication law, was hotly contested. In many ways it continued to be a battle between those with a journalism background and those with a broader communication theory background. The shift would not have taken place had not new faculty with broad communication interests been hired between 1982 and 1990. Implementing curricular change can be very traumatic for a department's faculty. New hires are often both the leaven and the catalyst for change.

Assessing Core Outcomes. Inherently linked with whether or not a unit develops a universal or sequence, practitioner or a studies core are the anticipated outcomes of the core. Do units want to be known because they teach skills, concepts, or some combination of both? The department's position at Trinity was that the students were best served with courses that provided conceptual maps to the field. In the core, we had moved away from industry-oriented courses like media writing to broader studies courses. (For a different perspective on what should be the characteristics of a core, see Sholle & Denski, 1994, pp. 164-169.)

The Core Today. In 1994-1995, the department made another change to the composition of the core. There had been a growing uneasiness with the upper division core course that addressed new technologies within a U.S. Media Systems approach. Students complained that it was not that much different than the Introduction to Mass Media class. The chairperson of the Department of Speech and Drama, Brooks Hill, came to the department with the idea of including a course in Human Communication Theory (Fundamentals of Human Communication) in the core of the Communication program. The department saw Professor Hill's recommendation as an ideal way of balancing out the department's core offerings and bringing the two departments closer together. The mass media class would teach industry structures stressing power relationships within the U.S. capitalist system. The media messages class would teach textual analysis and the human communication theory class would teach communication theory. The department voted for the new three-course core in late 1994. To summarize, the core now stressed theory, industry structure, and textual analysis.

Mission Statements

Mission statements are *political* documents that can be used to clarify or obfuscate a unit's reality (see Christ, 1995; Christ & Blanchard, 1994; Christ & Hynes, 1996). They can accurately mirror a vision or simply reflect a pipe dream. As Galvin (1992, p. 24) suggested, developing goals and mission statements can produce at least four benefits:

1. Clarifying organizational purpose.
2. Forcing consensus on what is important.
3. Creating a framework against which to evaluate resource allocation.
4. Reinforcing a commitment to student learning.

In a survey distributed to 258 member schools of the Broadcast Education Association (BEA), less than 56% of the large schools' departments and less than 50% of the medium and small schools' departments were identified as having mission statements (Warner & Liu, 1990). This is a surprisingly small number.

Apparently, many schools do not think explicit mission statements are needed. Departments might argue that they have implicit mission statements or that no matter what the mission statement says, it is the faculty, courses, and facilities that define a program. Although there is merit in this argument, explicit mission statements should be at the center of curricular discussion. Well-conceived mission statements provide vision and focus for a department, establishing a rationale for the allocation of limited resources. If taken seriously, they can be guideposts that remind people where a program has been and firmly point to the direction it is going.

The changes to Trinity's core courses can be seen within the context of its mission and anticipated outcomes. In 1982, with the first changes in the core, the overriding concern was on integration of the program. This concern can be seen in the part of the 1985 mission statement written as part of a self-study accreditation process for the Southern Association of Colleges and Schools:

> The Department of Communication's role in professional education is not solely to train people for a profession or for the current demands of professional practice. It is also to prepare students for membership in the public and for a future that transcends the limitations of both the traditional academic disciplines and contemporary institutional and professional practices and policies. (Trinity University Department of Communication, 1985, p. 2)

For the department, this mission represented a large step forward. The idea of moving beyond professional training was accepted but not embraced by some of the faculty. The idea of integrating traditional and contemporary disciplines and transcending the limited perspectives of both was relatively new (see *Planning for curricular change*, 1984). In 1994, the Department, in preparation for the 1995 Self-Study for the Accreditation by the Southern Association of Colleges and Schools, decided to rework the department's mission statement. A committee was convened and after a semester of work the department agreed on the following mission statement:

> The Department of Communication mission is to provide educational experiences that enrich and integrate the liberal arts and sciences with communication and media studies and practices. To this end, the Department of Communication seeks to educate students 1) to become communicators and media sense-makers, for themselves, their clients, and

their communities; 2) to understand their obligations as citizens within global and cultural communication contexts shaped by media; and 3) to recognize their opportunities and responsibilities as ethical, self-directed practitioners within changing information, technological, and communication environments. (Trinity University Department of Communication, 1995, no page number given)

In other words, the mission addressed students as future sense-makers, citizens, and practitioners. It provided a framework for defining where we were and where we thought we would be going. Of course, for the self-study, this mission statement was not enough. What also was needed was a method for assessing outcomes.

Assessing Outcomes

Assessment is the acid test for media educators. It requires a paradigm shift in a department's thinking. Instead of thinking what do faculty want to teach, the question becomes what do we want students to learn. The question "What is basic about the discipline?" becomes "What is basic about the discipline that students should learn and how do we know they have learned it?"

Programmatic assessment is like foul-tasting medicine: Not many enjoy the process of taking it, but most acknowledge that if it is done conscientiously it can help strengthen a program. There are not many faculty who would willingly give up teaching preparation or research time to devote their energies to the large time-consuming commitment needed to do assessment well. That is why the current assessment movement seems to be fueled more by outside forces and real fears of retrenchment, program elimination, and accreditation guidelines than by faculty needs (see Allison, 1994; Eshelman, 1991; Footlick, Wingert, & Leonard, 1990; Rosenbaum, 1994; Sykes, 1988; Wycliff, 1990).

Christ and Blanchard (1994) suggested that faculty should address both off- and on- campus challenges when approaching assessment. Off campus, they identified three challenges facing communication educators: (a) historical changes facing all colleges and universities in the mid-1990s; (b) emergent and converging communication technologies; and (c) the philosophical and theoretical ferment within the communication discipline. Because these "forces" are documented elsewhere, they are not discussed here (see Blanchard & Christ, 1993, chaps. 1-3, and Christ & Blanchard, 1994, pp. 31-55).

On campus, Christ and Blanchard (1994) suggested that faculty should ask (a) How and where their program fits within the university–how its mission, and curriculum fit the mission, philosophy, and anticipated outcomes of the university? (b) What outcomes are appropriate for the program as a whole? (c) What courses are appropriate to match those outcomes? (d) What outcomes are appropriate within a course?

The Department of Communication felt that it had addressed these questions in a number of ways. Level 1 was addressed, for example, with the department making a strong bid to become more central to the university by, among other things, placing its mass media and media messages core courses into the general education of the university. The liberal arts and sciences mission of the university suggested to the department the need to move toward a theoretical approach at the core level while encouraging application in later classes.

Assessing Core Courses

Haley and Jackson (1995) suggested a hierarchy of assessment that included four levels: (a) evaluation of individual program components (peer teaching review and course evaluations); (b) perceptions and performance of graduating seniors (survey of seniors, senior essays, university comprehensives, departmental comprehensives, and campaigns course); (c) evaluations of key constituents (faculty surveys, employer surveys, university alumni surveys, and department graduate surveys; and (d) comprehensive program evaluation (program review and accreditation). The department felt it could best address its program's educational impact by seeing how students were able to apply theory they had learned in their classes. We wanted our program evaluation (Level 4) linked to the performance of our students' learning (Level 2). (See Appendix A.)

A main concern we had about assessing the program was whether the assessment *instrument* could capture the program's flexibility and foundational nature. We had encouraged flexibility and experimentation. Now we were asking ourselves how we could assess the diverse educational experiences of our students. We prided ourselves that our students did not have to go lockstep through a rigid program. An assessment strategy was needed that would be true to our philosophy and mission and went beyond what faculty taught, to assessing what students learned.

We went through a list of options and determined that a portfolio might place undue emphasis on the "skills/practitioner" side of the program (see Orlik, 1994). An exit examination, unless it was very broad, was seen as going against the spirit of diversity we had tried to foster (see Eastman, 1994). An alumni survey was seen as an important component of our assessment program, but we wanted a vehicle that could give us more immediate feedback before the students headed off campus; more feedback about what they had learned.

The department decided on a senior seminar or capstone course (see Moore, 1994). We expect this course to pull together, to integrate, students' past undergraduate experiences building from the core courses that stress communication theory, industry structure/power relationships, and textual analysis. We expected our students to produce papers using all, but stressing at least one, of the three core areas. Students would be expected to apply what they learned in the core courses to issues, ideas, theories, or projects they had developed in other classes. For those working on production projects, the emphasis, however, would not be on the production, but on the critical analysis of the project.

As conceptualized, the department thinks there are at least two benefits to the capstone course. First, the course would bring majors back together as upperclass students. A "downside" of the current curriculum is that the flexibility stresses individuality in the upper grades. Students can lose a sense of belonging to a broader community of teachers, scholars, and students. The capstone course should have a positive "bonding" effect among students and with the department. Second, the course would continue to help the department strengthen its academic image on the campus. Presently, the program has been structured so that students can major by taking courses without being required to integrate their experiences. The capstone course would require students to make intellectual connections. It would require all majors to be reflective about what they have learned (see Sholle & Denski, 1994).

Conclusion

Over the last 15 years, Trinity University's Department of Communication has gone from a program that stressed sequences and a universal "journalism-oriented" core to a program with a broader communication orientation and a universal core of four courses. Over the years, lots of time and energy have been expended "fighting" over the core courses: What they should be, what should be in them, and who should teach them. With the understanding that core courses help define a program and the discipline to students and administrators, the department has felt that the battles have been instructive and "worth it" even though they have not always been pleasant. In some ways, the battles over the core became battles over the heart, soul, vision, and future of the department.

In our struggles over curricular reform we have learned at least three things. First, implementing curricular reform is a long, exciting, often contentious process. Having a vision, a mission, and a clear objective makes the trip, if not smoother, at least more directed. Second, core courses do matter and should be where a department puts a great deal of its resources. Finally, assessing student learning should be a key part of media education. Once the mission is clear and the courses are in place, faculty need to be able to assess student learning to be sure that what is basic and fundamental about the discipline and what we want our students to appreciate and learn is actually being learned.

DEPAUW UNIVERSITY'S
DEPARTMENT OF COMMUNICATION ARTS AND SCIENCES

Each of the subdisciplinary areas in communication study fundamentally focus on the process of human communication. That focus on process gives the discipline of communication a specific turf (Bohn, 1988; Turow, 1992). Although other disciplines are interested in certain aspects of what communication scholars do (learning–education and psychology; ethics–philosophy; effects–sociology and political sciences; aesthetics–art, creative writing; delivery–physics, computer science, etc.), only the communication discipline can fully and carefully draw together the principles and concepts of the overall communication process.

Once the scholars in the various subdisciplines of communication define process as the unifying agent, it is logical to determine some fundamental concepts that are deserving of study in each context. Although arguments could be made as to how long this list of communication concepts should be, few could argue against key fundamental concepts such as channels, symbols, interaction, feedback, credibility, structure, control, and ethics (McCall, 1994b; McCall, Weiss, & Sutton, 1994). Each of the concepts listed, and possibly others, have a clear relevance for any communication studies context. A 1995 special conference sponsored by the Association for Communication Administration sought to define the discipline by identifying and narrowing a list of concepts considered integral to the discipline. The strategy, as suggested in this writing, was to create a description of the communication process in a way that included all aspects of the discipline. The conference developed this definition of the discipline: "The field of communication focuses on how people use messages to generate meanings within and across various contexts, cultures, channels and media. It promotes the effective and ethical practice of human communication" (Berko, 1995, p. 12).

Some communication professors, particularly in mass media areas where the industry still demands vocationally based training, might worry that a process/concepts focus ignores the need for skill development. But that would be an unfounded fear. A process approach already assumes that messages must actually be delivered in any communication transaction, but, unlike a solely applied study, it starts studying and analyzing the process long before the actual application. This is obviously the case in every communication situation from public speaking to interviewing to stage productions to public relations to broadcast programming–there is much to study before the act of message dissemination. The key is that students, as they develop applied skills, will be studying communication in a more holistic manner, and they will understand the factors that impact effective communication. This overall approach removes the tired argument of whether to teach students skills or theory. Theory is provided as a foundation for students to better understand and appreciate practice.

Part of the beauty of the integrated program approach is that it allows the communication discipline to align itself clearly within the liberal arts and sciences. In this era of "back-to-basics" movements, this is a critical point. Integrated communication programs can point to specific academic turf to claim as their own, and demonstrate how understanding of this turf is essential to the education of any liberally educated person today. The discipline can no longer be dismissed as solely vocational.

Assessment for Communication Majors

The Department of Communication Arts and Sciences at DePauw University has operated for many years within a framework that expects students to function at all levels of communication study–praxis, theory, criticism, and research. This vision has been articulated and implemented largely through the leadership of Professor Robert O. Weiss. A formalized department goal to reflect this approach states, "Communication majors will be able to understand and participate fully in the human communication process through study in a liberal arts major in Communication Arts and Sciences that is based on praxis, theory, criticism and research." Five objectives have been drawn up to support the goal (see Appendix B).

The goal and the objectives were written in a manner that reflected the inclusive nature of the discipline. (Even the department name suggests that all contexts of communication and all approaches to their study are welcome here.) A student could meet and be assessed on the first objective by demonstrating practical competence in a variety of ways, but not necessarily in all ways–acting on stage, group leadership, media presentation or production, a public address, and so forth. A parallel case could be stated for objectives three and four. Thus, unlike some people mistakenly assume, an integrated program does not necessarily insist that a student become equally expert in all contexts of communication. But the student is expected to demonstrate understanding and competence of the communication process in some fashion.

Once the objectives are defined, strategies can then be implemented to meet them. DePauw's program utilizes several strategies to guarantee that communication majors are, indeed, developing understanding and ability in the communication process.

Capstone Course. Each major is required to meet a senior requirement, which is the culminating experience in the major. Students must enroll in a senior seminar where they will have the opportunity to display their accomplishment of the major objectives described above. (In some cases, students can meet the requirement in a faculty-directed independent study, but the wide majority of students meet the requirement in a senior seminar class.) Capstone experiences are winning favor in many programs (see Moore, 1994). There are several keys to an effective capstone seminar at DePauw. First, the seminar reaffirms the fundamental nature of communication as a discipline. It then focuses on a theme or concept of interest to the discipline, but it must be one that has application and mutual concern across the various communication contexts. Capstone issues presented successfully in recent semesters at DePauw include communication ethics, communication in social movements, controls in communication, communication and gender, communication as a liberal art, and communication and aesthetics. The seminar requires students to conduct and present a major, theoretically based research project. Obviously, this research project is essential in meeting objective four. (See the outcomes assessment flow chart model in Appendix C for an illustration of how this objective can be followed from overall goal to completion.) Finally, although individual faculty members have wide discretion in structuring the class, each is expected to provide assignments that require students to display their abilities to both analyze and deliver messages. Such assignments have included in-class debates, group presentations, and so on. At the conclusion of the semester, the professor should be able to determine for each student whether or not that student has successfully met the five objectives for a communication major at DePauw.

Structure of Major. The overall structure of the major is also critical to meeting the major goal and five objectives for communication majors in an integrated program. Except for the senior requirement, no specific course requirements exist for the communication major at DePauw. Students are required, however, to develop a program that reflects the nature of the integrated program. With the supervision of a faculty advisor, students design a major that includes coursework in three of the four broad communication content areas defined by the department. Those areas are speech communication, theatre, voice science, and mass communication. This system allows students some flexibility in designing their major programs, but ensures a degree of cross-context study. Communication majors at DePauw consist of 8 to 10 courses, so even with the three-course distribution requirement and the senior seminar, students have between four and six courses remaining to tailor a program to their specific interests (with the supervision of their faculty advisor). It should be pointed out that students are required to take at least three courses at the upper level, where theory, criticism and research methods will be more pronounced than at the freshman-sophomore level.

Introductory Course. The introductory course can play a key role in defining the discipline for prospective majors or even nonmajors taking an elective course. The course, Introduction to Communication Arts and Sciences, is designed to reflect the integrated nature of the department by studying communication not from a narrowing context-by-context approach, but from a process approach that identifies and analyzes the important concepts of communication. This approach differs from many programs where students might take one or more introductory courses called Introduction to Public Speaking, or Introduction to Interpersonal Communication, or Introduction to Mass Communication, and so on. Although each of these varied introductory courses might deal with core concepts somewhere along the way (credibility, channels, feedback, audience, ethics, etc.), students do not necessarily get sufficient depth in the key concepts and might well never get specific insight to the relevance of these concepts across the discipline. The course design can address each of the stated objectives for communication majors, thus providing students the department's vision of communication study and the opportunity to determine whether a major in this discipline is well suited to their interests. Whereas the introductory course is important in establishing key directions for a communication student, it is not specifically required for entry to the major. Some students, particularly late-declaring communication majors, have elected to bypass the course, which usually enrolls first-year students. The department continues to debate the need for making the course a requirement for all declaring majors.

Praxis Through Cocurricular Activities and Experiential Learning. A key strategy in meeting the objective of practical competence lies in providing students opportunities to apply their knowledge. Although some courses allow for some demonstration of practical communication competence (beginning acting, theatre production, group dynamics, video production, broadcast journalism, etc.), the classroom is generally considered a place for theory, criticism, and research. This approach diminishes the charge from certain quarters on campus that communication courses are purely vocationally based. It also provides that precious classroom time be used for conceptual and theoretical underpinnings that can be applied in practice in other places. In essence, the department uses class time to teach theory, criticism, and research, then provides avenues for praxis for those concepts to be applied. The practical avenues at DePauw include an active schedule of theatre productions, an intercollegiate and on-campus debate program, a campus FM radio station, and a cable television outlet to the community. (Students receive no academic credit for these activities. Participation credit is noted on the students' transcripts.) Other opportunities for practical application come from 1-month Winter Term internships (DePauw operates on a 4-1-4 academic calendar), domestic and international off-campus study semesters where half of the credit earned can be through internships, and even summer internships for which credit can be earned. The academic advisor plays a key role in directing students toward an appropriate number of cocurricular and internship experiences in which the students can demonstrate practical competence.

Alumni Surveys. Feedback from graduates of a program can be helpful in determining the impact of that program on the former students' careers and lives. The department of Communication Arts and Sciences at DePauw has done some limited alumni surveying, sometimes in cooperation with senior seminar classes. This sort of follow-up has provided a good deal of anecdotal and attitudinal information from a sampling of alumni. The department plans a thorough and broad-based alumni survey as part of preparations for a future North Central Association reaccreditation visit.

A good deal of survey data have been brought into the university by offices outside of the department. These data, gathered by both the Career Planning and Placement Center (CPPC), and the Office of Institutional Research, has proven to be particularly helpful in analyzing the utility of the major for the department's graduates. The CPPC findings, among other things, found that 96% of communication majors are employed or in graduate/professional schools within 9 months of graduation. That rate is higher than DePauw's all-campus average. The findings also report the nature and range of careers for which the communication major has prepared students. Although an extensive review of findings is not critical for this writing, it is easy to see the significance of this sort of data.

Portfolios. The department at DePauw has not previously been engaged in portfolio methods of assessment. But a department task force has been established to consider the viability of this technique. The task force will have to keep in mind the variety of communication contexts in which the department majors work. Unlike a department of speech, where all students might provide a videotaped speech for a portfolio, or a department of broadcasting, where all students might provide a résumé tape of productions, the integrated portfolio will need to allow for a range of materials that could demonstrate practical and conceptual insight.

"Care and Feeding" of Majors. Although outside the realm of more formal and content-related assessment, the department has historically viewed as essential what Professor Weiss calls the "care and feeding" of majors. This

notion refers to the broadbased department efforts to work with students in nonclassroom settings. The department has developed several objectives to help support and advise students in the communication program. These efforts include such items as: focusing on faculty academic advising as a central element in a student's college experience; sponsoring faculty/student discussions on topics such as graduate school, the utility of a communication major, placement, and so forth; maintaining student representation in departmental decision making; and, providing direct campus mailings to majors with information about department activities, registration, and so forth.

Assessment for Students Across the Academy

A department that expects to be vital to a university's overall educational mission must provide for assessing how well they contribute to the education of students who are not majors. Thus, a communication department should set a goal that includes contributions to the educational experiences of students across the campus. The DePauw Communication department goal to meet this priority states, "Communication Arts and Sciences department offerings will contribute to the broader institutional objective of developing liberally educated students." Five objectives have been drawn up to support this goal (see Appendix B).

These objectives make it clear that the department intends to be a player in meeting the institution's overall educational mission. Objectives two and three give the department specific roles to play in the campus-wide educational program. Objective two indicates the department's role in providing support for students meeting distribution requirements for graduation. All students must meet these general education distribution requirements, which include categories ranging from natural science to foreign language to social science. Objective three addresses the university-wide competence program that requires students to successfully complete at least one course in each quantitative reasoning (Q), writing (W), and spoken communication (S). These "across-the-curriculum" requirements can be met in any department as along as the courses have been designed appropriately and the faculty have completed the designated workshop. Communication course offerings can be found in each competence area–Q courses include communication research methods and theatre production, for example; W courses include theatre history, broadcast journalism, and so forth; and S courses could be virtually any upper level communication course, such as organizational communication, media criticism, rhetorical theory, and all communication seminars.

Cocurricular offerings, as indicated in objective five, provide another important way for the integrated communication department to impact the educational experiences of nonmajors, away from the traditional classroom setting. These offerings at DePauw include a 24-hour FM radio station, a cable access television operation, a debate organization that sponsors on-campus debate forums and competitive intercollegiate debate and individual speech events, and a theatre schedule that features six to eight productions per year. Opportunities to be involved in these activities are available to all students, regardless of major or year in school. There are no required communication courses to complete before joining these organizations, although such a foundation is obviously helpful to those students who do take departmental offerings. (See Appendix C for a flow chart model of this objective.) In many cases, students who participate in cocurricular activities without previous coursework later enroll in relevant communication courses to enhance their understanding of the particular application. Whereas many communication programs restrict cocurricular access only to majors, allowing nonmajors access is yet another signal that understanding and ability in communication should not be limited solely to communication students.

Assessment of the Department's External Reach

The vitality of a department can often be seen in how it impacts external constituencies. Although students and their progress must always remain the foremost priority of a department, it is also clear that what happens in an integrated communication studies department is of importance to other constituencies. With that in mind, the DePauw Communication Department has formulated this goal, "The Communication Arts and Sciences department will support the institution's external relations efforts to provide perspectives of DePauw to various external constituencies." Three objectives support this goal (see Appendix B).

With the possible exception of the varsity athletic program, no other university program reaches external publics as broadly as do the efforts of the DePauw Communication Department. This is not only an important service to these external publics, but such an effort tells the administration and the rest of the academic community that communication is an active discipline with particular outputs. The department has done a number of things in recent years that would show support of this goal–touring theatre performances, public debate programs, broadcast political candidate forums, faculty authored columns for newspapers, faculty participation in professional and community theatre, and so forth. All of these things are in addition to a regular schedule of broadcasting, theatre productions, and traditional faculty scholarship. The department also serves the discipline each year through sponsorship of the National Under-graduate Honors Conference in communication, where undergraduate researchers from around the country meet for 3 days on the DePauw campus for seminars with nationally recognized scholars. Although many possibilities exist for outreach, the key is that communication departments recognize and live up to the communication discipline's need to be actively and publicly displayed.

Assessment of Support for Communication Faculty

A department's faculty is the key ingredient for a program's success. Great facilities, a well-designed curriculum, budgetary support, and motivated students are important parts of the success equation, but the faculty are the strength of any program. A comprehensive assessment program should consider how to support the changing needs of faculty and keep them functioning effectively as teachers and scholars. The current goal for this area reads, "The Communication

Arts and Sciences department will work with its faculty members to provide professional support and development." (For current objectives see Appendix B).

These objectives are largely self-explanatory. But they demonstrate things that can be done within a department to support continued faculty energy and development. (It should be pointed out here that most other forms of faculty development–travel, financial support for research, course development, and so forth–are handled through DePauw's administrative channels and the university's Faculty Development Committee.)

A Closing Thought

Assessment in the integrated communication program poses different challenges than would be found in more narrowly focused programs. Student programs of study are likely to be less regimented in a broad-based integrated program where students have more freedom in the design of their majors. But the ultimate goal of any communication study program is to prepare effective and insightful communicators for the world of work and citizenship. The understanding of process, having "learned how to learn" about communication, should help students succeed throughout their communication lifetimes and in all contexts.

THE UNIVERSITY OF NORTH DAKOTA'S SCHOOL OF COMMUNICATION

Before we can assess our curriculum, we need to have a vision about what our curriculum should be and do. When we discuss curriculum, it is usually in terms of how to improve the skills students leave us with or how to add such topics as visual communication and new technologies to programs that are stretched to offer traditional areas. The very framework of our professional programs remains unexamined. Most programs continue to offer distinct majors or emphases around traditional career areas such as print journalism, broadcasting, advertising, and public relations. Despite the efforts of Blanchard and Christ (1993) to promote a curriculum founded in a "new professionalism," most medium and large-size professional programs remain untouched by calls for change.

Meanwhile, as the problems facing our programs grow more serious, communication issues have become, ironicallyk, among the most pressing issues of society. New means of storing, retrieving, and marketing information are presented to us as salvation for personal freedom and economic gain; new combinations of technology are being sold to us for our personal pleasure and escape. Despite this "information age" and "technological revolution" we are told we live in, the quality of our public conversations may never have been lower. For all of the information that is available, members of the public seem remarkably uninformed about public issues. For all of the communication technology available, the quality of understanding among groups seems to have deteriorated rather than improved. We feel we are literally and figuratively unraveling as families, workplaces, communities, and society.

The silence from schools of journalism and mass communication on these topics is a telling indictment. We seem to have nothing to contribute to the discussions that should be taking place about the critical communication issues of our day and their relationship to contemporary problems. We are too busy worrying about how far behind with technology our students will be when they leave us. We are too busy worrying about fluctuations in enrollments among the career paths we offer. We are too busy worrying that our media colleagues think our graduates are not well prepared for entry-level jobs. The analogy is apt: We have been fiddling while Rome is burning.

The solution to our inability to address this litany of problems–ours and society's–lies with our curricula. The University of North Dakota (UND) felt it was time for an innovative approach to curriculum design that abandoned a subservience to career tracks in favor of a curriculum organized around significant communication issues. Such a bold move, we felt, put us in sync with the needs of society and the needs of our universities; it enabled us to prepare students to enter an uncertain and changing communication world with the necessary skills and outlook to both adapt to and lead the changes that need to take place. We hope to be assuming a role in our universities and among media professionals as intellectual leaders rather than technical followers.

What Is an Issue-Oriented Curriculum?

The School of Communication at UND has implemented an issue-oriented curriculum. In the program, where speech and journalism have been merged for 10 years, we have streamlined our curriculum from five majors (journalism, broadcasting, public relations, advertising, and speech) to one; communication. Coursework is now organized, not around these career tracks, but around issues: *community, information,* and *technology.* Students still choose coursework that provides them skills in writing, speaking, editing, designing, and so forth, but courses are designed to lead them to understanding basic principles important to each of these three issues. Students will be required at the end of their program of study to demonstrate their mastery of 12 goals for student learning identified by the faculty. These goals, associated with each of the issues of community, information, and technology, provide students with the skills and knowledge we think *all* students should have, characterized by a holistic and integrated approach to understanding the role of communication and communication systems in contemporary life. (See Appendix D: The University of North Dakota's Goals for Student Learning.)

Students progress through a series of levels in the major. Level A requires two introductory courses that touch on all three issues of community, information, and technology. Levels B and C organize coursework around the three issues. Students choose five to six courses in Level B; these are courses that are recognized as specialized professional skills areas such as reporting, graphics, public speaking, and videography. In Level C, students choose four or five issue-related courses that provide history, analysis, and criticism. All students complete a practicum or internship or equivalent at Level D. Level E, which provides the assessment mechanism, requires all students to complete an academic portfolio, in which they demonstrate their mastery of the goals for student learning.

Students have considerable choice in arranging courses to constitute their major, but they are required to work with an advisor and to follow an approved plan of study. If they have a specific, traditional, career goal in mind, courses can be chosen to make a major that looks very like a traditional journalism, advertising, speech, broadcasting, or public relations major. Increasingly, however, we would expect to see and to encourage fewer of these traditional career paths because of the changing nature of communication industries and technologies. Students can put together innovative combinations of professional courses that will prepare them broadly. Most exciting about the curriculum is that it allows us to adjust to the changes coming in the future without the need for substantial changes in the basic framework.

Our curriculum truly balances skills courses with history and theory, a balance called for by guidelines of the Accrediting Council on Education in Journalism and Mass Communications. It is in our Level C that community, information, and technology can be seen as serious communication issues deserving of student and faculty attention. Alongside more traditional courses of communication law, community journalism, and media history, are new courses like The Social Consequences of an Information Society and New Technologies and the Future. In courses such as these, our students will be inquiring into the economic, political, and social implications of the future of communication. Shouldn't communication majors in every program be addressing the critical communication issues we face?

Why Has a Career-Oriented Curriculum Run Its Course?

An approach to curriculum design such as we have adopted at UND offers many advantages to the career-oriented design of the past, but it is not just the advantages of this new approach that led us to adopt it. We adopted the new approach because the traditional majors of our field are nearly obsolete. Sooner or later, all programs likely will have to device their own replacements to their current curricula. Consider these reasons that curricula organized around industry careers are no longer administratively nor intellectually viable:

1. Shifts in enrollment. What journalism and mass communication program has not felt the effects of declining enrollments in print journalism and broadcasting while facing enrollment surges in public relations and advertising? Now some are feeling the effect of declining advertising enrollments while print journalism enjoys a modest resurgence of popularity. The specifics for a particular program may vary within these enrollment trends, but the administrative effect is the same: staffing a curriculum with unstable and shifting enrollment patterns is difficult.

With budget and faculty cutbacks, some programs will have to face the unpleasant reality of ending certain areas of their curriculum if they continue a career-oriented curriculum. If they cannot continue to cover all areas, what will they be forced to cut out? And how long will the decision of which one or ones to cut out likely remain the correct decision?

2. Shifts in graduates' careers. Beyond shifts in enrollments that traditional programs are unable to accommodate easily are shifts in individuals' careers that make a traditional specialization increasingly limiting for a student. Because of changes in employment opportunities, students prepared for a particular professional area often find themselves searching for employment in another professional area. They quite possibly will find themselves moving from one professional area to another, as their careers lead them in and out of specializations. In any particular job, graduates increasingly will need skills that cut across print and visual media.

3. Inability to deal with future trends. Traditional curricula may have been appropriate for the way the world once was, but they will not take us into the future. No one knows precisely where the mixing and matching of technologies and industries will take us. Despite the predictions, the communication world of the future is not yet determined. What role will our graduates play? What will they be doing? What skills and knowledge will they need?

A program preparing students for careers of the past will be unable to deal with these shifts. Already we scramble to figure out how to include visual communication and new technologies in our curricula because they do not fit neatly under our career tracks. A proliferation of additional tracks only adds to the problem without addressing the underlying structure of the framework.

4. Mergers with speech communication. In 1984, UND, under the leadership of Vernon Keel, merged speech and journalism. Clearly it was a move still ahead of many universities. Now budget and staff reductions and hostile administrators are forcing other programs to contemplate merger with a department that may have been a competitor, if not an enemy, in the context of the university. The fact that programs of speech and mass communication are separate in so many universities and in our journals and professional associations should be cause for embarrassment to us. Speech programs are as much in the business of preparing professionals as journalism and mass communication (JMC) programs. JMC programs without speech communication run the danger of educating students with little or no understanding of the larger communication issues of which they will be a part. And JMC students need skills in public speaking, interpersonal relations, and organizational communication.

The reasons that departments resist mergers are many, but surely a prime suspect is the inability of faculty in both programs to see the possibilities for intellectual integration in the face of administrative integration. Speech programs fear losing their critical intellectual edge in the context of professional programs that have more often than not sacrificed media criticism for increased numbers of skills courses. Some JMC faculty may disdain the theoretical and research perspective of their speech communication colleagues.

Traditional curricula make administrative integration difficult; they make intellectual integration impossible. Intellectual integration, accomplished through curricular change, however, makes administrative integration logical. The route to intellectual integration involves finding our commonalities across sequences and specializations. The arbitrary boundaries between interpersonal, family, organizational, and mass communication must come down, just as they must between professional areas. What do we all have in common? The study and practice of communication, of being and knowing, of the human capacity for creating relationships and making meaning. An integrated program can have a professional orientation, preparing students to be ethical communication professionals, regardless of the specific organizational or technological context in which they find themselves.

5. Academic illegitimacy. Our traditional curricula have contributed to the indifference or outright hostility so many journalism and mass communication programs face in the academy. We often claim we are made to feel we are illegitimate members of the university because of our professional orientation. Yet schools of law and medicine do not face the same scorn as we face. Why? The mission of journalism and mass communication programs to produce journalists and broadcasters and public relations and advertising practitioners is insufficient to justify or define the social and intellectual contribution that we should be making as academic units. Schools of medicine and law do not see themselves simply as creators of doctors or lawyers. They see themselves as sites for the study of law and medicine. New legal theory and new medical insights come from these schools. They do not serve the professions of law and medicine so much as they serve the public through the study and evaluation of legal and medical practice, leading the very professions for which they have supplied new members.

We need stronger, more socially conscious missions if we are to assume a legitimate role in the academy. A mission of serving media industries is insufficient and inappropriate, just as it would be inappropriate for media industries to see themselves as serving the State. We must provide a critical check and balance to the media much as the media provides such a check on government. Especially for those of us in public institutions, we have an obligation to serve the public rather than a particular special interest group that may have the political and economic power to affect us.

In a similar way, a mission of training students for media careers is insufficient and inappropriate. We must ask, toward what end? For whose ends? Like schools of medicine and law, we should prepare students to serve the public by becoming ethical professional communicators. Our obligation is to the *profession* of communication practice, not to particular industries or employers.

With a career-oriented curriculum, we are trapped into obligations to media industries and employers. This is not to say that our curricula should not lead to students having careers; it is to say that a career is the means to the end of serving the public through ethical communication practices, not the end in itself.

What Are the Advantages to an Issue-Oriented Curriculum?

There might be any number of models to consider in replacing a career-oriented curriculum. An issue-oriented curriculum, however, has a number of advantages that address problems specific to mass communication programs as well as to higher education in general.

1. Staffing and planning. An administrator of an issue-oriented curriculum is to be envied. Because all students, regardless of their career goals, need coursework in these significant issues, enrollments can be predicted and planned for. In the North Dakota model, we have designed the curriculum so that students have choices of skills and theory courses related to each issue. Enrollment targets can be set for each course scheduled. When a course fills, students can be directed to another course. Changing a few individual courses will not have a serious impact on the student's program of study. Heavy or light demand for particular courses can be much more easily met than can an imbalance of demand for entire sequences or majors.

2. Student flexibility. Programs that emphasize issues rather than careers are doing their students a favor. Students will leave these programs with a strong grasp of where a professional communicator fits into larger social needs and concerns. They should have a broad base of skills and exposure to a spectrum of communication areas to make adaptation and change feasible. The design of our curriculum means students can study a far broader range of areas of communication than we could support if forced to staff complete majors in each.

An issue-oriented curriculum can be built on more choices than a traditional specialized skills program. The choices built into our model mean that students will have a much easier and faster time getting through their program of study. We have reduced prerequisites and requirements to enable students to complete their major in a maximum of four semesters rather than the six or seven our traditional programs of study required.

3. Intellectual integrity. We no longer need to feel like illegitimate members of the academy with an issue-oriented curriculum. Showcasing important communication issues in the curriculum directs the attention of students and our faculty and administrative colleagues to the substantive content of our field. These issues should be used as a framework to link together important research and outreach initiatives. They should serve as the focus for the important intellectual discussions we initiate and lead on and off campus. Given the importance most universities are placing on such communication issues as diversity and technology, identifying issues that link a program of communication to university priorities is a step in the right direction to making the program "central to the mission of the university."

For example, now that we have identified what we see as the most significant communication issues for us to address, we are able to use them as a framework for judging priorities of the School and for giving focus to what we do. We traditionally have held an annual editors and broadcasters day each fall. We will use our three issues to provide different themes each year. Our Communication Research Center has begun a publication, *Communication Issues,* that will present faculty research and opinion about topics related to our three program themes. The first issue is on funding for public broadcasting. Because the curriculum is explicitly linked to the research and outreach priorities of the faculty, we are making better use of our time and energies.

4. Service to society. A curriculum that deals explicitly with significant social issues is a curriculum that puts its obligations to society at the forefront. If we do not ensure that these critical communication issues receive attention and public discussion, who will? The answer is that no one else will or is, to the potential detriment of the quality of our public and personal lives. We have an obligation, as members of universities entrusted with the production and critique of knowledge, to raise issues about the quality and purpose of our communication systems and of their future design. We must ensure that we represent the public interest in those discussions rather than market or industry interests.

An issue-oriented curriculum could be a model for other university departments, illustrating a means by which we can create a better fit between what we study and teach with the pressing needs of society.

But Is It Accreditable?

Accreditation may be the most serious of any obstacles to significant curriculum change. Programs will be hesitant to risk losing accreditation; others interested in becoming accredited will not want to take the chance that they do not "look" like a traditional career-oriented professional school. In other words, accreditation has led to imitation rather than innovation.

But why should not an issue-oriented curriculum be accreditable? Ours provides students with a breadth of professional specializations. It provides a balance of skills with theory and history. It provides practical experience. It ensures the quality of our graduates because students will not leave us without demonstrating what they know and can do. Our goals for student learning, comprehensive and general, stress what we think students need to know in order to be broadly prepared, adaptable, and ethical communicators.

But Won't the Media Object?

Journalism and mass communication programs who worry too much about offending media industries should examine their relationship with the media more carefully. Do media industries worry about offending us? Do we want them to have that kind of control over our curricula? Preserving the autonomy and independence of our programs for our intellectual and ethical integrity is as important as the news media's insistence on its autonomy and independence from government.

If, however, we view media professionals as one constituent among many, who have in common with us a mission of serving the public interest through ethical communication practices, we should not fear their reactions. In fact, the support we have received from North Dakota media, advertising, and public relations professionals has been strong and enthusiastic. Endorsements for our curriculum have arrived from the four largest daily newspapers in the state, from the largest broadcast station owner, and from public relations and advertising executives. Contrary to the perceptions of many academics, these media professionals do not insist that graduates take numerous specialized professional courses. They do not care what the major is called. They see the value of students taking courses in speech communication. And they appreciate our focus on the very communication issues that are of concern to them and to their readers, viewers, and clients.

In short, an issue-oriented curriculum offers numerous advantages without the problems of its predecessor career-oriented curriculum. It offers the kind of bold curricular reform that is necessary in this time of economic and technological uncertainty. It enables a program to place itself at the heart of important university and societal concerns. It positions a program as an innovative model within a university, responding creatively to internal and external demands for change. The alternative is to run the greater risk of doing nothing.

Assessing the Issue-Oriented Curriculum

A typical approach to assessment of student learning in a professional media program is to test how prepared students are for entry-level media careers. An issue-oriented, integrated curriculum, on the other hand, requires that we assess how well students understand the holistic nature of communication issues and how those issues might be addressed. Ideally, the assessment program will require students to review and reflect on what they have learned and to synthesize the learning that has taken place in a variety of courses and experiences. For these reasons, a curriculum should be preceded by the articulation of what faculty want all students to have learned when they leave the program. Only such explicit articulation will enable the faculty to assess at the end of a student's program of study whether or not the curriculum has accomplished its purpose.

At UND, we identified 12 goals for student learning that form the basis for assessment. These goals reflect the integrated, issue-oriented intent of the program and guide student selection of courses (with an advisor's approval). Students are informed throughout the program that they will be held accountable for these goals in a senior academic portfolio course. Individual courses emphasize selected goals, reflecting the course's location in the community, information, or technology category of the curriculum. Students are advised to retain work they do in their courses for use in the portfolio.

The new curriculum was implemented in the fall of 1995 as the old five-major curriculum was being phased out. In 1996-1997, the first graduates of the new program will be coming through the senior portfolio course. Students will be required to review the coursework they have taken, to make connections between the coursework and the goals for students, and to provide examples of work they have done on each of the goals. They will be demonstrating in the portfolio that they understand and have achieved a level of competence in each of the goals, with the opportunity to correct or address any shortcomings during the course. The portfolio course will provide us feedback about the level of achievement of our students, but just as importantly, it will provide us feedback about what we are doing in our program. We will be able to determine if individual courses are making the contribution to the curriculum that we had envisioned and whether or not the programs of study that students are following produce the results we want. In other words, students will know how they have done and we will know how well we have done and why.

Assessment, although often viewed as a bureaucratic intrusion from administrators and outsiders, can provide the opportunity to rethink our mission, our purpose, and our curricula. It calls for us to struggle with our internal differences–within departments and across campus–by beginning, not with what has always been done in the past, but with what needs to be done to address an uncertain future where we can only be sure of the fact that we will need to be able to explain what we do and how well we do it. A strong assessment program enables us to justify and measure the success of the kinds of changes called for in these times: changes in what and how we teach as well as mergers and reconfigurations of traditional areas of communication.

APPENDIX A: TRINITY UNIVERSITY'S DEPARTMENT OF COMMUNICATION'S TEACHING, ADVISING, RESEARCH, AND SERVICE OBJECTIVES

In assessing the Department of Communication and constructing its goals, the faculty endorses the concepts of scholarship espoused by Ernest L. Boyer (1990), former President of the Carnegie Foundation for the Advancement of Teaching. He advocates a four-part definition of scholarship: the scholarship of teaching, integration, discovery, and application. Adopting this definition, the faculty assesses its activities.

The Scholarship of Teaching (Assessing Student Learning)

By considering teaching as a form of scholarship, Boyer transforms the routine of teaching and its artificial separation from research into an active, exciting, frontier-crossing activity that creates an intellectual environment where critical thinking thrives long after the last class is taken:

> [G]ood teaching means that faculty, as scholars, are also learners. All too often, teachers transmit information that students are expected to memorize and then, perhaps, recall. While well-prepared lectures surely have a place, teaching, at its best, means not only transmitting knowledge, but *transforming* and *extending* it as well. (p. 24)

The scholarship of teaching is central to education at Trinity University and is formally manifested in terms of instruction *and* advising. (The headings below are part of a form developed by the Southern Association of Colleges and Schools.)

Instructional Objective. Of persons earning degrees with a major in communication, at least 80% will successfully complete (with a grade of B or better) a final paper/project that integrates a student's understanding of mediated communication: its theories, industries, and texts.

Advising Objective. All majors will have a faculty advisor who will help them develop a coherent degree plan.

Method for Assessing the Instructional Outcomes. A senior-level course (i.e., capstone course) will provide students with an opportunity to integrate their undergraduate experience in the major. The emphasis of the course will be on critical reflection about media, theories, industries and texts.

Method for Assessing the Advising Outcomes. Names of faculty advisors and their advisees will be published and distributed each semester. Each year, approximately 10% of the advisees will have their records and degree plans audited and interviews will be conducted if deemed necessary. Faculty advising self-evaluations are also part of the yearly review process.

Timing of the Instructional Assessment. Students will take the capstone course in their senior year, or in rare cases approved by the department chair, as rising juniors.

Timing of the Advising Assessment. Advising will be assessed each semester with audits and faculty self-evaluations taking place at early intervals.

Responsibility for Instructional Assessment The faculty will be responsible for developing the capstone, senior-level course and ensuring that this integrative function is carried out. The instructor of record will read all papers and assign letter grades. The chair will be responsible for assuring that the better papers and projects are kept in a departmental archives and sent to undergraduate competitions where appropriate.

Responsibility for Advising Assessment. The chair is responsible for assessing advising.

The Scholarship of Discovery/Integration (Assessing Research)

The scholarship of discovery is closest to what is normally known as research:

> The scholarship of discovery, at its best, contributes not only to the stock of human knowledge but also to the intellectual climate of a college or university. Not just the outcomes, but the process, and especially the passion, give meaning to the effort. (Boyer, 1990, p. 17)

The scholarship of discovery is a central activity of the academy. It is challenging, rewarding, and helps define the college/university experience.

The scholarship of integration is:

> Serious, disciplined work that seeks to interpret, draw together, and bring new insight to bear on original research. . . . The distinction we are drawing here between "discover" and "integration" can be best understood, perhaps, by the questions posed. Those engaged in discovery ask, "What

is to be known, what is yet to be found?" Those engaged in integration ask, "What do the findings *mean*?" (p. 19)

The scholarship of integration, like the scholarship of discovery, may take the form of speeches, reviews, papers, articles, book chapters, and books.

Objective. Over a 2-year cycle, all faculty will either deliver a paper, publish an article, book chapter, or book in the area of their expertise. (This was considered a minimal criterion that has been easily met in the past. The two year cycle was chosen to take into account those working on long-term projects.)

Assessment Method for Assessing the Outcomes. Annual reviews will be used to assess research productivity.

Timing of the Assessment. In January, faculty will complete annual reviews for the preceding year.

Responsibility for Assessment. The chair will monitor and evaluate annual reviews.

The Scholarship of Application (Assessing Service)

The scholarship of application is not simply the act of doing good, rather:

> To be considered *scholarship*, service activities must be tied directly to one's special field of knowledge and relate to, and flow directly out of, this professional activity. Such service is serious, demanding work, requiring the rigor–and the accountability–traditionally associated with research activities. (Boyer, 1990, p. 22)

Objective. Over a 2-year cycle, all faculty will actively serve the community, the university, and the profession by giving talks, speeches, and/or interviews; being on committees and/or task forces; holding offices in professional associations; or being actively involved in other "community" services.

Assessment Method for Assessing the Outcomes. Annual reviews will be used to assess service commitment.

Timing of the Assessment. In January, faculty will complete annual reviews for the preceding year.

Responsibility for Assessment. The chair will monitor and evaluate annual reviews.

Results from assessment should lead to affirming the present direction of the program of where changes need to be made.

APPENDIX B: DEPAUW UNIVERSITY'S DEPARTMENT OF COMMUNICATION ARTS AND SCIENCES OBJECTIVES (MCCALL, 1995)

Communication Major

1. The communication major should demonstrate practical competence in communication through one or more media.
2. The communication major will be able to identify and articulate the fundamental theoretical approaches to the study of human communication.
3. The communication major should be able to identify, synthesize, analyze, and evaluate a variety of communication issues within a variety of interaction settings.
4. The communication major should be able to use a variety of methods or tools in researching and examining topics of relevance, thus producing fresh knowledge about communication.
5. The communication major should be able to articulate and defend the nature of the discipline to various constituencies.

Assessment for Students Across the Academy

1. Students in communication classes will develop philosophical and citizenship values in order to become participants in the institutional decision making of our society.
2. The department will support the general education requirements of the university by consistently offering courses that meet group six (self-expression) and group three (literature and the arts) requirements.
3. The department will support the university competence program through annually offering courses in each quantitative reasoning, written expression, and spoken expression.
4. As the academic department best suited to understand and promote the central role of spoken communication in the learning process, the department will provide expertise and coordination of the "S" speaking-across-the-curriculum program.
5. The department's cocurricular offerings (student media, theatre, debate) will provide out-of-classroom communication experience for all interested DePauw students, regardless of major.

Assessment of the Department's External Reach

1. Department sponsored activities in electronic media, debate, and theatre will provide information and entertainment to the DePauw, Greencastle, and west Indiana communities through public performances.
2. Department faculty will continue to lend support for admissions efforts through various group presentations and individual conferences.

3.   Department faculty will share their expertise with professional associations and the public at large through professional conferences and publications, and popular media.

Assessment of Support for Communication Faculty

1. Faculty will be provided opportunities to teach in new areas through an ongoing series of topics courses.
2. Faculty will share ideas and practices in a newly established mentoring system.
3. Opportunities will be provided for collaborative teaching, particularly in sharing instructional responsibilities in the introduction to communication arts and sciences course.

APPENDIX C: DEPAUW UNIVERSITY'S DEPARTMENT OF COMMUNICATION ARTS AND SCIENCES ASSESSMENT FLOW CHARTS

Student Research

Objective: Produce new knowledge in communication through a variety of methods

Method: Have each student conduct independent and original research under the direction of a faculty member.

Results: Determine number of students who produce work at a given faculty standard. Note number of student projects selected for outside presentation.

Improvements: Encourage more awareness of the need for research and provide research possibilities in lower level classes. Promote more submissions of student research projects to outside conferences and so forth.

Cocurricular Activities

Objective: All students, regardless of major, will have access to participate in department cocurricular activities.

Method: Tally participant lists of various cocurricular activities.

Results: Determine number of total nonmajors who are active in communication department cocurricular activities.

Improvements: If the number is less than agreed on target, then expand promotion of opportunities available.

APPENDIX D: UNIVERSITY OF NORTH DAKOTA'S SCHOOL OF COMMUNICATION GOALS FOR STUDENT LEARNING

Community:

1. To understand how *language* and communication *processes* create communities.
2. To understand the role of community and *identity* in how individuals see the world and others see them.
3. To understand the *interactions* of individuals, organizations, groups, and social movements and the conflicts and opportunities that can result.
4. To use an ethical framework to *analyze and address* the communication problems and opportunities of individuals and groups.

Information:

5. To understand the diverse and changing ways we acquire, produce, and share *knowledge* about the world.
6. To understand various kinds of *messages, stories, images and texts* and how and why they are constructed.
7. To understand the role of *interpretation* in how we respond to messages and texts.
8. To *research* and *create socially responsible* oral, written, and visual communication.

Technology:

9. To understand the *historical and contemporary context* (political, economic, legal, and social) of communication institutions and technologies.
10. To understand the *consequences* for individuals and communities of the use and content of communication media.
11. To understand *alternate possibilities* for having access to, using, and arranging communication technologies and institutions.
12. To *use* communication technologies ethically in conventional as well as imaginative ways.

REFERENCES

Allison, T. (1994). Regional association requirements and the development of outcomes statements. In W. G. Christ (Ed.), *Assessing communication education: A handbook for media, speech, and theatre educators* (pp. 57-86). Hillsdale, NJ: Lawrence Erlbaum Associates.

Berko, R. (1995, October). ACA conference defines the field. *Spectra, 31*(10), 12.

Blanchard, R. O., & Christ, W. G. (1985). In search of the unit core: Commonalties in curricula. *Journalism Educator, 40*(3), 28-33.

Blanchard, R. O., & Christ, W. G. (1990). Broadcast curriculum: Essential outcomes. *Feedback, 31*(3), 6-7.

Blanchard, R. O., & Christ, W. G. (1993). *Media education and the liberal arts: A blueprint for the New Professionalism.* Hillsdale, NJ: Lawrence Erlbaum Associates.

Bohn, T. W. (1988). Professional and liberal education. *ACA Bulletin, (64),* 16-23.

Boyer, E. L. (1990). *Scholarship reconsidered: Priorities of the professoriate.* New York: The Carnegie Foundation for the Advancement of Teaching, Princeton University Press.

Brock, S. S. (1996). Core curriculum outcomes: Discrepant beliefs about the field. *Journalism and Mass Communication Educator, 51*(1), 4-14.

Christ, W. G. (Ed.). (1994). *Assessing communication education: A handbook for media, speech, and theatre educators.* Hillsdale, NJ: Lawrence Erlbaum Associates.

Christ, W. G. (1995, Winter). J/MC agenda for the 90's . . . the role of journalism and mass communication in the university of the future. *Insights,* 1-5.

Christ, W. G., & Blanchard, R. O. (1994). Mission statements, outcomes, and the new liberal arts. In W. G. Christ (Ed.), *Assessing communication education: A handbook for media, speech, and theatre educators* (pp. 31-55). Hillsdale, NJ: Lawrence Erlbaum Associates.

Christ, W. G., & Hynes, T. (1996). *Missions and purposes of journalism and mass communication education: Joint AEJMC-ASJMC task force report.* Columbia, SC: AEJMC.

Christ, W. G., & McCall, J. (1994). Assessing "the what" of media education. In S. Morreale & M. Brooks (Eds.), *1994 SCA Summer Conference Proceedings and Prepared Remarks* (pp. 477-493). Annandale, VA: Speech Communication Association.

Christ, W. G., & Williams, S. (1993). Developing THE pre-production course: The war of the worlds. *Feedback, 34*(2), 14-19.

Dates, J. L. (1990). The study of theory should guide curriculum. *Feedback, 31*(3), 10-11.

Dickson, T. (1995). *JMC education: Responding to the challenge of change. A report of the AEJMC Curriculum Task Force.* Columbus, SC: AEJMC:

Eastman, S. (1994). Exit exams and the media major. In W. G. Christ (Ed.), *Assessing communication education: A handbook for media, speech, and theatre educators* (pp. 351-382). Hillsdale, NJ: Lawrence Erlbaum Associates.

Eshelman, D. (1991, April). *Outcomes assessment strategies: Implications for broadcast education curricula.* Paper presented at the 36th annual Broadcast Education Association Convention, Las Vegas, NV.

Finney, R. G. (1990). Wanted: Reading and writing skills. *Feedback, 31*(3), 9.

Fletcher, J. E. (1990). Toober ain't couch potatoes. *Feedback, 31*(3), 9.

Footlick, J. K., Wingert, P., & Leonard, E. A. (1990, December 10). Decade of the student. *Newsweek,* pp. 70, 72.

Galvin, K. N. (1992). Foundation for assessment: The mission, goals and objectives. In E. A. Hay (Ed.), *Program assessment in speech communication* (pp. 21-24). Annandale, VA: Speech Communication Association.

Haley, E., & Jackson, D. (1995). A conceptualization of assessment for mass communication programs. *Journalism & Mass Communication Educator, 50*(1), 26-34.

McCall, J. M. (1995, November). *Assessing communication education at a small university.* Paper presented at the Speech Communication Association Convention, San Antonio, TX.

McCall, J. M. (1994a, November). *Affirming commonalties–curriculum directions to support the study of all contexts of communication.* Paper presented at the Speech Communication Association Convention, New Orleans, LA.

McCall, J. M. (1994b). Assessment at DePauw University. In S. Morreale & M. Brooks (Eds.), *1994 SCA Summer Conference Proceedings and Prepared Remarks* (pp. 297-300). Annandale, VA: Speech Communication Association.

McCall, J. M. (1990). Beyond the Roper report. *Feedback, 31*(3), 9-10.

McCall, J. M., Weiss, R. O., & Sutton, L. (1994, November). *The study of communication arts and sciences at DePauw University.* Paper presented at the Speech Communication Association Convention, New Orleans, LA.

Moore, R. (1990, April). *Pro: Core courses.* Paper presented at the Broadcast Education Association Convention, Atlanta, GA.

Moore, R. (1994). The capstone course. In W. G. Christ (Ed.), *Assessing communication education: A handbook for media, speech, and theatre educators* (pp. 155-179). Hillsdale, NJ: Lawrence Erlbaum Associates.

Orlik, P. (1994). Student portfolios. In W. G. Christ (Ed.), *Assessing communication education: A handbook for media, speech, and theatre educators* (pp. 131-154). Hillsdale, NJ: Lawrence Erlbaum Associates.

Planning for curricular change in journalism education. (1984). (A Report of the Project on the Future of Journalism and Mass Communication Education) The Oregon Report. Eugene, OR: School of Journalism, University of Oregon.

Quenzel, G. (1990, April). *Against: Core courses.* Paper presented at Broadcast Education Association Convention, Atlanta, GA.

Rakow, L. (1995). New curricular categories for the future: University of North Dakota School of Communication. *Journal of the Association for Communication Administration, 3*, 211-215.

Rosenbaum, J. (1994). Assessment: An overview. In W. G. Christ (Ed.), *Assessing communication education: A handbook for media, speech, and theatre educators* (pp. 3-29). Hillsdale, NJ: Lawrence Erlbaum Associates.

Sholle, D., & Denski, S. (1994). *Media education and the (re)production of culture.* Westport, CT: Bergin & Garvey.

Sykes, C. J. (1988). *ProfScam: Professors and the demise of higher education.* New York: St. Martin's Press.

Trinity University Department of Communication (1985). *Self-study.* San Antonio, TX: Author.

Trinity University Department of Communication (1995). *Self-study.* San Antonio, TX: Author.

Turow, J. (1992). On reconceptualizing 'mass communication.' *Journal of Broadcasting and Electronic Media, 36*(2), 105-110.

Warner, C., & Liu, Y. (1990). Broadcast curriculum profile (a freeze-frame look at what BEA members offer students). *Feedback, 31*(3), 6-7.

Wartella, E. (1994). Challenge to the profession. *Communication Education, 43*, 54-62.

Wycliff, D. (1990, September 4). Concern grows on campuses at teaching's loss of status. *New York Times,* pp. A1, A9.

3

Telecommunications Programs

Peter Orlik
Central Michigan University
Ralph Donald
The University of Tennessee at Martin

Telecommunications programs typically are distinguished by a high number of student majors served by a small number of faculty. Thus, to accurately evaluate the professional preparation of such a large student body, assessment activities in academic units that teach telecommunications must make frugal use of limited resources and also enlist widespread faculty support. The two case studies in this chapter detail a pair of successful but divergent responses to this assessment challenge. Central Michigan opted for a Senior Seminar that combines capstone course and exit examination strategies whereas the University of Tennessee at Martin chose to focus on a portfolio approach. The selection and implementation of both of these plans demonstrate that the best campus assessment vehicle is one that respects a department's culture and resource limitations, keeping telecommunications students' career paths and postgraduation needs uppermost in mind.

INTRODUCTION

For a telecommunications unit, the assessment task can be more challenging than it is for colleague academic departments because of two key factors. First, the comparative high cost of its equipment-dependent instruction when compared to "chalk-intensive" units (such as English and history) makes the telecommunications curriculum more susceptible to heightened scrutiny from dollar-strapped upper administrators. Second, the relatively small faculty size of radio-television departments means there are fewer professors among whom the assessment task can be spread–and less faculty time to divert to assessment-related activities.

Consequently, self-evaluative mechanisms in a telecommunications program must defend that program's worth and effectiveness while expending a minimum of scarce staff time in assessment implementation. Nevertheless, the unit still must produce an assessment plan that provides: (a) a mechanism for prescriptive programmatic analysis and change; and (b) a vehicle by which its students can ascertain, on an individual basis, their own professional strengths and weaknesses. As with any curriculum, assessment activities that only serve the institutional needs of the department will not spark enthusiastic student participation. On the other hand, plans that solely focus on individual student diagnostic needs will not generate the data that oversight agencies demand.

In the latter half of this chapter, Ralph Donald discusses how a portfolio approach can meet institutional assessment needs while, at the same time, creating a "trickle down effect" that benefits multiple aspects of the telecommunication program's operations. In the first half of this chapter, meanwhile, Peter Orlik presents a cost-effectiveness case for a hybrid assessment plan that blends two evaluative procedures: the *capstone course* and the *exit examination.*

SELECTING THE ASSESSMENT PLAN BY PROCESS OF ELIMINATION

In the 1994-95 school year, Central Michigan University's Broadcast & Cinematic Arts (BCA) Department, like all academic units within the institution, was charged with developing a comprehensive assessment plan that could be phased in over a 2-year period. This task was complicated by the fact that the unit had suffered four successive cuts in its faculty allocation–cuts not motivated by any drop in the department's student credit hour production but rather by the forced budgetary downsizing of its parent College of Arts & Sciences. Thus, an additional programmatic burden was placed on a unit that continued to attract as many students as before, but could call on fewer staff to service them.

Given these constraints, a number of otherwise appealing evaluative mechanisms had to be ruled out. The BCA faculty member serving as the department's assessment director, for instance, possessed over a decade of experience in supervising prior-learning portfolio assessment activities for the university's College of Extended Learning. In this capacity, he had been ultimately responsible for hundreds of portfolio evaluations annually; assessments that translated students' prior learning from work, avocational, and noncollegiate training activities into academic credit. However, because BCA lacked the availability of faculty "load" (or the funds to pay for professor portfolio evaluations as an *overload* activity), the director's past portfolio experience and continuing portfolio preference had to be set aside. The benefits of the portfolio approach–as detailed later in this chapter and by Orlik (1994)– were well recognized. But so were the insufficient resources at hand to harvest these benefits. An alternate strategy had to be found.

Alumni questionnaires, another valid assessment procedure, were also rejected for budgetary reasons. Telecommunications programs often produce a large number of graduates and the BCA Department was no exception. But tracking all of these graduates, delivering a valid questionnaire to them, and then tabulating and analyzing the results were tasks far beyond the resources of an already multiactivity department served by a single secretary. And if a broad and "escape-proof" net cannot capture a large and diversified percentage of alumni, such questionnaires can be the source of significant distortion through sample insufficiency and imbalance.

The department's records were far more complete than those of the campus Alumni Office but still suffered from the gaps and omissions that are inevitable when budgetary and support staff shortages make continuous and frequent mailings and record updating impossible. Under these conditions, one may end up with assessment results that are unrealistically positive because only the successful graduates have taken the initiative to stay in touch (the "bragging conduit" phenomenon). Conversely, such one-shot or underfunded questionnaire activities are just as likely to yield assessment findings that are unrealistically negative. This can result when, for example, a high percentage of responses comes from mailings sent to graduates' parents with whom these alumni are once again living because they have failed to secure decent-paying positions.

This left the *exit examination* and the *capstone course*. The exit examination requires a venue that can somehow guarantee broad-based and serious senior participation; no easy task in the multidirectional world of the telecommunications department with its numerous cocurricular involvements and their conflicting schedules and time demands. Meanwhile, the capstone course, particularly in its conventional 3-credit-hour configuration, consumes significant amounts of faculty load–especially in programs like radio-television that are likely to produce a sizable number of graduating seniors each year. Further, the very nature of the capstone course requires small, seminar-size sections if the individual and small-group activities essential to a well-focused crowning experience are to be accommodated. Even more of that scarce faculty time thereby must be expended to staff these multiple sections. (See Prus and Johnson [1993] for a thorough inventory of advantages and disadvantages associated with these and other assessment options.)

Consequently, neither the exit examination nor the capstone course initially seemed likely to meet the needs of a resource-strapped telecommunications program. However, as the BCA program at Central Michigan University discovered, an efficient combination of the two strategies could viably garner mandated institutional assessment data *and* provide student self-assessment servicing at the same time.

THE SENIOR SEMINAR: A HYBRID APPROACH

Realistically then, devoting already-scarce assets to an additional telecommunications course only makes sense when that course does "double duty." That is just what a Senior Seminar can accomplish if it is designed with both capstone course and exit examination justifications fully in mind. According to Moore (1994), a telecommunications *capstone course* is meeting student needs when it "integrates course work, knowledge, skills, and experiential learning to enable the student to demonstrate a broad mastery of learning across the curriculum for a promise of initial employability and further learning and career advancement" (p. 163). Note the emphasis here on the student's own professional entry and enhancement. Meanwhile, Eastman (1994) discovered in her research that, if critical objections can be overcome, an *exit examination* can be "useful in providing feedback to the faculty about the weaknesses and strengths of course work, curriculum, and teaching. The results of tests can be compared over time to demonstrate improvements in curriculum" (p. 378). Note the emphasis here on *departmental* servicing and validation.

As envisioned at Central Michigan, the capstone course, which incorporates an exit examination, would be positioned to meet both student-oriented and departmentally oriented goals while blunting many of the most common objections to exit testing that Eastman uncovered. It would ensure student participation in the departmentally assessing exit examinations for two reasons. Most obviously, this is achieved by tying the tests to a required culminating course. Just as important, the scheduling of these tests as measures for self-comparison among graduating (and therefore competing) seniors impinges on the students' lives at the very time they become most concerned about their after-campus prospects. Thus, attention to student needs is further reinforced through the timely use of examination results *within* the course as a student-servicing prescriptive tool.

In addition, as a locally developed instrument, this examination has the potential consistently to reflect the faculty-accepted goals for the curriculum and to take into account the type of student who enrolls in it. Given resource constraints, however, the design of this vehicle was required to achieve both departmental and student goals in an efficient manner with the total staff availability of only .25 of one faculty member's load (the allocation that had been squeezed out to compensate the faculty member serving as BCA assessment director.) Thus, the Senior Seminar was born.

DEVELOPING THE SENIOR SEMINAR

In constructing the framework for the Central Michigan capstone course–and the vital exit examination contained within it–the following developmental process ensued.

Stage 1

During the initial semester of planning, faculty were asked to identify the central objectives for (a) the department's core courses (required of all majors and most minors), and (b) the elective course clusters outside the core. This decision reflects Nichols' (1991) caution that, "No institution or department has the resources or time to assess all possible aspects of each degree program. . . . Hence, it is logical to begin by focusing the department's assessment efforts on those expectations for graduates that have been identified as of primary importance" (p. 17). Consequently, each professor isolated only *a single and fundamental* objective of the core course or elective cluster for which she or he was responsible. For core courses or elective clusters taught by more than one individual, the staff members involved collaborated in the formulation of an objective statement. Ultimately, each student's attainments are to be tested in each core area and in the single elective cluster on which that student primarily has chosen to focus.

Stage 2

During the second semester of the Seminar's development, these objectives were submitted to the BCA Industry Advisory Board–a group of media executives that helps the unit maintain its interface with a wide variety of electronic media enterprises. (For departments without an advisory board, this objective validation could alternatively be accomplished by submitting the objectives list to the unit's internship supervisors–those media professionals who regularly oversee the program's upper level students in off-campus work situations.)

Stage 3

As a result of this feedback (which came via both written and group discussion formats) fine-tuning of BCA's objective statements was accomplished. Listed in Appendix A are the original statements as modified by this subsequent dialogue. Although the changes were relatively minor, the exercise proved very valuable, not only in honing the statements, but in mutual clarification and consensus-building among faculty and industry parties.

As Nichols (1991) reminded all academics, the most appropriate objective statements "are nontechnical expressions offered by the faculty in the department regarding what they believe students should know, be able to do, or think upon completion of their programs" (p. 28). Given the preprofessional thrust of most telecommunications departments, these statements also should positively register with industry executives.

Stage 4

With programmatic outcomes thus identified, the third semester of BCA's assessment plan development was devoted to finalizing the actual syllabus for the Senior Seminar. This course would constitute the vehicle through which the exit examinations would be administered and serve as the diagnostic culmination of the student's undergraduate major or minor. Several implementing decisions were made at this point.

Resource limitations determined that the Senior Seminar would be a 1-semester hour course. Senior participation imperatives decreed that it be part of the curriculum's required core and taken in one of the student's final two semesters so as to properly function as a programmatic capstone. In order further to intensify the experience, keep each seminar section size small, and conserve faculty resources devoted to the task, the Seminar would be offered in half-semester laboratory format. This meant that each section of the class would meet 4 hours per week for a total of 8 weeks with 4 separate sections mounted every academic year. Given the 4 contact hours per week and amount of paperwork entailed, the available .25 of one professor's load for the year could sufficiently and justifiably service the Seminar's needs. With students experiencing a total of 32 contact hours (4 hours x 8 weeks), adequate time was available to cover what were deemed the *three* essential components of the course:

Essential Component 1. Administration of a battery of tests over each core area as well as the test covering whichever elective cluster each student chooses to take. In this way, it is possible to evaluate the central and universal elements of the curriculum while still allowing for the diversity which, as Eastman (1994) pointed out, is the hallmark of many media departments. For programmatic assessment purposes, it was determined that statistics would be compiled as to how many times the student took each core course. (Department requirements specify that a minimum grade of C must be earned in every class in the core.) Excessive repeating of one course by a multitude of students would obviously raise concerns about curricular design and/or delivery.

Data would also be collected to discriminate between courses taken within the BCA Department and those brought in as transfer credit. This would provide valuable comparisons between objectives attainment among students enrolled in the course at Central Michigan and those exposed to the subject area at another university. In addition to the tests' objective and short-answer questions, other open-ended items would allow students to identify their self-perceived strengths and weaknesses and the strengths and weaknesses of the education received via the department's cocurricular offerings. The continuing monitoring of test results and test items by the department faculty as well as by members of its Industry Advisory Board serve, over time, to further refine individual items and suggest new areas for scrutiny.

Essential Component 2. Subsequent feedback to students about their performance on these objectives' attainment tests as well as class discussions exploring ways for them to exploit strong points and mitigate weak ones.

To facilitate this process, it was decided that the test batteries needed to be broken up into discrete sections, interspersed with in-class analysis of the results of each section. Students could thereby benchmark their own competencies with those of their peer group and become more aware of their own comparative potential.

Essential Component 3. Refining of student strategies for their entry into the job market and heightening their sensitivity to anticipated changes in the field that will impact long-term career prospects.

A three-pronged strategy was selected to serve this function. First, seminar students would be required to refine their professional résumés in response to class and instructor discussion and suggestions. Second, each student would be guided in the construction and polishing of whichever one of the following was most appropriate to their job-seeking strategy: performance audition tape, production reel, writing or sales portfolio. Finally, each student would prepare a brief research paper focusing on trends in the industry area of most interest to them and speculating about the impact of those trends on their own career programming.

Components 2 and 3 also address aspects of objective attainment most central to a given student's chosen career path that may not fully be measurable by the Senior Seminar's examination component alone. For example, production students would be able actually to demonstrate their *advanced* manipulation of equipment, advertising/sales students could showcase *detailed* marketing strategies they had formulated, and all students would have the opportunity to evidence writing and research ability by probing an industry area in which they claim to have acquired more specialized expertise than minimal objective passing would require.

Stage 5

The department's assessment process, and the Senior Seminar, which is its prime vehicle, are very much works in progress. As of this writing, faculty are engaged in the formulation of the questions that will make up the exit examination test batteries. These are of both objective and open-ended varieties. Faculty are also encouraged to share their test items with same-specialist colleagues at other institutions as another means of item validation. As mentioned earlier, however, different institutions possess differing curricular philosophies and student body characteristics. Thus, a program's own faculty must remain the final arbiter of questions that assess its own students.

It is important to note that the actual student scores on the exit tests will *not* be factored into the student's grade for the Senior Seminar. The reason for this is twofold. First, a double jeopardy mechanism is not advisable. Students have already been tested on these subject areas in their past coursework and have met minimum competency levels or they would not have attained the required minimum grade of C in each core experience. In the case of the elective clusters, students seldom continue to pursue a self-chosen option in which they do poorly. Instead, they naturally gravitate toward a strength area. Second, the goal of departmental assessment is to measure the residual effect of earlier training and therefore its effectiveness. Encouraging exit examination cramming would only contaminate the process.

During debate on the new Senior Seminar, a member of the University Curriculum Committee argued that not tying student exit test scores to their Seminar course grade gave students no incentive to put their best effort into these tests. Other members, however, were convinced by the argument that these are preprofessional students about to enter a daunting job market. Whatever they could do to spotlight their own strengths and weaknesses and ratify pride in their past accomplishments was clearly in their own self-interest.

Stage 6

Once the Senior Seminar and its exit examination test batteries have actually been put on line (final curricular approval has recently been granted for the course), results of the Seminar's testing activities will be regularly shared with the department's Industry Advisory Board. Their suggestions will continue to be solicited; not only about test item validation but as to: (a) how weaknesses in objectives attainment might be rectified, and (b) whether new objectives (and perhaps courses) need to be added and/or existing ones deleted.

Although much of the emphasis in this assessment plan has been placed on courses, it is important to note that the cocurricular activities of the department (FM radio station, municipal cable television channel, and chapters of Alpha Epsilon Rho–the National Broadcasting Society and the Radio-Television News Directors Association) play important roles in the integration and application of knowledge and skills first introduced in classes. Open-ended questions are being designed to evaluate the importance of these activities in student professional preparation and to detect any dissonance between course-taught and activity-taught lessons.

It must be reemphasized that to be successful, any assessment plan must meet both the corporate evaluative needs of the sponsoring department and the self-evaluative needs of each student. This requires the isolation of common preferences and purposes linking academic unit and individual learner as well as the coherence of these purposes with the accountability standards embraced by the institution. As Banta (1993) put it, the preeminent task is to "build a sense of shared purpose among students, faculty, and administrators based on clearly articulated and communicated statements of mission and educational goals" (p. 365).

The developing Senior Seminar just described (and more officially evidenced in the syllabus in Appendix B) attempts to isolate and summarize those goals in a way that speaks to professional demands of the telecommunications industries and measures the academic experiences intended to address those demands. It strives to accomplish its assessment task in a cost-effective manner that expends only .25 FTE or Faculty Teaching Equivalent (one FTE is equivalent to one full-time teacher's time). And its structural progression helps remind students of past accomplishments and sensitize them to future challenges.

PORTFOLIO ASSESSMENT

Media practitioners constantly remind telecommunications educators that the kind of graduates they seek for entry-level positions are those who both write well and are well versed in the liberal arts and sciences. But telecommunications educators also know from experience that employers value graduates who can additionally demonstrate competence in the basic practical skills of the profession. Employers may value a liberal arts education, but when the time comes to actually hire someone for an entry-level position, the graduate who also knows how to compose a camera shot, edit tape, write continuity or a broadcast news story has a distinct advantage (Steinke, 1993).

These days, the typical credentials electronic media graduates bring to the job market are a bachelor's degree in their field plus an eclectic collection of experiences while working on campus media and/or on an internship. Some graduates of electronic media programs may also possess some form of résumé tape (one outcome of Peter Orlik's capstone course, discussed previously).

However, the majority of students lack this important tool. Graduates often send out hundreds of cover letters and résumés to potential employers announcing that they are ready, willing, and college-prepared for an entry-level job in electronic media, but few can provide potential employers with concrete evidence of their readiness. And employers, many of whom were not top students themselves, are not overly impressed by grades (Cappelli, 1992).

In 1991, the faculty of the Department of Communications at the University of Tennessee (UT) at Martin discussed strategies for increasing the success rate of graduates in obtaining media jobs and overcoming the inherent problems of the academic assessment tools in use. Tennessee requires many forms of higher education assessment, including enrolled student and alumni surveys, American College Test (ACT) entrance and exit tests to measure improvement in basic skills, and some form of major achievement test administered to graduates and reported to the state. Through a system of performance-based funding, state colleges and universities receive additional budget allocations based on measured achievement. One of these measures is based on the annual improvement of scores in the major achievement test. Mostly, campus departments may determine what kind of tool is used in major achievement testing and whether or not students are required to achieve a certain score to graduate. UT Martin's Communications Department had used a comprehensive, objective 100-question senior exit exam, a mandated exercise in the department's Senior Seminar capstone course, that required students to remember facts learned in coursework over 4 years. None of the department's faculty had been happy with this test, nor were the results ever used to evaluate either student achievement, readiness for graduation or programmatic success. All the test did was meet Tennessee's major achievement test requirement. Not surprisingly, students considered the test a monumental waste of time and were unmotivated to study for it, which further reduced its validity as a measure of anything.

The faculty decided to try another approach: to adopt a senior portfolio as the official Senior Seminar graded exit test requirement for all communications majors. Scores of 0 to 100 are possible, but a score of 70 was required to graduate. A student who might fail to achieve a 70 may resubmit a revised portfolio after either its contents are revised or enlarged, or, in an unusual case, additional coursework or practicum experience is obtained.

As discussed in the first part of this chapter, it is not universally believed that comprehensive testing is a valid measure of achievement after 4 years of electronic media education. On the other hand, Haley and Jackson (1995) called portfolio assessment "authentic," maintaining that this means of assessment ". . . replicates the challenges and standards of performance" encountered in the workplace (p. 30). For this department, the faculty hoped that because a satisfactory portfolio score would be required to pass the Senior Seminar and thus qualify for graduation, and because the end product would also be perceived by students as worthwhile, portfolio assessment might provide more valid assessment plus programmatic feedback. Then, portfolio in hand, students would leave the university with a professionally prepared, persuasive "sales brochure" to assist them in the job search. And because achievement of a satisfactory portfolio score required them to produce more quality media products while enrolled in the program, students, through experience, would become more adept at the basic skills of the profession.

The senior portfolio requirement commands students' attention by asking them to demonstrate a certain standard of holistic competence before they are permitted to graduate. Borrowing from the jury system used to assess the synthesis of learning and skills in the disciplines of music, art and theatre, the faculty believe that the quality of the media products students have learned to create (e.g., radio news stories, scripts, TV commercials, public service announcements, TV programs, multimedia presentations, etc.) holistically represents the educational objectives of the entire curriculum better than any other single evaluative measure.

As the last hurdle to jump in Comm 492, Senior Seminar, students prepare a portfolio of the best work they have completed both on campus and in part-time media employment during the time they have been at the university. Portfolios are submitted for approval by a jury of faculty in their major sequence (the department has three: Broadcasting, the largest; Public Relations, and News-Editorial).

Besides creating an arguably more valid evaluation device, the faculty have found that portfolio assessment has generated a positive qualitative ripple effect throughout the entire program. The remainder of this chapter discusses some of these advantages and provides a glimpse at how the senior portfolio requirement is operationalized at UT–Martin.

Faculty members actively support the portfolio requirement in all their courses, identifying in their syllabi which projects are appropriate to save for senior portfolios. As a result, faculty report a surprising benefit: Before they required senior portfolios, a professor might pass back a student's script project for a radio commercial, which would be marked up with the usual red pen. That script would next end up in a trash can 99 times out of 100. But now the student, who knows that this project is a possible portfolio element, not only saves his or her work, but also reads the professor's criticism more carefully, makes corrections to the original on the computer, and saves it on both hard copy and disk for the senior portfolio. As an advertising practitioner might phrase it, portfolios provide professors with "more bang for the buck" in each class assignment.

Other examples of the senior portfolio's ripple effect:

• Faculty can individually review the success of the individual objectives within each course they teach in light of the competencies displayed by students about to graduate. Then, as a committee, faculty within each sequence can assess how these objectives work together.

• Some faculty give Communications Department majors extra course credit for "mini-portfolios"–final compilations of student work throughout the semester in a single course. Assignments are rewritten, reshot, or reedited to reflect the improvements on the original assignments suggested by their professors.

• Students seem to take their classes and their class projects more seriously. Because they are required to display greater competence, *learning* the task assigned rather than just completing assignments is on the rise.

• Students volunteer for work on UT Martin's campus media outlets for many more hours than required. They are "staying with it" until they master the skills, rather than just earning departmentally mandated practicum credits to "cash in" for graduation. Surveys such as those by Becker, Kosicki, Engleman, and Viswanath (1993) routinely demonstrated that success in the job market is much more likely for those with significant experience in campus media.

• Students seem more confident in their ability to compete for jobs after they prepare a portfolio of their work: They *know* they can do professional-quality work because they have a faculty-reviewed portfolio to prove it to a potential employer. Through this process, students also learn another valuable job skill: evaluating their own work, culling through their accomplishments, choosing and polishing their very best–also demonstrating to potential employers that they know quality work when they see it (Forrest, 1990; Hutchings, 1990).

• Because the faculty in each sequence sit on juries together to evaluate these senior portfolios, they learn more about what their colleagues are doing in the classroom. Redundancy in the curriculum is reduced through enhanced faculty communication.

• Faculty also can more easily evaluate the results of their courses. This is especially helpful in coordinating the content of courses that build on each other.

• Also, identifying uniform weaknesses among graduating seniors prompts faculty to alter course content and/or create new curriculum or requirements.

These last two benefits are significant. The usual objective student evaluation survey forms tell faculty little about what students have really learned in a course. Correct his or her assignment, give out a grade, but what can the student really do, what has he or she been able to synthesize after finishing a course? But look at an end-of-semester mini-portfolio assignment and one can readily see if the student really "got it." Evaluate that same student's portfolio as a graduating senior and faculty can more easily track a student's overall improvement, increased sophistication and ability to judge the quality of his or her own work.

And when faculty see the results of their efforts *in context* with the rest of student experiences and achievements in the curriculum, they can more easily pinpoint programmatic strengths and weaknesses. Every semester when UT Martin's telecommunications faculty meet around a table to evaluate senior portfolios, they discuss alterations in both course and curriculum content to improve the "product." After such changes have been in place for a period of time, they evaluate effectiveness in subsequent portfolios. Across the board in education, portfolios are used–and praised–for the feedback they provide those who teach (Schilling & Schilling, 1993). (The portfolio instructions handout students receive is in Appendix C and an abridged senior seminar syllabus is found in Appendix D.)

But portfolio assessment would not be effective if students first heard about it in their senior year. High school students who visit the Department of

Communications learn about portfolios before they choose to come to the university, and new communications majors enrolled in Communications Department-sponsored sections of the university's first-year student orientation course are introduced to the senior portfolio and given a handout describing portfolio aims and content. Additional information on portfolios is usually provided in the department chair's annual summer letter to communications majors.

It is very clear to UT Martin's Department of Communications how advantageous portfolios are to the success of the program. But potential employers are impressed as well. Many graduates report that listing on their résumé that a portfolio and tape are available has prompted employers to ask to see them. Graduates are advised to use this request as an excuse to visit the station, studio, and so forth, and deliver the portfolio in person–one additional chance to make a positive impression. For example, during a recent field trip visit to WTVF-TV News in Nashville, an executive producer mentioned how impressed he was with the portfolio of one of UT-Martin's graduates whom he had interviewed for a videotape editor/Chyron operator job the day before. A few days later she was offered the job.

However, no evaluation system is perfect, and portfolio assessment has some potential pitfalls to consider. The most frequently cited concern with portfolios is the issue of authenticity. How can you be sure that students are turning in their own work? In huge programs with many hundreds of undergraduate majors, this could conceivably present a problem. But in moderately sized programs such as the UT-Martin (210 majors in fall 1995), professors are well aware of whose work they are seeing–and seeing for perhaps the third or fourth time. This is key to the authenticity issue: The same professors who have assigned, evaluated, graded, and sometimes evaluated the same work again in mini-portfolios at the end of the semester are the faculty judging these final senior portfolios. In a system such as this, there is little chance for student dishonesty.

The other possible criticism is perhaps more valid: How do you assess the more theoretical, less demonstrable kinds of knowledge students should have before graduation? For example, in Communications Law and Ethics, one of the course units calls for students to learn, discuss, and evaluate the codes of ethics espoused by the major telecommunications associations, such as the Radio-Television News Directors Association. Only by qualitatively evaluating the content of a broadcast journalism student's writing and résumé tape, and only then by inference, can faculty determine if students learned, understood and perhaps adopted the organization's major ethical precepts.

But portfolio evaluation is and should never be the entire evaluative package. Graduate students undergo comprehensive assessment only after the successful completion of their coursework, and the juries that music, art, or theatre students encounter are scheduled only after passing a battery of courses. Any system of evaluation of potential graduates should consider both grades in coursework and the holistic results demonstrated in a device such as the portfolio.

CONCLUSION

It must be reemphasized that to be successful, any assessment plan must meet both the corporate evaluative needs of the sponsoring department and the self-evaluative needs of each student. This requires the isolation of common preferences and purposes linking the academic unit and individual learner as well as the coherence of these purposes with the accountability standards embraced by the institution. As Banta (1993) put it, the preeminent task is to "build a sense of shared purpose among students, faculty, and administrators based on clearly articulated and communicated statements of mission and educational goals" (p. 365).

The developing Senior Seminar utilized by the BCA Department at Central Michigan University, which was described in the first part of this chapter, attempts to isolate and summarize those goals in a way that speaks to professional demands of the telecommunications industries and measures the academic experiences intended to address those demands. It strives to accomplish its assessment task in a cost-effective manner that expends only .25 FTE. And its structural progression helps remind students of past accomplishments while sensitizing them to future challenges.

When summing up the faculty's experience with the senior portfolio requirement adopted by the UT at Martin's Department of Communications, one can only add that it serves the combined objectives of a holistic measure of student achievement, to encourage student participation in active learning, to provide a once-per-semester outcome evaluation of a department's curriculum and course content, to coordinate the activities of all faculty in a sequence, and to deliver a valid assessment of applied student learning. And the end result is a portfolio students can also use to assist them in obtaining employment.

APPENDIX A: OBJECTIVES FOR CENTRAL MICHIGAN'S ASSESSMENT PLAN

To denote the modifications that took place, deletions from the original objective statements are in (parentheses) and additions are CAPITALIZED.

Core Objectives

1. Students will exhibit familiarity with multiple theories of mass communication and the roles of media in society and will be able to apply these theories in analyzing media production, content and utilization within historical, social, cultural, psychological, and artistic contexts. [*This objective statement was not changed.*]

2. Students will be able to perform basic audio production functions including operation of equipment, use of sound support (mechanisms) TOOLS and organizing of appropriate behaviors necessary (to) FOR the creation of industry-acceptable packages of audio communication.

3. Students will be able to integrate the sound, (illumination) LIGHTING, and pictorial elements of video production to create purposeful (television)

communication(s) via effective manipulation of equipment and technical personnel.

4. Students will be able to identify and describe the impact of important individuals, organizations, SYSTEMS, and technologies on the historic and projective development of electronic communication in the United States.

5. Students will be able to write effective (radio and television) ELECTRONIC MEDIA continuity through formulation of a copy strategy, construction of a message that meets that strategy, and formatting of that message in industry-accepted script and storyboard form.

6. Students will be able to dissect and evaluate mass media messages of varying lengths and types by application of several different critical yardsticks –economic, aesthetic, ethical, sociological, psychological, and structural–and will be capable of addressing key continuing conflict points with which media professionals must cope. [*This objective statement was not changed.*]

7. Students will be able to apply federal STATUTES, administrative rules and regulations as well as judicial precedents to everyday electronic media situations, discriminating between those that can be dealt with by the media practitioner and those requiring professional legal advice.

Elective Cluster Objectives

Advanced Audio Production: Students will be able to demonstrate appropriate selection and placement of microphones for (both stereophonic and) multitrack studio recordings as well as (evidence) appropriate (mixdown) MIXING techniques for a variety of audio production (tasks) APPLICATIONS.

Advanced Video Production: Students will be able to integrate the elements and techniques of studio (and) AS WELL AS field production and postproduction to create a variety of TARGETED video program types (that clearly communicate with the desired audience).

Electronic Journalism: Students will be able to produce news for (radio and television) ELECTRONIC MEDIA by application of ORGANIZATIONAL, reporting, interviewing, writing, EDITING, packaging, and (direction) DIRECTING techniques.

Electronic Media Performance: Students will be able to execute and critically evaluate a variety of performance tasks including (radio) announcing, (radio and television) newscasting, reporting, HOSTING, and interviewing.

Film Theory and Criticism: Students will be able to describe the social, political, economic, technical, and aesthetic development of the American and international film industries from their origins to the present and demonstrate how individual films and film trends HELP TO CREATE, reflect, reinforce, exploit and/or challenge prevailing cultural values and shifting social attitudes.

Media Management: Students will be able to identify and apply relevant strategic approaches to issues and challenges in a variety of decision-making situations, including facility management, programming, sales, and promotion. [*This objective statement was not changed.*]

APPENDIX B: CENTRAL MICHIGAN UNIVERSITY DEPARTMENT OF BROADCAST AND CINEMATIC ARTS SYLLABUS

BCA 499   SENIOR SEMINAR   1(0-2) (no lecture/two lab hours)

Bulletin Description

Capstone assessment of the student's professional strengths and weaknesses plus refinement of strategies for establishing a successful post-graduation career.

Prerequisites

Signed BCA major or minor and senior standing. Must be taken in one of the last two semesters prior to graduation.

Textbooks and Other Required Student-Furnished Materials

None. Some very current articles and similar supplementary readings will be provided by the instructor.

Special Requirements

This class is part of the BCA major/minor "core." As with all core courses, students are required to earn a minimum grade of "C" for successful course completion.

General Methodology Used in Teaching the Course

As a seminar, the bulk of this class will be devoted to two key types of discussion:

   1) *Retrospective* discussions that isolate key issues and skills to which each student has been exposed during his/her involvement in BCA courses and co-curricular activities;

   2) *Projective* discussions that focus on key trends in the industry and what these trends might require of (a) entry-level and (b) veteran media professionals.

The course will also involve the administration and subsequent analytical discussion of a battery of tests designed to assess the level of student mastery in the "core" and "elective cluster" subject areas taught by the department. "Core" courses are those required of every BCA major and most minors. "Elective cluster" subject areas are more specialized/advanced studies that students choose in order to round out their programs.

Course Objectives

Upon completion of the Senior Seminar, students will be able to:

1) Identify and rank order their own professional strengths and weaknesses.
2) Determine how this strength/weakness inventory corresponds to the requirements and emphases of the type of industry position each is seeking.
3) Describe key trends in the electronic media and how these trends will influence the number and configuration of the industry position being sought.
4) Create:

   (a) a résumé conforming to industry expectations and

   (b) patterns for customizing it in order to target specific job classifications.
5) Produce one of the following: audition tape, production reel, writing or sales portfolio suitable for showing to potential employers.

General Course Outline

NOTE: THE COURSE WILL BE OFFERED EACH SEMESTER IN TWO HALF-SEMESTER BLOCKS. THUS, EACH SECTION WILL RUN FOR EIGHT WEEKS WITH FOUR HOURS OF MEETING TIME PER WEEK. EACH OF THE FOLLOWING UNITS IS ONE WEEK IN LENGTH.

UNIT I: Discussion: "What attracted me to study electronic media and is this element still the profession's prime attraction for me?" "Does this particular attraction realistically translate into a career opportunity for me?"

UNIT II: Diagnostic tests over the first three core course objectives in the areas of:
Survey of the Mass Media
Audio Production
Video Production

UNIT III: Analytical discussion of the results of the first three core objective diagnostic tests. Audition tape and production reel construction principles.

UNIT IV: Diagnostic tests over the last four core course objectives in the areas of:
History & New Technologies
Electronic Media Copywriting

Mass Media Criticism
Electronic Media Law & Regulation

UNIT V: Analytical discussion of the results of the last four core objective diagnostic tests. Writing and sales portfolio construction principles.

UNIT VI: Administration of the elective cluster objective test of each student's choosing; discussion of résumé construction and customization techniques.

UNIT VII: Analytical discussion of the results of the elective cluster diagnostic tests; discussion of current industry trends and dynamics and their implication for career launch.

UNIT VIII: Résumé and reel or portfolio revisions; dovetailing of professional aspirations with self-competency and industry realities.

Evaluation

One quarter (25%) of the student's grade will depend on completion of each of the seven "core" test batteries and at least one "elective cluster" battery. Because the prime purpose of these tests is that of individual and departmental assessment rather than mastery of *new* material, the *score* on each test will not be factored into the student's grade. The student will be considered to successfully have completed this portion of the course by taking the core and elective cluster batteries within the time frames specified in the course outline.

The remainder of the student's grade will be based on the following, with each of these factors constituting another 25% of the course grade:

1) The quality of informed participation in class discussions.
2) A short paper on industry trends most relevant to each individual's career goals and the competencies these trends most likely will place in demand. The paper's conclusion will compare/contrast student aspirations with that student's diagnostic test results. (Are the strength areas as ratified by the test results among the key components of professional positions being sought?) A finalized professional résumé will serve as the paper's Appendix.
3) Construction and refinement of *one* of the following:
    performance audition tape
    production reel
    writing or sales portfolio.

APPENDIX C:
A HANDOUT ON PORTFOLIO PREPARATION FOR UNIVERSITY OF TENNESSEE AT MARTIN COMMUNICATIONS DEPARTMENT SENIORS

A portfolio is an elegant binder, folder, or other neat, organized-looking device full of the best work you have done while enrolled at UT-Martin. Its immediate purpose is to demonstrate to a jury of department faculty in your sequence what you have learned to do (and do well) during your time here. But portfolios have a very valuable and practical purpose: When you graduate, you cannot expect to be hired as a professional communicator (especially in this combination depressed/competitive job market) *if you can't prove that you can do the work*– and do it better than all those other hundreds of communications graduates out there. As this department's faculty has stressed throughout your time here, the contents of a Communications Department graduate's stringbook, P.R. portfolio, or résumé/audition tape plus various samples of outstanding writing can be that extra bit of evidence that will get you your first job as a professional communicator.

If for one reason or another, you may not now possess all the items you need, I strongly suggest that you sign up for additional practicum (or simply volunteer to join the staff) at the *Pacer*, WUTM, WLJT, UTPM, etc., this semester–do a lot, and *save everything*. To help you understand what we're talking about, here are some examples of typical portfolio materials:

- Since you will learn effective résumé writing in senior seminar, your current résumé should be the first document in your portfolio. There is no need to include a cover letter.
- Radio production air checks and radio news air checks (well-edited with perfect levels: dubbed to cassette with great care and carefully cued to first sound minus two seconds).
- Television résumé tapes you produced as projects in TV News and ENG/EFP.
- Individual tapes, or excerpts from tapes of radio or television programs or program elements you produced.
- Broadcast copy (news, continuity, commercials, documentaries, entertainment scripts–Comm 315 is a great source for these).
- Professionally-oriented class projects (sales presentations, professional-looking projects such as an ad campaign or TV programming simulation, a research class survey, etc.).
- Clippings of your published newspaper or yearbook stories or photos.
- Newspaper or P.R. publication page layouts you have designed.
- News stories and research papers written for class assignments.
- P.R. news releases written for various course assignments.
- P.R. or other class project presentations, pamphlets, folders, research, etc.
- *Almost all* of your Desktop Publishing class assignments.
- *Any work similar to the above produced while working in the professional media and/or on an internship.*

Note: Failing to remove instructor comments, grades, notes, errors noted, etc., on any of these portfolio elements is just *not acceptable*. Any copy, paper, project or assignment worthy of inclusion in your portfolio should be reedited, sharpened, fixed, reprinted, etc., *prior* to inclusion in your portfolio. *Never* show off your mistakes to potential employers; *always* put your best foot forward. Also, when you get around to presenting some kinds of class projects in your portfolio, they may require some amount of introductory explanation. This is usually handled on title pages that precede these projects.

REGARDING QUANTITY, THESE ARE THE MINIMUM REQUIRE-MENTS:

• *News-editorial* students must present no less than TWENTY news stories, editorials, or feature stories, plus samples of publications you've edited (e.g., *Pacer* or *Spirit* pages you designed, Desktop Publishing class newsletter project, etc.) See the note below for a hint on how to reduce your large page layouts to fit the 8 1/2 x 11 size pages in your portfolio.

• *P.R. students* must present at least TEN news releases, plus TEN stories published in the *Pacer* or any other newspaper or magazine, plus samples of P.R. publications you've edited. You may also add any good broadcasting products you may have produced. If you've completed Desktop Publishing class, include the best of those projects. Hint: To get a job in P.R., it's important to show off your versatility. Do so with these samples.

• *Broadcasting students* must present no less than TEN separate examples of broadcast news, commercial or PSA copy and/or other continuity, written in perfect professional broadcast style, as you learned in Comm 315. Fill up *one complete page* of short radio copy to equal one of the ten examples required. All copy must be your original work, not rewrites of other people's copy. Among these examples, you must display AT LEAST one commercial, one broadcast news story, and one PSA. Also, broadcasting students must submit *3-6 sample pages from no less than one long-form TV show script, plus a treatment for that script*. All broadcasting students must submit either a TV or a radio résumé tape of between 5 to 10 minutes in length. You *may* turn in both radio and TV résumé tapes, but you *must* submit one or the other.

Also remember UTM's rules of academic honesty: The work you display in your portfolio must be your own: You may include something you did in a group project, providing the portion you include is entirely your own.

Standards for résumé tapes are as follows:

• TV production résumé tapes should begin with a slate, followed by 10 seconds of black, followed by your program audio and video. Also, tail slate the tape.
• Among your other clips, résumé tapes for *TV production students* must contain at least one commercial.

- Résumé tapes for *TV news students* should strictly adhere to the instructions in Don Fitzpatrick & Associates booklet, *How to Prepare and Improve Your Television News Audition Tape.*
- Résumé tapes for radio news should feature you reading copy in a short newscast (2 min or less), plus short clips from a few radio documentaries you produced and clips from one or more interviews you've conducted. Be sure to pepper your news stories with actualities (sound bites).
- Résumé tapes for radio production must include a radio air check, clips of you doing live commercials/PSAs, clips of you reading a short (30-45 second) headline newscast, followed by clips from some of your best production work, including PSAs, commercials, liners, etc.

Helpful Hints:

Borrowing tips from successful portfolios in prior semesters, be sure to do the following:

- Present your work in a classy-looking binder, folder or other neat, organized-looking device.
- Present no "bare pages": Insert *each individual page* into plastic, see-through material.
- Be sure to label each section with tabs and with title pages explaining the *kind* of work the prospective employer will be looking at (e.g., for a P.R. student, labels might separate news releases written while on internship from those written for P.R. classes, stories published in the *Pacer*, stories published elsewhere, desktop publishing, ad layouts, and P.R. research projects. Hint: Especially for P.R. research and broadcast sales projects, carefully label and explain what your potential employer is about to read).
- If your portfolio includes tapes, the formats should be audiocassette for radio and U-matic for television. These tape boxes will fit inside the back cover of your portfolio (Velcro is preferred to attach the tape boxes). *Label both these tapes and the boxes neatly and professionally,* and be sure that they are cued. Later on, when you're using your portfolio to help you get a job, don't forget to recue the tapes after each use.
- All copy should be incredibly neat and tidy and free from errors. Any copy not originally laser printed should probably be reprinted *with a laser-quality machine.* Professional employers look for evidence of quality in every aspect of the work you show them. This tells them what level of excellence you are capable of delivering on the job. And the reverse is true: They are also on the lookout for sloppy work, which tells them something bad about you and your work quality potential. If you can't do professional work when your very job is on the line, what level of quality can they expect from you every day?
- Since portfolios generally contain 8 1/2 x 11-sized documents, larger newspaper page layouts and other printed materials you have produced may not fit. To solve this problem, use a high-quality copier capable of doing reductions, and reduce these layouts to 8 1/2 x 11 size. If you can't get

satisfactory reductions over at the university printers, have them done at a professional copy shop.

APPENDIX D:
THE UNIVERSITY OF TENNESSEE AT MARTIN
DEPARTMENT OF COMMUNICATIONS COMM 492, SENIOR
SEMINAR SYLLABUS (ABRIDGED)

Course Description

Topics include an examination of communications theories and current issues through discussion, research and presentations, research and presentations on the cultures and media systems of other countries, plus activities to assist in preparation for graduates to successfully search for jobs in the communications industry. (Comm. 492 should ideally be taken during a student's last semester in residence at UT Martin.) *Prerequisite: Senior standing, and a nearly-completed major in Communications.*

Textbooks

A text designed especially for this class, *Readings in Mass Communication*, edited by Michael Emery and Ted Curtis Smythe; also *Naked at the Interview*, by Burton Jay Nadler, a book designed to prepare students to effectively search for and interview well for your first job.

Major Course Objectives

Upon successful completion of this course, students should be prepared to:
   a. understand and discuss selected major theories of mass communication;
   b. understand and discuss many of the major professional and social issues confronting communications practitioners today, such as first amendment issues, the status of women and minorities in the various communication industries, racial and gender discrimination in the media today, and social constructions of reality created by the media of mass communications.
   d. understand the cultures and governmental/regulatory structures in relation to the communications systems utilized in other countries, and compare them with those in America;
   e. create an attractive, persuasive cover letter and résumé and know how to compete effectively for entry-level positions in either the electronic media, print journalism, or public relations, or, use similar skills to compete successfully for acceptance and fellowships in M.A. degree programs in our discipline;
   f. use various kinds of resources to develop a long list of prospective employers to utilize in the job search;
   g. create a portfolio for prospective employers that demonstrates a graduate's ability to do the work required of an entry-level communications practitioner.

The Course Plan

We will conduct lecture-discussion sessions in which we will cover the major communication theories. To learn about current mass communication issues, you will choose readings from our textbook, report to the class, and actively participate in any discussion or debate that develops. To learn about world communication systems, you will investigate another country's system in depth, prepare a handout which includes the major statistics found in your report (everything from the literacy rate to the number of TV stations, networks, newspapers, magazines, cable TV systems, etc.) and present an oral report on that topic. Your professor will work with the class both as a whole and one-on-one to achieve Senior Seminar's fourth major course objective, personal preparation to compete for employment in the profession, or to obtain graduate school admission. To assist you in implementing an effective employment search, you will be assigned to research and develop a number of real "leads" for potential jobs. Also, in lieu of a written, university-required exit test, you will prepare, present, and be graded on a portfolio of the best work you have done during your time at UT-Martin.

Graded Assignments

Immediately purchase and read the two textbooks. Take notes on what we talk about in class during issues discussions, and study for an essay exam on *Readings in Mass Communications,* based on these readings and our class discussions. There is no need for an exam on *Naked at the Interview,* because if you really want to become employed after graduation, you *will* read it, cover-to-cover, more than once. Those who don't will very likely find employment alongside Al Bundy at the shoe store.

After lecture, discussion, handouts and readings in *Naked at the Interview,* you will choose an actual job advertisement, write a cover letter to apply for that job, and write a résumé, which you will use both for this job application and later for your portfolio.

During the portion of the course designated on the schedule for "Communication issues and discussions," each of you will present and discuss an article you've chosen from the text, and give opinions about the opinions offered by the writer. You will be graded on your preparation, knowledge of the subject, and your presentation skills.

You will research the media system of a country other than the U.S. You choose the country. The purpose of this research is to gather information for an informative, *extemporaneous* speech (that means you do not *read* your speech) to our class. On the assigned day, you will make a presentation to the class on your chosen country. For full credit, your oral presentation must address the following topics:

• *Briefly* outline the country's history, culture (try to find out the literacy rate) and politics (presentations which feature a lot to say about these topics and little to say about the media system will not earn full points);

- Discuss which of the five theories of the press the country utilizes (you'll learn the five theories in class), and justify your choice;
- Detail the country's media history;
- Include a description and evaluation of all mass media, from broadcasting to cable to newspapers to magazines and books, etc.,
- Detail the country's media regulatory and operational frameworks (laws and regulations, financial support structure, popular participation in media content, etc.,)
- Finally, if possible, do some "show and tell." Display as many examples of your chosen country's indigenous print and/or broadcast products as you can.
- You will also be graded on how well you present these topics. You'll have half the class to make your presentation. This means organization, oral presentation skills, visual aids, etc., all the things you were taught in Speech class. Also, on the day you are assigned to make your presentation, you will duplicate and hand out to all members of the seminar a "Media Fact Sheet" on your country. *Suggestion:* Start research on this project *early* in the semester. Some countries are harder to research than others, and if you are unsuccessful, you may need time to change countries and start over. That is hard to do late in the semester, when you are concerned about finishing your other courses well and preparing a good senior portfolio. Students in prior semesters who have been successful in this assignment say it takes more lead time than you think. *Take their advice.* Complete your research for this assignment before mid-term time.
- The job search mailing list project "jump starts" your efforts to find potential job leads and develop a professional approach to difficult task of finding employment after you graduate. You must submit a list of 100 names, titles, addresses, phone numbers and fax numbers of potential employers in your specialty area.

THE SENIOR PORTFOLIO

The senior portfolio is a compilation of your best work done at UT Martin, during your internship, and in the professional media job/s you have had. Along with this syllabus you will receive detailed instructions on how to put together your portfolio. Your grade for the portfolio is based on 100 points, and is submitted to the Tennessee Higher Education Commission as your score on the Communications major achievement test, a state graduation requirement. If your portfolio grade is below a 70, you will not pass Senior Seminar–and thus not graduate–until you resubmit and achieve a score of 70. However, 70 is the highest grade you can earn for any re-submission after the final portfolio deadline date. You may come to my office *at any time this semester* prior to the deadline date for help, or for me to "preview" your portfolio. You are urged to take advantage of this service. Nothing would please me more than for *all of you* to earn high scores on this project.

You should wait to enroll in Senior Seminar until your last semester at UT Martin so you can compile the most comprehensive, impressive portfolio. However, if the portfolio contents can be improved by adding items you will produce soon afterwards (eg., in an internship), you can receive an "I" grade for the semester and then resubmit your portfolio later on.

REFERENCES

Banta, T. W. (Ed.). (1993). *Making a difference: Outcomes of a decade of assessment in higher education.* San Francisco: Jossey-Bass.

Becker, L. B., Kosicki, T., Engleman, T., & Viswanath, K. (1993). Finding work and getting paid: Predictors of success in the mass communications job market. *Journalism Quarterly, 70* (4), 919.

Cappelli, P. (1992, November-December). College, students and the workplace: Assessing performance to improve the fit. *Change,* p. 57.

Eastman, S. (1994). Exit exams for the media major. In W. G. Christ (Ed.), *Assessing communication education: A handbook for media, speech, and theatre educators* (pp. 351-382). Hillsdale, NJ: Lawrence Erlbaum Associates.

Forrest, A. (Project Director). (1990). *Time will tell: Portfolio-assisted assessment of general education,* (Report of the American Association for Higher Education Assessment Forum)

Haley, E., & Jackson, D. (1995). A conceptualization of assessment for mass communication programs. *Journalism and Mass Communication Educator, 50*(1), 30.

Hutchings, P. (1990, April) Learning over time: Portfolio assessment. *AAHE Bulletin,* 6-8.

Moore, R. (1994). The capstone course. In W. G. Christ (Ed.) *Assessing communication education: A handbook for media, speech, and theatre educators* (pp. 155-179). Hillsdale, NJ: Lawrence Erlbaum Associates.

Nichols, J. (1991). *The departmental guide to implementation of student outcomes assessment and institutional effectiveness.* New York: Agathon Press.

Orlik, P. (1994). Student portfolios. In W. G. Christ (Ed.), *Assessing communication education: A handbook for media, speech, and theatre educators* (pp. 131-154). Hillsdale, NJ: Lawrence Erlbaum Associates.

Prus, J., & Johnson, R. (1993, June). *Student assessment options: A review and critical analysis.* Paper presented at the American Association for Higher Education 8th conference on higher education assessment, Chicago.

Schilling, K. M., & Schilling, K. L. (1993, March 24). Professors must respond to calls for accountability. *Chronicle of Higher Education,* p. A40.

Steinke, G. (1993). Tennessee broadcasters prefer workers with college communications training. *Feedback, 34*(1), 8.

4

Journalism and Mass Communication Programs

Judy VanSlyke Turk
University of South Carolina

Although there is no known automatic relationship between *teaching* and *learning*, journalism and mass communication faculty and administrators in today's "age of accountability" wrestle with the questions of how to document that their students learn, and how to document that the faculty's instructional efforts have something to do with that learning. A survey of journalism and mass communication administrators and a "mini" case study of how the College of Journalism and Mass Communications at the University of South Carolina developed its plan to measure learning shed light on how journalism and mass communication programs can and do involve themselves in outcomes assessment. The chapter includes model learning objectives and a checklist for successful outcomes assessment.

INTRODUCTION

Teach it and they will learn.

Journalism and mass communication educators are not likely to accept this prophecy as self-fulfilling, any more than they are likely to believe in the cinematic fantasy of "build it and they will come."

But while they know full well there is no automatic causal or correlational relationship between the concepts of teaching and learning, faculty and administrators in colleges of journalism and mass communication nevertheless struggle with demands from both internal and external constituencies that they document that their students *do* learn, and that the faculty's instructional efforts in the classroom and laboratory have something to do with that.

Although they may not call what they do "outcomes assessment," journalism and mass communication faculty and administrators are involved in assessing outcomes, what Erwin (1991, p. 15) described as "the process of defining, selecting, designing, collecting, analyzing, interpreting. and using information to increase students' learning."

The College of Journalism and Mass Communications at the University of South Carolina did not call its measurement of student learning outcomes assessment until it formalized a process of assessment in the 1995-1996 academic year. Without a formal process, the measurement of student learning that took place–from assignment of grades on student assignments to critiquing student performance in a capstone senior year course–did not specifically address any particular instructional goals. The purpose of this measurement had never been articulated but it was loosely assumed that faculty evaluated students to make sure the students had learned something necessary for successful performance in their chosen career fields.

But with rumblings in 1995 from both the South Carolina legislature and the state's Commission on Higher Education that additional data on student performance might well be required of public higher education institutions, the College's faculty agreed that designing a formal outcomes assessment program for the College might preempt imposition of a state-drafted plan.

Work on a formal plan began in the summer of 1995. The plan was approved in the spring of 1996, and its implementation will be carried out over the next academic year. What follows is a discussion of some of the questions the College addressed in developing its plan, and a synthesis of some of the issues other larger journalism and mass communication colleges might wish to address as they develop their own formal assessment programs.

KEY ISSUES AND CONCEPTS

Journalism and mass communication educators, not unlike their colleagues in other disciplines, must answer several questions as they develop and implement their outcomes assessment processes. Here are the questions the faculty at the University of South Carolina addressed in developing their outcomes assessment program:

1. *Why* do outcomes assessment? For what purpose(s)?
2. *What* do we assess?
3. *How* do we assess whatever it is we decide to assess? What techniques do we use?
4. How do we take advantage of *incentives* for assessment, and eliminate the *obstacles*?
5. How can we make our assessment process *successful*?

PURPOSES OF OUTCOMES ASSESSMENT

The literature of outcomes assessment suggests several purposes that may be served by measuring student outcomes. A 1995 survey of the 203 journalism and mass communication administrators whose academic units are members of the Association of Schools of Journalism and Mass Communication (ASJMC) indicated that identifying what students should be learning and evaluating the extent to which that learning occurs is the primary purpose of those who have implemented assessment programs. (A questionnaire was mailed to the 203 journalism and mass communication academic units that are members of the ASJMC. Two thirds of those who received questionnaires completed and returned them: 136 completed questionnaires were received, for a response rate of 67%.)

Almost 7 of 10 of the administrators who responded to that survey said evaluation of learning was the primary purpose of their units' assessment efforts. Other frequently mentioned purposes were the gathering of information for curriculum and course development, of prime importance to about 2 of 10 respondents, and measurement of faculty-teaching effectiveness, of prime importance to another 10% of the administrators.

Even though outcomes assessment is required of almost one third of the respondents by their state legislatures, and of almost 6 of 10 of the respondents by either the regional association that accredits their institution or their institution itself, few administrators (about 9%) said providing data for accountability to accreditors or for how public or institutional funds were spent was an important purpose of their outcomes assessment programs.

At the University of South Carolina, the purpose of developing a formal outcomes assessment program was twofold. One purpose was to beat the state legislature and/or higher education governing body "to the punch" and develop an assessment program before one was imposed by individuals likely to be less informed about journalism and mass communication education than the College's administrators and faculty. A second purpose was that mentioned most frequently in the ASJMC survey: to evaluate what, and how well majors in the College were learning.

WHAT TO ASSESS

Measurement and testing experts generally classify student outcomes as either cognitive, having to do with knowledge and the use of higher order mental processes; behavioral, having to do with the students' ability to perform specific tasks; or affective, having to do with students' feelings, attitudes, values, beliefs, self-concepts, aspirations, and social and interpersonal relationships (Astin, 1993). The literature (Association of American Colleges, 1985, pp. 15-24; Boyer, 1987, pp. 92-99; U.S. Department of Education, 1991) suggests a variety of outcomes that can and should be measured.

A list that includes cognitive, behavioral, and affective outcomes appropriate to professional education proposed in the Michigan Professional Preparation Network Report is of particular value to journalism and mass communication educators. That list includes communication competence, critical thinking, contextual competence, aesthetic sensibility, professional identity, professional ethics, adaptive competence, leadership capacity, scholarly concern, and motivation of continued learning.

Another taxonomy of outcomes developed by Alverno College combines the cognitive and affective outcomes of communication skills, analytical ability, problem-solving ability, social interaction, taking responsibility for the environment, involvement in the contemporary world, aesthetic responsiveness, and development of values (Jacobi, Astin, & Ayala, 1988).

Educators–including journalism and mass communication faculties and administrators–have tended to focus on measuring cognitive and behavioral outcomes such as subject-matter knowledge, academic ability, critical-thinking ability, special aptitudes, vocational achievement, and awards and recognition received.

The journalism and mass communication administrators surveyed in 1995 emphasized measurement of skills and professional competencies–cognitive outcomes–over measurement of affective outcomes. For instance, 9 of 10 respondents agreed or strongly agreed that outcomes assessment was most valuable when it measured experiential outcomes. An equal number said they had identified specific professional competencies and abilities they wanted their students to learn, and that they even had identified the specific courses or experiences through which they expected students to learn those competencies and abilities. A smaller number–7 of 10–said assessment of student learning must include attention to student values.

At the University of South Carolina, the emphasis in the learning objectives set by faculty–the objectives against which student learning is to be measured–is on performance of specific tasks and use of particular skills or knowledge (see Appendix A). But some attention is paid to affective outcomes, especially in terms of students' awareness of professional ethics and their ability to make ethical judgments and decisions. Inclusion of these ethical objectives was particularly appropriate given the wording of the University of South Carolina's motto that stressed the value of higher education in building character. The motto, in the original Latin translates, "Learning humanizes character and does not permit it to be cruel."

HOW TO ASSESS OUTCOMES

It is a truism of assessment that *how* you measure depends on *what* you measure. Respondents to the 1995 journalism and mass communication administrator survey indicated that even *whether* they measured outcomes depended in part on their ability to identify what they considered appropriate measurement tools. About 2 of 10 of the respondents who said they did not engage in outcomes assessment cited "no clear methods available to evaluate" or "no good instruments to use" as a reason. Complicating the issue is the reality that assessment can take place at the individual student, class, sequence, program, department, college, and/or university levels (Christ & McCall, 1994).

Given the preference of journalism and mass communication educators for measuring whether students have learned specific professional competencies and abilities, it is not surprising that most of the assessment that occurs is at the individual student level. Generally, this assessment infers that learning has occurred if the student can perform tasks that require use of specified competencies and abilities.

At the University of South Carolina, for example, we began the process of designing an outcomes assessment plan by enumerating the core and disciplinary-specific competencies we expected each student to demonstrate by the time degree requirements were completed (see Appendix A).

The literature of journalism and mass communication outcomes assessment (Ervin, 1988; Haley & Jackson, 1995) supported that preference for experientially based measures, with standardized testing generally used only when it is mandated by a university or a state legislature.

Based on responses to the 1995 survey of administrators, the most frequently used outcomes assessment technique in journalism and mass communication programs today is evaluation of student performance by an internship or job supervisor (92% used this technique).

Evaluation of student performance in a capstone course or experience was a technique used by three quarters of the respondents. Other frequently used techniques were evaluation of a portfolio of student work by a faculty member (65%), exit interviews of students by a faculty member (43%), and exit interviews of students by an administrator (37%). Evaluation of a portfolio of student work by a professional or advisory board member (23%) and administration of a comprehensive exam (20%) were techniques used by fewer than 1 of 4 respondents.

As the administration and faculty at the University of South Carolina began to consider which in the array of assessment techniques held the most promise for its formal program, the realization dawned that the College already was using several of these techniques. The College already had capstone courses in place that were required of all majors. Although internships were not required, they were encouraged and involved careful screening and evaluation of both the student and sponsoring organization. Certain courses included portfolio reviews.

Some faculty conducted brief, informal exit interviews with graduating advisees; faculty consensus was that those exit interviews should be "institutionalized" and expanded into a series of focus group interviews, conducted by the dean, associate deans and sequence directors, with approximately 20% of the graduating students each semester.

In other words, the wheel did not need to be invented and reinvented. Rather, the task of formalizing would involve examining techniques already in place and deciding, perhaps, to modify some while adding others.

SPECIFIC ASSESSMENT TECHNIQUES

Internships

Internships are used by many journalism and mass communication colleges to measure the extent to which students can successfully synthesize and apply skills and competencies they have been taught in a variety of classroom and laboratory situations. As such, an internship "could also be considered the final test for a sound curriculum in preparing the student for a profession," according to Limburg (1994, p. 192). Because a college degree alone is generally not enough to land a student a first full-time job after graduation, the internship also provides students with the professional experience that employers increasingly seek even in entry-level employees (Limburg, 1994).

At the University of South Carolina, students are encouraged to complete internships to validate their choice of a particular career field and to ascertain whether they are adequately prepared to enter that profession. Faculty and professional supervisors evaluate, as they assign a grade to student internship performance, how effectively students apply the variety of skills and the contextual knowledge they have been taught in already-completed courses.

Students acquire a portfolio of work that is examined by faculty and professional supervisors as part of the process of grading the internship. Feedback to the faculty from the intern in journal entries or final self-evaluation reports as to which courses and college experiences were most valuable in preparing the student for the internship, and for which on-the-job tasks the curriculum had not prepared the student, can be used by faculty to redesign or refine the curriculum (see chap. 3).

Capstone Courses

Capstone courses also provide students with an opportunity to demonstrate that they have learned and can use the knowledge and skills they have been taught in their coursework. As a form of summative evaluation, the capstone course provides an in-depth opportunity for students to demonstrate they have met a program's curricular goals and objectives as they apply their accumulated learning, in a single experience or opportunity, by developing creative products and solutions (Moore, 1994).

At the University of South Carolina, the capstone courses in the print and electronic journalism sequences are called *senior semesters*. A student in one of the senior semesters is simultaneously enrolled in 12 credit hours of advanced courses in the major (and is discouraged from enrolling in any other courses during that semester). The courses, a combination of reporting, writing, editing, and production, focus on preparation of a specific news product: a weekly laboratory newspaper for the print students, and daily television and radio newscasts for the electronic journalism students. The students function as the full-time staff of these news products, with the faculty serving as coaches and executive editors. For advertising and public relations majors, the capstone course is a campaigns course in which students working as a team research, plan, and often implement an advertising or public relations campaign for a client.

The University of South Carolina faculty adopted the view that the approaches students take and the decisions they make in solving the practical problems they encounter in these capstone courses reflect not only skills and knowledge but also attitudes, values, feelings, and beliefs, making it possible to judge the appropriateness of cognitive, behavioral, and affective learning to students' chosen professions.

The Carnegie Foundation recommended three instruments for measuring outcomes be incorporated into a capstone course: a senior thesis, which draws on the historical, social, and ethical perspectives of the major; an oral presentation of the thesis with peer critique; and preparation of a portfolio (Boyer, 1987).

At the University of South Carolina, the primary measure of learning in its capstone courses is the portfolio of work students accumulate: the articles they report, write, and edit or the page layouts they design; the on-air tapes of news packages they produce for radio and/or television; and the advertising or public relations campaign "book" to which the student contributes. In the advertising and public relations campaign course, students generally present their campaign plans. But there is no senior thesis or oral presentation of a thesis in any of the College's capstone courses.

Production or performance of a senior project provides an opportunity for the student to implement a workable solution to a problem or issue, applying skills and abilities learned in the curriculum. Wallace (1988, pp. 35-36) noted several advantages of the project: it puts students in close contact with faculty "coaches," and it "provides practical career-related experiences . . . (and) offer(s) the students a sense of accomplishment as they serve . . . in a quasi-professional practical capacity." At the University of South Carolina, for example, the campaigns courses link advertising and public relations students to real or hypothetical clients in the community. The senior semester projects for print and electronic journalism students assign students to work collaboratively on producing daily television and radio newscasts or weekly lab papers. Such collaborative effort "develops interpersonal skills and uses evidence as a support for plans and decisions. Additionally, the concept of deadlines, persuasive argument, and personal responsibility are developed" (Moore, 1994, p. 164). (For a list of advantages and disadvantages of capstone courses see Moore, 1994.)

Exit Interviews

Exit interview are employed to assess learning as students leave a journalism and mass communication program to enter a professional career or practice. Although the exit interview is typically a sit-down interview with the dean, department chair or faculty adviser, local practitioners or members of a program's professional advisory board may conduct the interview.

Limburg (1994) suggested the exit interview also can involve the equivalent of a mini-portfolio review when they include reviewing and critiquing with students the assignments they completed in key courses and assessing the degree of improvement in a student's work over time, and identifying areas of strengths and weaknesses in the student's overall performance.

The interview typically focuses on academic performance–acquisition of cognitive, behavioral, and affective skills and knowledge–and how this performance relates to expected career requirements. At the University of South Carolina, that certainly will be the focus when a form of exit interview is introduced in 1996. Rather than attempting to meet with each of the College's approximately 150 graduates each year in individual exit interviews, the faculty agreed that the Dean's Advisory Council (comprised of dean, associate deans, and sequence directors) should conduct two focus group interviews of approximately 15 graduating students each spring semester. Questions will focus on the degree to which students feel prepared to enter the professional workforce, on which of their college academic experiences most (or least) prepared them for their career and on their ability to articulate ethical and social values that should and do guide the fields of journalism and mass communications.

Portfolios

Portfolios provide a panoramic view of a student's development of professional skills and abilities over time. The primary task of the portfolio assessment process examines what Orlik (1994, p. 133) called "experience that often *already has been transcripted*." The portfolio, he said, ratifies what each student individually has achieved, compares this to what other students exposed to the same curricular structure have learned, and validates that each student possesses the fundamental skills and insights needed in his or her chosen career field (see chap. 3).

Portfolios frequently consist of samples of classroom or laboratory assignments completed, with written instructor comment; samples of work produced; performance evaluations by supervisors; and awards or commendations received. The portfolio has clear benefits for both the student and the academic program. The student acquires a job-seeking tool and the needed assurance that he or she possesses the skills and competencies needed for success in a chosen profession.

The journalism and mass communication college can examine the effectiveness of its curriculum in delivering its desired instructional outcomes, provided that the unit has determined and agreed on those desired outcomes *before* implementation of the portfolio assessment technique.

But the disadvantages outweighed these potential advantages when the faculty at the University of South Carolina considered adding a comprehensive portfolio review to its required assessment practices. Several professional courses required of the College's majors, from the beginning Writing for the Media course to capstone courses in both print and electronic journalism, include portfolios as key components of measuring student learning. But the faculty decided against a portfolio review that covered the student's entire college career largely because the time required for thorough review and feedback would detract from the College's realization of its high-priority goal to expand faculty scholarship, especially externally funded research. The faculty also expressed concern about the authenticity of portfolio work. They asked, at what stage might a piece of student work already critiqued and corrected (perhaps even multiple times) by a faculty member become something other than the student's own work?

Comprehensive Examinations

Comprehensive examinations administered to students as they graduate seem to have raised the most apprehension nationwide of any assessment technique, and certainly are among the least-used assessment techniques in journalism and mass communication colleges and departments. In the 1995 survey of administrators, only 20% used comprehensive examinations, and virtually all of these were in states where such a comprehensive examination is required by the state legislature. A 1992 survey of 276 institutional members of the Broadcast Education Association (BEA) who had undergraduate degree programs showed the same disdain for comprehensive examinations as the 1995 study of members of the ASJMC. In the BEA study, only 6% of the programs used any kind of comprehensive exit examination even though many reported using other assessment mechanisms (Eastman, 1994).

Objections to standardized testing abound. Nielsen and Polishook (1990) claimed that standardized tests are as likely to confuse as to inform. Eastman (1994) noted that because students do not start with the same knowledge or skills, and learn different things from the same experiences, standardized tests are meaningless except as a measure of one student's ability to perform well on future similar tests.

Although many fields and disciplines have developed national standardized exams, the Assessment Resource Center at the University of Tennessee reports that more than 40 fields–including journalism and mass communication–lack such national testing instruments (Eastman, 1994). So on those rare occurrences when comprehensive examinations *are* used in journalism and mass communication programs, the instruments are developed locally.

Faculty generally are suspicious of and resistant to developing and using standardized tests "partly because they are wary about the uses to which assessment findings will be put, especially in state systems, and partly because of the predictable costs in faculty time and energy" (Wolf, 1989, p. 8). Quantitative examination results might be twisted into measures of teaching achievement, thus affecting retention, promotion, and salaries.

Eshelman (1991) outlined several ethical dangers associated with exit testing including coercion of units into adopting tests lacking educational validity in response to political pressure and the encouragement of "teaching to the test."

At the University of South Carolina, faculty briefly discussed using a media organization's employment test (usually a combination of writing, editing, and current events) as a standardized measure of learning for print and electronic journalism students. But unwillingness of media organizations to share examples of such examinations, and lack of a valid comparable professional instrument for advertising and public relations professions, resulted in the decision against any standardized testing.

ASSESSMENT OBSTACLES AND INCENTIVES

Opponents of outcomes assessment argue that setting goals, measuring outcomes, and being accountable for results works well in business settings but not in the academy (Rosenbaum, 1994). Skeptics say outcomes assessment is a lockstep process that goes against the grain of individual autonomy and academic freedom, and that it has no value unless it is tied to rewards and incentives, such as increased funding, which is too rarely the case.

Respondents to the 1995 survey of journalism and mass communication administrators who said their units were not involved in outcomes assessment were most likely to give as a reason the fact that they were *not required* to do assessment (one third of the respondents). Other prevalent reasons were lack of a clear assessment methodology (18%) or of assessment instruments (21%). Some cited the expense involved in assessment as a deterrent (15%), and a handful (3%) mentioned fears that assessment data might be misused. Nine percent cited a lack of faculty support within the unit for assessment procedures.

These findings parallel in many respects those of a 1986 survey of colleges and universities by the American Council on Education that identified five major obstacles to outcomes assessment (presented in order of frequency of mention with most mentioned listed first): lack of funds to develop assessment procedures, no clear methods to evaluate, fears that assessment data would be misused, lack of faculty support, and no good instruments (Sims, 1992).

But just as there are obstacles to adoption of outcomes assessment, so are there incentives, some of them certainly of the "if you can't lick 'em, join 'em" variety. Being required by law, regulation, or accreditation standard is one sure incentive. Another is that many of the techniques of outcomes assessment are not new and are, in fact, already in place in many journalism and mass communication colleges. Outcomes assessment may just be making explicit what faculty and administrators have been doing all along through internships, portfolio reviews, capstone courses, and even exit interviews.

As mentioned earlier, the University of South Carolina's College of Journalism and Mass Communications sought to introduce its own program of outcomes assessment to preempt imposition, by legislature or state governing board, of an assessment plan it might find less palatable than one of its own devising. And the administration and faculty took stock of what measurement of learning already was talking place so that its formal assessment plan became, in many ways, only an explicit articulation of what already had been going on informally.

A third incentive–that outcomes assessment can lead to improving teaching and learning–also helped tip the scales at the University of South Carolina. The College's tenure and promotion guidelines, and its requirement of formal annual performance reviews, place heavy emphasis on quality of teaching. Many faculty were quick to grasp that a formal program of outcomes assessment would give them "hard" data regarding their effectiveness in teaching.

As Astin (1993, p. 130) noted, "The role of assessment is to enhance the feedback available to faculty and staff in order to assist them in becoming more effective practitioners (to) enhance practitioners' understanding of the connections between their actions and the talent development process." And research has begun to show that outcomes assessment does, indeed, lead to improvement in learning and teaching when designed for these purposes and when conducted properly (Banta, 1993).

INGREDIENTS OF SUCCESSFUL ASSESSMENT

Perhaps the seminal assessment issue for journalism and mass communication educators is how to ensure that when it is done, it is done well. (see Appendix B: Checklist for Successful Outcomes Assessment). The literature and the experience of the University of South Carolina tell us that successful outcomes assessment can be distilled into five points.

First, successful outcomes assessment begins with clarification of the goals and values of the educational experience. The University of South Carolina faculty began by asking themselves what they wanted their students to know or do, and then linked those goals to the College mission.

Second, successful outcomes assessment links learning goals and objectives to particular courses or curricular requirements. At the University of South Carolina, each objective was matched to a particular course in the curriculum where it should be taught. When it appeared that an objective was not met by the present curriculum, suggestions for course enhancements and improvements were made to the curriculum committee to ensure that all objectives were consciously addressed in the curriculum.

Third, successful outcomes assessment uses multiple approaches so that the complex relationships between learning and teaching can be fully explored in a variety of contexts. The University of South Carolina faculty concluded that use of multiple approaches–a blend of the traditional such as test and exams with some less traditional alternatives such as exit interviews or capstone courses–provides more reliable, valid, and meaningful results than assessment based on just one measure.

Fourth, successful outcomes assessment involves everyone who is part of the learning-teaching process, with faculty taking responsibility for leading and designing the assessment. Journalism and mass communication administrators may initiate the planning process, but the faculty must own it and play the lead role in clarifying mission, setting goals and objectives, and determining how to measure student achievement.

Fifth, successful outcomes assessment requires clear and frequent communication among all the stakeholders to avoid confusion and mistrust and to ensure that the results are used. At the University of South Carolina, the results of each outcomes assessment measure will be communicated back to both students and faculty so they can use the results for the improvement of learning and teaching. The results also will become part of regular reporting to the University's central administration and the self-study conducted for review every 6 years by the Accrediting Council on Education in Journalism and Mass Communications (ACEJMC). Faculty also are expected to incorporate some of this information in their tenure and promotion dossiers and in their annual performance reviews to demonstrate effective teaching.

Evidence of success will come from longitudinal measurement of student performance, with the expectation that student performance will show continuous improvement as data from one year's measurement are used to improve instruction in subsequent years. At South Carolina and elsewhere, therefore, we must await the "proof of the pudding" of outcomes assessment implementation.

APPENDIX A: CORE COMPETENCIES AND LEARNING OBJECTIVES

Core Competencies for All Undergraduate Students

WRITING: The core skill is the ability to write well. This simple objective provides students with occupational insurance.   Good writing is THE characteristic most in demand by our partner employers.

SPEAKING: Presenting one's ideas and work in a professional manner is necessary for any graduate. Our students should be able to adequately articulate their thoughts.

THINKING: Logical manipulation of facts combined with insightful interpretation is mandatory for each student.

COMMUNITY: To reweave the frayed fabric of society each student must understand his/her role in community building.

Learning Objectives For Electronic and Print Journalism Undergraduates

BASIC KNOWLEDGE

An undergraduate student who completes the degree requirements in the electronic and print journalism sequence should possess basic knowledge of:

- The role and history of journalism in American society.
- The First Amendment foundation of journalism.
- The legal parameters of journalism, libel, slander, invasion of privacy, telecommunications regulations, etc.
- The telecommunications industry as it now operates and its future prospects.
- The relation of wire services, syndicates, and news video providers to media outlets.
- The economics of journalism.
- The influences of technology and computers on the information delivery process.
- The retrieval and use of information from electronic data bases in news stories. The use of quantitative and qualitative research in the daily practice of journalism.
- The importance of the written word as a method of conveying information.
- The manipulation of words, sound, graphics, still and moving visual images to construct journalistic messages.
- The moral and ethical considerations of journalism.
- The diversity / ethnicity / racial / gender issues in news coverage and in news operations.
- The role of journalism in affecting public policy.
- Propaganda and its use in the news process.

BASIC SKILLS

An undergraduate student who completes the degree requirements in the electronic and print journalism sequence should demonstrate the ability to perform these journalistic tasks:

- Gather information through interviewing, observation and the use of documents, printed and computerized, to write fair and balanced news, news-feature stories.
- Access information via Freedom of Information Acts, understanding the rights and restrictions of such acts.
- Access and analyze quantitative data (like government budgets and tax rates) and describe their potential impact on people and society.
- Read a legislative bill and explain how it becomes law.
- Access the criminal justice system and write appropriate stories.
- Use news judgment to identify newsworthy events and sources.
- Deal fairly with public officials, politicians, public and private persons who are in the news.
- Develop and cultivate sources and properly use confidential sources and off-the-record and background information.
- Handle quotes, including sound bites, from sources correctly and ethically.
- Use computers to gather data, write and edit stories.
- Write accurate, fair, and balanced news stories, news-features, and features.
- Write and edit copy, including spelling, punctuation, and grammar, in conformance with standard English and journalistic style, such as Associated Press style.
- Cover, write, revise, and edit stories under deadline pressure.
- Shoot, select, edit, and present pictures, graphics, and video with an appreciation of the ethics of the manipulation of visual images.
- Design news presentations: newspaper layout or broadcast newscast.
- Use the accepted journalistic, legal, and cultural standards for publishing profanity.
- Work effectively and fairly with supervisors and coworkers.
- Prepare appropriate résumé material to find the first and next job.
- Read and circulate reports, evaluate coverage and operations to identify areas in need of improvement.

GENERAL KNOWLEDGE

- The differences between American journalism practices and those in other countries.
- The management skills needed in mass media operations, such as personnel practices, legal procedures, accounting principles, etc.
- The skills needed to survive in a business-based working environment, such as time management and interpersonal interaction.

Learning Objectives for Advertising Undergraduates

GENERAL

An undergraduate who completes degree requirements in the advertising program should:

- Understand the origin and evolution of advertising, including major events and key historical figures and their contributions (e.g., figures such as those featured in Bart Cummings' book *The Benevolent Dictators*).
- Know the different roles that advertising plays for various organizations and how it fits into the overall marketing mix. Know what "integrated marketing communications" refers to and know the difference between advertising and marketing, sales promotions, publicity, public relations, and personal selling.
- Be aware of the major social and ethical issues in advertising: deception, puffery, taste, stereotyping (women, Hispanics, Blacks, the elderly), advertising to children, advertising controversial products, subliminal advertising, intercultural differences, political advertising, influence on the media.
- Understand the major economic issues of advertising: advertising and . . . prices, added value, consumer choice, industry concentration, influence on business cycle, aggregate consumption, and advertising as a media subsidy. Also be aware of international ownership and mergers or consolidations in the field.
- Understand the major regulatory constraints of advertising: (1) areas of advertising control (content, type of product advertised, fairness, and barriers to competition); (2) government regulation: federal (FTC and other agencies); state and municipal; (3) self-regulations; and (4) other influences: the media, associations, the trade press.
- Know the "players" that make up the advertising industry: (1) advertisers (clients): national and local (retail); (2) agencies (full service–including all marketing communication functions–and specialized); (3) media and media reps; and (4) suppliers.
- Know how ad agencies and corporate/retail ad departments are organized and what functions are performed by each department within those organizations. Also know what organizational trends have taken place in agencies and advertisers in recent years.
- Understand what services agencies perform for their clients, how agencies and the services they provide have changed over time, how agencies are compensated, how staff time is billed, how agencies win and lose accounts, and how they handle the issue of competing accounts.
- Know the major methods of budgeting used in advertising and the advantages and disadvantages of each (objectives and task, percent of sales, unit of sale, competitive spending, quantitative and experimental, affordable and arbitrary).
- Know the major methods of primary and secondary research used in the following types of research activities: general market information; competitive marketing and promotional activities; consumer attitudes, brand and theme awareness; consumer product and media usage patterns; audience

and circulation data; pretesting and posttesting individual ads and commercials and evaluating entire campaigns.

- Know advertising media: their evolution; recent trends in media usage; characteristics and relative advantages and disadvantages of various media types; how their audiences are measured and by whom; how time and space are bought and sold; how advertisers and agencies compare the relative efficiency of various media types and vehicles.
- Know target marketing: ways advertisers classify consumer segments (demographics, geodemographics, psychographics, benefit segmentations, etc.) and how is that information obtained and by whom.
- Know advertising creative: how message strategy is arrived at, who is involved in its creation, how it is tested, and how the creative process is carried out from initial problem to creative workplan to final execution.
- Understand the various types of sales promotions and event marketing activities and how they are employed in different market situations.
- Understand the concept of database marketing and how it is employed by marketers.
- Know the major elements that must be considered when developing print and electronic messages–e.g., headlines, body copy, layout styles, layout principles, typography/color, printing methods, etc. in print; scripts, storyboards, taping and filming in electronic messages.
- Be familiar with major published literature and reference material in the discipline: have read some of the major books in the field that touch on the business (e.g. *Ogilvy on Advertising*), the people (*From Those Wonderful People Who Brought You Pearl Harbor* or *Leo*) or the issues; should be familiar with the key business magazines in the field (*Ad Age, AdWeek, American Demographics,* etc.), major syndicated services (MRI, Nielsen), specialized reference books (*SRDS* catalogs), key academic journals (*Journals of Marketing, Journal of Advertising,* etc.), and other more general sources that cover the field on a regular basis (*The New York Times, The Wall Street Journal*). And, they should be aware of major advertising organizations such as 4As, ANA, AAF, etc.
- Know the jargon of the business. (Maybe we just require students to learn an assigned glossary of terms for one of our upper level courses.)
- Be knowledgeable about various career opportunities in the field and be aware of the skills needed to excel in each of these career areas.

SPECIFIC

An undergraduate who completes degree requirements in the advertising program should:

- Be able to do secondary research on a market, an industry, a geographical area, a consumer group or a company through conventional "hard copy" library resources and CD-ROMs and online sources.
- Be able to do primary research (survey or observation) to determine current and potential customers' attitudes, awareness, and usage of client and competitive products or services.

- Be able to develop a creative workplan . . . and create the subsequent creative executions for an entire advertising campaign in a variety of media.
- Be able to do a small-scale pretest of rough versions of ads/spots; be able to set down a campaign evaluation plan; and be able to set up an experiment to determine the relative effectiveness of different messages.
- Be able to do an entire media plan, from objectives to tactics.
- Be able to do an entire sales promotion plan, from objectives to tactics.
- Be able to do an entire publicity/event marketing plan, from objectives to tactics.
- Understand (though not necessarily be able to do it) enough about what takes place in the production of a TV and radio commercial that they could ask intelligent questions of the producer of the spot. Ditto on print production.
- Be able to write the script and all the slides for an A-V presentation to be made to a client or to top management and any of the topic areas listed above.

Learning Objectives for Public Relations Undergraduates

BASIC KNOWLEDGE

An undergraduate student who completes degree requirements in the public relations program should possess basic knowledge of:

- The role and function of public relations within business, not-for profit, and government organizations.
- Options for staffing the public relations function: internal department v. external firm, technician v. manager practitioner roles, and interaction of public relations practitioners with other organizational employees, suppliers, and vendors.
- The range of activities that may be performed by public relations practitioners: publicity, promotion, public education, public affairs, lobbying, media relations, marketing public relations, community relations, financial relations, employee relations, customer relations, relations with special interest and activist groups, issues management.
- The societal benefits provided by the practice of public relations and the degree to which those benefits are recognized and acknowledged by employers, clients, the mass media, and the public.
- The relationship between First Amendment rights and the practice of public relations.
- The historical development of the public relations function, historical figures who have played major roles in development of the practice, and historically significant case studies that have shaped the field.
- Contribution women and minorities have made to the development of the public relations practice, and the roles and status of women and minorities in the current public relations workforce.
- The variety of models used to depict how public relations is practiced in a variety of organizational settings and situations: press agentry/publicity, public information, two-way asymmetric, two-way symmetric.
- Trends and issues likely to influence the future practice of public relations: internationalization/globalization of organizations; downsizing of internal

public relations staffs and resultant outsourcing of public relations tasks; growing public distrust of businesses, institutions, government and the media; ethical dilemmas arising out of conflict of interest, conflict of commitment, and cross-cultural differences.

- Leading sources of information on current practices in the field of public relations: PRSA's Body of Knowledge; publications such as *PR Tactics and Techniques, PR Strategist, PR Reporter, PR Quarterly, Public Relations Review, Journal of Public Relations Research.*
- Characteristics, member services and codes of ethics of major professional organizations: PRSA, IABC, IPRA.
- Concepts and theories of persuasion and the formation and change of attitudes and opinions.
- The history and current roles, functions, and practices of mass and specialized media and their utilization in public relations communication.
- Concepts and theories that help explain and predict which channels and media of communication are most effective with a variety of target publics and in a variety of communication situations.
- The roles of research at various stages of the public relations process and research methodologies that are appropriate to each stage.
- Interconnectedness of public relations, advertising, and marketing in an organization's overall communication efforts and the differences among these communication-related disciplines.
- Symbiosis of visual and nonvisual communication in public relations communication.
- Legal constraints on the practice of public relations: libel, slander, privacy, copyright, contracts, government regulations, freedom of information laws, proposals to license the practice of public relations.
- Ethical constraints on the practice of public relations: PRSA and IABC codes of ethics, concepts of social responsibility, PRSA and IABC accreditation of practitioners.

BASIC SKILLS

An undergraduate student who completes degree requirements in the public relations program of study should demonstrate the ability to perform these public relations tasks:

- Write news and feature releases for a variety of types of announcements and types of organizational employers or clients.
- Plan and implement a news conference or news briefing, including preparation of a media kit and preparation of executives for media interviews.
- Write copy for an employee, member and/or customer newsletter.
- Write copy for a promotional or educational brochure.
- Write a script for a video news release.
- Write a script for both a radio and a television public service announcement.
- Write a speech or text for an oral presentation.
- Write a business memo and/or business letter.
- Write and design an issues, image, or advocacy advertisement.
- Design and execute a layout for a flyer, newsletter, and brochure.

- Write and design a résumé that effectively markets the student's experience and skills for entry-level employment.
- Write a report summarizing and drawing conclusions from data and information collected in a survey, content analysis, and/or background search of the literature.
- Write, pretest, administer, and analyze a public opinion/attitude survey and/or a communication audit or readership study.
- Gather demographic and behavioral characteristics and media usage patterns of target publics using library resources and online methods of accessing secondary research data.
- Develop and write a strategic plan/proposal that identifies and defines a public relations problem; identifies goals, objectives, and target publics; identifies appropriate techniques and tactics to solve the problem and meet objectives; determines a budget and timetable to carry out those techniques and tactics; and sets forth a plan to evaluate results.
- Develop and write a crisis communication plan.
- Plan and implement a special event (tour, groundbreaking, anniversary, open house, etc.), including the marketing and publicizing of that event.
- Script and deliver an oral presentation, with visual aids, of a proposal for a project or campaign.
- Script and deliver an oral presentation, with visual aids, evaluating the results of a project or campaign.

APPENDIX B: CHECKLIST FOR SUCCESSFUL OUTCOMES ASSESSMENT

Does our journalism and mass communication unit have a clear and articulate mission statement?

Does it meet the needs of our institution and of our constituencies?

Do we have consensus on the values and goals of the educational experience with which we provide our students?

Have we agreed on what it is we want our students to know or to be able to do by the time they graduate?

Have we identified competencies we want to teach, and linked them with specific courses or educational experiences in our curriculum?

Are the competencies we've identified consistent with our mission?

Do we agree on the purpose of our assessment program?

Are we measuring student outcomes to improve teaching?

Or are we measuring outcomes to be more accountable for how we are using and investing faculty and monetary resources?

Are we prepared to examine not only the outcomes of teaching–what students learn–but the processes of teaching and learning?

Do we acknowledge that different learning styles among students mandate a variety of teaching styles to ensure that all students have the opportunity to learn?

Do we differentiate between "experiencing" and "learning?"

Have we devised multiple means for measuring what students are learning?

Do we go beyond the mundane classroom measures of tests and graded assignments?

Do we blend faculty or "outsider" examination of student outputs–portfolio reviews, internships, capstone courses–with student self-evaluation of what they have learned?

Is everyone involved in the teaching and learning process involved in planning and administering our outcomes assessment program and measures?

Are faculty in charge?

Was input from students and from professionals such as advisory board members or local employers sought in the initial planning stage of the program?

Are we committed to using the results of outcomes assessment?

Do we have a plan to communicate the results of the measurements we take to both faculty and students?

Have we identified specific ways–curriculum review, course revision, input into faculty performance, tenure or promotion reviews–in which the results can be used?

REFERENCES

Association of American Colleges (1985). *Integrity in the college curriculum: A report to the academic community.* Washington, DC: Author.

Astin, A. W. (1993). *Assessment for excellence: The philosophy and practice of assessment and evaluation in higher education.* Washington, DC: American Council on Education.

Banta, T. W., & Associates (1993). *Making a difference. Outcomes of a decade of assessment in higher education.* San Francisco: Jossey-Bass.

Boyer, E. L. (1987). *College: The undergraduate experience in America.* New York: Harper & Row.

Christ, W. G., & McCall, J. (1994). Assessing "the what" of media education. In S. Morreale & M. Brooks (Eds.), *1994 SCA Summer Conference Proceedings and Prepared Remarks* (pp. 477-493). Annandale, VA: Speech Communication Association.

Eastman, S. T. (1994). Exit examinations for the media major. In W. G. Christ (Ed.), *Assessing communication eduction: A handbook for media, speech, and theatre educators* (pp. 351-382). Hillsdale, NJ: Lawrence Erlbaum Associates.

Ervin, R. F. (1988, October). Outcomes assessment: The rationale and the implementation. *Insights* (pp. 19-23). Columbia, SC: Association of Schools of Journalism and Mass Communication.

Erwin, T. D. (1991). *Assessing student learning and development.* San Francisco: Jossey-Bass.

Eshelman, D. (1991, April). *Outcomes assessment strategies: Implications for broadcast education.* Paper presented to the Courses and Curriculum Division of the Broadcast Education Association, Las Vegas, NV.

Haley, E., & Jackson, D. (1995). A conceptualization of assessment for mass communication programs. *Journalism & Mass Communication Educator, 50*(1), 26-34.

Jacobi, M., Astin, A., & Ayala, F., Jr. (1988). *College student outcomes assessment: A talent development perspective.* Washington, DC: Association for the Study of Higher Education.

Limburg, V. E. (1994). Internships, exit interviews, and advisory boards. In W. G. Christ (Ed.), *Assessing communication eduction: A handbook for media, speech, and theatre educators* (pp. 181-200). Hillsdale, NJ: Lawrence Erlbaum Associates.

Moore, R. C. (1994) The capstone course. In W. G. Christ (Ed.), *Assessing communication eduction: A handbook for media, speech, and theatre educators* (pp. 155-179). Hillsdale, NJ: Lawrence Erlbaum Associates.

Nielsen, R. M., & Polishook, I. H. (1990, April 11). Taking a measure of assessment. *Chronicle of Higher Education*, p. A14.

Orlik, P.B. (1994). Student portfolios. In W. G. Christ (Ed.), *Assessing communication eduction: A handbook for media, speech, and theatre educators* (pp. 131-154). Hillsdale, NJ: Lawrence Erlbaum Associates.

Rosenbaum, J. (1994). Assessment: An overview. In W. G. Christ (Ed.), *Assessing communication eduction: A handbook for media, speech, and theatre educators* (pp. 3-29). Hillsdale, NJ: Lawrence Erlbaum Associates.

Sims, S. J. (1992). *Student outcomes assessment: A historical review and guide to program development.* New York: Greenwood.

U.S. Department of Education. (1991). *America 2000: An Education Strategy.* Washington, DC: Author.

Wallace, R. C. (1988, January). A capstone course in applied sociology. *Teaching Sociology, 16*, 34-40.

Wolf, B. L. (1989, November 28). *The assessment initiative at Indiana University-Bloomington.* Unpublished paper, Indiana University, Bloomington.

5

Distance Learning

Kathy A. Krendl, Ron Warren, and Kim A. Reid
Indiana University

If technology does anything at all, it makes us creatures of habit. On our university campus, we are habitual users of computer E-mail systems, but we are seldom as aware of this as when we need to deal with students who do not share our computer dependence. Our communication technology is not an issue when we all are familiar with it and use it every day. When something this basic becomes an issue, however, we are reminded that our means of communication are still quite new (and that we all became techno-dependents rather quickly).

As we write this chapter, we are involved in a course called Living in the Information Age, which asks students to discuss the technological developments of present-day society and their social implications. A handful of the students live quite a distance away and "attend" the class via video- and audio-teleconferencing technologies. The course asks students to use E-mail, computer, conferencing, fax, telephone, and audiovisual technologies to complete basic tasks like submitting assignments, gathering and sharing research materials, and even attending class. As one might imagine, some people need more help with these tasks than others who are "habitual users" of electronic mail, computer conferences, and electronic databases.

What we have done is no different from other instructors who have offered college courses at a distance. We have asked people to change the way they communicate in their courses, and, therefore, the way they learn. The small step to an electronic mail account can be an enormous leap for many people, especially nontraditional students who are most attracted by distance education opportunities. In essence, such issues of connectedness are our focus in assessing learning at a distance. This chapter looks at the nature of educational communication, distance learning, and the implications of recent technologies for those wishing to determine the effectiveness of such programs for their own educational institutions.

LEARNING CONTEXTS AND EDUCATIONAL COMMUNICATION

Although the tendency among researchers has been to base comparisons of distance education and traditional classes specifically on what transpires in the classroom, the range of learning contexts and experiences associated with most traditional instruction is actually quite broad. Students attend lectures, participate in discussions, avail themselves of the instructor's office hours, break into small groups, go to the library for required readings and research exercises, and so on.

Our goal in designing a distance-education course was to adopt a broad definition of learning contexts associated with instruction and attempt to integrate technology as fully as possible into a wide range of activities. That is, we attempted to use technology to provide a diverse array of learning activities similar to the array of activities that students experience in traditional educational contexts. For example, in the traditional classroom students meet face-to-face with the instructor during scheduled class meetings. In the distance-education class, interactive audio and video capabilities were utilized so that students participating from a distance were able to interject questions and comments throughout the class sessions. In addition, instructors typically hold office hours for students to meet with them on a one-to-one basis, creating an environment conducive to the development of a mentoring relationship. In the distance-education context, this function was fulfilled through faculty-student meetings conducted via telephone (using a toll-free number) during regularly scheduled hours in real time or asynchronously by E-mail, providing students more flexibility to communicate with the instructor at their convenience. Students conducted research online, investigating Internet resources and online information services, rather than physically traveling to the campus library. The research process–asking focused questions, identifying key terms and concepts, selecting appropriate resources, and so on–is not altered by the mode of delivery. Whether residential students conduct their research within the walls of the library, from a dorm room, or from a site distant from campus makes little difference. The process of conducting information searches and locating relevant resources remains intact. Finally, collaborative learning experiences were arranged electronically using computer conferencing to facilitate communication and learning among small groups of students, just as students participating in traditional classes often form or are assigned to discussion groups or study groups that meet informally.

DEFINING DISTANCE LEARNING

For many of those who have been instructors or students in distance-education courses, the differences between so-called "traditional" classroom instruction and distance learning are at once fundamental yet nonexistent. That is, the change in classroom technology introduces new and varied teaching-learning experiences. Yet, the fundamental practice of education remains. Although the separation of teacher and student brings profound changes to any course, a well-designed and managed experience yields learning that may surpass the lecture/discussion, or "chalk talks," that many associate with higher education. To assess distance learning, we must first understand exactly what we mean by the term and identify the nature of learning at a distance. This section discusses a definition of distance education, the concepts related to the assessment of distance learning, and the focal concerns of these processes.

Distance Education

As may be expected, there are literally dozens of definitions of "distance education" offered in the literature. Some scholars trace distance education back to the earliest days of correspondence study in Europe and the United States (Holmberg, 1986). Consequently, many definitions of distance education begin (and some end) with the physical separation of teacher and student (Holmberg, 1977; Moore, 1973). Of course, with this physical and sometimes temporal separation come important features that characterize distance education (Keegan, 1988):

1. The use of technical media to permit teacher-student communication and deliver course content and instruction.
2. The provision of two-way communication that allows students to benefit from or initiate dialogue.
3. The teaching of students as individuals, cut off from other students and other means of learning not directly associated with the teacher.
4. The influence of an educational organization in preparing and delivering instructional materials and student support services.

This list of characteristics is clear on one point–distance education is a product of the Industrial Age. Peters (1973, as cited in Keegan, 1988. p. 6) stated that distance education's emphasis is on reproduction of quality learning materials for a growing number of students. He unequivocally stated that, "It (distance education) is an industrialized form of teaching and learning."

Some scholars have criticized such definitions for emphasizing "distance" and the technological means of bridging the teacher-student gap. Larsen (1986) pointed out that although content can be transmitted by many media, be it print or electronic, learning remains an inductive process. Garrison and Shale (1987) argued that the essential criteria that identify the distance-education focus on teacher-student communication processes. In their view, such communication is noncontiguous, technologically mediated, and facilitates/supports the educational process. Smith (1988) saw this as a dialogical process that necessarily reaches beyond course materials. In short, a meaningful dialogue among teachers and students is not bound to books and videotapes.

Communication and Delivery Technology

In essence, a communicative approach to distance education takes a very different view of what delivery technology means. The correspondence perspective sees media as a means of delivering course materials from the school to the home. In most cases, the goal is to let these materials stand on their own–students learn from them independent of teachers. The focus here is on a clear transmission of information with at least one channel of two-way communication (usually the mail or telephone). The alternative, which we shall call a communication perspective, looks at delivery technologies for their impact on the communication process. Rather than a means of transmitting information, technologies are assessed for their effects on instructional interaction, collaboration, and learning.

The blend of delivery technologies used in 1990s distance courses (e.g., video conferencing, computer conferencing, online databases, World Wide Web sites) may be seen as a way of producing knowledge rather than simply receiving it. If they have access to such technologies, students have easier access to vast arrays of information about any subject. At the same time, however, students must assume more control over and responsibility for their learning. They must explore wider bases of material on their subject matter, assemble this information into personally meaningful forms of knowledge, and bring this meaning to bear on the course's content and agenda. This information and knowledge, particularly with current computer technologies, can be shared in an increasingly horizontal manner. Information, both good and bad, may flow across students as readily as it flows from instructors to students. In short, knowledge and content material no longer come exclusively from the professor. Students must more actively construct their own learning experience with these technologies. Access to a wider variety of information and a different communication environment facilitates collaborative efforts at knowledge building.

Knott (1994) laid out six components necessary for distance education: (a) target learners to whom the courses are directed, (b) instructors, (c) an educational organization to administer the course(s), (d) a communications system or network (often employing multiple media), (e) communications equipment at local and distant learning sites, and (f) policymaking organizations that develop and/or regulate distance-education programs. To this we would add the professionals required to provide academic, financial, technical, and other services to students at local and distant learning sites. Present-day distance courses are more than well-designed content materials. They take the combined effort of dozens of professionals within and often between various institutions. The creation of "electronic" classrooms via computer systems and teleconferencing has shifted the focus from the classroom to the entirety of the educational experience, including everything that happens prior to and between class meetings.

Student- and Client-Centered Distance Education

By definition, distance-education courses and programs are designed to bring higher learning to those who are not able to get to a "traditional" classroom. The reasons such students enroll in such courses are both personal (self-enrichment and -discovery) and professional (acquiring new skills, promotions, or earning potential). Whatever the reasons are, the central focus of distance-education programming is meeting the needs of nontraditional students. In many cases, distance students are not subject to the same pressures for grades, degrees, or internships. Many of their reasons for higher learning are much more compelling and pragmatic: job layoffs, opportunities for promotions and/or career changes, and decreases in earning potential. When educational organizations target such people with college courses, they necessarily place those people's needs ahead of everything else involved in designing and offering distance courses. In short, distance-education is now based on the adage: "We are not educators if we have no students."

A corollary of this is the client-centered approach to the assessment of distance-education. Many distance-education programs take the sponsoring institution beyond its walls and into the larger community. As a result, many more people have a stake in the outcomes of distance learning. These "stakeholders" include students and the institution itself, but may also include businesses and government agencies, as well as the larger economic communities that exist within regions and states across the country. Because all of these groups want to see some return on their academic and financial investments, distance-education has many audiences to address. The nature of evaluation changes as the audience seeking information changes. Students are concerned primarily with gaining the knowledge and skills they need in their personal and professional lives. Faculty members may be concerned with this and distance-education technologies' potential for quality instruction. Administrators and program sponsors may be concerned that such programs meet the economic and social needs of larger communities. In any of these cases, the needs of the client are the driving concern of the evaluator.

Two final distinctions should be made before any discussion of evaluating distance learning can take place. The first is the difference between assessment and evaluation. Assessment refers to any process that measures what students have learned from teaching strategies, including course-specific methods (e.g., assignments, class activities, and tests) and programmatic strategies (e.g., exit interviews or honors theses) designed to test specific content knowledge. This primary focus on academic content is a defining characteristic of student assessment. Evaluation, on the other hand, looks beyond this to examine the entire educational experience. The mesh between students' needs and their experiences during a course or program is the primary criterion in evaluation. Beyond teaching strategies, then, evaluation examines classroom interaction, the effectiveness of course/program administration, the quality of student support services, access to and quality of technical equipment, and cost-benefit analyses of distance-education programs. In short, every aspect of a distance course or program can be evaluated, whereas only students' mastery of course content is assessed (Rowntree, 1992).

The second important distinction is the difference between course and program evaluation, which is a matter of scale. Although individual courses may be taught at a distance by several departments within a college, contemporary distance-education is often organized on a much larger scale. Courses are offered by several academic disciplines, and technology-based degree programs are becoming more common at many institutions. In fact, the 1980s and 1990s have witnessed an increase in interinstitutional efforts at distance-education. Colleges, universities, vocational and trade schools, and other bodies of higher learning have joined forces to offer courses and certificate/degree programs to students within numerous states and regions of the United States. In conducting programmatic assessment of distance learning these considerations are fundamental.

INFLUENCES ON (UN)SUCCESSFUL DISTANCE LEARNING

The conception of distance-education we have offered has some significant implications for teaching, learning, and evaluating these kinds of courses. Some research has indicated that several factors are associated with student success in distance learning, including personal characteristics, study behaviors, students' preferred learning styles, and the academic or learning environment created by distance courses (James, 1982; Whitlock, 1989). The primary concern with distance courses is not that students become experts with delivery technologies, but that the academic environment is conducive to learning. This section of the chapter discusses five influences on this environment: students' motivations for learning, teaching and learning styles, teacher-student power relations, course design, and coordination of evaluation and assessment.

Student Motivations and Needs

We have alluded to the notion that distance-education is designed as a means of reaching out to a school's larger community. In higher education, this is often an attempt to bring college coursework to populations that have not been able to attend on-campus courses or have not considered higher education an option when preparing for employment. The lesson here is fairly clear: Distant students are not the 18- to 22-year-olds that come in search of a bachelor's degree. The "distance" they feel from conventional classrooms may be geographic, psychological, and social. They come from vastly different segments of the surrounding society, with varying life experiences, employment histories, and personalities. No one can assume that all distant students are enrolled in the same course for the same reason (e.g., see the evaluation survey of Livieratos & Frank, 1992). These students have a variety of motivations, both personal and professional, for taking distance courses.

Evaluation of distance learning needs to focus on this assumption. Quantitative measures of learning or information retention may not provide a true picture of what students learn at a distance. When students are motivated by factors aside from factual knowledge of the content, assessment of their achievement and evaluation of their experience must take such factors into account. Gupta and Arun (1986) argued that effective evaluation must assess changes in the learner's experiences, personality, and behaviors consequent to distance learning.

Motivation has been identified as an important factor contributing to success in distance-education (Oxford, Park-Oh, Ito, & Sumrall, 1993). Indeed, differences in students' personal background have been correlated with varying levels of success in distance courses (Stone, 1990). Kirkwood (1987) suggested that prospective distance students record a full inventory of their desires, expectations, and support systems before embarking on such studies. The task for evaluation is to discover students' places in the institution's academic environment and the institution's place in students' personal and professional environments (Dirr, 1987). An additional concern is the accompanying social atmosphere. A common argument for pursuit of extracurricular activities, internships, and the like is the opportunity students have to learn from applying their knowledge and working with one another. Distant students may be shortchanged when it comes to interacting with and learning from their fellow students outside the classroom (Verduin & Clark, 1991).

With significant diversity in students' motivations and backgrounds, student success becomes a relative matter. In traditional courses, high levels of motivation lead to high grades; in distance-education, high motivation levels are vital to finishing the course. Many studies have identified factors that lead students to drop out of distance courses at all types of higher education institutions (Chacon-Duque, 1985; Coldeway, Spencer, & Stringer, 1980; Cookson, 1989; Dille & Mezack, 1991; Eisenberg & Dowsett, 1990; James, 1984). Some common reasons are provided:

1. In many cases students drop out due to course difficulty.
2. At times, students drop a course when they feel they have learned what they want to learn–any additional material is superfluous.
3. In some cases students did not receive the academic or personal support they needed to keep working.
4. In other cases, communication among teachers and students did not provide an effective learning atmosphere.
5. Family or job-related factors are also tremendous pressures on distant students (Kember, Lai, Murphy, Siaw, & Yuen, 1994).

Teaching and Learning Styles

Because of the changes in the traditional classroom power structure, as well as the types of students attracted by distance-education programs, instructors must frequently build their instructional strategies around the learning styles that best suit their students. Although it may seem an obvious statement, not everyone learns well from correspondence study or video conferencing or any other single technology (Oxford et al., 1993). Many students are able to learn factual material from course readings or lectures. Few are able to practically apply material just by reading about it. Some students prefer visual presentations of course content, via computer or videotapes, others must be able to interpret and express content material in their own words. Some students work well in-dependently, but many others prefer to interact with groups of their colleagues to learn the subject matter. In short, students in any single course will possess a mix of learning styles, hence the course should provide for materials and activities that are flexible enough to address multiple styles of learning. Some argue that learning styles affect students' achievement and attitudes in any class-room situation, perhaps particularly in distance-education (Gee, 1990).

A blend of pedagogical strategies are required to meet this challenge. The use of multiple-teaching strategies can also provide new insights and perspectives on course material. Just as course content may shift from week to week, so will the ways students learn that content. Thus, it seems important to consider how students learn when evaluating their performance and the effectiveness of the distance-education course. Some research has already examined students' learning and study experiences in distance-education, underscoring the importance of considering learning styles when assessing student achievement and evaluating instruction (Peruniak, 1983). It seems vital that such assessment ask students to think and talk about their perceptions of course instruction and its value in light of their own educational goals. Further, educational technologies are one factor that must figure prominently in the evaluation of instructional quality.

Our feeling is that students should evaluate the context of their learning experience rather than focus on a course's content or subject matter. Students' ability to assess content is limited. Their novice status in the field does not inform them enough to permit a professorial evaluation of course content. It seems pointless, then, to ask students if they have learned everything they should have learned when, by definition, they do not know what "everything" includes. However, the student is a very well-informed observer of the educational process. Learners are highly qualified to evaluate the experience of distance-education, having been in many other classrooms in their lifetimes, having a wealth of experiences against which to judge the distance classroom, and having the ultimate expertise–being a student in the class.

Teacher-Student Power Relations

In the distance classroom, the traditional roles of teacher and learner are altered. The restrictions on the communication process inherent in many forms of educational technology (e.g., correspondence study, use of prerecorded videotapes) often grant students more power over their own learning and knowledge production. Many authors argue that distance-education results in a shift in the responsibilities of teacher and learner, that the distance classroom is a setting suited to collaboration (Harasim, 1993; Hiltz, 1993; Laszlo & Castro, 1995; Thach & Murphy, 1994). The authority of the teacher is reduced; the responsibility of the student for his or her learning, and the learning of others, is heightened (Morgan, 1978). In terms of evaluation, the relative importance of process and product is called into question. In other words, the distance-education class adopts a strong student-centered orientation. Evaluation procedures should reflect this orientation.

The shift in the power structure of a distance-education classroom has an impact on evaluation in that a course's schedule and content are less stable. That is to say, in the traditional classroom, a teacher might cover a specified curriculum, rarely straying from a predetermined path. In this teacher-centered model, the instructor determines and controls the instructional path. In the distance classroom, when students can exert more influence over the learning process, course content may shift and adapt in directions that students wish to pursue. From semester to semester a course may begin from the same starting point, yet arrive at different destinations depending on the interests and needs of the students enrolled. Evaluating course content and the quality of instruction is difficult in these settings. The shifting course content provides no common ground on which to compare courses. The focus is instead on the construction of communication and learning processes within each course.

Course Design

Although our discussion has tried to counter the notion that distance learning is a process of programmed, independent instruction, we by no means wish to suggest that the design and development of a distance-education course or program is unimportant. The use of electronic media forces an instructor to carefully consider the content covered as well as the means by which it will be delivered. In addition, the design of activities and assignments becomes even more crucial as students will gain experience with content material in a very different setting than that of traditional courses. The use of collaborative learning techniques, multimedia instructional packages, and a wide variety of new tools for gathering and sharing information will make students as important to one another's learning as the instructor.

There is no doubt that this evaluation approach requires careful planning and effort well in advance of any distance-education course. Teaching at a distance requires careful thought about content, media, teaching methods, learning activities, and measurement of learning. Likewise, evaluation involves planning what issues will be covered in the evaluation, how evaluation data will be used, how the data will be collected, and how much the evaluation will cost. Distance education experts emphasize the importance of early planning and pilot testing of instructional units, materials, and activities (Bernard & Lundgren, 1994; Meacham & Evans, 1989; Willis, 1994), as well as carefully weaving evaluation strategies and methods into the course (Mani, 1988).

One advantage of ongoing reflection on the learning process is that it permits formative evaluation of a course–improvements can be made before the course is finished. A second advantage is that these reflective activities permit students to learn by thinking about how they are taught and how they discover and explore course content. A dialogue about learning can often unlock a student's understanding of how she or he learns (Beaty & Morgan, 1992).

Coordinating Evaluation and Assessment

As our discussion previously indicates, the distance-education course must expand its evaluative focus to the performance of all course participants, from the exclusive focus on students and teachers to include administrators and support staff as well. It is the entire educational experience that occupies center stage, not simply the products of student knowledge created in coursework and examinations. Consequently, all facets of the course must be evaluated, from in-class activities and faculty office hours to the myriad services that offer library resources, access to various media, and academic services necessary to completion of coursework. Another important area of assessment is the impact of student attitudes about all of these elements. On a program level, this includes curricular, technical support, and administrative services and facilities students must deal with in the process of accessing academic advising, registering for courses, completing assignments, and earning degrees (Bates, 1987; R. Clark, 1989; Grimes, Krehbiel, Nielsen, & Niss, 1989; Grundlin, 1983; Johnson & Silvernail, 1994; Knott, 1994; McBeath, 1986; Silvernail & Johnson, 1992; Smith & McNelis, 1993).

The argument here is that the nature and extent of communication in the distance classroom are the cornerstones of the learning experience offered to students (Shale & Garrison, 1990). The communication process should, therefore, be the cornerstone of course evaluation. A crucial quality of communication in distance-education is that communication issues are not confined to any particular group–students, faculty, support professionals, librarians, and administrators can all inform evaluators on this process from their unique perspectives. In making this argument, however, we must emphasize that a focus on classroom communication should not be equated with ignoring assessment of students' learning. We offer a warning about any artificial separation of "process" from "product."

It is possible, however, that the two can be assessed simultaneously. Content material and an instructor's educational philosophy will determine the kinds of pedagogical strategies used in various courses. These strategies are, in turn, significant factors contributing to student learning. The quality of the process necessarily determines the quality of learning in any course, and distance-education courses are particularly good examples of this truism. That is, different types of courses will have qualitative differences in content that influence the process of student-teacher and student-student interaction. Humanities courses, for example, may rely on strategies such as writing research papers more than computer courses taught primarily through laboratory work. Some instructors may prefer to have students present material to the class, others may prefer to present their own lectures at every class meeting. Hence, assessments of content should be sensitive to the nature of pedagogical practices and strategies used in a particular course or program.

Evaluating Distance Education Programs

Scriven (1991) gave a basic definition of evaluation: "Evaluation is the process of determining the merit, worth and value of things, and evaluations are the products of that process" (p. 1). It is not enough to gather data about a program blindly. The evaluator, by definition, is coming to some judgment or interpretation about the success and/or failure of the program. In order to determine merit or worth, the evaluator must be aware of the standards against which a program will be judged. Thus, the activity of evaluation includes a considerable amount of investigation into reasonable standards for assessing and evaluating the program. Furthermore, these standards are rarely obvious or objective. Any number of sets of standards can apply to a program. The more important question is which set of standards will be most useful to the purpose of a particular evaluation.

Scriven (1991) put it succinctly, saying that ". . . evaluation has two arms, only one of which is engaged in datagathering. The other arm collects, clarifies, and verifies relevant values and standards." In many ways the identification of values and standards is the more elusive task. Before the evaluator can begin to think of what data are appropriate and what methods should be employed to collect these data, she or he must explore the possible frameworks for evaluating the program.

The Joint Committee on Standards for Educational Evaluation (1994) defined a program as "educational activities that are provided on a continuing basis" (p. 3). Distance-education programs may range in scale from local efforts based in community colleges to consortia of major universities reaching out across states. Furthermore, distance-education programs consist not only of the course content, but are also defined and shaped by the faculty, students, and administrators involved in the delivery of the instructional materials. We can examine these programs from many perspectives: within courses, within institutions, across courses, and across institutions.

In our conception of evaluation, it is the evaluator's job to examine how the parties involved in the process communicate, and ultimately to assess whether they have created a unified experience or one fractured by miscommunication and misunderstanding. Further, many elements of this process are unique to each classroom setting. The same set of evaluation procedures may not work for every class. Several researchers (Braskamp, Fowler, & Ory, 1982; Lewy, 1988; Wagner, 1993; Webber, 1987;) have argued that effective evaluation must be locally sensitive, taking into account the specific needs and design of each course.

Accountability

Distance-education efforts must be particularly sensitive to the notion of accountability. These technology-based programs are often high profile and high cost, thus encouraging the careful scrutiny of legislators and the public. Educators, too, are suspicious of the overt changes that distance-education technologies introduce into the teaching and learning process. The suggestion that student evaluations should be part of assessing distance learning is often met with considerable skepticism. Our experience has taught us that faculty are leery, in some cases justifiably so, of how evaluation data will be used. For example, if such data are to be used as the basis of granting tenure or promotion, a course evaluation certainly has implications beyond the classroom walls. Many faculty members and administrators are fascinated by the potential of reaching out to new audiences, but also fearful of the potential criticism that will undoubtedly arise in response to distance-education initiatives.

House (1993) proposed three different types of accountability that institutions of higher education face: state- or public-controlled accountability, professional control (by professors and administrators), and consumer control. Naturally, each of these types of accountability is always present. The problem for the evaluator is how to identify standards that address the disparate concerns of these groups with vested interests in the program. "The basic question, then, is what kind of evaluation will preserve the disciplinary and teaching processes that produce knowledge for faculty and students, while at the same time providing necessary information to the state and the public" (p. 61). House concluded that there is no answer to this question. We cannot identify one method of evaluation that will, without fail, address all of the appropriate concerns. He proposed that evaluators be mindful of the particular context of distance-education programs.

Communication-Based Evaluation

Distance-education program evaluation is, at bottom, the gathering of data from a variety of viewpoints with the goal of assessing, sustaining, and improving pedagogical support systems designed to serve the needs of distant learners. A complex array of factors influences the learning process and must be considered in program evaluation. Mani (1988) described a model of the evaluation process that places the evaluator at the center of the learning process. In contrast, our conception of distance learning and evaluation places the student at the center of the learning process, and focuses evaluation on learning as manifested in the communication processes among participants. This view of evaluation stresses a focus on classroom communication as a key to understanding learning. In the evaluation of distance-education programs we must examine communication within and across specific sites, within and between groups and individuals, and within and between institutions.

Because course content becomes more variable in the distance classroom, and because students may be afforded more opportunities to direct their own learning in these settings, we emphasize a focus on the learning process as opposed to the learning product. The distance classroom and distance-education programs challenge the communication skills of teachers, students, and support staff. The learning process is embedded in the ways that these stakeholders use the available lines of communications.

Goals for a process-oriented evaluation should address the key issues of how communication proceeds within and among the students, faculty, and administrators that make up the program. In effect, our strategy for evaluating distance-education programs looks more at whether or not the program is successful in creating good learning environments than it does at traditional educational outcomes.

Because distance-education programs vary widely in their scope and structure, we offer a strategy for identifying standards and value constructs rather than a method for evaluating distance-education programs. In addition, we propose a number of potential sources of data that speak to these standards. The metaphor for evaluation of distance-education is less a process of following a recipe and more a process of pursuing an investigation (Smith, 1992). That is, a recipe is prescriptive and preordained, resulting in a known object, whereas an investigation is a process of continual discovery, resulting in the emergence of an object constructed by the process of investigation. In this case, the object is a distance-education program that is built on a foundation of values and beliefs held by the various stakeholders in the program, as interpreted or mediated by the evaluator.

Smith (1992) offered a view of evaluation in which "four mental abilities or powers–knowledge, observation, reasoning, and intuition–are employed in an alternatively exploratory and confirmatory, emergent process of investigative inquiry to develop and justify claims in the construction of multiple lines of argument designed to fully explain a problem that has been posed within the given context of a particular investigative game" (p. 9). Evaluation is an investigative game that is much akin to problem solving. The parameters of the problem are unknown at the outset, and must be defined as part of the process of solving the problem. An evaluator must explore the potential issues of an evaluation, then act to confirm whether or not these issues really are important.

One can pose the problem simply. First, how does one identify the purposes of the evaluation–what does the evaluator want to know? Second, how does one identify the data sources that address those concerns? Finally, how does one interpret the results? The challenge of identifying what one needs to know is not always transparent. Thus, the first step in an evaluation of a distance-education program should be to identify the stakeholders in that program. That is, the groups of people who hold an interest in the program and the resulting evaluation should be identified at the outset.

Guba and Lincoln (1987) identified the concept of "stakeholder constructions" as a primary concern in evaluation. This type of evaluation, sometimes called stakeholder responsive (Stake, 1983) or fourth generation evaluation, rests on the notion that evaluations create reality rather than objectively discovering it (Guba & Lincoln, 1987). The evaluator is the agent of this construction, at times teaching others about stakeholder values, and at times learning about stakeholder values.

According to Guba and Lincoln (1987), once the important stakeholders in the program have been identified, the evaluator enters a process of negotiation. She or he negotiates with stakeholders about relevant standards and important issues in the program. From these discussions with stakeholders, the evaluator draws a list of issues that are central to the particular evaluation.

Guba and Lincoln (1987) stressed that, in this model, evaluation is a social-political process, saying that "consequently any individual or group with a stake in the evaluator (i.e., put at risk by the evaluation) has a right to provide input based on its own value position, to have that input honored, and to be consulted in any decision making that results" (p. 80).

The evaluator cannot possibly address all of the concerns and issues brought out in the preliminary discussions with stakeholders. The evaluator must negotiate with these stakeholders to arrive at a set of issues that focus the evaluation, that set the boundaries of the evaluation. For example, in an evaluation of a distance-education program, three obvious sets of stakeholders arise–the students who are being served by the program, the faculty and staff who teach and administer the program, and any private or governmental bodies who endorse and pay for the program. The evaluator would begin the process by having informal conversations with members of each of these stakeholder groups. Through this informal discussion of the program the evaluator will discover the various concerns of the stakeholders. Acting almost as a mediator between stakeholder groups, and armed with a good idea of the concerns people have, the evaluator negotiates, in more formal terms, which of these concerns are relevant to the purpose of the evaluation (Guba & Lincoln, 1987).

These concerns become the framework for evaluation. For example, in an evaluation of a distance-education program that delivers several courses to sites in large institutions as well as community centers. The evaluator would meet with students enrolled at the large institution, with students at the community centers, with faculty who teach the courses, with the technical staff, and with administrators that oversee the program. The students at community centers might express concerns about their lack of communication with the other students, or their ability to communicate with the instructor. Instructors might be concerned with ways of involving students at all sites in their courses. Administrators might be concerned with maintaining quality across all courses.

The next step of the evaluation would be for the evaluator to formally present a set of issues that she or he thinks are important (based on information gleaned in informal conversations). From our earlier example, an evaluation strategy might highlight communication between origination and remote sites, instructional strategies, and quality control issues. The evaluator would send a preliminary evaluation strategy out to stakeholders, asking them to give their feedback on the proposed plan. After a process of negotiation, the evaluator and the representatives of stakeholder groups should come to a consensus as to which of the issues laid on the table will be part of the evaluation. This is very much a political process, in which the evaluator must be sensitive to the needs of the stakeholders. The role of the evaluator is to provide advice about doing evaluation, while being careful to listen and learn about the program from the stakeholders. In the previously mentioned example, the stakeholders might decide to address all of the issues raised, or they might decide to focus the evaluation on a particular issue.

Having set the boundaries for the evaluation, the evaluator must turn to the identification of guiding questions as well as appropriate methods or types of data that will help inform or answer the questions. The guiding questions of the evaluation will come from the issues identified by the stakeholders. For example, if an important issue is communication between sites, the evaluator will come up with a set of questions that address that issue. How do students communicate between sites? How do teachers communicate with students at origination and remote sites? Is there a difference in the way the instructor communicates with students at different sites?

These questions in mind, the evaluator must find opportunities for collecting data that speak to these questions. The evaluator could find answers to these questions by, for example, analyzing conversational turn-taking in class, by interviewing students, by analyzing E-mail traffic. Two topics are of particular interest to evaluators of distance-education programs–the distance itself, and the fact that distance-education programs are made of diverse courses that have an internal structure all their own. In planning for an evaluation, an evaluator must characterize the disparate sites that comprise the program. For example, a telecommunications suite at a major university has a different feel (and a different set of students) than a remote site located at a local public library. Furthermore, the relationship between faculty and students will shift depending on individual faculty members' pedagogical styles and course content.

In distance education it is particularly important to plan evaluation so that the variety of contexts across which the program occurs may be captured. A good evaluation serves both to describe the program as it exists, as well as to make some evaluative judgment about the program. Furthermore, a thoughtful evaluation serves a particular purpose and takes on a certain role in relation to the evaluator.

Scriven (1967) made a fundamental distinction between the *formative* role of evaluation and the *summative* role of evaluation. Formative evaluation is evaluation that feeds directly back into the program as the program continues to evolve. The purpose of formative evaluation is to provide information that serves to aid in making fairly immediate improvements in the program being evaluated. For example, an evaluation might find that E-mail as a means of communication between teachers and students in a course delivered by distance-education is inadequate for creating discussion outside of class. The immediate result might be that the instructor decides to use computer-conferencing software instead (see Kulik & Kulik, 1987; Kulik, Kulik, & Schwalb, 1986).

Summative evaluation, by contrast, is typically conducted at the end of a program's life in order to judge its overall effectiveness. Distance-education programs may not have clear end points. However, universities and legislatures conduct periodic large-scale analyses of these programs to justify expenditures. The decisions that they come to, based on summative evaluation, often change the course of the program.

The line between formative and summative evaluation is often blurred, but the distinction is relevant. Both types of evaluation are necessary and useful as they relate to distance-education programs.

The important steps in the process of creating an evaluation plan (for review, see Franklin, Yoakam, & Warren, 1995):

- Stakeholder identification. In this step the evaluator seeks to discover players. Who are the people who have an important stake in the program being evaluated?
- Negotiation of relevant standards. Having identified the stakeholders, which of their concerns are most relevant to the purpose of the evaluation?
- Focusing the evaluation. One evaluation cannot address issues. Powerful evaluations are focused on a handful of key issues, not on dozens of related topics.
- Guiding questions that fulfill the strategy. What are the research questions that best get at the issues at hand in the evaluation?
- Identification of appropriate data sources. Given your guiding questions, what types of data are likely to yield the best information to answer the question?

Methods

Obviously the methods of any program evaluation are dependent on the needs and goals of the program itself.   In dealing with a large interinstitutional consortium, for example, these goals and needs are not completely manifest at the interinstitutional level.   They reside also in the people involved in the program within each institution, within each course.   Just as goals and needs change from one course to the next, evaluation is dependent on the goals and needs of faculty and students in a particular situation.   Because the model of program evaluation described here relies on multiple evaluation approaches, it must also accommodate multiple methods of gathering data.

Many scholars have argued for using multiple methods in evaluation research. Perhaps the most compelling argument for multiple methods concerns the potential for enhanced data quality.   A blend of quantitative and qualitative analyses can provide the breadth and depth of information that large and complex evaluation programs require.   Some refer to this multiple methods approach as *triangulation* (Coldeway, 1988; Lafleur, 1990; Lewy, 1988).   Researchers can also use a single method to triangulate on data collected from several viewpoints (e.g., instructors, students, support personnel).   Other scholars (Lafleur, 1990; Rothe, 1985) speak of "complementarity," or using different methods to gather data on *outside* and *inside* learning factors.   That is, one gathers surface-level information about students' and instructors' communication behaviors (outside factors), and in-depth information on the nature of their experience and the meanings given to it (inside factors).

For example, in evaluating a distance-education course, one might look at how students and instructors use a computer conference.   The evaluator might approach the problem by examining the conference itself as a document.   This analysis could produce quantitative information about usage of the conference. It would also provide data for qualitative interpretations of the conference text. Furthermore, the evaluator might interview the users of the conference in order to ascertain their attitudes toward using the computer conference.   Each of these different examinations gives a different perspective on how the students used the conference.   They all converge to give an overall picture of how the conference was used to support the course.

In short, by approaching a phenomenon from different perspectives, multiple methods may increase the validity and reliability of the data (Lewy 1988; Lincoln & Guba, 1985).   This practice also encourages the evaluator to question assumptions about distance-education and the learning process by searching for confirmation from parallel but independent data sources (Burge, 1990).

Although these arguments are not new, recent models of program evaluation (e.g., Eastmond, 1991) argue that quantitative and qualitative methods can and should be incorporated into the design of distance-education evaluation research. Some authors (Burge, 1990; Webber, 1987) have gone so far as to state that evaluation studies not using multiple-method designs must justify their selection of a single method.   Because quantitative and qualitative data illuminate different aspects of the program and because distance-education evaluation has diverse goals, justification of a single-method approach is difficult.

House (1994) argued that methods are important but subordinate to the subject matter being explored and that the quantitative-qualitative debate is the result of a fixation on methods. Further, he believes that making judgments in evaluation requires defining the context of the judgment. This setting of the context rests in both quantitative and qualitative methods. The primary responsibility in evaluation is to paint a complete picture of the evaluand, not to adhere to methodological constraints. To that end, the evaluator should be able to use various methodological tools to paint such a picture.

Because each situation gives new opportunities for collecting data, the possibilities for data collection are almost endless. With the expansion of the classroom beyond a traditional setting, potential data sources have proliferated. The important factor in deciding whether or not to collect a certain type of data resides in whether or not those data will inform the issues and guiding questions that the evaluator has identified as important.

Rowntree (1992) suggested possible data collection methods for evaluating distance-education programs, such as examining routine statistics and student records, program documentation, naturalistic observation, informal conversations, and structured interviews.

For example, at our institution we teach a course about information and its role in society. This course is delivered by distance-education technology throughout the state. One of the features of the course is that students keep an electronic journal of their experiences with the information technologies that they are introduced to over the course of the semester. In evaluating this course, we used the electronic logs as data that might inform the issue of how the students dealt with the array of new technologies used to teach the course.

Communicating and Using Evaluation Results

Designing an evaluation and collecting appropriate data to respond to the guiding questions that have been identified as relevant to the particular application are formidable tasks. However, the most delicate task is how to report the data. The purpose of evaluation is to provide information that helps people–teachers, students, administrators, legislators–make good decisions. Those decisions can be quite varied across the various constituencies. An evaluation report must be tied to the needs and interests of the stakeholders in the program.

For example, in evaluating a distance-education consortium of public universities, the issue of public accountability and overall value to residents of the state is paramount. Just as the collection of data is focused on issues raised by stakeholders, so must the report be focused on their information needs. The evaluator has the responsibility of constructing a fair characterization of the program and its effectiveness. The primary stakeholders in the program may have blinders on that allow them to see only the issues that are important to them. According to Stake (1967), the purpose of evaluation was to tell the story of what happened based on the evidence gathered and to provide a credible explanation of the events and outcomes including multiple perspectives.

CONCLUSION

The evaluation of distance-education programs is a complex task because the stakeholders are enormously diverse and the programs themselves are distinct. The very nature of distance-education programs, bringing together groups of people in locations that are geographically, culturally and institutionally quite different, presents a profound challenge to researchers. The model proposed here, focusing on communication processes between instructor and students, students and students, instructor and support staff, and students and support staff, adopts the perspective that communication is the key to understanding and evaluating learning in the distance-education context. Various types of communication data may be collected to examine the distance-education program from the viewpoints of the various constituents. We argue that distance learning evaluation must move beyond the narrow assessment of learning in a particular course and focus, instead, on the learning process as manifest in the communication that occurs in various contexts using diverse modes of delivery between students and faculty, support staff, administrators, and other students.

REFERENCES

Bates, A. W. (1987). *The Open Learning Institute and Knowledge Network. A proposed programme for institutional research and evaluation summary of recommendations.* (I.E.T. Paper No. 259.) (ERIC Document Reproduction Service No. ED 298 959)

Beaty, E., & Morgan, A. (1992). Developing skill in learning. *Open Learning, 7*(3), 3-11.

Bernard, R. M., & Lundgren, K. M. (1994). Learner assessment and text design strategies for distance education. *Canadian Journal of Educational Communication, 23,* 133-152.

Braskamp, L. A., Fowler, D. L., & Ory, J. C. (1982). *Faculty uses of evaluative information.* (ERIC Document Reproduction Service No. ED 218 308)

Burge, E. J. (1990). *Marrow bone thinking: A plea for strengthened qualitative research in distance education.* Paper presented at the Conference on Research in Distance Education, Caracas, Venezuela. (ERIC Document Reproduction Service No. ED 328 228)

Chacon-Duque, F. J. (1985). *Building academic quality in distance higher education. A monograph in higher education evaluation and policy.* University Park: Pennsylvania State University Center for the Study of Higher Education. (ERIC Document Reproduction Service No. ED 267 673)

Clark, R. E. (1989). *Evaluating distance learning technology.* Paper prepared at the invitation of the United States Congress, Office of Technology Assessment. (ERIC Document Reproduction Service No. ED 325 097)

Coldeway, D. O. (1988). Methodological issues in distance educational research. *The American Journal of Distance Education, 3*(2), 45-54.

Coldeway, D. O., Spencer, R., & Stringer, M. (1980). *Factors affecting learner motivation in distance education: The interaction between learner attributes and learner course performance* (REDEAL Research Report #9). Project REDEAL Research and Evaluation of Distance Education for the Adult Learner. (ERIC Document Reproduction Service No. ED 249 346)

Cookson, P. S. (1989). Research on learners and learning in distance education: A review. *American Journal of Distance Education, 3*(2), 22-34.

Dille, B., & Mezack, M. (1991). Identifying predictors of high risk among community college telecourse students. *American Journal of Distance Education, 5*(1), 24-35.

Dirr, P. J. (1987). *Critical questions in the evaluation of distance education. Keynote address to the Annual Conference on Teaching at a Distance*, Madison, WI. (ERIC Document Reproduction Service No. ED 307 849)

Eastmond, J. N. (1991). Educational evaluation: The future. *Theory Into Practice, 30*(1), 74-79.

Eisenberg, E., & Dowsett, T. (1990). Student drop-out from a distance education project course: A new method of analysis. *Distance Education, 11*, 231-253.

Franklin, N., Yoakam, M., & Warren, R. (1995). *Distance learning: A guide to system planning and implementation. Indiana University*. Bloomington: Indiana University.

Garrison, D. R., & Shale, D. (1987). Mapping the boundaries of distance education: Problems in defining the field. *American Journal of Distance Education, 1*(1), 7-13.

Gee, D. B. (1990). *The impact of students' preferred learning style variables in a distance education course: A case study*. (ERIC Document Reproduction Service No. ED 358 836)

Grimes, P. W., Krehbiel, T. L., Nielsen, J. E., & Niss, J. F. (1989). The effectiveness of "Economics U$A" on learning and attitudes. *Journal of Economic Education, 20*, 139-152.

Grundlin, H. U. (1983). *Audio-visual media in the Open University: Results of a survey of 93 courses* (I.E.T. Papers on Broadcasting No. 224). (ERIC Document Reproduction Service No. ED 253 199)

Guba, E., & Lincoln, Y. (1987). The countenances of fourth-generation evaluation: Description, judgment, and negotiation. In D. S. Cordray & M. W. Lipsey (Eds.) *Evaluation studies review annual* (Vol. 11, pp. 70-88). Newbury Park, CA: Sage.

Gupta, A. K. & Arun, R. (1986). Effective pupil evaluations in distance learning systems. *University News, 24*(8), 6-11.

Harasim, L. (1993). Collaborating in cyberspace: Using computer conferences as a group learning environment. *Interactive Learning Environments, 3*(2), 119-130.

Hiltz, S. R. (1993). *The virtual classroom*. Norwood, NJ: Ablex.

Holmberg, B. (1977). *Distance education: A survey and bibliography*. London: Kogan Page.

Holmberg, B. (1986). *Growth and structure of distance education*. London: Croon Helm.

House, E. (1993). *Professional evaluation*. Newbury Park, CA: Sage.

House, E. (1994). Integrating the quantitative and qualitative. In S. Rallis (Ed.), *The qualitative-quantitative debate: New perspectives* (pp. 23-37). San Francisco: Jossey-Bass.

James, A. (1982). *Exploring strategies of assessment and results in the Spanish Universidad Nacional de Educacion a Distancia and the United Kingdom Open University*. London: The Open University. (ERIC Document Reproduction Service No. ED 228 910)

James, A. (1984). Age-group differences in the psychological well-being and academic attainment of distance learners. *Distance Education, 5*, 200-214.

Johnson, J. L., & Silvernail, D. L. (1994). Impact of interactive television and distance education on student evaluation of courses: A causal model. *Community College Journal of Research and Practice, 18*, 431-440.

Joint Committee on Standards for Educational Evaluation. (1994). *The program evaluation standards (2nd ed.)*. Thousand Oaks, CA: Sage.

Keegan, D. J. (1988). On defining distance education. In D. Sewart, D. Keegan, & B. Holmberg (Eds.), *Distance education: International perspectives* (pp. 6-33). London: Routledge & Kegan Paul.

Kember, D., Lai, T., Murphy, D., Siaw, I., & Yuen, K. S. (1994). Student progress in distance education courses: A replication study. *Adult Education Quarterly, 45,* 286-301.

Kirkwood, A. (1987). *Enabling new students to examine their expectations of distance learning. Some examples from British and Australian tertiary institutions.* Paper presented at the International Conference on The First Year Experience, Southhampton, England. (ERIC Document Reproduction Service No. ED 304 121)

Knott, T. (1994). *Planning and evaluating distance education: A guide to collaboration.* Memphis, TN: Diaphera.

Kulik, C. L. C., Kulik, J. A., & Schwalb, B. J. (1986). The effectiveness of computer-based adult-education: A meta-analysis. *Journal of Educational Computing Research, 2,* 235-252.

Kulik, J. A., & Kulik, C. L. C. (1987). Review of recent research literature on computer-based instruction. *Contemporary Educational Psychology, 12,* 222-230.

Lafleur, C. (1990). *Complementarity as a program evaluation strategy: A focus on qualitative and quantitative methods.* Paper presented at the Annual Meeting of the Canadian Evaluation Society, Toronto, Canada. (ERIC Document Reproduction Service No. ED 348 390)

Larsen, S. (1986). Information can be transmitted but knowledge must be induced. *Programmed Learning and Educational Technology, 23*(4), 331-337.

Laszlo, A., & Castro, K. (1995, March-April). Technology and values: Interactive learning environments for future generations. *Educational Technology,* 7-13.

Lewy, A. (1988). *Issues in curriculum evaluation.* Jerusalem: Israel Ministry of Education and Culture. (ERIC Document Reproduction Service No. ED 317 590)

Lincoln, Y. S., & Guba, E. G. (1985). *Naturalistic inquiry.* Beverly Hills, CA: Sage.

Livieratos, B. B. & Frank, J. M. (1992). *Alternative learning modes: Spring '92 telecourse & weekend college enrollees.* Columbia, MD: Howard Community College Office of Planning and Evaluation. (ERIC Document Reproduction Service No. ED 352 105)

Mani, G. (1988). Evaluation of distance education. In B. N. Koul, B. Singh, & M. M. Ansari, (Eds.), *Studies in distance education* (pp. 68-83). New Delhi, India: Indira Gandhi National Open University.

McBeath, C. (1986). *Curriculum decision making in TAFE.* (ERIC Document Reproduction Service No. ED 275 842)

Meacham, D., & Evans, D. (1989). *Distance education: The design of study materials* (5th ed.). (ERIC Document Reproduction Service No. ED 321 754)

Moore, M. G. (1973). Toward a theory of independent learning and teaching. *Journal of Higher Education, 44,* 661-679.

Morgan, A. R. (1978). *Student learning in the Open University–the provision of diversity in a distance education system.* AIR Forum Paper 1978. (ERIC Document Reproduction Service No. ED 161 396)

Oxford, R., Park-Oh, Y., Ito, S., & Sumrall, M. (1993). Learning a language by satellite television: What influences student achievement? *System, 21*(1), 31-48.

Peruniak, G. (1983). Interactive perspectives in distance education: A case study. *Distance Education, 4,* 63-79.

Peters, O. (1973). *Die didaktische Strukur des Fernunterrichts. Untersuchungen zu einer industrialisierten Form des Lehrens and Lernens.* Weinheim: Beltz.

Rothe, P. J. (1985). *Linking quantitative and qualitative distance education research through complementarity.* ZIFF Paper 56. (ERIC Document Reproduction Service No. ED 290 011)

Rowntree, D. (1992). *Exploring open and distance learning.* London: Kogan Page.

Scriven, M. (1967). The methodology of evaluation. In *Perspectives of curriculum evaluation.* AERA Monograph Series on Curriculum Evaluation, no. 1. Chicago: Rand McNally.

Scriven, M. (1991). *Evaluation thesaurus* (4th ed.). Newbury Park, CA: Sage.

Shale, D., & Garrison, D. R. (1990). Education and communication. In D. R. Garrison, & D. Shale, (Eds.), *Education at a distance: From issues to practice* (pp. 1-21). Malabar, FL: Krieger.

Silvernail, D. L., & Johnson, J. L. (1992). The impact of interactive televised instruction on student evaluations of their instructors. *Educational Technology, 32*(6), 47-50.

Smith, D. L., & McNelis, M. J. (1993). *Distance education: Graduate student attitudes and academic performance.* Paper presented at the Annual Meeting of the American Educational Research Association, Atlanta, GA. (ERIC Document Reproduction Service No. ED 360 948)

Smith, J. K. (1988). The evaluation/researcher as person vs. the person as evaluator/researcher. *Educational Researcher, 17*(2), 18-23.

Smith, N. (1992). Aspects of investigative inquiry in evaluation. In N. Smith (Ed.), *Varieties of investigative evaluation* (pp. 3-11). San Francisco: Jossey-Bass.

Stake, R. E. (1967). The countenance of educational evaluation. *Teachers College Record, 68,* 523-540.

Stake, R. (1983). Program evaluation, particularly responsive evaluation. In G. F. Madaus, M. S. Scriven, & D. L. Stufflebeam (Eds.), *Evaluation models: Viewpoints on educational and human services evaluation* (pp. 287-310). Hingham, MA: Kluwer Academic.

Stone, H. R. (1990). *A multi-institutional evaluation of video-based distance engineering education.* Paper presented at the Frontiers in Education Conference, Vienna, Austria. (ERIC Document Reproduction Service No. ED 325 072)

Thach, L., & Murphy, K. L. (1994). Collaboration in distance education: From local to international perspectives. *The American Journal of Distance Education, 8*(3), 5-21.

Verduin, J. R., & Clark, T. A. (1991). *Distance education: The foundations of effective practice.* San Francisco: Jossey-Bass.

Wagner, E. D. (1993). *Evaluating distance learning projects: An approach for cross-project comparisons.* Paper presented at the Annual Meeting of the Association for Educational Communications and Technology, New Orleans, LA. (ERIC Document Reproduction Service No. ED 363 273)

Webber, C. F. (1987). *Program evaluation: A review and synthesis.* (ERIC Document Reproduction Service No. ED 291 771)

Whitlock, Q. (1989). Student failure in open learning. *Educational and Training Technology International, 26,* 141-144.

Willis, B. (Ed.). (1994). *Distance education: Strategies and tools.* Englewood Cliffs, NJ: Educational Technology Publications.

II Knowledge, Skills, and Attitude Assessment

6

Media Literacy

Sherry Wulff
Alverno College

This chapter presents an initial conceptualization of media literacy and its development within an innovative college context. Embedded in an educational program that features an ability-based curriculum with assessment-as-learning as a crucial part of the learning process, media literacy at Alverno College holds the position of a specific, integral ability within the general ability of communication. Effective communication is one of eight general abilities that all Alverno students develop and demonstrate prior to graduation. The first section, Conceptualizing Media Literacy, focuses concurrently on the construction of a shared understanding of media literacy across the curriculum as well as on the initial positioning of media literacy within an ability-based curriculum. The second section, Assessment and Media Literacy, profiles Alverno's approach to assessment-as-learning and provides a sketch of media literacy assessment within a discipline course. Alverno College, a small, midwestern, liberal arts women's college, has committed to media literacy as a significant communication ability that empowers students to participate actively and responsibly in contemporary society.

INTRODUCTION

Although media may not be solely responsible for turning [social/cultural] events into media events, all events that matter in a postmodern society must be multimediated, and the way we know them will always depend upon media technology. Knowledge is a production of mediatech, and those who are media illiterate and technophobic will be cut off from producing it, from circulating it, and from engaging in the struggles over it: in a mass-mediated culture they are sidelined.

—Fiske (1994, p. xxii)

CONCEPTUALIZING MEDIA LITERACY EDUCATION

How does a small, midwestern, liberal arts college for women prepare students to guide such powers as those associated with contemporary media and technology, powers connected to traditional media technologies, such as print publishing and television broadcast industries, as well as to powers emerging and evolving in the realms of computer multimedia and the World Wide Web? How does this type of college facilitate for all students in all disciplines and professional fields the development of media literacy as a crucial communication ability, encouraging them to embrace technology as a communication tool and mode for acting within and on the world in local as well as global contexts? These are several of the primary questions driving this chapter on media literacy. (Parts of this chapter were first presented in Wulff, 1994.)

Currently media literacy education in the United States, unlike Canada or Germany, remains in the beginning stages of development and effective practice, yet it is slowly gaining recognition as a viable component in general education (Aufderheide, 1993; Brown, 1991). Fortunately, a growing number of K-12 and postsecondary educators in language arts, communication-related disciplines, and visual arts support media literacy education in their classrooms, institutions, and in such professional organizations as the Speech Communication Association, the Association of Educational Communications and Technology, the International Visual Literacy Association, and the National Council of Teachers of English (Brown, 1991; Considine & Haley, 1992; Eisner, 1991; Foster, 1995; McLaren, Hammer, Sholle, & Reilly, 1995; Self, 1990; and Shutkin, 1990).

However, in many K-12 and postsecondary educational environments, media literacy education either has no place in general education and/or exists only as a specialized area of study linked with language arts/communication units (K-12) or communication departments (postsecondary). Despite a growing social concern with the role(s) and impact of media as well as with the necessary skills and abilities students must develop for life in a media-oriented and technological society, relatively little has been done in the United States to establish, implement, and evaluate credible media literacy education in general curriculum (Aufderheide, 1993).

In higher education the progress toward the incorporation of media literacy as an essential ability in higher education appears minimal (Aufderheide, 1993; Brown, 1991). Alverno College, with a mission that focuses on the academic, personal, and professional development of women, stands among the few U. S. higher education institutions working toward media literacy within and across the curriculum. Indeed, educators at Alverno have begun positioning media literacy as a viable component of general education in an ability-based curriculum. Media literacy fits into Alverno's ability-based curriculum as a specific, integral communication ability, which involves, in part, the development and demonstration of critical thinking and production skills (see Loacker, Fey, Cromwell, & Rutherford, 1984). At Alverno, all students must develop and demonstrate media literacy as one means to act effectively as competent communicators participating in a democratic and technological society as well as interacting in global contexts.

Overview of Alverno's Ability-Based Curriculum

A small, urban, Catholic, liberal arts college for women located on the south side of Milwaukee, Wisconsin, Alverno's mission centers on the personal, academic, and professional development of women. With traditional weekday and nontraditional weekend college programs, Alverno prides itself as a community of learning for more than 2,450 students and approximately 210 full-time and part-time faculty (Alverno College, 1994). As a community of learning, Alverno faculty, staff, and students ground their pursuit of knowledge in a curriculum centering on student development and demonstration of eight general abilities: communication, analysis, problem solving, valuing in decision, social interaction, global perspectives, effective citizenship, and aesthetic response (Alverno College Faculty, 1994, pp. 12-13). These general abilities are considered "as integrated, developmental, and transferable" (Alverno College Faculty, 1994, p. 9). All students demonstrate competency in at least four levels of development in each of the eight abilities prior to graduation with a bachelor's degree. (Note: Four levels of development are broadly defined later in a discussion of the general communication ability.)

Organized into distinct campus-wide committees (departments), each general ability committee includes faculty from diverse disciplines. More often than not, Alverno faculty belong to an ability committee as well as their discipline departments. In the ability committees, faculty participate in an ongoing process of refining the ability according to the demand of contemporary life and student needs. They construct and refine criteria for the development and assessment of the ability across the disciplines as well as align ability learning and assessment with courses in general education and the discipline departments. For example, a nursing faculty member may also belong to the aesthetic responsiveness ability committee or a chemistry faculty member may also belong to the communication ability committee. In a general education and in discipline courses, students study and demonstrate competence in not only the content but in the ability (ies) linked to the course. For instance PCM 170, an introductory-level visual communication course in the Professional Communication Department (PCM), not only facilitates students' learning in design and desktop publishing, but also facilitates students' development of competence in computer literacy, analysis, problem solving, and valuing.

Before proceeding into an overview of the process for conceptualizing media literacy at Alverno, and in order to facilitate an understanding of how media literacy is positioned as a specific communication ability, more context about Alverno's ability-based curriculum with emphasis on the general communication ability is needed. For all Alverno students, the general ability of communication involves development and assessment of performance in seven specific abilities: writing, reading, speaking, listening, using/reading media, computer literacy, and quantitative thinking. (Note: Media Literacy will replace Using/Reading Media as a specific ability in communication.)

Prior to graduation, all students achieve and demonstrate four levels of development in each of the seven specific communication abilities (as well as in each of the eight general abilities: communication, analysis, problem solving, valuing in decision making, social interaction, global perspectives, effective citizenship, and aesthetic response). Each developmental level of an ability assumes mastery of, while building on, the prior level. Levels 5 and 6 of the general eight abilities are developed and demonstrated in students' major and minor fields of study. Discipline departments select three to five of the eight abilities associated with Alverno's curriculum for their students to develop and demonstrate at levels 5 and 6. For example, elementary education majors must demonstrate levels 5 and 6 of analysis, communication, problem solving, valuing, and social interaction. Majors in professional communication must demonstrate levels 5 and 6 of analysis, problem solving, and valuing.

The PCM faculty chose these three general abilities (analysis, problem solving, and valuing) because of their recognized value by those in communication professions and because of their significant value as support for specific communication abilities generally considered as inherent in the communication discipline and in the department's curriculum. For example, media literacy, speaking, listening, writing, and reading are firmly embedded in the structure and content of professional communication courses.

As mentioned earlier, for all Alverno students, communication across the curriculum explicitly involves assessment of the first four levels of development in each of the specific communication abilities (writing, reading, speaking, listening, using/reading media, computer literacy, and quantitative thinking, i.e., math). These levels can be broadly defined as follows:

Level 1: Self-Recognition. For example, students identify their own strengths and weaknesses as a communicator
Level 2: Awareness. Students communicate with analytic consciousness of the process. They perceive and know components in the process.
Level 3: Making Relationships. Students understand and connect components in the communication process in order to communicate with effective control of the process.
Level 4: Integration. Students unify components and effective control of the communication process with discipline frameworks. (Loacker, 1984)

Level 1. Level 1 acknowledges students' history of communication experience. At this level, students concentrate on exhibiting an awareness of their communication strengths and areas to improve. Students, through self-assessment, identify what they know and what they can do as writers, readers, speakers, listeners, media users/readers, computer users, and quantitative thinkers. They reflect on how and why they performed as they did, as well as on what components they could strengthen and build on in future communication assessments. Overall, students identify their communication needs through self-assessment and gain self-assurance through productive feedback.

Before starting their academic studies at Alverno, entering students take the New Student Assessment coordinated by Alverno's Assessment Center. They attend an orientation seminar prior to the assessment. The writing and reading components are used with other traditional pieces (ACT scores, high school transcripts, etc.) for acceptance decisions. Math (quantitative thinking) results are used primarily as placement indicators. The New Student Assessment also opens two portfolios for each student: a writing portfolio and a speaking/media video portfolio. These portfolios are maintained for every student until they graduate. After graduation, students can pick up their portfolios from the Assessment Center. Frequently students use portions of their portfolios as evidence of their communication capabilities in career interview situations.

Level 2. At Level 2 students carefully examine the communication performances of others, heightening their awareness and inferring from these performances a variety of effective communication styles and strategies employed in the construction and conveyance of meaningful messages for specific audiences. Students consider the contexts, participants (e.g., producer- sender-audience), components, processes, and products of diverse communications. Through focused study and practice, they become increasingly conscious of the components and structures of effective communications as well as how they function. At Level 2, students are also introduced to explicit, public criteria that Alverno faculty collaboratively formulated. (The media literacy criteria, see Appendix B, are an example of collaboratively produced, public criteria.)

Students work with communication content as they observe, practice, and receive feedback in 1 semester hour labs for speaking/media, writing, and quantitative thinking. The assessments for these communication abilities occur in introductory writing, speaking, and quantitative thinking courses. Reading, listening, and computer literacy learning experiences as well as assessments take place in introductory discipline courses. Writing, along with speaking and using media video portfolios continue as performances are recorded in introductory courses.

Level 3. At Level 3 of communication development, students progress from a consciousness of communication processes toward effective control of processes. They communicate in multiple modes through expressive, substantial writing and speaking, critical reading, active listening, and accurate media interpretation, purposeful computer use, and relevant media production. In their communications, they perceive and draw on the relationships between the parts of communication processes and perceive how the whole reaches a level that is greater than the sum of its parts. At Level 3, students achieve a consistency of communication fitness, for example, of selecting (and practicing) communication styles and strategies to fit specific contexts.

As preparation for work with more complex material, students gain experience and self-assurance through practice in advanced communication labs. Writing, reading, speaking/using media, and listening labs supplement ongoing, developmental work on these specific communication abilities in 300-level (junior level) discipline and/or general education courses. Assessments for each of these abilities as well as the computer literacy ability generally occur in the context of the 300-level courses, although, Alverno's Assessment Center coordinates a performance assessment of reading, listening, and reading media.

Writing portfolios and speaking and using media video portfolios continue with additions of Level 3 performances.

Level 4.   Integration stands as the primary descriptor of Level 4 communication performances.   Students bring together communication skills and discipline content.   In a coherent manner and in different discipline courses and external (i.e., outside of the classroom and course environments) assessments, students habitually demonstrate the ability to convey discipline concepts and frameworks through diverse communication modes and through a fine control of the process.   Indeed, students at Level 4 unite process with content.   Learning experiences at Level 4 occur within the course context, whereas assessments occur inside as well as outside of the classroom.   Students also take extensive Level 4 multicommunication assessments.   In these assessments of performance, students exhibit critical communication skills in integrated multiple modes of writing, reading, speaking and using media, and listening.   Writing and speaking portfolios continue at Level 4, documenting student development as they position themselves for advanced ability work (Levels 5 and 6) in their major and minor fields of study.

Constructing a Shared Understanding of Media Literacy

Currently in Alverno's ability-based curriculum, media as part of the general communication ability centers on two aspects of media communication: (a) using media effectively when communicating in oral modes such as stand-alone speeches or group presentations and (b) reading (decoding and examining) media. At Alverno, using media and reading media have traditionally been considered significant strands to develop in the process of becoming a competent communicator.   Using media has been closely connected with speaking as a specific ability of communication.   Generally, when students are assessed for speaking they are also assessed for using media.   The reading media assessment occurs independently from other communication ability performances and assessments for all students.   However, weekday college professional communication majors and minors, as well as all students in the weekend college program, take the reading media assessment in the context of an introductory speech course.

In Fall 1991, several members of the communication ability committee began to reconsider the college's approach to media as a communication ability. There was concern that current campus practice was not fully meeting student needs to be able to use or think about media in a critical manner, especially in light of media's pervasiveness in diverse modes and formats of communication (e.g., personal, small group, and/or mass-audience messages), and media's position as social agents reflecting, representing, influencing, and/or constructing culture.

These perspectives of media as well as society's pervasive reliance on media technology as communication tools and channels for message construction and transmission changed the parameters of media education, calling for more depth and breadth.   It was no longer enough to be able to use media effectively in oral communication contexts or to be able to read media at an introductory level. Rather it was important to examine not only the changes in media's communication roles and social position, but students' needs relative to what it means to be literate in media communication and what it means to become effective communicators in today's society.

Initially it seemed vital that: (a) students know and feel confident using media technology to construct and/or present specific communications such as designing computer-generated transparencies for a speech; (b) students understand the advantages and disadvantages of diverse media modes in order to select carefully the most appropriate medium(s) to convey their messages; and (c) students examine and evaluate diverse media as messages in themselves in order to get at the deeper meanings potentially conveyed as well as the potential social agency of the medium(s).

In preparation for coordinating a media literacy subcommittee, which was formed by the communication ability committee in January 1992, the author spent Fall 1991 synthesizing background material in media studies as well as related theoretical standpoints in communication and education to not only facilitate the construction of a rationale and definition for media literacy as well as criteria for assessing media literacy development at Alverno, but to address the needs of students and the needs of instructors from diverse disciplines who would be respectively learning and supporting media literacy in their courses.

Influenced by post-masters' coursework in educational communications and technology at the University of Wisconsin-Madison, semiotics quickly moved into the foreground of the author's thinking about media literacy (at that time) because of its attempts to consider the foundation of communication and meaning making from a broader perspective. Semiotics recognizes and goes beyond language-based symbol systems that rely on letter forms or characters for written expression to investigate sign-based symbol systems of communication that take into account how we make meaning from a diverse range of symbols structured into grammars/codes and texts, for example, constructed and culturally accepted codes of visual techniques in film and television, page design in print media, or screen and document design in computer-generated media. (The following readings were used to construct a foundation in semiotics and to inform the links between semiotics and media literacy. See Barthes, 1968; Berger, 1984; Clarke, 1990; Cunningham, 1984; Deely, 1982; DeVaney, 1991; Eco, 1979b, 1984; Fiske, 1982; Guiraud, 1975; Hammer & McLaren, 1991; Hawkes, 1977; Hylynka & Belland, 1991; Noth, 1990; Sebeok, 1989, 1991; Siegel & Carey, 1989; Suhor, 1984; and Tufte, 1990.)

Although, in the author's opinion, semiotics as a science and art of signs appears to lack a complete formulation of a common base of elements and principles, its value as a framework for media literacy remains significant. Educators from diverse disciplines need not necessarily know the complex details of semiotic theory to implement a semiotic perspective when developing and integrating media literacy curriculum. Semiotics as a study of how we make meaning from and express our thoughts through signs within codes has solid potential for heightening awareness and understanding of nonverbal symbol systems. A focus on central semiotic concepts, such as sign, signification, signifier, signified, codes, and so forth, could encourage a paradigm shift from a linguistic bias to more balanced visual-verbal mode of analysis that would better accommodate interdisciplinary media education. For effective media literacy programs, educators must create an ongoing process to establish and refine core content and skills that students should know and develop as well as the degree and level that students should demonstrate their media literacy knowledge. Semiotics can serve as a tool and possibly theoretical framework for constructing content and determining skills.

For groups, such as women, subject to negative image perceptions and/or in subordinate power positions, media literacy becomes especially significant as a set of skills necessary for not only understanding the role(s) and power of media as a cultural agent, but as a set of skills for taking action as when designing, composing, using, and/or responding to media-based communications.

In February 1992, the media literacy subcommittee, informed by a synthesis of readings, began drafting a rationale, definition, and criteria for media literacy development and assessment within the Alverno College context. To keep their work learner centered, the subcommittee, composed of faculty from English, communication, nursing, and the sciences, discussed critically in a series of Friday afternoon meetings what it means to be a media-literate person. In other words, they asked: "What does a media-literate person know and what can she do?" They placed media literacy within the framework of an ability-based curriculum by considering it as a specific ability within a general communication ability to be developed by all students. In other words, at Alverno, the concept of media literacy was framed and grounded by the concept of what it means to be an effective communicator in any discipline. In fact, prior to graduation (and as mentioned earlier), students in all disciplines at Alverno currently develop their ability as effective communicators in speaking, using and reading media, listening, reading, writing, computer literacy, and quantitative literacy (mathematics).

The subcommittee concluded that students must be more than simply aware of media's powerful force and role in contemporary society. Instead, all students whether music, chemistry, English, nursing, or business majors must critically know and critically act with as well as on media. Moreover, media literacy as defined at Alverno, that is, the developed abilities of proficient use, effective creation , and critical interpretation of diverse media (see Appendix A), serves as a direct avenue to ownership of media's powers. Media literacy must be an important component in a contemporary higher education curriculum that has been designed to prepare and develop students for active participation in a democratic society and within global contexts. At Alverno, the conceptualization of media literacy rests on these assumptions: (a) media holds sociocultural agency in broad- and narrowcast contexts; (b) media literacy must be positioned as a crucial, specific ability within general communication as part of an ability-based program that focuses on the personal and professional development of women through liberal arts higher education.

In 1993 during the period that the media literacy subcommittee was drafting and revising a media literacy rationale, definition, and assessment criteria for students and faculty at Alverno, the Aspen Institute published *Media Literacy: A*

Report of The National Leadership Conference on Media Literacy. The conference ran under the auspices of The Aspen Institute's Communications and Society Program. Not surprising to those involved in media education, the report considered the need and/or rationale for media literacy and media literacy-oriented education among our citizenry a given. Overall the report focused its content by first providing two central definitions:

> 1. Media literacy: The movement to expand notions of literacy to include the powerful post-print media that dominate our informational landscape, helps people understand, produce and negotiate meanings in a culture made up of powerful images, words and sounds. (p. 1)
> 2. A media-literate person: Can decode, evaluate, analyze and produce both print and electronic media. The fundamental objective of media literacy is critical autonomy in relationship to all media. Emphases in media literacy training range widely, including informed citizenship, aesthetic appreciation and expression, social advocacy, self-esteem, and consumer competence. The range of emphases will expand with the growth of media literacy. (Aufderheide, 1993, p. 1)

Following the definitions, the Aspen report continued by presenting an overview of media educators' assumptions about media and of their shared pedagogical approach in developing media literacy skills, as well as an overview of media literacy education in Canada, Germany, and the United States. According to the report, media present and shape reality; media have inherent commercial, ideological, and political implications. Furthermore, each medium has developed a specific rhetoric and aesthetic associated with form and content. And "receivers negotiate meaning in media" (p. 2).

The 1993 Aspen Report reflected a closely related trend of thinking about media literacy by educators from various disciplines (not just communication or English educators) at Alverno College. As noted earlier, semiotics provided a theoretical framework to inform the start of conceptualizing media literacy at Alverno. After considerable reading and discussion, within the subcommittee, media literacy emerged during the 1992-1993 academic year as composed of three developmental strands: proficient use, effective creation, and critical inter-pretation. These strands were further defined by the formulation of developmental assessment criteria, which are presented later and in Appendix B.

The subcommittee also prepared a contextual definition and rationale along with criteria for four levels of development in each of the strands. A process of debate and refinement occurred over 2 years until the communication ability committee as a whole reached consensus and approved an evolved draft in May 1994. (See Appendix A.) A great deal of time was necessary to discuss thoroughly and come to consensus as a faculty about shared criteria defining developmental levels of a specific ability such as media literacy. Without the support of time and critical talk, a task often becomes sidelined, remaining on an abstract bench rather than on a playing field and in a mode of dynamic use.

Although the Aspen Institute Conference Report on media literacy did not inform the subcommittee's or the communication ability committee's thinking when conceptualizing media literacy and the developmental criteria for assessment, the correlation between the Aspen Report and the media literacy work at Alverno illustrates a common fundamental understanding of what media literacy is; an understanding shared on a national and perhaps international level, but adapted for local, contextualized practice.

As the media literacy subcommittee moved into final preparation stages of the definition, rationale, and assessment criteria, the communication ability committee reconceptualized and restructured how the majority of specific communication abilities (writing, reading, speaking, listening, media literacy, and computer literacy) were learned and assessed at Alverno. The committee determined to move beyond an approach emphasizing discrete development of specific communication abilities in separate labs and courses to an integrated approach. Consequently, positioning media literacy learning and assessment across the curriculum was reserved for incorporation into the new learning and assessment approach of specific communication abilities as restructured by the communication ability committee.

During the 1994-95 and 1995-96 academic years, media literacy learning and assessment was moved into the restructuring process of the communication ability At present, new integrated communication seminars rather than labs are being designed to promote this change in our vision of learning and our process of developing students' communication ability. Currently, media literacy learning and assessment experiences are being incorporated into these new integrated communication seminars, which are scheduled to begin in Fall 1996. Faculty across the disciplines will be asked to support media literacy learning and assessment in their courses just as they presently support the other specific communication abilities (i.e., writing, reading, listening, speaking, computer literacy, as well as quantitative literacy) in their courses. In order to facilitate this support process for across-the-curriculum media literacy learning and assessment, the communication ability committee will prepare resource materials and conduct in-service activities for faculty.

Facilitating media literacy learning and assessment in the Alverno context assumes an ongoing process. To meet the needs of all Alverno students as they individually as well as professionally develop, and as faculty educate them for the demands of contemporary life and for effective participation in an ever-changing environment, faculty must continually revisit their curriculum and practice, evaluating and refining it for viability and integrity. Even though the conceptualization process of media literacy learning and assessment has reached a final stage before implementation, the communication ability committee expects to revisit and continually refine it as they judge the effectiveness of the process and practice, and as they keep in the foreground what it means for Alverno students to be media literate as one means to act as competent communicators, participating in a democratic and technological society as well as interacting in global contexts.

ASSESSMENT AND MEDIA LITERACY

Nationally and internationally recognized for its innovative ability-based curriculum, Alverno employs a complex, nongraded system guided by educational principles that link learning with assessment. Student development and achievement take primary positions in Alverno's educational process. In multiple assessments of performance in and outside of the classroom, students learn how to integrate their abilities, to transfer and apply knowledge in diverse contexts, and to use their abilities and knowledge holistically in order to act effectively in personal, academic, and professional realms. Constructive feedback and reflective self-assessment also play vital roles in students' learning and achievement. Both enable students to take careful responsibility for their learning, becoming autonomous lifelong learners. Throughout the learning process in Alverno's ability-based curriculum, the principle of assessment-as-learning plays a key role in student development and achievement.

Assessment Assumptions

The concept of assessment in higher education evokes a diverse range of reactions among faculty, staff, and administration. At Alverno assessment holds a central position in the learning process. In fact, the Alverno community has been working with assessment as an integral component in student learning and achievement for over 20 years. At Alverno the concept of assessment opens with an etymological, and perhaps metaphorical, consideration of the infinitive, to assess, which originally meant to sit down beside [late ME < ML < L *assess(us)* ptp. of assidere *(as + sidere)*] (Alverno College Faculty, 1994, p. 1). Whether course-based or institutional, assessments at Alverno are occasions of learning. They are occasions for people to sit down beside each other in a democratic position of close observation and careful judgment based on explicit, public criteria. Assessment is not where teachers stand over students in an authoritarian position of scrutiny and arbitrary examination based on implicit, private standards or rules.

Consequently, in a position beside students, faculty at Alverno define student assessment-as-learning as "a process, integral to learning, that involves observation and judgment of each student's performance on the basis of explicit criteria, with resulting feedback to the student" (Alverno College Faculty, 1994, p. 3). Key assumptions about assessment at Alverno include the following descriptors: public, expected outcomes/ developmental criteria; performance; feedback; self-assessment; multiplicity; cumulative; expansive; and, externality (Alverno College Faculty, 1994).

Public, Expected Outcomes/Developmental Criteria. Ability-related outcomes and criteria are public in the sense that they are made known to students along the learning path. For example, course outcomes, what we expect a student to know and do by the end of the course, are often stated in the syllabus and explained at the semester's start. Explicit assessment criteria, "indicators of an ability as seen in its performance" (Alverno College Faculty,

1992, p. 32), are stated up front for students, when they receive assignments and projects that function as assessments.

Performance. Consequently, due to the explicit assessment criteria, there are no surprises about instructor and/or assessor expectations. Students know the criteria and strive to achieve the criteria through their assessment performances. And performances serve as demonstrations or samples of students' ability to do what they know. These performances often integrate one or more of the eight abilities (communication, analysis, problem solving, valuing, social interaction, global perspectives, effective citizenship, and aesthetic response) with discipline or interdisciplinary content and knowledge.

Feedback. Instructors, peers, or outside assessors, those not affiliated with a specific section of a course or set of students, provide structured commentary or feedback to students about their performances. Feedback based on student performance presents a diagnostic perspective of student progress as observed in their assessment performances. Moreover, feedback prompts questions, stimulating students to judge their performances from perspectives other than their own. The emphasis on observed behavior assists students in focusing on their strengths within an ability as well as on areas that require improvement (Alverno College Faculty, 1994).

Self-Assessment. Whereas constructive feedback connected to explicit criteria may target strengths and areas for improvement, self-assessment concentrates on learner knowledge of (and experience with) what was achieved, how and why it was achieved, as well as what could or should be done in the future to continue or reinforce ability development. In reflective, discerning self-assessments students make judgments based on specific criteria and provide evidence to support those judgments (Alverno College Faculty, 1994). In other words, they learn to take responsibility for and ownership of their education.

Based on the author's experiences with self-assessment, students through self-assessment essays addressing explicit criteria appear to reinforce and significantly extend their learning. This form of reflection adds depth and breadth to their learning. They learn to articulate process and components of content in a connected manner. Self-assessment, depending on the approach, may also honor or respect mistakes. Mistakes can be experienced as important, positive learning occasions especially in student apprehensive situations such as technophobic students working with equipment operations.

Multiplicity. The aspect of multiplicity in assessment takes into account the following: (a) number of opportunities, (b) diverse contexts, and (c) different modes. Every student has numerous assessment opportunities within courses and outside of or external to courses. In assessments of performance, students practice and demonstrate the one or more of the eight abilities in diverse settings (e.g., an in-basket assessment is assessment that includes diverse, multiple tasks presented in a business-style in-basket, which students peruse, prioritize, and complete or make plans for completion within a set time frame.) Each assessment performance at Alverno provides a sampling of a student's progress along with her level of ability. Together the samples form a picture of student development within an ability as well as across the eight abilities. Multiplicity also relates to assessment mode. Assessments can target a single or multiple mode (e.g., writing, or listening, reading, writing, speaking, and using media (Alverno College Faculty, 1994).

Cumulative and Expansive. Furthermore, assessments of performance can focus on specific developmental levels of ability and/or on an integration of abilities and their levels. This picture of development evolves as students add sequential assessment samples throughout their academic career at Alverno. In this way, assessment can be thought of as cumulative as well as expansive. As students move from beginning to advanced levels of ability development, prior levels of ability are reconstructed, reinforced, and strengthened in assessments. On first impression, this process may seem quite linear and rigid. However in practice, each student's sequence of assessments reflects individual paths of expanding development and achievement. These paths may appear linear, spiral, branched, and so forth, depending on student learning styles, environmental factors, and so forth. (Alverno College Faculty, 1994).

Externality. Distance between learning contexts and assessments establishes the degree of externality in assessments. Achieving distance in self-assessment can be a difficult process. Nevertheless, faculty assist students in their attempts to sit outside of their performances to evaluate their own progress. Faculty also work toward a measure of distance when they employ criteria in a specific assessment. Also, Alverno students take a series of extensive, external assessments designed by various committees and departments. These external assessments, that is external to the classroom, often integrate several of the eight abilities. And, the assessments are usually evaluated by someone other than their current course instructors. Externality, then, compounds the number of standpoints on students' learning thereby enhancing the picture of student development with more detail and depth (Alverno College Faculty, 1994).

Woven together these assumptions of assessment, public, expected outcomes/developmental criteria, performance, feedback, self-assessment, multiplicity, cumulative, expansive, and externality, support a practice of teaching and learning that is open to ongoing refinement by the entire Alverno College community.

Assessing Media Literacy

Presently media literacy learning and assessment primarily resides in discipline courses. However, that paradigm shifts in Fall 1996 when the new integrated communication seminars take their place in Alverno's general education curriculum. In order to address media literacy assessment in any substantial manner at this point, examples are presented in Appendix C. This appendix illustrates curriculum materials relevant to media literacy development, assessment, and achievement within a discipline course context. Media literacy is explicitly identified as a course learning outcome and embedded in the nature of course assignments and assessments.

CONCLUDING REMARKS

Assessment of students' specific and general communication abilities at Alverno College engages faculty and students in the learning process. Faculty facilitate the learning context and within that context they observe students' performances in multiple communication modes. These assessment performances occur along a developmental learning path guided by expected outcomes and public criteria. After their performances, students metaphorically and, perhaps, literally sit down to reflect on the process and outcomes. They identify their learning needs to become responsible, aware, confident, and lifelong learners who own such specific communication abilities as speaking, listening, writing, reading, quantitative thinking, computer literacy and, of course, media literacy.

Through a developmental process of assessment-as-learning that is supported across Alverno's curriculum, all students become media literate. On a consistent basis, they proficiently use, effectively create, and critically interpret media communications. Media-literate students own a specific communication ability and set of communication skills necessary for active, responsible participation and interaction in contemporary society.

APPENDIX A: ALVERNO COLLEGE COMMUNICATION DEPARTMENT MEDIA LITERACY RATIONALE & DEFINITION

Media are pervasive forces in local and global contexts. As a result, media literacy is crucial to being a well-educated and effective communicator. Yet, traditionally media literacy has not been a significant component of general education. At Alverno, media literacy is considered as important as other abilities that students are required to demonstrate across the curriculum.

Media literacy requires the development of knowledge and abilities in the use, creation, and interpretation of diverse media.

Media are varied representations of communication purposely created to convey information and influence the perceptions of others in local and global contexts. This interpretation distinguishes media literacy from other abilities developed in reading, writing, listening, computer literacy, and aesthetic response. In courses at Alverno that provide learning experiences in media literacy, we focus on typography and graphics, whether generated by hand or through the use of technology, as well as productions in visual, audio, and multimedia formats.

Media literacy centers on developing these abilities: proficient use, effective creation, and critical interpretation.

APPENDIX B: ALVERNO COLLEGE COMMUNICATION DEPARTMENT   MEDIA LITERACY VALIDATION CRITERIA: LEVELS 1-4

Using Media: Selection and Incorporation of Media in Own Presentations

Level 1
* Demonstrates some awareness of her ability to use media related to her own presentation.
* Demonstrates some awareness of potential for influencing the intended audience through media.

Level 2
* Uses media purposefully, not cosmetically.
* Reveals understanding of how to support concepts through her use of media.

Level 3
* Includes appropriate and diverse media (e.g., overheads, slides, videos) in discipline-related presentations.
* Uses high-quality, aesthetically pleasing media.
* Expresses specific relationships between media and message of presentation.

Level 4
* Selects and incorporates professional-quality media within a specific context to clarify frameworks from academic disciplines.

Creating Media: Development or Adaptation of Media for Own Presentations

Level 1
* Demonstrates ability to create media that assist audience understanding of content.
* Demonstrates some awareness of potential for influencing the intended audience through media.
* Creates media that are readable and accessible to an audience (hand-created media are accessible).

Level 2
* Reveals awareness of audience need for clarity and right to be interested ("audience-friendly").
* Reveals understanding of how to support concepts through her creation of media.
* Draws upon available technology to create media.

Level 3
* Selects/designs appropriate and diverse media to convey discipline concepts.
* Shapes media to influence audience response.

- Expresses specific relationships between media and message of presentation.

Level 4
- Develops, within discipline-related context, relationships among frameworks, knowledge, and outcomes.

Interpreting Media: Analysis and Evaluation of Media Messages

Level 1
- Assesses effectiveness of own media message (understandable, appropriate, legible).

Level 2
- Observes elements of form and function.
- Explains how personal experiences influence her response to media messages.

Level 3
- Infers relationships between form and function of media.
- Infers underlying values/ethics inherent in media messages.

Level 4
- Builds on perceived relationships between form and function of media to take and defend a position on how media reflect personal and cultural values/ethics.

APPENDIX C: ASSESSMENT MATERIAL (INSTRUCTOR, PEER SELF)

Instructor's Assessment

Presenters:_____

Assessor: _____   Date: _____

Title: _____

Presentation Components
____   Content: rationale, analysis, theoretical framework, ethical considerations, findings, action plan
____ Bibliography   ____ Agenda   _____ mins. Time frame
____ Media (two):_____

Production and Ability Criteria

A. ___ Students, through the project and presentation, formulated "new" perspectives about the impact of media on a significant cultural issue/subject by

1. ___ appropriately applying theory associated with mass or micro media.

2. ___ critically examining the relationship between the issue/subject and its representation in the media.

   a. ___ identifying and credibly interpreting the techniques used to shape/manipulate the content and form of media sources in order to influence viewers/readers.

   b. ___ carefully evaluating the effectiveness of intent, execution, and outcome of media source(s).

   c. ___ thoroughly considering the ethics involved.

B. ___ Students produced two professional-style speaker support media demonstrating an informed use of technology, i.e., each media piece enhanced the presentation and exhibited good to strong production quality.

Feedback

Peer Assessment

Presenters:_____

Peer: _____ Date: _____

Title: _____

Production and Ability Criteria

___ appropriately applied theory associated with mass or micro media.

Strengths/Recommendations

___ critically examined the relationship between the issue/subject and its representation in the media.

Strengths/Recommendations

___ identified and credibly interpreted the techniques used to shape/manipulate the content and form of media sources in order to influence viewers/readers.

Strengths/Recommendations

____   carefully evaluated the effectiveness of intent, execution, and outcome of media source(s).

Strengths/Recommendations

____   thoroughly considered the ethics involved.

Strengths/Areas to Improve

____   produced 2 professional-style speaker support media demonstrating informed use of technology.

Strengths/Areas to Improve

Self-Assessment & Self-Evaluation Essay
DUE:_____

Project Self-Assessment:

To self-assess your final project, apply the following format as well as production and ability criteria to the process and outcomes. Use specific, concrete examples from your research work and formal presentation to support your judgments.

A. How did you (your group) through research and a formal presentation, formulate "new" perspectives about the impact of media on a significant cultural issue/subject by

1. appropriately applying theory associated with mass or micro media.

2. critically examining the relationship between the issue/subject and its representation in the media through

a. identification and credible interpretation of the techniques used to shape/manipulate the content and form of media sources in order to influence viewers/readers.

b. careful evaluation of the effectiveness of intent, execution, and outcome of media source(s).

c. thorough consideration of the ethics involved.

B. How did you (your group) produce two professional-style speaker support media demonstrating informed use of technology, i.e., each media piece enhanced the presentation and exhibited good to strong production quality.

Course Self-Evaluation:
To self-evaluate course learning experiences, first review the explanation of competence validations in your syllabus, then respond to the following questions:

- What were your strengths and areas for improvement relative to multimedia production? Consider your slide-tape program and computer work.
- Overall, what did you learn about media research, presentation, and multimedia production? Consider the research strategies, presentation preparation, and production process you used throughout this course.
- How did you develop and/or reinforce upper-level competence in Analysis, Problem Solving, and Valuing? Refer to your mid-term slide-tape program as well as your final project.
- How will course learning experiences influence your future academic and professional work?

REFERENCES

Alverno College. (1994). *Alverno facts 1994-95.* Milwaukee, WI: Alverno College Productions.
Alverno College Faculty. (1992). *Liberal learning at Alverno College* (5th ed.). Milwaukee, WI: Alverno College Productions.
Alverno College Faculty. (1994). *Student assessment-as-learning at Alverno College* (3rd ed.). Milwaukee, WI: Alverno College Institute.
Aufderheide, P. (1993). *Media literacy: A report of the national leadership conference on media literacy.* Queenstown, MD: The Aspen Institute
Barthes, R. (1968). *Elements of semiology.* (A. Lavers & C. Smith, Trans.). New York: Hill & Wang. (Original work published 1964)
Berger, A. A. (1984). *Signs in contemporary culture: An introduction to semiotics.* New York: Longman.
Brown, J. A. (1991). *Television "critical viewing skills" education: Major media literacy projects in the United States and selected communities.* Hillsdale, NJ: Lawrence Erlbaum Associates.
Clarke, D. S., Jr. (1990). *Sources of semiotic: Readings with commentary from antiquity to the present.* Carbondale: Southern Illinois University Press.
Considine, D. M. & Haley, G. E. (1992). *Visual messages: Integrating imagery into instruction.* Englewood, CO: Teacher Ideas Press.
Cunningham, D. J. (1984, April). *What every teacher should know about semiotics.* Paper presented at the Annual meeting of the American Educational Research Association, New Orleans, LA. (ERIC Document Reproduction Service No. ED 250 282)
Deely, J. (1982). *Introducing semiotic: Its history and doctrine.* Bloomington: Indiana University Press.
DeVaney, A. (1991). A grammar of educational television. In D. Hylynka & J. Belland (Eds.), *Paradigms regained: The uses of illuminative, semiotic and post-*

modern criticism as modes of inquiry in educational technology (pp. 241-280). Englewood Cliffs, NJ: Educational Technology Publications.

Eco, U. (1979a). *The role of the reader: Explorations in the semiotics of text.* Bloomington: Indiana University Press.

Eco, U. (1979b). *A theory of semiotics.* Bloomington: Indiana University Press.

Eco, U. (1984). *Semiotics and the philosophy of language.* London: Macmillan.

Eisner, E. W. (1991). Rethinking literacy. *Educational Horizons, 69*(3), 120-128.

Fiske, J. (1982). *Introduction to communication studies.* London: Methuen.

Fiske, J. (1994). *Media matters: Everyday culture and political change.* Minneapolis: University of Minnesota Press.

Foster, B. G. (1995). Helping children cope in the information age. *Educational Horizons, 73*(4), 174-180.

Guiraud, P. (1975). *Semiology* (G. Gross, Trans.). Boston: Routledge & Kegan Paul (Original work published 1971)

Hammer, R., & McLaren P. (1991). Rethinking the dialectic: A social semiotic perspective for educators. *Educational Theory, 41*(1) 23-46, .

Hawkes, T. (1977). *Structuralism and semiotics.* Berkeley: University of California Press.

Hylynka, D., & Belland, J. C. (1991). Critical study of educational technology. In D. Hylynka & J. Belland (Eds.), *Paradigms regained: The uses of illuminative, semiotic and post-modern criticism as modes of inquiry in educational technology* (pp. 5-20). Englewood Cliffs, NJ: Educational Technology Publications.

Loacker, G., Cromwell, L., Fey, J., & Rutherford, D. (1984). *Analysis and communication at Alverno: An approach to critical thinking.* Milwaukee, WI: Alverno Productions.

McLaren, P., Hammer, R., Sholle, D., & Reilly, S. (1995). *Rethinking media literacy: A critical pedagogy of representation.* New York: Lang.

Noth, W. (1990). *Handbook of semiotics.* Bloomington: Indiana University Press.

Sebeok, T. A. (1989). *The sign and its masters.* Lanham, MD: University Press of America.

Sebeok, T. A. (1991). *A sign is just a sign.* Bloomington: Indiana University Press.

Self, W. (1990). Teacher, media, technology, and the imagination. *Virginia English Bulletin, 40*(1), 1-2.

Siegel, M. & Carey, R. R. (1989). *Critical thinking: A semiotic perspective.* Urbana, IL: National Council of Teachers of English.

Shutkin, D. S. (1990). Video production education: Towards a critical media pedagogy. *Journal of Visual Literacy, 10*(2), 42-59.

Suhor, C. (1984). Towards a semiotic based curriculum. *Journal of Curriculum Studies, 16*(3), 247-257.

Tufte, E. R. (1990). *Envisioning information.* Cheshire, CT: Graphics Press.

Wulff, S. (1994). To sit down beside: Assessment and communication competence at Alverno College. In S. Morreale & M. Brooks (Eds.), *1994 SCA summer conference proceedings and prepared remarks* (pp. 217-233). Annandale, VA: Speech Communication Association.

7

Critical Thinking

Henry Ruminski and William Hanks
Wright State University

This chapter reviews literature relevant to assessment of critical thinking, including several standardized tests of thinking designed for college students, and it reviews advice from authorities on how to assess critical thinking in open-ended formats. Suggestions are offered on how assessment can be conducted in several subject areas of media education. As defined in this chapter, assessment is the "process of defining, selecting, designing, collecting, analyzing, interpreting and using information to increase students' learning" (Hutchings, 1993, p. 15). We describe several methods of assessment that are useful either within a course and/or for periodic evaluation of student achievement. But we do not suggest specific timetables for assessment, because various regional accrediting associations and schools establish varying time lines and general assessment models (see Allison, 1994).

INTRODUCTION

In 1990, Congress passed the "Goals 2000: Educate America Act," which included this goal: "The proportion of college graduates who demonstrate an advanced ability to think critically, communicate effectively, and solve problems will increase substantially" (U.S. Department of Education, 1990). Both before and after "Goals 2000," journalism and mass communication educators claimed critical thinking to be a major goal in media education (Blanchard, 1988; Blanchard & Christ, 1993; Brown, 1991; Mullins, 1987; Shoemaker, 1993; Stark & Lowther, 1988; Steiner, 1993).

Steiner (1993) succinctly stated the reasoning: "The considerable overlap in descriptions of the liberally-educated critical thinker and the ideal journalist (one who is curious, skeptical, rational, logical, persistent, open-minded, fair, intellectually flexible) suggests that critical thinking skills are at the heart of the journalistic enterprise, yet critical thinking as such is an unstated curricular goal" (p. 98).

Steiner is probably correct. A survey of Association for Education in Journalism and Mass Communication (AEJMC) members revealed that most respondents agreed that teaching critical thinking is important in journalism and mass communication. However, there was little agreement as to a definition of critical thinking and most respondents seemed to think critical thinking did not require explicit instruction. Most respondents believed their textbooks lacked explicit instruction in how to think critically (Ruminski & Hanks, 1995), which is consistent with Shoemaker's (1987) analysis of 31 popular mass communication textbooks. Apparently Shoemaker (1993) was correct in saying critical thinking in mass communication and journalism is rarely "dealt with systematically or given priority among various associations for professional education in communication" (p. 99). For example, the Accrediting Council on Education in Journalism and Mass Communication (ACEJMC) does not list critical thinking as one of its standards, noting only that students should learn to "gather, organize, synthesize, and communicate information" in formats to fit media (ACEJMC, 1991, p. 9).

None of the other professional associations that relate to media education, including the Broadcast Education Association (BEA), the Speech Communication Association (SCA), and the International Communication Association (ICA), have published critical thinking standards although each association's members no doubt share a commitment to critical thinking in various ways. Worthy of note, by way of contrast, is the careful attention SCA has given to defining and assessing speaking and listening competence (Morreale, Moore, Taylor, Surges-Tatum, & Hulbert-Johnson, 1993).

Defining Critical Thinking

American education in general has not been systematic about defining and measuring critical thinking. Robert H. Ennis (1993), a major figure in the critical thinking movement in the United States, wrote: "Although critical thinking has often been urged as a goal of education throughout most of this century (e.g., John Dewey's *How We Think*, 1933; and the Educational Policies Commission's *The Central Purpose of American Education*, 1961), not a great deal has been done about it" (p. 17). And critical thinking assessment, he noted, "has been neglected even more than critical thinking instruction" (p. 179). Why? Mainly because defining and measuring critical thinking in a valid way are difficult tasks. However, several authorities on critical thinking do try to define critical thinking in a broad way that captures its complexity and is measurable (see, e.g., Ennis, 1993; Facione, 1991; Paul & Nosich, 1991).

Christ and Blanchard (1994) correctly noted that the starting point for assessment should be "agreement about what should be assessed" (p. 479). Probably most media educators would agree that critical thinking should be assessed. There is little apparent agreement, however, among those media educators as to definition.

Surveys of both SCA and AEJMC members revealed a wide range of definitions, with respondents generally agreeing that critical thinking involves analysis (Ruminski & Hanks, 1995; Ruminski, Spicer, & Hanks, 1994). These surveys also revealed a fairly widespread belief that improvement in critical thinking simply results from 4 years of college, despite significant evidence to the contrary (Keeley, Browne, & Kruetzer, 1982; King, Kitchener, Davison, Parker, & Wood, 1983; Nickerson, 1988; Perkins, 1985; Welfel, 1982). These two topics–definition and assumption of improved thinking–are related. For if critical thinking is only vaguely defined, it can be pretty much anything students do after 4 years of college and a few years in a major. But, as Chesebro (1991) noted regarding oral communication competency, some degree of standardization is desirable so we know what we mean by competency. Therefore, the discussion that follows assumes standardization is desirable to establish some common ground.

Dozens of definitions of critical thinking have been published, just as over 1,000 personality traits have been identified. But as Sternberg (1987) pointed out, "The problem is not that there are close to 1,000 personality traits . . . or thinking skills . . . but that there are many different names for the same thing" (p.252). Sternberg unified the various skills and dispositions that cognitive psychologists, learning theorists, philosophers and others have discussed as higher order thinking under three learned functions: (a) the executive function, or metacognitive; (b) the specific thinking skills, such as inferences; and (c) the ability to acquire and organize knowledge. These higher order skills stand in contrast to lower order skills such as rote memorization and simple recall. A definition that represents these three components of critical thinking, and one that lends itself to assessment, is found in *Critical Thinking: A Statement of Expert Consensus for Purposes of Educational Assessment and Instruction* (Facione, 1990). The definition, a product of an American Philosophical Association (APA) Delphi research project involving 46 experts in thinking, states:

> We understand critical thinking to be purposeful, self-regulatory judgment which results in interpretation, analysis, evaluation, and inference, as well as explanation of the evidential, conceptual, methodological, or contextual considerations upon which that judgment is based. . . . The ideal critical thinker is habitually inquisitive, well-informed, trustful of reason, open-minded, flexible, fair-minded in evaluation, honest in facing personal biases, prudent in making judgments, willing to reconsider, clear about issues, orderly in complex matters, diligent in seeking relevant information, reasonable in the selection of criteria, focused in inquiry, and persistent in seeking results which are as precise as the subject and the circumstances of inquiry permit. Thus, educating good critical thinkers means working toward this ideal. It combines developing CT skills with nurturing those dispositions which consistently yield useful insights and which are the basis of a rational and democratic society. (p. 2)

Although wordy, complex, and expressed in typical committee language, this definition does seem to cover the elements included in most other definitions. For example, Paul and Nosich in their *Proposal for the National Assessment of*

Higher-Order Thinking, commissioned by the U. S. Department of Education (1991), wrote:

> Critical thinking is the intellectually disciplined process of actively and skillfully conceptualizing, applying, analyzing, synthesizing or evaluating information gathered from, or generated by observation, experience, reasoning, or communication as a guide to belief and action. . . . It is based on universal values. . . clarity, accuracy, precision, consistency, relevance, good reasons, depth, breadth and fairness. . . . It entails the examination of those structures or elements of thought implicit in all reasoning: purpose; questions-at-issue; assumptions; concepts; empirical grounding; inferences; implications and consequences; objections from alternative viewpoints, and frame of reference. . . . It entails . . . traits of mind . . . independence of thought . . . and critical reading, writing, speaking and listening skills. (pp. 4, 5)

Both definitions subsume the Stark and Lowther (1988) idea of critical thinking (CT) as "the ability to examine issues rationally, logically and coherently" (p. 23). They also overlap D'Angelo (1971): "Critical thinking is the process of evaluating statements, arguments, and experiences" (pp. 7-8); McPeck (1981): "The core meaning of critical thinking is the propensity and skill to engage in an activity with reflective skepticism" (p. 8); Kurfiss (1988): "An investigation whose purpose is to explore a situation, phenomenon, question, or problem to arrive at a hypothesis or conclusion about it that integrates all available information and that can therefore be convincingly justified" (p. 2); Norris and Ennis (1989): "Reasonable and reflective thinking that is focused upon deciding what to believe or do" (p. 25); Brookfield (1991): identifying and challenging assumptions; recognizing contexts; exploring alternatives; and general skepticism about that which is assumed (pp. 7-9); and Paul (1990): the ideal critical thinker is fair-minded "about beliefs and viewpoints that are diametrically opposed to her own" (pp. ii-iii).

Operationalizing Critical Thinking

Of all the definitions, the only one that has been operationalized in standardized instruments measuring both thinking skills and dispositions (or attitudes) is the Delphi consensus. Both skills and dispositions seem to be required of any definition of critical thinking and both should be assessed in order to reflect the theoretical characterizations of CT commonly found and noted by Facione, Sanchez, Facione, and Gainen (1995), and including Dewey (1933), Sheffler (1965), D'Angelo (1971), Passmore (1972), Glaser (1984), Meyers (1986), Mayfield (1987), Kurfiss (1988), Browne and Keeley (1990), Paul (1990), Chaffee (1992), Oxman-Michelli, (1992), Wade and Tavris (1993), and Gray (1993).

The research literature on assessment of instruction in critical thinking reveals some of the strengths and weaknesses of various operational definitions of critical thinking. As Halpern (1993) reminded us, "Any assessment of student gains in the ability to think critically needs to be based upon an operational definition. . . . Although there is no absolute agreement on what constitutes critical thinking, there is sufficient overlap [among definitions] . . . to allow an evaluator to move beyond the definitional stage" (p. 240). Some of the definitions used in assessment studies were operationalized in commercial standardized tests such as the Watson-Glaser Critical Thinking Appraisal (WGCTA) (1980), and others were devised by the researchers. See, for example, Fox, Marsh, and Crandall (1983). The WGCTA, the oldest and most used critical thinking test, contains 80 response items across five types of thinking: (a) induction, (b) deduction, (c) assumption identification, (d) interpretation of data, and (e) identification of strong versus weak arguments. There are two matching forms of the test that can be used in pre- and posttest designs. A description of commercial thinking tests designed for college-age students follows a brief review of research on teaching critical thinking in college.

Teaching Critical Thinking

Relatively few empirical studies have been reported. Fox, Marsh, and Crandall (1983) measured college students' cognitive growth using Piagetian measures of thinking and found that college students who had been directly instructed in problem-solving skills showed significantly higher gains in intellectual maturity than students who had not received such instruction. Gibbs (1985) reviewed empirical studies and found none that satisfied rigorous requirements for experimentation (namely the use of experimental and control groups and random assignment of students to groups). However, he found that the WGCTA was the most frequently used test of critical thinking, followed by the Cornell test. He also noted that a carefully designed essay-type test, such as the Ennis-Weir Essay test (Ennis & Weir, 1985) and a carefully designed essay test by Browne, Haas, and Keeley (1978), had clear-cut criteria for evaluation and interrater reliability. Gibbs concluded that "conventional curricula, not designed specifically for critical thinking instruction can produce weak positive or even negative results" (p. 147).

Halpern (1993) concluded her review by saying, "Better thinking can be learned with appropriate instruction" (p. 250). This conclusion seems to hold in studies with varying operational definitions in critical thinking tests. Bangert-Drowns and Bankert (1990) conducted a meta-analysis of 20 studies of effects of explicit instruction in critical thinking. Ten of them used the WGCTA, five used the Cornell Thinking test, and five used various noncommercial tests. The authors found that "results consistently favored programs that use explicit instruction methods" (p. 2), that is, defining thinking tasks and providing training on those tasks. Facione (1991) developed and published a commercial multiple-choice critical thinking test to compare college students in a general education course in critical thinking to a comparable group. The group from the critical thinking course scored significantly better than the control group.

In speech communication, published research on effects of instruction on critical thinking has focused on formal debate, and the WGCTA was the instrument most often used to define critical thinking (Beckman, 1955; Brembeck, 1947; Colbert, 1987; Cross, 1971; Howell, 1943; Huseman, Ware, & Gruner, 1972). But debate and any other training said to improve critical thinking as measured by standardized tests should also transfer improved thinking to other contexts.

Should Critical Thinking Be Transferable?

In all fields reporting research on effects of instruction, evidence of transfer of training is slight. Halpern (1993) asserted that "The goal of any instruction designed to improve thinking is transfer of training . . . [i.e.] use of critical-thinking skills in a wide variety of contexts. The whole enterprise would be of little value if these skills were only used in the classroom or only on problems that are very similar to those presented in class" (p. 249). However, she cited only one source that has produced evidence of "spontaneous transfer of thinking skills to real-world problems that occur outside the classroom" (see Lehman & Nisbett, 1990). Norris and Ennis (1989) notes the problem of transfer, observing lack of consensus among experts as to whether people apply specific thinking skills they learn in one context to another context. And there is disagreement among experts as to whether real-world thinking can or should be taught only within subject matter (Ennis & Norris, 1990).

There is no standardized subject-specific test of critical thinking that covers the several thinking skills and dispositions noted in several prominent conceptual definitions of critical thinking. But there are many standardized commercial tests of critical thinking, each focusing on sets of distinguishable critical thinking tasks (Ennis, 1993).

Critical Thinking Measurement Tools

There are seven measurement tools suitable for undergraduate college students that address various thinking skills. However, of these only one instrument is specifically designed to measure college students' critical thinking predispositions: The California Critical Thinking Dispositions Inventory (Facione & Facione, 1992). Another instrument, the Holistic Critical Thinking Scoring Rubric (HCTSR), lists several criteria that can be used to judge open-ended or performance-based tests (Facione & Facione, 1994). A summary of the dispositions inventory and the rubric follow later, after Norris and Ennis' (1989) description and commentary on college-level thinking tests. (See Appendix A)

As noted earlier, the Watson-Glaser Critical Thinking Appraisal is the oldest and most widely used test. The test, by G. Watson and E. G. Glaser, is published by Psychological Corporation (555 Academic Court, San Antonio, TX 78204), and is aimed at Grade 9 through adulthood. Norris and Ennis (1989) noted that it does not ask for judgments about the credibility of sources, semantics, or predispositions.

Overall, Norris and Ennis regard the WGCTA as fairly well-balanced in testing for a variety of thinking skills. However, we think it important to note that 16 of the 80 items on the test are deductive logic questions for which necessarily there is only one possible answer. Critics, such as McPeck (1981), understandably question the value of deductive logic in real-world reasoning. Reliability estimates for the WGCTA range from .70 to .82, and the test has a long history of testing for construct and predictive validity (Kramer & Conoley, 1992).

The Cornell Critical Thinking Test, Level X (1985), was written by R. H. Ennis and J. Millman and published by Midwest Publications (PO Box 448, Pacific Grove, CA 93950), and is aimed at junior and senior high school and college students. It has 72 items, with sections on induction, credibility, observation, deduction, and assumption.

There is another, somewhat different version of the Cornell Critical Thinking Test, called the Level Z test (1985), which is aimed at Grades 7 through college, and it contains sections on prediction and experimental planning, fallacies, and definition, as well as induction and credibility. Ennis himself noted the weaknesses in both the tests he coauthored, as well as other tests. He cautioned that such tests should be used mainly for teaching purposes rather than "high-stakes" purposes such as placement or program accountability (Ennis, 1993).

Ennis also coauthored the only commercial essay test of critical thinking, The Ennis-Weir Critical Thinking Essay Test (1985), with E. Weir, published by Midwest Publications (address given earlier). The test, aimed at Grades 7 through college, tests for getting the point, identifying reasons and assumptions, stating a point, giving good reasons, seeing options, and reacting to equivocation, irrelevance, circularity, reversal of "if-then" relationships, overgeneralization, credibility, and emotive language. Examinees are given a fictitious letter to the editor of a newspaper and asked to evaluate the thinking in each of the letter's eight paragraphs and in the letter as a whole. Graders give credit, for example, for pointing out an analogy does not fit; noting an incorrect definition, or noting the shift in meaning of words. Graders score each paragraph in a similar manner, following the instructions in the manual. Estimates of interrater reliability range between .86 and .82, but Norris and Ennis (1989) specified that "these numbers only mean that different graders tend to rank students the same, not that they tend to give about the same level of score. Different graders may rank examinees responses in the same order but still have widely different average scores" (p. 8).

The California Critical Thinking Skills Test (CCTST; Facione & Facione, 1992) has two statistically matched forms and is described by its authors as the operationalization of the APA Delphi panel (1990) definition of critical thinking: "The process of purposeful, self-regulatory judgment" (p. 2). The manual says, "The CCTST is a standardized, 34-item, multiple choice test which targets those core critical thinking skills regarded to be essential elements in a college education. The items range from those requiring an analysis of meaning of a given sentence, to those requiring much more complex integration of CT skills"(p. 2).

The authors of this chapter have used the CCTST for diagnostic and teaching purposes in media classes and have found most of the questions useful in identifying careless errors in reading and systematically analyzing information in the question scenarios. Ennis (1993) also noted that parts of the CCTST can be useful in identifying students who are weak in critical thinking predispositions. We agree with Carter-Wells' (1992) judgment that CCTST is the best available standardized test.

Disposition Tests

A companion instrument to the CCTST is the California Critical Thinking Dispositions Inventory (CCTDI; Facione & Facione, 1992). The instrument "derives its conception of the disposition toward CT from the APA Delphi Report" (Facione, Sanchez, Facione, & Gainen, 1995). The CCTDI has 75 Likert-style items over seven dispositions, each of which is computed as a subscore. A total composite score is computed by adding the subscores. The seven scales are: (a) Inquisitiveness, (b) Open-mindedness, (c) Systematicity, (d) Analyticity, (e) Truth-seeking, (f) CT Self-confidence, and (g) Maturity (Facione & Facione, 1992).

The authors of this chapter have used CCTDI to explore tendencies toward thinking, and we have generally found that students in our classes who scored well on predispositions were also the students who supported their opinions and positions with reasons. We were somewhat surprised to find out that students who were predisposed not to think critically did not try to give "the expected answers" to inventory prompts, but without embarrassment agreed with statements such as, "The best way to solve problems is to ask someone else for the answer."

The CCTDI and the other standardized instruments that measure features of critical thinking can be criticized for being reductionist and for not testing students' ability to think well in specific subjects they have studied. These criticisms apply to all general knowledge thinking measures, as does the objection that the general knowledge subjects in questions are frequently trivial.

Yet some critical thinking tests can provide valuable information about students' thinking, especially if, as Norris (1985) and Ennis (1993) suggested, students can write down or explain orally why they gave certain answers. And, we would add, if students understand we are not interested in the subject matter of the questions, but rather in how the students approach the questions.

Use of Measurement Tools in Assessment

In assessing courses and program effectiveness in improving critical thinking in media education, some standardized instruments can help measure the "repertoire of thinking strategies that will enable [students] to acquire, evaluate, and synthesize information and knowledge [and to] develop analytical skills to make decisions in both familiar and unfamiliar circumstances" (Stark & Lowther, 1988, p. 23). That is, standardized instruments can measure some aspects of critical thinking in media education that relate to decision making in unfamiliar circumstances, which require general thinking strategies, including knowledge of logical fallacies, how to break down a complex idea into manageable parts, and the disposition to use those strategies.

But we have to know what thinking strategies we want to measure, and then we can decide what instruments to use. Ennis (1993) offered good advice: "For comprehensive assessment, unless appropriate multiple-choice tests are developed, open-ended assessment techniques are probably needed" (p. 184).

Although the WGCTA and/or the Ennis-Weir Essay test can reveal certain strengths and weaknesses in students' thinking, such tests cannot tell us how a student would approach solving an unstructured problem such as developing a public relations plan. Such tests cannot tell us how a student in advertising might develop an ad strategy or copy objectives.

Multiple measures should be used to measure critical thinking in media education, just as multiple measures should be used for assessment in general (Erwin, 1991). First, although there are general thinking skills, there also is empirical evidence that critical thinking entails subject-specific thinking. For example, experts in thinking about subjects also know a lot about those subjects. Bransford and Vye (1989), in *A Perspective on Cognitive Research and Its Implications for Instruction*, stressed the point that competent thinkers in various fields have competence in the skills and information and have practiced on problems in those fields.

CRITICAL THINKING IN MEDIA EDUCATION

Ideally, a stand-alone thinking course in critical thinking should be required of media education majors. But the definition, skills, and predispositions entailed in the definition established by the program for assessment purposes should be the basis of instruction for such a course (see Shoemaker, 1993).

Expert advice to Association of Schools of Journalism and Mass Communication (ASJMC) would seem to support the view that critical thinking should be assessed using measures both of thinking skills that are subject- specific and those that are not. Ewell (1991) offered three general principles of assessment: (a) assessment should cover knowledge and skills taught throughout the program's curriculum; (b) assessment should provide multiple measures of student performance; and (c) assessment procedures should provide information on multiple dimensions of student performance; that is, they should yield more than a single summative grade. At minimum, critical thinking as broadly defined to include skills and dispositions should be taught throughout the media-education curriculum, and critical thinking should be assessed as majors complete the curriculum. Every level of thinking skills need not be taught in every course, but those skills should be taught and predispositions nurtured over the entire curriculum. At completion of the student's course of study, in some senior-level course such as a capstone course, multiple measures of student performance should be taken.

Assessment of critical thinking within a media education program might use a "value-added" approach in which students coming into the major are tested for critical thinking and given posttests as they complete the major. However, such an approach makes sense only if general thinking skills are tested either with multiple-choice instruments or essay tests because new majors are presumed not to possess the knowledge required for subject-specific thinking tests. Also, such testing obviously could not be conducted under rigorous conditions using control groups and random selection.   Halpern (1993) pointed out, even without control groups students can be used as their own controls, and taken together with other information, pre- and posttests could provide evidence of effectiveness of critical thinking instruction.

THE ASSESSMENT PLAN

• Step 1: Give all students who enter the major a standardized critical thinking test and a dispositions inventory to provide a baseline. We recommend the CCTST and the CCTDI.
• Step 2: Interview each student and point out the strengths and weakness shown by the standardized tests. Explain the results.
• Step 3: Using the HCTSR as a guide, design media course assignments that utilize critical thinking skills. In evaluating those assignments, use the HCTSR to point out to students how their critical thinking weaknesses affect their level of achievement.
• Step 4: Give all exiting seniors the CCTST and CCTDI. Compare to baseline to assess critical thinking growth.

We do not recommend creating your own multiple-choice test to measure general critical thinking skills or dispositions. Instead, we recommend selecting one of the standardized instruments already discussed. Although the multiple-choice exam does offer savings in time in administering and grading, it requires much more time in the initial construction, trials, and revisions needed to develop a valid and reliable instrument.

If you choose to construct your own multiple-choice exams there are a number of sources offering advice (Costa, 1985; Jacobs & Chase, 1992; Norris & Ennis, 1989).   Statistical analysis of the results of the initial administration of the instrument will help to identify items that may be poorly worded or have confusing options and will provide reliability estimates for individual items. The initial administration of any instrument should be used only to refine the instrument. If needed for assessment purposes, the results should be used cautiously and only after a careful analysis. If essay tests are used, intercoder reliability should be measured to ensure that coders are evaluating answers in a consistent, systematic way.   In addition, all the points about reliability and validity raised in earlier discussions of testing apply to any effort to create your own test, whether general or subject specific. To achieve the most comprehensive measure of critical thinking we recommend a combination of general critical thinking skills tests, essay instruments and various performance measures.

Open-ended information-gathering techniques can take several   forms, including performance-based assessment techniques. "Performance-based assessment is a type of testing that calls for demonstration of understanding and skill in applied, procedural, or open-ended settings" (Baker, O'Neill, & Linn, 1993, p. 1211).

This type of assessment, also referred to in testing literature as authentic assessment, direct assessment, and alternative assessment, is defined by these general characteristics:

1. Uses open-ended tasks.
2. Focuses on higher order or complex skills, for example, evaluation as opposed to simple recall.
3. Employs context-sensitive strategies.
4. Often uses complex problems requiring several types of performance and significant student time.
5. Consists of either individual or group performance.
6. May involve a significant degree of student choice.

Performance assessment is an alternative to pencil-paper tasks that call for a single correct answer and it may include a variety of projects such as case studies, research reports, and portfolios. Performance assessment can measure higher order thinking, including critical thinking (Resnick & Resnick, 1992). However, higher order thinking as measured in performance assessments should be linked to other measures of thinking ability as a check on validity. Criteria for performance evaluation include the following:

1. Have meaning for students and teachers and motivate high performance.
2. Require the demonstration of complex cognitions, for example problem solving, knowledge representation, explanation, applicable to important problem areas.
3. Exemplify current standards of content or subject matter quality.
4. Minimize the effects of ancillary skills that are irrelevant to focus of assessment.
5. Possess explicit standards for rating or judgment. (Baker, O'Neill, & Linn, 1993, p. 1214)

Performance-assessment techniques designed to fit these criteria would seem to be ideal instruments for critical thinking in media education, assuming acceptable reliability can be established. And such reliability estimates probably can be established if performance tasks are specific and raters are trained (see, e.g., Baker, et al., 1993, p. 1213; Morreale, et al., 1993, pp. 18-21). Scoring rubrics should match the tasks and the definition of critical thinking.

We know of no standardized CT test that matches elements of the CT definition on which it is based to a scoring rubric for open-ended, or performance-based test, except the CCTST and its companion rubric, the Holistic Critical Thinking Scoring Rubric (HCTSR). The rubric also incorporates features that can measure critical thinking dispositions.

Facione and Facione (1994) illustrated how HCTSR, which is based on the APA Delphi definition of CT, can be applied to assess open-ended performance. The definition in brief is "purposeful, self-regulatory judgment which results in interpretation, analysis, evaluation and inference, as well as the explanation of the evidential, conceptual, methodological, and criteriological criteria on which it is based" (Facione, 1990, p. 3). HCTSR is in the public domain for educational purposes. It lists several broad criteria that roughly match elements of the CT definition. The HCTSR form is in Appendix B.

The authors designed the rubric to rate classroom project presentation and assigned papers but note that it "can be used to achieve one data point in a multi-modal plan for curriculum assessment by providing a rating of a representative sample of student work which demonstrate the students' critical thinking" (p. 9). They exemplify the kinds of instructions that might be given to students to be sure they know they are to demonstrate critical thinking:

> The following guidelines for preparation of your presentation . . . should not be approached in a step-wise or linear fashion. Rather, they are suggested as an interactive framework to drive your presentation. . . . You should provide your audience with knowledge of your thinking process and criteria in choosing the position you plan to defend rather than merely listing possible opinions or conclusions. It is important that you demonstrate how you considered alternatives fairmindedly by providing the reasons and evidence for the positions you take, descriptions of the other alternative positions you considered but rejected, and the considerations you found to be most decisive in forming your judgment. (p. 10)

Then they instruct the student to be sure to present definitions, the main arguments, evidence, pro and con considerations, assumptions, and a justification for the position taken. The idea behind the rubric and directions is to assess both critical thinking ability and some critical thinking predispositions Thus use of the rubric allows matching significant elements with any given students' score on the standardized CT skills test (CCTST) on the dispositions inventory (CCTDI).

Some adaptation of the HCTSR is feasible in several areas of media education, as we hope to illustrate with the examples that follow. Media writing assignments of various kinds could be used as critical thinking performance assessments. For example, students can be asked to write an opinion piece based on assigned readings that contain opposing views. They can be informed of the purpose of the writing assignment and the critical thinking rubric by which they will be evaluated. Raters should have carefully read the information that the student uses as source material and generally agree on such things as credibility and validity of evidence, logic, interpretation of data, clarity, and so forth, related to the various sources given to the student.

Information-gathering performance assessments might include a written and/or oral report on a given topic, an annotated bibliography on a topic, a list of sources and reasons why such sources might be useful for such things as radio or television news, features, commentary or interview. Evaluators of this kind of performance should know in advance the kind and relevance of sources in order to judge whether the student had considered the purpose of the information-gathering assignment, important definitions, relevance of various sources to the topic and purpose. Not all the critical thinking criteria presented in the HCTSR need apply to all performance tasks, so for example, an information-gathering assignment that simply requested information might not require an evaluation of evidence.

In the area of ethics, however, there may be a long list of criteria that would be applied to a performance assessment, such as the presentation of a position a student journalist might take on whether he or she would deceive potential sources in order to get information.

A production performance assessment might call for development of a TV and/or audio production for a specified purpose. The performance could include the preproduction plan, production plan, and postproduction plan, along with justification for the plans, including such things as budget constraints. It might also include an actual production. But in order for the criteria to be applied the task should be fairly well-constructed by the faculty who evaluate the performance so that they will have considered the various possibilities involved in making decisions involving the production, such as the technical capabilities of the available production facility, available time, money, and so forth.

A media management decision-making case study would be an excellent performance assessment vehicle to test real-world critical thinking. For example, Sherman (1987) presented several scenarios for management decisions. Some involve personnel decisions that could affect a broadcast station's status with the Federal Communications Commission regarding equal opportunity employment policies of the Commission. Others involve programming decisions in which there are simply no right or wrong answers, decisions that require one to be clear about management objectives. Sherman's scenarios are constructed tightly enough, and his textbook provides enough information, that raters who judge the presentations of students can have considered various options, the evidence, and the arguments that could be advanced (see chap. 12).

A student in an advanced reporting or editing class, which has covered the reporting of quantitative data, could be presented with brief results of a public opinion survey and asked to evaluate its newsworthiness for a particular audience. The evaluator would judge whether the student's comments examined the adequacy of the research method, the relevance of the sample used and the real versus statistical significance of any findings. The evaluator also would examine the student's ability to explain why particular items would be of interest to a specific audience or challenge the conclusion based on the information presented.

A public relations assignment might involve asking the student to develop a strategy for communicating a new company policy that requires a restocking fee on returned, nondefective merchandise. The student would be told to identify the relevant publics and the potential effects of the change, indicate how and what types of information would be gathered for planning and suggest communication strategies and objectives that might be useful in announcing the change. See an evaluation form in Appendix C.

Evaluators can judge whether the student accurately identified those who would be affected by the change, both internally and externally, and whether the student clearly differentiated between the potential effects of the change on each public. The student also can be judged on the adequacy of the information on which any plan would be based. For example, what kind of information is sought to serve as evidence to justify the fee and what types of arguments are used in the communication strategy? The objectives can be judged on whether they accurately reflect the problem, are achievable and can be measured.

An advertising student could be asked to create a series of statements about a new product and explain why each statement should be considered for an advertising campaign. The instructions should be clearly constructed so that the student will know which critical thinking criteria will apply. For example, the student could be presented with a technical fact sheet and reminded that any claims about physical product qualities must be supported by factual data. The evaluator could then determine if the student has accurately assessed the evidence and interpreted it accurately.

SUMMARY

We began this chapter by discussing developing of critical thinking skills as a goal for media education. We agreed with Shoemaker who said critical thinking in mass communication and journalism is rarely "dealt with systematically or given priority among various associations for professional education in communication" (p. 99). However, several authorities on critical thinking were cited who do try to define critical thinking in a broad way that captures its complexity and is measurable.

We agreed with Christ and Blanchard (1994), who noted that the starting point for assessment should be "agreement about what should be assessed" (p. 479). We acknowledged that although most media educators might agree that critical thinking should be assessed, there is little apparent agreement among those educators about how to define and measure critical thinking.

For this chapter we used a definition of assessment as the "process of defining, selecting, designing, collecting, analyzing, interpreting and using information to increase students' learning" (Hutchings, 1993, p. 15). The published definition of critical thinking that probably best represents its major components and one that lends itself to assessment is found in "Critical Thinking: A Statement of Expert Consensus for Purposes of Educational Assessment and Instruction" (Facione, 1990).

We found no standardized subject-specific test of critical thinking that covers the several thinking skills and dispositions noted in several prominent conceptual definitions of critical thinking. We found five critical thinking tests and one inventory of critical thinking dispositions suitable for undergraduate college students. We agreed with Carter-Wells' (1992) judgment that CCTST is the best available standardized forced-choice test.

In assessing courses and program effectiveness in improving critical thinking in media education, some standardized instruments can help measure how well students acquire, evaluate, and synthesize information. However, multiple measures should be used to measure critical thinking in media education, just as multiple measures should be used for assessment in general (Erwin, 1991). Open-ended information-gathering techniques can be useful in media education and can take several forms, including performance-based assessment techniques that call for demonstration of understanding and skill.

We know of no standardized CT test that matches elements of the CT definition on which it is based to a scoring rubric for open-ended, or performance-based tests, except the CCTST and it companion rubric, the HCTSR. The rubric also incorporates features that can measure critical thinking dispositions. The HCTSR is in the public domain for educational purposes. The rubric, as discussed in the chapter, allows matching significant elements with any given student's score on the standardized CT skills test (CCTST) or on the dispositions inventory (CCTDI).

We noted that some adaptations HCTSR can be used in media education. Given the difficulty in preparing and establishing reliability and validity for a multiple-choice instrument we would argue for using a forced-choice test with opportunity to explain, and/or essay or performance-based assessment techniques if a standardized test does not meet your requirements.

APPENDIX A: CRITICAL THINKING ASSESSMENT TOOLS

Title	Aspects Measured	Strengths and Weaknesses
Watson-Glaser Critical Thinking Appraisal test	Induction, deduction, assumption-identification, interpretation of data, evaluation of strength of argument.	Tests variety of skills, but relies heavily on deductive logic; test is long and may fatigue examinees.
Cornell Critical Thinking Test, Level X	Induction, deduction, credibility of sources, observation, assumption-identification.	Tests a variety of skills, including evaluation of source credibility, but credibility items seem too simple and answers likely depend on background beliefs.
Cornell Critical Thinking Test, Level Z	Induction, deduction, credibility judgment, predication, experimental planning, fallacies, definitions, assumption-identification.	Relatively short test that tests some scientific method knowledge; some items unchallenging.
Ennis-Weir Critical Thinking Essay Test	Identification of strengths and weakness of arguments, judging relevance of arguments, evidence, analogies, accuracy of definitions.	Only standardized essay CT test, requires writing justifying judgments; but reliable only for reliable ranking and not for actual score.

APPENDIX A (Continued)

Title	Aspects Measured	Strengths and Weaknesses
The California Critical Thinking Skills Test	Inductive and deductive inferences, analysis of meaning, identification of cogent reasons, evaluations of objections to conclusion.	A short test (34 items) that tests a variety of skills, does not rely heavily on deductive logic; but contains a few convoluted word-puzzles.
The California Critical Thinking Dispositions Inventory	Measure inquisitiveness, open-mindedness, systematicity, analyticity, truth-seeking, CT self-confidence, intellectual maturity.	Only standardized measure of predispositions, good face-validity, seems to predict actual performance; but some items may signal desirable responses.
The Holistic Critical Thinking Scoring Rubric	Provides guide for judgment of critical thinking within subject matter contexts calling for examinees to produce rather than simply respond.	Adaptability to a variety of subject-specific contexts; but reliability must be established for each task.

APPENDIX B: HOLISTIC CRITICAL THINKING SCORING RUBRIC (HCTSR)

4. Consistently does all or almost all of the following: Accurately interprets evidence, statements, graphic, questions, etc. Identifies the salient arguments (reasons and claims) pro and con. Thoughtfully analyzes and evaluates major alternative points of view. Draws warranted, judicious, non-fallacious conclusions. Justifies key results and procedures, explains assumptions and reasons. Fairmindedly follows where evidence and reasons lead.

3. Does most or many of the following: Accurately interprets evidence, statements, graphics, questions, etc. Identifies relevant arguments (reasons and claims) pro and con. Offers analyses and evaluations of obvious alternative points of view. Draws warranted, non-fallacious conclusions. Justifies some results or procedures, explains reasons. Fairmindedly follows where evidence and reasons lead.

2 Does most or many of the following: Misinterprets evidence, statements, graphics, questions, etc. Fails to identify strong, relevant counter-arguments. Ignores or superficially evaluates obvious alternative points of view. Draws unwarranted or fallacious conclusions. Justifies few results or procedures,

seldom explains reasons. Regardless of the evidence or reasons, maintains or defends views based on self-interest or preconceptions.

1. Consistently does all or almost all of the following: Offers biased interpretations of evidence, statements, graphics, questions, information, or the points of view of others. Fails to identify or hastily dismisses strong, relevant counter-arguments. Ignores or superficially evaluates obvious alternative points of view. Argues using fallacious or irrelevant reasons, and unwarranted claims. Does not justify results or procedures, nor explain reasons. Regardless of the evidence or reasons, maintains or defends views based on self-interest or preconceptions. Exhibits close-mindedness or hostility to reason. (Facione & Facione, 1994, p. 8)

APPENDIX C: EXAMPLES OF CRITICAL THINKING TASKS

CT Elements	Problem	Student Demonstrates CT
Definitions of terms, evaluation of source credibility, fair-minded look at opposing views, identification of assumptions, inductive and deductive inferences.	Write editorial on controversial topic.	Write editorial for or against banning books that contain racial slurs from school libraries.
Definitions, identification of assumptions, selection of relevant facts, documents, interpretation.	Write interpretive piece based on legal documents.	Write a feature explaining a given state's open-records law and how it affects the public.
Definitions, identification of assumptions, inductive and deductive inferences, evaluation of alternative positions vis-à-vis goals and values, reasoned justification of ethical choice.	Take a position on a question of journalism ethics.	Write a position paper for professional journalists on ethics of deceit in order to gain information about a religious cult by joining it for the purpose of publishing stories.
Definitions (of purpose, objectives) vis-à-vis a video production, analysis of audience, resources, i.e., time, budget, personnel, equipment, interpretation of objectives in visual terms.	Design a video production.	Write a preproduction plan, production schedule, and budget.

APPENDIX   C   (Continued)

CT Elements	Problem	Student Demonstrates CT
Definitions, selection of relevant information, fair-minded consideration of alternatives, selection and analysis of data, interpretation of data.	Respond to FCC Inquiry about minority hiring policy of station.	Write an affirmative action policy for a given television station.
Definitions, selection and evaluation of evidence, interpretation of data, identification of assumptions, evaluation of credibility of sources, synthesis of research.	Write story interpreting and evaluating a topic in scientific research.	Write an article that interprets, evaluates, and synthesizes research on genetic basis of homosexuality, based on research and review and evaluation of scientific opinion.
Definitions, selection of information, analysis, interpretation, evaluation.	Develop a strategy to communicate new policy for customer returns.	Write a public relations plan to communicate a policy of charging a restocking fee for the return of undamaged merchandise.

REFERENCES

Accrediting Council on Education in Journalism and Mass Communication. (1991). *Accredited journalism and mass communication education, 1991-92.* Lawrence: University of Kansas.

Allison, T. (1994).   Regional association requirements and the development of outcomes statements.   In W. G. Christ (Ed.), *Assessing communication education: A handbook for media, speech, & theatre educators* (pp. 57-88). Hillsdale, NJ: Lawrence Erlbaum Associates.

Baker, E. L., O'Neill, H. F., & Linn, R. L. (1993).   Policy and validity prospect performance-based assessment. *American Psychologist, 48*(12), 1210-1218.

Bangert-Drowns, R., & Bankert, E. (1990). *Meta-analysis of effects of explicit instruction for critical thinking.* (ERIC-Document Reproduction Service No. ED 328 614)

Beckman, V. (1955). *An investigation of the contributions to critical thinking made   by   courses   in   argumentation   and   discussion   in   selected   colleges.* Unpublished doctoral dissertation, University of Minnesota, St. Paul, Minnesota.

Blanchard, R. O. (1988). Our emerging role in liberal and media studies. *Journalism Educator, 43*(3), 28-31.

Blanchard, R. O., & Christ, W. G. (1993). *Media education and the liberal arts: A blueprint for the new professionalism.* Hillsdale, NJ: Lawrence Erlbaum Associates.

Bransford, J. D., & Vye, N.J. (1989). In L. B. Resnick & L. E. Klopfer (Eds.), *Toward the thinking curriculum: Current cognitive research* (pp. 173-205). Alexandria, VA: Association for Supervision and Curriculum Development.

Brembeck, W. (1947). *The effects of a course on argumentation on critical thinking ability.* Unpublished doctoral dissertation, University of Wisconsin-Madison, Madison, WI.

Brookfield, S. D. (1991). *Developing critical thinkers: Challenging adults to explore alternative ways of thinking and acting.* San Francisco: Jossey-Bass.

Brown, J. A. (1991). *Television critical viewing skills education: Major media literacy projects in the United States and selected countries.* Hillsdale, NJ: Lawrence Erlbaum Associates.

Browne, M. N., Haas, P., & Keeley, S. (1978, January). Measuring critical thinking skills in college. *The Educational Forum,* 219-226.

Browne, M. N., & Keeley, S. M. (1990). *Asking the right questions.* Englewood Cliffs, NJ: Prentice-Hall.

Carter-Wells, J. A. (1992, January). *Defining, teaching, and assessing critical thinking in a multicultural context.* Paper presented at the meeting of the Association of American Colleges, Washington, DC.

Chaffee, J. (1992, Spring). Teaching critical thinking across the curriculum. *New Directions for Community Colleges, 77,* 25-35.

Chesebro, J. W. (1991). Oral communication competency and assessment. *The Carolina Speech-Communication Annual, 7,* 6-22.

Christ, W. G., & Blanchard, R. O. (1994). Mission statements, outcomes, and the new liberal arts. In W. G. Christ (Ed.), *Assessing communication outcomes: A handbook for media, speech and theatre educators* (pp. 31- 55). Hillsdale, NJ: Lawrence Erlbaum Associates.

Colbert, K. R. (1987). The effects of CEDA and NDT training on critical thinking ability. *Journal of the American Forensic Association, 23*(4), 194-201.

Costa, A. (Ed.). (1985). *Developing minds: A resource book for teaching thinking Part X.* Alexandria, VA: Association for Supervision and Curriculum Development.

Cross, G. (1971). *The effects of belief systems and the amount of debate experience on the acquisition of critical thinking.* Unpublished doctoral dissertation, University of Utah, Salt Lake City.

D' Angelo, E. (1971). *The teaching of critical thinking.* Amsterdam: B. R. Gruner N. V.

Dewey, J. (1933). *How we think: A restatement of the relation of reflective thinking to the educational process.* Lexington, MA: Heath.

Educational Policies Commission. (1961). *The central purpose of American education.* Washington, DC: National Education Association.

Ennis, R. H. (1993). Critical thinking assessment. *Theory Into Practice, 32*(3), 179-186.

Ennis, R. H., & Millman, J. (1985a). *Cornell critical thinking test, level x.* Pacific Grove, CA: Midwest Publications.

Ennis, R. H., & Millman, J. (1985b). *Cornell critical thinking test, level z.* Pacific Grove, CA: Midwest Publications.

Ennis, R. H., & Norris, S. P. (1990). Critical thinking assessment: Status, issue needs. In J. Algina & S. Legg (Eds.), *Cognitive assessment of language and math outcomes* (pp. 1-42). Norwood, NJ: Ablex Publishing.

Ennis, R. H., & Weir, E. (1985). *The Ennis-Weir critical thinking essay test.* Pacific Grove, CA: Midwest Publications.

Erwin, T. D. (1991). *Assessing student learning and development.* San Francisco: Jossey-Bass.

Ewell, P. T. (1991). *Benefits and costs of assessment in higher education: A framework for choice-making.* Boulder, CO: National Center for Higher Education Management Systems.

Facione, N. C., & Facione, P. A. (1994). Critical thinking disposition as a measure of competent clinical judgment: The development of the California, *Nursing Outlook,* 1-13.

Facione, P. A. (1990). *Critical thinking: A statement of expert consensus for purposes of educational assessment and instruction.* (ERIC-Document Reproduction Service No. ED 315 423).

Facione, P. A. (1991). *Using the California critical thinking skills test in research, evaluation, and assessment.* Millbrae, CA: The California Academic Press.

Facione, P. A., & Facione, N. C. (1992). *The California critical thinking dispositions inventory (CCTDI), and test manual.* Millbrae, CA: The California Academic Press.

Facione, P. A., & Facione, N. C. (1993). *The California critical thinking skills test.* Millbrae, CA: The California Academic Press.

Facione, P. A., & Facione, N. C. (1994). *Holistic critical thinking scoring rubric (HCTSR).* Millbrae, CA: The California Academic Press.

Facione, P. A., Sanchez, C. A., Facione, N. C., & Gainen, J. (1995). The disposition toward critical thinking. *The Journal of General Education, 44*(1), 1-24.

Fox, L. S., Marsh, G., & Crandall, J. C. (1983, April). *The effect of college classroom experiences on formal operational thinking.* Paper presented at annual convention of Western Psychological Association, San Francisco, CA.

Gibbs, L. (1985). Teaching critical thinking at the University level. *Informal Logic, 7*(2-3), 137-149.

Glaser, R. (1984). Education and thinking: The role of knowledge. *American Psychologist, 39*(2), 93-104.

Gray, P. (1993). Engaging students' intellect: The immersion approach to critical thinking in Psychology instruction. *Teaching Psychology, 20*(2), 68-74.

Halpern, D. F. (1993). Assessing the effectiveness for critical thinking instruction. *The Journal of General Education, 42*(4), 238-254.

Howell, W. (1943). The effects of high school debating on critical thinking. *Speech Monographs, 10,* 99-103.

Huseman, R., Ware, G., & Gruner, C. (1972). Critical thinking, reflective thinking and the ability to organize ideas: A multivariate approach. *Journal of American Forensic Association, 9*(4), 261-265.

Hutchings, P. (1993). Principles of good practice for assessing student learning *Assessment Update, 5*(1), 6.

Jacobs, L. C., & Chase, C. I. (1992). *Developing and using tests effectively: Guide for faculty.* San Francisco: Jossey-Bass.

Keeley, S., Browne, M. N., & Kruetzer, L. (1982). A comparison of freshmen and seniors on general and specific essay tests of critical thinking. *Research in Higher Education, 17*(2), 139-154.

King, P. M., Kitchener, K. S., Davison, M. L., Parker, C. A., & Wood, P. K. (1983, March-April). The justification of beliefs in young adults: A longitudinal study. *Human Development, 26,* 106-116.

Kramer, J. J., & Conoley, J. C. (Eds.). (1992). *The eleventh mental measurements yearbook.* Lincoln, NE: The Buros Institute of Mental Measurements.

Kurfiss, J. G. (1988). *Critical thinking: Theory, research, practice, and possibilities.* Washington, DC: ASHE-ERIC.

Lehman, D., & Nisbett, R. (1990). A longitudinal study of the effects of undergraduate training on reasoning. *Developmental Psychology, 26*(6), 952-960.

Mayfield, M. (1993). *Thinking for yourself: Developing critical thinking skills through writing.* Belmont, CA: Wadsworth.

McPeck, J. E. (1981). *Critical thinking and education.* Oxford, England: Martin Rober.

Meyers, C. (1986). *Teaching student to think critically.* San Francisco: Jossey-Bass.

Morreale, S. P., Moore, M. R., Taylor, K. P., Surges-Tatum, D., & Hulbert-Johnson, R. (1993). *The competent speaker.* Annandale, VA: Speech Communication Association.

Mullins, E. (1987, May). *Task force report on liberal arts and sciences in journalism/mass communication.* Paper presented to the Association of Schools of Journalism and Mass Communication, New York.

Nickerson, R. S. (1988). On improving thinking skills through instruction. In E. Rothkopf (Ed.), *Review of research in education* (pp. 3-57). Washington, DC: American Educational Research Association.

Norris, S. P. (1985, May). Synthesis of research on critical thinking. *Educational Leadership,* 40-45.

Norris, S. P., & Ennis, R. H. (1989). *Evaluating critical thinking.* Pacific Grove, CA: Midwest Publications, Critical Thinking Press.

Oxman-Michelli, W. (1992). Critical thinking as critical spirit. *Resource Publication Series: Montclaire Institute for Critical Thinking, 4*(7), 1-13.

Paul, R. (1990). *Critical thinking: What every person needs to survive in a rapidly changing world.* Rohnert Park, CA: Center for Critical Thinking and Moral Critique, Sonoma State University.

Paul, R., & Nosich, G. M. (1991). *A proposal for the national assessment of higher-order thinking.* Sonoma, CA: Center for Critical Thinking, Sonoma State University.

Passmore, J. (1972). On teaching to be critical. In R. F. Deardon, P. Hirst, & R. Peters (Eds.), *Education and the development of reason* (pp. 415-433). Boston: Routledge & Kegan Paul.

Perkins, D. N. (1985). Postprimary education has little impact on informal reasoning. *Journal of Educational Psychology, 77*(5), 562-571.

Resnick, L. B., & Resnick, D. P. (1992). Assessing the thinking curriculum: Tools for educational reform. In B. R. Gifford & M. C. O'Connor (Eds.), *Changing assessments: Alternative views of aptitude, achievement, and instruction* (pp. 37-76). Boston: Kluwer.

Ruminski, H., & Hanks, W. (1995). Critical thinking lacks definition and uniform evaluation criteria. *Journalism and Mass Communication Educator, 508*(3), 4-11.

Ruminski, H., Spicer, K., & Hanks, W. (1994, May). *Critical thinking in speech communication: A survey of speech communication educators.* Paper presented at Eastern States Communication Association, Washington, DC.

Sheffler, I. (1965). *Reason and teaching.* Indianapolis, IN: Hackett.

Sherman, B. L. (1987). *Telecommunications management: The broadcast & cable industries.* New York: McGraw-Hill.

Shoemaker, P. (1987). Mass communication by the book: A review of 31 texts. *Journal of Communication, 37*(3), 109-131.

Shoemaker, P. (1993). Critical thinking for mass communication students. *Critical Studies In Mass Communication, 10*(1), 99-111.

Stark, J. S., & Lowther, M. A. (1988). *Strengthening the ties that bind: Integrating undergraduate liberal and professional study.* Ann Arbor: University of Michigan.

Steiner, L. (1993). Critical thinking. *Critical Studies In Mass Communication, 10*(1), 98.

Sternberg, R. J. (1987). Questions and answers about the nature and teaching of thinking skills. In J. B. Baron & R. J. Sternberg (Eds.), *Teaching thinking skills: Theory and practice* (pp. 250-262). New York: Freeman.

U.S. Department of Education. (1990). *National goals for education.* Washington, DC: Government Printing Office.

Wade, C., & Tavris, C. (1993). *Psychology.* New York: Harper Collins.

Watson, G., & Glaser, E. (1980). *Watson-Glaser critical thinking appraisal.* San Antonio, TX: Psychological Corporation.

Welfel, E. R. (1982). How students make judgments: Do educational level and academic major make a difference? *Journal of College Student Personnel, 23*(6), 490-497.

8

Media Writing

Seth Finn
Robert Morris College

Traditionally media writing courses have called on students to perform real-life newswriting and scriptwriting assignments, thereby adopting a model of performance assessment. Public demand for institutional accountability has motivated an extension of assessment activities to faculty performance as well. This chapter explores five topics related to improving student performance and its assessment in media writing courses: (a) reorienting students to media writing strategies and the demands of an invisible audience; (b) structuring the course syllabus and media writing assignments so that students know what is expected of them; (c) relating course content to models of media theory and practice that support the entire media studies curriculum; (d) employing modern techniques of analytical scoring to provide diagnostic assessment of student writing; and (e) implementing a program of holistic scoring by instructor groups to monitor student achievement and fine-tune course content.

INTRODUCTION

Assessment in media writing courses is both simple and complex. Simple because the end result of all media writing assignments is an explicit real-world product–the script. Complex because the writer is a student, not a professional. Nothing is as effortless to grade as a script that meets standards of professional quality. Nothing is as disheartening as dealing with a script that has totally missed the mark. In the real world, anything less than an "A" can be discarded. In the academic world, anything less than an "A" implicitly demands a diagnostic assessment. One purpose of this chapter is to explain how this academic ideal might be realistically pursued to the benefit of students, instructors, and academic institutions. A second, and no less challenging purpose, is to describe how systematic procedures for assessing the success of a media writing course might be implemented to serve the same constituencies.

PREPARING STUDENTS FOR ASSESSMENT

In the language of educational testing, assigning a real-life task, such as writing a newspaper article or broadcast script, and evaluating it to determine a student's mastery of the skills involved falls within the domain of performance assessment. As Stiggins and Bridgeford defined it:

> Performance assessment is . . . a systematic attempt to measure a learner's ability to use previously acquired knowledge in solving novel problems or completing specific tasks. In performance assessment, real life or simulated assessment exercises are used to elicit original responses which are directly observed and rated by a qualified judge. (quoted in Gipps, 1994, p. 99)

When one contrasts the concept of performance assessment with the traditional practices used to assess learning in a liberal arts environment, then it is immediately recognizable that most students have had little experience with performance assessment when they enroll in their first media writing class. Up to this point, students are much more likely to have developed competence in taking exams that tested their knowledge, comprehension, and analytical abilities, but not the application of their acquired knowledge to a real-life or simulated exercise.

Even students who have demonstrated their competence in writing essays and term papers now have to come to terms with a new set of circumstances, including an invisible audience and a new role for the instructor. The conventional composition text admonition to "know your audience" takes on a new meaning when that audience is an abstract construct rather than an instructor or classmates. For the most part, students have been conditioned to write essays and term papers for their teachers and professors, who are specialists and experts. They have been rewarded for revealing every relevant item they have uncovered in their research or can recall from their studies. Often the presentation of ideas can be somewhat unclear, but instructors, whose primary goal is to assess their students' success at acquiring knowledge about a subject, may rely on their own expert knowledge to give a sympathetic reading to their students' writing.

Mass media writing courses, however, force a new set of circumstances on students and instructors. The audience for a script is an imaginary public. Most members of the audience know much less about the information to be communicated than the writer. Suddenly students function as experts–not by choice, but by virtue of their role in the production process–writing to an audience that cannot be relied on to use expert knowledge to decode the intended message. If the writer is hazy about the ideas to be communicated, the members of the audience are likely to become confused or impatient. Certainly they cannot be relied on to dispel the foggy notions of a poorly encoded message.

This predicament of writing to an inexpert and invisible audience–typical of a mass media environment–is novel in an academic setting. Suddenly the instructor who traditionally plays the role of motivator and sympathetic reader of student writing moves to the sidelines as a "qualified judge." Based on his or her experience, an evaluation must be made. Does the script generate a meaningful message for the imagined audience? The instructor assumes the role of editor or producer. The fundamental assessment of the message is based not on what the student knows about the topic, not even what the instructor can infer, but on what it communicates to an unknowing public. The student writer as expert, the instructor as judge of an invisible audience's sensibilities; this new assessment procedure must be made explicit to the media writing student.

A second major adjustment for the media writing student is the adoption of a series of peremptory writing conventions. Writing for the media requires changes in structure, strategy, and style. Print journalists have long insisted that traditional techniques of composition taught in high school and college were worse than useless. Edwin L. Shuman's 1903 text, *Practical Journalism*, underscored this point with a list of exaggerated imperatives: "Put the point of your whole story into the first sentence, and the shorter the sentence the better. Whether the story be two columns or two inches long, cram the marrow of it into the first paragraph. Banish the school-essay idea that there must be an introduction or preliminary explanation of any kind" (Shuman, cited in Adams, 1993, p. 107).

In recent years, the notions underlying college composition courses have been under scrupulous review, often leading to revolutionary new approaches (Faigley, Cherry, Jolliffe, & Skinner, 1985). Nevertheless, the differences between academic writing and media writing are not always so obvious to inexperienced students. When asked to write nonfiction scripts, such as radio public service announcements (PSAs), feature interviews, or minidocumentaries, they may–unless carefully coached–employ expository writing styles that have afforded them success in other writing classes. Worse yet, they may become mired in complexity, abstraction, and inflated vocabulary, because they have been encouraged, beginning with their high school English teachers, to believe that those devices provide convincing evidence of their intellectual growth (Hake & Williams, 1981).

MAKING A SYLLABUS ASSESSMENT-FRIENDLY

Investing time in the development of a comprehensive syllabus is one especially effective way to improve the validity of student assessment in media writing courses (Tucker, 1994). First and foremost, students need an explicit description of each writing assignment if assessments of their writing are to be valid. For example, instructors often assume that students can use sample scripts in their texts as examples of correct format. Yet many times when textbook authors collect copies of real-world scripts to exhibit differences in content, they inadvertently introduce an excessive amount of variance in formats. Novice students, trying to interpolate rules from many examples, may needlessly devote large blocks of time to resolving such issues as proper margins and headings when they should be concentrating on formulating their message and revising it.

To forestall this misplaced effort, the syllabus, as well as other written materials distributed throughout the semester, should spell out the nature of each written assignment in a way that relieves the student from the burden of working out routine procedures. That way the student's effort and the focus of an instructor's assessment is on the essential skills to be acquired and demonstrated. One of the major differences between novices and experts in undertaking a task is that the experts can isolate important elements of the task from the menial ones and focus their attention where needed. In explicitly describing writing assignments–in essence giving away the answers to the simple questions–students will remain focused on essential components rather than trivial ones.

Another way a syllabus can facilitate assessment is in the careful structuring of assignments in terms of their complexity. The proper order for acquiring skills in media writing is not always as clear cut as it is in arithmetic where, for instance, multiplication precedes division. And yet, it is clearly useful for instructors to consciously build one assignment on another, so that lessons learned–or not learned–in one exercise can be tested in the next. Media writing students who begin the semester by creating a 30-second live radio PSA based on material published in a free pamphlet should be reminded 10 weeks later, as they embark on a 15-minute screenplay based on a favorite short story, that once again they are adapting published material to a nonprint medium. This time, however, they will exploit both a visual and an audio channel, using varied shots, voices, and sounds as well as elements of dramatic structure in a manner that is consistent with the techniques they have learned in their intervening assignments. Thus, the last assignment in the course explicitly functions as a capstone exercise.

There is a point, however, at which extensive direction of a student on a particular assignment creates an environment in which the instructor provides all the "answers." At that point, the student is responding rather than thinking. Too much "practice on the task" can subvert the instructor's intention to measure higher order thinking skills. The instructor ends up teaching the student to complete the performance assessment task–no matter how realistic in design–on automatic pilot rather than provoking the high order application of knowledge skills it was designed to assess (Gipps, 1994). This subversion of thinking through rote learning is the Achilles' heel of performance assessment and thus remains a constant concern in media writing instruction.

COMMUNICATION THEORY AND WRITING ASSESSMENT

The major safeguard against teaching rote skills in a media writing course is the instructor's explicit concern with communication theory. There are, of course, rules of spelling, grammar, and punctuation that a good writer must observe just as a good driver must be cognizant of motor vehicle laws and rules of the road. In both cases, however, a finite list of rules cannot account for every contingency. Eventually the rules must give way to a conceptual model of a complex system that can be used to guide behavior. As scholars and researchers, communication faculty are dedicated to devising and refining models of a communication system. In general, understanding the system serves to expand the repertoire of effective behaviors, provide rationales for what previously may have been perceived as arbitrary rules, and give the individual confidence to assess the effectiveness of his or her own behavior, even to the point of breaking fundamental rules in instances when they prove counterproductive. In short, a model of communication should facilitate the student's transition from novice learner to competent practitioner, with the additional benefit of identifying criteria for assessing effective media writing.

Different writing instructors may find different models of communication particularly suitable to their teaching approach, but even a model as simple as Shannon's schematic of a general communication system–although often criticized for its lack of an explicit feedback mechanism (Rogers & Kincaid, 1981)–can be effectively employed to explore media writing principles and practices (Finn, 1991). What makes Shannon's linear model especially appropriate (see Fig. 8.1) is its focus on the encoding and decoding of messages as the essential element of a communication system.

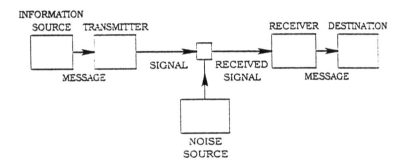

FIG. 8.1. Schematic diagram of a general communication system.

Note. Figure from Shannon, 1949. Copyright ©1949 by the Board of Trustees of the University of Illinois Press. Used with permission of the University of Illinois Press.

The order of events–devising a message (at the source), encoding the message in representative symbols (at the transmitter), receiving the symbols that stand for the message (at the receiver), and inferring the message by decoding the symbols (at the destination)–denotes in precise terms the semiotic nature of all communication; in short, that the explicit meaning of a message never travels through a channel, but must be reconstituted at the destination. The job of the source–the media writer–is to devise a set of symbols capable of conjuring up in the minds of the intended audience the message meant to be conveyed.

Accordingly, Shannon's model underscores the reality that effective communication is based on the careful structuring and selection of symbols in an environment where writers must project what meanings audiences will attach to the words they have selected. Shannon's model is not unique in this focus on the intricacies of coding systems. Rather, this short discussion of its attributes is meant to reinforce the notion that the assessment of media writing can be meaningfully drawn from theory as well as practice in a manner that integrates media writing courses with the broader field of communication studies.

Other Goals in Media Writing Courses

Directing serious attention to theoretical models in a media writing course contests as well the presumption that the primary educational goal of media writing courses is to develop competence in one or more specialized forms of scriptwriting. Such a singular goal is unrealistic and unproductive for a number of reasons. It is unrealistic, for instance, to believe that every student who enrolls in an introductory media writing course has either the inclination or the talent to become a professional media writer. Nor could the various mass media industries employ all of them. With the possible exception of students enrolled in a traditional print journalism curriculum, most communication studies students initially register for a media writing course only because it is a required part of the curriculum or serves as the prerequisite to a production course that they truly desire. More importantly, however, it would be unproductive to overlook the possibilities that an introductory media writing course provides in reinforcing other components of a departmental curriculum. Thus, there may be other types of assessments in media writing courses besides the evaluation of print copy or production scripts.

One area that requires serious consideration is the assessment of student knowledge and understanding of the primary script formats used in print, broadcast, film, and multimedia production. For most students, these formats–some traditional, many still evolving as a result of computer technology–appear to be full of arbitrary conventions, and yet each element–from headings to line lengths–has evolved from particular demands of production. Whereas journalistic copy may undergo minimal reconfigurations during the production process, broadcast and film scripts are often as removed from the final product as architectural drawings are from a constructed building. Moreover, multimedia scripts and storyboarding envision a perpetual reconfiguration of text, audio, full-motion video, animation, and graphics. Thus, internalizing the logic of script formats as well as inferring production details from actual scripts reinforces knowledge that can be usefully applied across a continuum of courses from media criticism to media management to media ethics, not to mention advanced writing and production courses.

Script formats are only one example of substantive knowledge that may be introduced in a media writing course. Accordingly, testing students on other types of knowledge derived from a media writing course need not be a trivial or tedious exercise as long as it advances the broader goals of the faculty's core curriculum. Even traditional essay exams make sense if questions are centered on such topics as contrasting the formal characteristics of different media channels, critically analyzing and comparing the techniques used in single and multimedia productions exhibited in class, and recounting the significant problems students encountered and the solutions they devised in completing their own assignments.

The potential benefits are twofold. Assessing students' analytical understanding of print, broadcast, film, and multimedia programming and its creation provides a legitimate method to reward students, if only partially, for their serious commitment to a required course in which disparities in creative or technical skills give some students an initial advantage. Furthermore, expanding the focus of the course to include the assessment of intellectual competencies other than media writing skills helps reinforce the liberal arts objectives of the curriculum and avoid the tendency to "duplicate in the classroom the occupational culture of the newsroom and other media 'shops'" (Blanchard & Christ, 1993, p. 63).

THE NEW MECHANICS OF WRITING ASSESSMENT

Over the past 2 decades dissatisfaction with the writing skills of secondary school students across the United States has generated intense support for improved methods of assessing writing instruction. Whereas none of these programs has been focused on media writing, communication faculty can exploit the wealth of experience derived from writing assessment trials to devise improved methods for assessing media writing. Spandel and Stiggins (1990), although addressing primary and secondary school English teachers in their text, provide an excellent introduction to the various forms of assessment, their rationale, and effective implementation. To fully comprehend the literature of writing assessment, the uninitiated must first acquire a precise understanding of its terminology.

Writing assessment methods fall into two major categories: indirect and direct. Grammar and spelling tests that are commonly used to screen registration for journalism or media writing courses are a good example of indirect assessments of writing skill. The examiner infers a student's current writing ability from his or her skill in responding to objective questions that are believed to be empirically correlated with success in writing courses. Most writing instructors believe indirect methods provide only a crude approximation of the mental capabilities necessary for good writing. They put their trust in direct assessments of writing ability, that is, the evaluation of actual pieces of writing a student has been assigned to complete.

Direct assessments fall into three categories, distinguished by the scoring method employed: primary-trait scoring, holistic scoring, and analytic scoring. Primary-trait scoring presumes that writing is successful if it appears to achieve one or more desired effects on its intended audience. Primary-trait assessment puts particular emphasis on the "rhetorical situation created by the purpose, audience, and writing assignment" (Huot, 1990, p. 238). Media writing textbooks are replete with primary traits for each writing assignment. Student writers are admonished, for example, to write news stories that are informative yet effortless to read, radio commercials that motivate the listener to buy the product, or sitcom dialogue that generates a chuckle every 30 seconds.

Although primary traits are often the focal point of classroom discussion and instructor feedback, in the realm of composition instruction critics complain that primary-trait scoring often fails to reveal the nexus of writing qualities that undergird all effective writing. One antidote to this deficiency is analytic scoring, which is designed to explicitly identify for students a set of five or six traits that constitute the recurring qualities of good writing. The advantages of analytic scoring can be best appreciated, however, after a brief explanation of yet a third procedure, holistic scoring, which attempts to approximate the rigor of analytic scoring, but with a reduced burden on the evaluator's time.

Holistic Scoring

Holistic scoring comes in two types–general impression scoring and focused holistic scoring. The distinction is based on whether or not the evaluation is linked to a set of specific written criteria. When the instructor foregoes such a list, deferring instead to his or her intuitive judgment of good and bad writing, then the system of assessment is known as *general impression scoring.* Quite often this amounts to a rank ordering of students' written assignments from best to weakest performances, a strategy that is routinely employed by instructors trying to assure relative fairness in their subjective evaluations of student work. The alternative, *focused holistic scoring,* furthers this quest for fairness by requiring instructors to consciously attend to specific criteria when rating student writing assignments. Spandel and Stiggins (1990), for example, proposed a list of six criteria: (a) ideas and content, (b) voice, (c) organization, (d) sentence fluency, (e) word choice, and (f) conventions in their text on writing assessment.

Interestingly, advocates of direct assessment are rarely daunted by fears of subjectivity, pointing out that intense training of raters by expert evaluators can lead to a very consistent level of evaluation of student samples, especially when raters are guided not only by a list of criteria but exemplars of high, middle, low, and unacceptably poor student work for any particular writing task. They often point to the methods used by experienced judges at diving, gymnastics, and figure-skating competitions, whose subjective ratings are nevertheless accepted as valid because they are based on a rigorous set of criteria (Frederiksen & Collins, 1989).

Subjectivity aside, holistic scoring still suffers from a serious deficiency. The final result of holistic scoring, even when focused by a set of written criteria, is a single score, usually on a rating scale with no more than four or five levels. Its usefulness in a media writing curriculum is thereby limited in ways that Spandel and Stiggins (1990) previously noted for general composition courses: "Holistic scoring is an efficient method of selecting students who show the most promise with respect to writing skills or of selecting those students who are most in need of special assistance. Thus, it's ideally suited to selection or placement decisions that can be made on the basis of an overall impression of writing proficiency" (pp. 6-7).

What holistic scoring readily offers is speed and efficiency. Trained assessors can reliably score at a rate of one page a minute (Spandel & Stiggins, 1990). At such speeds, a department-wide assessment of student writing portfolios approaches the realm of practicality, thereby providing the means for evaluating the aggregate success of a media writing course or program. In addition, a team of media writing instructors or even a single faculty member can employ holistic assessment to rank applicants seeking to enroll in beginning media writing courses or demonstrate sufficient competency to take advanced ones.

Analytic Scoring

Once inside the classroom, however, progress in student writing hinges on providing practice and diagnostic feedback. Analytic scoring is designed to optimize such feedback by standardizing its form. Although most media writing instructors no doubt employ some form of holistic assessment when grading assignments, their verbal feedback may be an ad hoc response based on the premise that each sample of writing is a unique "work of art." The instructor's comments focus accordingly on what the student has done well and what problems remain. In the process, the instructor may ignore many essential components of good writing because their implementation was not noteworthy in that particular case.

Analytic scoring raises questions about the efficacy of letting the results of written assignments direct the form–if not the content–of instructor feedback. As in focused holistic scoring, analytic scoring requires instructors to devise a set of specific written criteria to guide the assessment, but this time they actually award scores for each of the designated traits. Those scores represent a diagnostic evaluation of the writing from which students can then plan their revisions. If analytic scoring is to work effectively as a diagnostic tool, then the choice of criteria is especially critical. Taken together the individual criteria must constitute the "whole" of writing traits that adhere to create a successful script. Furthermore, these criteria must be established early on in the dialogue between instructors and students if instructors want to empower their students to initiate their own revisions on the basis of such scores.

Therefore, the decision to adopt some form of analytic scoring extends far beyond the implementation of a new grading system. It requires a mini-revolution in teaching strategy, as implied in Spandel and Stiggins' (1990) discussion of the differences between holistic and analytic scoring: "Analytical scoring acknowledges the underlying premise of holistic scoring that the whole is, indeed, more than the sum of its parts, but it adds that if we're to teach students to write, we must find a way to define the components of good writing and to talk intelligently about them in a language that student writers can understand and use in revision" (p. 7). Articulating a need "for a language that student writers can understand and use in revision" is certainly easier than inventing that language, especially when it is difficult to envision how a half-dozen writing characteristics might be equally applicable to the multiple forms of media writing–from newspaper reports to TV spots to feature length screenplays.

Scaling Up for Systematic Assessment

From the outset it should be clear that implementing a systematic assessment plan for media writing course requires a substantial investment of time and thought. The argument in its favor is that without systematic assessment, instructors and institutions have no clear cut evidence of their successes and their failures and may waste even more time and thought on academic enterprises, which do little or nothing to improve their students' competencies (Frederiksen & Collins, 1989).

However, just because media writing instructors rely on direct assessments of their students' learning does not guarantee that the evaluations are valid or reliable. Validity may be skewed by an idiosyncratic set of criteria, and reliability by failure to rigorously adhere to the selected criteria. Analytic scoring was developed by Diederich (1974) at least partially in response to a study he published in 1961 that reported ratings by 53 readers of 300 papers collected from four Northeastern colleges. Ninety-four percent of the papers were assigned at least seven different scores. On average only 3 times out of 10 did readers assign the same paper the same score (Huot, 1990).

As an example of the improvements that can occur after implementing a systematic approach to educational assessment, Frederiksen and Collins (1989) point to results from the National Assessment of Educational Progress in which students were "given a writing assignment with a particular goal, such as writing a letter to the chairman of the school board on the advisability of instituting a 12-month school year" (p. 29). Raters who were trained to evaluate a set of primary traits, such as persuasiveness, recorded interscorer agreements of 91% to 95% although part of this improvement must be attributed to the adoption of a much simplified rating scale–4 points instead of 9.

The more pressing problem, however, is the selection of assessment criteria if the techniques of focused holistic or analytic scoring are to be used. The literature of assessment is notably silent on the subject of specific criteria that might be employed in media-writing assessment. Centered as that literature has been on evaluating the writing abilities of primary and secondary school students; this is not especially surprising. But as Huot (1990) pointed out in his extensive review, the advancement of programs of direct writing assessment seem to have been spurred in the past more by the need "to turn the tide against the use of indirect testing" (p. 258) than the development of a theory of how the rating process itself should work.

Given the proportion of media writing faculty who have practiced writing as a profession before returning to academic life, one has every reason to be optimistic that their entry into the field of writing assessment could well revitalize the field's theoretical core. However, until media writing instructors become fully engaged in this debate, devising procedures that grow out of strictly theoretical assumptions is likely to remain an elusive goal. Nevertheless, a number of ideas for implementing systematic assessment procedures can be explored guided by the simple dictum that the first thing to examine in adopting a writing assessment system is "who wants what information for what purpose" (Faigley et al., 1985, p. 210). Because the most insistent *who* may well be students and university administrators, the next two sections of this chapter are lengthy ones devoted to (a) analytic scoring for diagnostic assessment of student writing in the classroom, and (b) holistic scoring for institutional assessments of media writing courses.

Diagnostic Assessment in the Classroom

In the classroom, students need diagnostic evaluations of their written assignments that only analytic scoring procedures can provide. However, developing an analytic scoring instrument broad enough to evaluate the variety of written assignments in an introductory media writing course is a daunting task for which media writing instructors will find few precedents. One useful point of departure is a form developed at Alverno College that, although not strictly used as a scoring device, nevertheless identifies and rates student achievement in written expression on six basic traits at three levels of ability.

In the early 1970s, Alverno made a radical departure from the mainstream by devising a competence-based curriculum that evaluated students in eight intellectual areas of which communication is just one (Ewens, 1979; Loacker, Cromwell, Fey, & Rutherford, 1984; Magner, 1989). Ever since then, students at Alverno have demonstrated their academic progress on a track that begins at Level 1 for first-year students, continues to at least Level 4 in all domains for all graduates, and further to Levels 5 or 6 in those intellectual areas closely allied to a student's major. For purposes of illustration, this discussion highlights the assessment form used in a sophomore-level professional communication course titled Writing: The Editing Process. Students in this course are expected to demonstrate through a series of writing assignments that they have achieved, on average, a Level 3 or better rating for their abilities in communication. The assignments, selected by the instructor, may typically include a 750-word personal essay, a 550-word opinion column, and a 750-word profile of a professional writer. Many of these articles are submitted for publication in area and campus publications. In preparation for that, students are required to choose two articles for polished revisions at the end of the semester (M. McLaughlin, personal communication, September 8, 1995).

For evaluation purposes, the communication faculty have devised a seven-item *Writing Feedback Sheet,* which enumerates the criteria for evaluation. Students submit the completed evaluation sheets with their assignments, providing a self-evaluation by judging their success–either Level 1, 2, 3, or higher–on each of the criteria. Instructors then make their evaluations, checking corresponding boxes for Levels 1, 2, 3, or higher, and provide verbal comments as they think appropriate. The description of criteria is premised on a model of communication that focuses on the interface between the writer and the receiver. Thus, the six criteria all make reference to "connecting with audience." They are designated on the *Writing Feedback Sheet* as follows:

1. CONNECTS WITH AUDIENCE through *ESTABLISHING CONTEXT.*
2. CONNECTS WITH AUDIENCE through *VERBAL EXPRESSION* (word choice, style, and/or tone).

3. CONNECTS WITH AUDIENCE through *APPROPRIATE CONVENTIONS* (usage, spelling, punctuation, capitalization, sentence structure, format).
4. CONNECTS WITH AUDIENCE through STRUCTURE (sense of introduction/development/conclusion; focusing by main point made; major/minor connections).
5. CONNECTS WITH AUDIENCE through *SUPPORT/DEVELOPMENT.*
6. CONNECTS WITH AUDIENCE through *APPROPRIATE CONTENT.*

A seventh item lets the instructor rate the student's self-evaluation.

In a manner typical of analytic scoring, each criterion is matched to a description of what Level 1, 2, and 3, and additionally Level 4 quality work entails. For example, the levels for *SUPPORT/DEVELOPMENT* are specified as:

Level 1. Shows ability to use examples and/or evidence meaningful to the audience.
Level 2. Supports most generalizations with examples and/or evidence meaningful to audience.
Level 3. Uses appropriate development for clarification of message.
Level 4. Uses development of appropriate length and variety and of sufficient interest to convince audience of worth of message.

A full set of these detailed descriptions for criteria on an assessment form is commonly called a *rubric*. The rubric, however, is just an index of the assessment process. In well-directed programs, instructors continually refine their notions of assessment criteria and calibrate their judgments of corresponding competency levels at faculty workshops where examples of student writing are analyzed and compared. At Alverno, new instructors are also assigned senior faculty as mentors to provide them further advice as they begin to evaluate their students' writing.

Although the Alverno instrument provides insight into a rigorously administered writing assessment program, it is unlikely to serve as a model for most conventional schools of journalism or communication studies departments. For one, the abstract language of the instrument reflects not only the needs of the particular writing course for which it was designed, but also a college-wide assessment program that has been only hinted at in describing the context in which the Alverno evaluation sheet is used. By virtue of their receiving assessments rather than grades from the onset of their college program, Alverno students enter a discourse with their faculty that is completely familiar to them by their sophomore year, but alien to outsiders (Alverno College Faculty, 1994). In addition, this first professional writing course–as well as others to follow–seeks to advance students' abilities in analysis, problem solving, and valuing, in addition to communication. Thus the wording of the *Writing Feedback Sheet* reflects concerns with abilities in four intellectual areas, not simply communication, a fact that should reinforce a point made earlier that assessment in media writing courses need not be limited to the immediate goal of article or script production.

To return to this section's primary focus, however, if the media writing assessment methods employed at Alverno College are not wholly generalizable to other institutions, how might media faculty proceed to develop their own writing assessment procedures? One scenario based on personal experience is to bring faculty together to revise or build from the ground up a new media writing course that at least initially is team taught by the participating faculty. At the University of North Carolina at Chapel Hill, I first taught broadcast and film writing as part of a four-member team chosen to develop a uniform syllabus for the department's introductory course. Each of us had a well-developed expertise in media writing (advertising, news, documentary, and drama), and each of us subsequently took responsibility for lecturing combined sessions of our classes and designing two of the eight scriptwriting assignments for the joint syllabus. Between the lectures in which we explained to the students the media writing skills they were to develop and our private meetings in which we justified our choices for assignments and explained the criteria by which they should be evaluated, we were all able to generalize from our in-depth knowledge about one type of media writing to all the other types offered in the course.

Although our charge to devise a uniform curriculum for the introductory course did not include the development of a complementary assessment system, we began informally articulating criteria for assessment in our weekly meetings. The key here seemed to be that the need to identify characteristics of good media writing naturally accompanied our decision to let each expert devise what he or she believed to be pedagogically sound and realistic scriptwriting assignments for all of us–without regard to the inexpertness of fellow instructors. Colleagues, thus, had to look for similarities between assignments and the criteria used in assessment rather than emphasizing differences. Otherwise, they would feel as if they lacked the competence to evaluate their students' work. No doubt, there was some anxiety as well as resistance. But the experience suggests that agreement on assessment criteria even for diverse types of writing may be greatly facilitated by team teaching efforts where the justification for specific curricular innovations must be developed and explained to team members.

An alternative to building a course from the ground up is to look for an assessment format from the field of composition studies that is sufficiently generalizable to be adapted to a media writing course. This strategy should appeal to social scientists who have opted in the course of their research to build on a measurement system that has already been put into practice and tested in the field. There is no sense in reinventing the wheel when one can benefit from the experience of fellow practitioners. In this regard, the list of six essential traits of good writing advanced by Spandel and Stiggins (1990)–ideas and content, voice, organization, sentence fluency, word choice, and conventions–is especially attractive. Their claim to the validity and reliability of these six traits is based on its use "by hundreds of teachers to score thousands of student writing samples, from kindergarten through college level (and some professional adult writing, as well)" (p. 149). The intellectual challenge that remains for media writing instructors, however, is to elaborate on these six traits in a meaningful way that suggests how this list can be used to evaluate the broad range of writing assignments made in a typical media writing course.

Tables 8.1 through 8.3 summarize the results of such an intellectual enterprise by identifying those qualities or techniques that provide evidence of writing skill in completing three print journalism (Table 8.1), three radio (Table 8.2), and three television (Table 8.3) writing assignments typical of introductory media writing courses. Spandel and Stiggins' six traits remain fundamentally the same, except for accommodations that must be made to a multimedia environment. First, the concept of *voice* is expanded to *voices*, because most extended media writing presents multiple voices within a single "composition." Second, the notion of *word choice* must give way to the concept of *symbol choice* because the media writing student is learning how to manipulate not only text, but full-screen video, graphics, and sound. That means many of the references listed under other traits will also signify visual and aural as well as verbal concepts.

The entries in these matrices are meant to be suggestive rather than comprehensive. Nevertheless, the exercise demonstrates how terminology of media writing need not be divorced from the vocabulary of other writing courses at the college level. Thus, if an assessment system has already been established as part of the university's freshman composition program, then the list of criteria already in place may well be a starting point for devising a broadly based evaluation procedure for media writing. Not only is it valuable to integrate writing programs across the curriculum, but building on a conceptual system students already know may help them better understand the messages that their media writing instructors are trying to convey.

Tables 8.1 through 8.3 do not, of course, constitute an actual form to use in assessing writing assignments. Rather, the specific characteristics listed under a general trait, such as content and ideas or voices, provide the parenthetical explanation for that trait in the context of a particular writing assignment. And unlike the Alverno form described earlier, in an introductory media writing course with numerous and diverse assignments, a set of evaluation sheets with different parenthetical explanations may be necessary for each assignment. Furthermore, a rubric would have to be devised that describes achievement for each trait on a 4- to 6-point scale that ranges from "rudimentary" to "polished" levels of writing. Finally, the evaluation form itself would only be as good as the consistency with which it was applied. Thus, its effective use would require substantial discussion and training among media writing instructors.

Holistic Scoring for Institutional Assessment

Once a faculty devises an analytic scoring procedure, much of the difficult conceptual work for implementing institutional assessments is complete. At the institutional level, the purpose of writing assessment is typically to evaluate students for course placement decisions or aggregate the scores of many students to evaluate the effectiveness of a particular media writing course or a sequence of courses. In both instances, focused-holistic scoring should generate sufficiently

TABLE 8.1.
Elements to Be Evaluated in an
Assessment of Print Journalism Assignments
Based on a Taxonomy of Writing Traits
Developed by Spandel and Stiggins (1990)

Assignment	Ideas and Content	Voice(s)	Organization	Sentence Fluency	Symbol Choice	Conventions
Speech Story	•participants •issues/themes •circumstances •background •so-what factor	•speaker •audience •supporters •opponents •authorities	•inverted pyramid •multiple elements •list of minor topics	•clarity •appropriate pace •transitional devices	•precise •unbiased •unobtrusive •"said"	•direct quotes for unique or important statements •rules of attribution
Crime Story	•who •what •where •when •why •how	•law officers •victims •witnesses •suspects	•summary lead •chronology of events •sidebars	•short active sentences •metaphorical images •detail and dialogue	•accurate •unprejudiced •non-inflammatory •obscenity-free	•verifying charges •attributing opinions •libelous expressions
Developing Business Story	•records •reports •meetings •news conferences •impact	•officials •spokespersons •analysts •pressure groups	•lead •tie-back •transition •return to story	•analogies for numbers •varied sentence length •coherent references	•jargon-free •technical words add meaning	•direct quotes for unique expression •guidelines for citing sources

TABLE 8.2
Elements to be Evaluated in an Assessment of Radio Scriptwriting Assignments Based on a Taxonomy of Writing Traits Developed by Spandel and Stiggins (1990)

Assignment	Ideas and Content	Voice(s)	Organization	Sentence Fluency	Symbol Choice	Conventions
Radio PSA	•useful •salient •imaginable	•authoritative •persuasive	•problem/ solution •fantasy/ fulfillment	•active •concise •conversation- like	•precise •familiar •readable •speakable	•radio drama format •announcer •dialogue •testimonial •vignette
Radio Interview Feature	•informative •revealing •insightful •entertaining	•probing •engaged •friendly •unique •candid •thoughtful	•thematic •chronological •general to specific •abstract to concrete	•continuity •paraphrasing •soundbites •set-ups	•colorful •active •defining •clarifying	•radio drama format •timing •editing •pacing
Radio News	•accuracy •impact •surprise •timeliness •proximity	•informed •credible •impartial •aggressive	•effects then causes •recent to past •update then background	•leads •attributions •verb tenses	•objective •unbiased •concrete •non- inflammatory	•radio news format •names •titles •numbers •punctuation

TABLE 8.3
Elements to Be Evaluated in an
Assessment of Television Scriptwriting Assignments
Based on a Taxonomy of Writing Traits
Developed by Spandel and Stiggins (1990)

Assignment	Ideas and Content	Voice(s)	Organization	Sentence Fluency	Symbol Choice	Conventions
Political Ad with Storyboard See also Radio PSAs (Tab. 8.2)	•name recognition •policies •social vision •opponent negatives	•diverse •approachable •genuine •recognizable	•master shots •visual logic	•repetition •slogans	•logos •political symbols •candidate poses	•live-TV format •shot types •storyboard symbols
TV News See also Radio news (Tab. 8.2)	•video events •aftermath •interviews •still pictures •graphics	•anchors •reporters •officials •witnesses •victims	•establishing shots to key details •continuous chronologies •interrupted chronologies	•anchor lead-ins and tags •fluent non-redundant narration	•matching words to elements in frame	•TV news format •VO •SOT •character generator
Sit-Com Dialogue	•conflict •character •setting	•distinctive •attractive •irritating •irrepressible •empathetic	•conversation •discussion •argument •activity	•set-ups •punchlines •rejoinders •comebacks •one-liners	•odd words •ambiguities •slapstick •mishaps	•three-camera format •scene setting •directions

valid data for the purposes of making administrative evaluations. If instructors have already devised a measurement system to support analytic scoring in the classroom, then they can, in fact, simplify its use–keeping the enumerated list of traits in mind, but not individually scoring them–to give a quick, rough rating for institutional use.

One promising example of how an institutional assessment system might be instituted for media writing courses comes from a case study of a technical writing course at the New Jersey Institute of Technology (NJIT; Elliot, Kilduff, & Lynch, 1994). A concise description of the NJIT assessment program and the results its authors derived from their study highlights the benefits of adopting systematic assessment for institutional evaluation.

In 1989, the present and former instructors for English 342, a junior-level technical writing course at NJIT, met collectively to design a new course that integrated the aims and goals of technical writing. Chief among their objectives was "to develop a sense of community among instructors and their students . . . [and] an empirical measure of the performance of these students" (p. 5).

Especially salient to the focus of this chapter, the course incorporated a variety of specific assignments that reflected real-life situations, such as writing "memoranda, letters, résumés, job posting notices, technical translations, feasibility reports, case studies, and proposals" (p. 7). Student drafts would be critiqued by peers using primary trait evaluation sheets. Final copies could then be submitted to the instructor for an initial grade and feedback for subsequent revisions. Students eventually placed each assignment in their portfolios when they thought it was completed to the best of their ability and ready for a final evaluation.

Although the portfolios were designed to provide a record of growth in the student's writing ability, it soon became clear that it would not be feasible for the instructors as a group to evaluate each portfolio. Thus grading for each assignment as well as the student's course grade remained the responsibility of his or her instructor, but all students–in consultation with their instructors–were asked to submit a cover letter, résumé, and their two strongest writing samples for further evaluation. The evaluation took place at a 4-hour reading session near the end of the semester. Each student's portfolio selections–designated a *cluster* to denote a combination of writing samples–were evaluated by two instructors who headed other sections of the course. To achieve a consensus on assessment criteria and scoring levels, a scoring rubric "based on presentation of ideas, cohesion, style, usage, and overall reader response" (p. 25) was jointly tested and calibrated on a 4-point scale. A cluster exhibiting a high level of student performance was awarded 4 points; one exhibiting a low performance received 1 point. A student cluster had to accumulate 4 points from its two readers to be accepted as a passing performance.

Over the four semesters for which data were reported, the instructors evaluated clusters from 308 students. On average, they achieved an interreader agreement rate of 93%, which matched the optimum rates for holistic assessments of student essays submitted to the Educational Testing Service. Furthermore, their assessments showed very stable results from semester to semester, with about 80% of their students achieving a passing performance under these circumstances. Finally, the holistic assessment scores consistently correlated with students' course grades ($.65<r<.69$), providing evidence of their concurrent validity.

From an institutional point of view, the procedure permitted NJIT instructors to make two extremely useful analyses. In one case, they were able to compare holistic cluster assessments for junior-transfer students with those who had begun their course of study as freshmen at NJIT. Although both groups achieved comparable passing rates, the 4-year students achieved a statistically significant higher mean score on the assessment of their clusters. In another analysis, the instructors investigated results among Asian, Black, and Hispanic students to see if the assessment criteria favored a particular cultural or ethnicity group. Interestingly, the analysis suggested that "language background, rather than race or ethnicity, explain[ed] the lower success rate of underrepresented students" (p. 15).

Whereas the authors of this study are constrained in assessing their own achievement, there is much to learn from this case study. The first question one must ask is what is the reward for such an enterprise? Elliot and his colleagues (1994) answered cautiously: "It is necessary to anticipate realistically the assessment effort. The study . . . took three years to complete. It took two years of scoring the clusters before we had enough data even to begin an analysis. Literally hundreds of hours were spent in designing the course, developing the scoring methodology, reading the clusters, gathering the data and drawing conclusions" (p. 17).

The enterprise may well be beyond the scope of many departments and many courses. During this period at NJIT, nine sections of technical writing with about 17 students each were offered each year. For a course that is offered to only one section a semester, it would take 9 years before a comparable amount of data could be collected for statistical analysis. But for courses with large enrollments, some of the questions that can be asked and answered are quite striking. Although in many media writing programs it would be reassuring just to provide evidence that individual instructor grades correlate with departmental criteria, the NJIT instructors took the data one step further to investigate differences in performance between various segments of the student body. These results were used to help them identify areas where institutional or curricular changes were needed.

Most intriguing is the opportunity that their baseline data provided to monitor diverse aspects of their technical writing course. If some types of assignments were disproportionately underrepresented among those selected for evaluation, then the instructors would have an initial indication that students were not able to master specific types of assignments and corresponding skills. In addition, if the portfolios of the lowest 20% were submitted to analytic as opposed to holistic scoring, regular patterns of low scores on one or more individual traits could identify precise skills that the poorest performing students lack (and might be required to bolster before registering for the course). With such knowledge in hand, instructors can then experiment with new strategies and examine the results. Thus, the assessment process, which in this case began with the design of a new course, evolves into a process of continual course development. To quote Elliot et al. (1994): "A program of assessment . . . is never finished; rather, assessment is a process that is as recursive as writing itself" (p. 17).

A NOTE ON PORTFOLIO ASSESSMENT

The NJIT study's use of selected assignments from student portfolios requires some additional background on the concept of portfolio assessment itself. Ironically, if one were to turn back the clock on writing assessment to the mid-1980s, then one would be embroiled in a controversy that pits portfolio assessments against holistic assessments, which were then exclusively associated with impromptu, timed writing samples. Classroom teachers and composition theorists were unnerved by the single-shot (or scattershot) nature of holistic assessments (Camp, 1993), which were often mandated by school officials in search of cost-effective, large-scale evaluations of student writing skills. The teachers and theorists argued strenuously that holistic assessments based on timed tests sent students the wrong message about good writing because reading, reflection, discussion, feedback, and revision were all eliminated from the process (Elbow & Belanoff, 1986).

As White (1993) pointed out, "portfolios refer to a method of collecting materials for evaluation, rather than to an evaluation method itself" (p. 101). The use of portfolios does allow instructors to mark students' improvement over the course of an entire semester, their dedication to revision, and their ability to write in various formats when determining student grades. However, in the case of the NJIT faculty attempting to assess the impact of their new technical communication course, it was soon obvious to everyone involved that it would be impractical as well as unnecessary to evaluate the entire portfolio of every enrolled student. A multielement sample of student work–the cluster–was sufficient for assessment at the institutional level.

Interestingly, many of the decision points in devising writing assessment procedures parallel the methodological problems that communication researchers must resolve when conducting content analytic studies. Portfolios raise issues in sampling. Likewise, the development of assessment forms and rubrics raises issues in the validity and reliability of coding procedures. According to White (1993), the proponents of portfolio assessment are still far from devising efficient or reliable procedures for characterizing or synthesizing the rich sampling of writing behaviors that portfolios reflect. As a result, he predicts that "portfolio assessment is likely to become the next chapter for holistic scoring, with results that are now hard to foresee" (p. 101).

ADDING UP SYSTEMATIC ASSESSMENT

This chapter began with the observation that assessment procedures in media writing classes are in one sense very much on target because of the natural inclination of instructors to adopt the methods of performance assessment, that is, measure student achievement by assigning and evaluating real-life journalistic and scriptwriting tasks. This has been the norm if not the rule in media writing courses since the inception of journalism studies on college campuses, and in this regard media writing courses may stand up to external evaluation better than other communication offerings.

Furthermore, few external evaluators have cause to criticize the dedication of media writing instructors who not only constantly revise and update realistic writing assignments but devote countless hours to providing students verbal feedback on their articles and scripts. It is often solitary, exhausting work, for which there seem to be few available shortcuts. Nevertheless, in this chapter some initial steps that can make assessments more effective have been outlined. Among these strategies are orienting students to the invisible public that constitutes their real audience, making concrete for them the difference between academic and media writing, investing time in writing the course syllabus to make sure assignments are explicit, and employing communication models to help students construct a framework for judging their own writing.

However, the bulk of this chapter has been devoted to a much more revolutionary concept–the implementation of programs of systematic assessment. The pressure for such programs is most likely to be felt in the near future, if not already, from administrators who know nothing about the teaching of media writing but are responding to political forces who want *scientific* evaluations of academic programs. Not only is this bound to create added work, but the assessment system that suits administrators may fail to connect in any meaningful way with the impressionistic and individualistic approach media writing instructors typically employ in the classroom. Worse yet, many may find themselves "teaching to a test" that distorts their teaching philosophy (see White, 1994, pp. 171-173, on the negative consequences of artificial criteria).

The alternative is to "bite the bullet" at this early stage and devise an analytic scoring system for student writing that neatly incorporates a holistic scoring system for institutional review. As previously suggested, this may occasion a complete revamping of media writing courses as faculty sort out exactly what competencies they want students to strive for and at what levels they think students should perform. At a minimum faculty will have to deconstruct current media writing courses to see how component parts of typical assignments correspond to general traits that are embodied in all forms of written expression. Such a task promises much trial and error, but by articulating exactly what they are seeking in student writing, faculty may come to better understand what they are trying to teach.

In asserting the benefits of analytical scoring, Spandel and Stiggins (1990, pp. 15-16) listed five factors for instructors to ponder:

1. [Analytical scoring will] yield useful information to students who need to know how to make their writing better . . . if the criteria for scoring are clear, well defined, and truly reflective of what classroom teachers value.
2. When teachers . . . and students agree on a common vocabulary to use in talking about writing, communication becomes more efficient . . . Suddenly, students know what grades mean.
3. Teachers who use written scoring guides to assess writing don't have to write lengthy comments all the time . . . [S]tudents who have (and use) their

own copies of the scoring guide know what the scores mean, so extensive comments become less critical.

4. In evaluating students' writing, many teachers regardless of the general method they use, feel compelled to serve as private editors for their students. . . . A good writing assessment bypasses all this editing.

5. *Most* important, a good writing assessment system helps teachers and student writers to think and talk about writing.

The focus on establishing a dialogue with students and diminishing the adversarial stance exhibited by instructors acting as gruff, no-nonsense editors is curiously similar to the concept of editorial "coaching" advanced by the Poynter Institute for Media Studies (Clark, 1988; Fry, 1988). Nevertheless, the caveat for media writing instructors at this early stage in implementing such procedures is whether the experience of composition instruction is generalizable to all the types of applied writing taught in media writing courses. Only through personal experience will instructors discover if and when systematic assessment procedures truly add up.

RECOMMENDED READINGS

It should be evident by this point that the vast preponderance of literature on writing assessment has been generated in the field of composition studies. For the media writing instructor, there is no neat strand to follow. At best, interested readers can immerse themselves in the literature of writing assessment, which begins with Diederich's (1974) *Measuring Growth in English*, a classic that set the groundwork for analytic scoring procedures. A truly remarkable compendium of experience and insight on how to design writing assessment programs is White's (1985, 1994) *Teaching and Assessing Writing: Recent Advances in Understanding, Evaluating, and Improving Student Performance.* The 1994 edition incorporates a second decade of experience in the field. Two edited volumes (Greenberg, Wiener, & Donovan, 1986; Williamson & Huot, 1993) that include chapters by White and many other practitioners are also well worth perusing.

The ideas expressed in this chapter draw heavily on Spandel and Stiggins' (1990) *Creating Writers: Linking Assessment and Writing Instruction.* Their text is a "how-to" guide for establishing analytical scoring procedures in the classroom with a lot of practical "why-to" incorporated in the text. Elliot, Kilduff, and Lynch's (1994) article is strongly recommended to appreciate the full scope of establishing a systematic assessment program to monitor a college-level applied writing course. Also Frederiksen and Collins' (1989) article concisely outlines the rationale for systematic assessments. Their rationale for the legitimacy of subjective judgments will appeal to anyone who has ever grappled with coding latent meaning in a content analytic study. Finally, the theory and practice of assessment developed over the past 2 decades at Alverno College deserves further scrutiny as described in this volume by a current faculty member (see Wulff, chap. 6, this volume), in an early book chapter by Ewens (1979), and two softbound volumes available from the Alverno College

Institute, *Student Assessment-As-Learning At Alverno College* (Alverno College Faculty, 1994) and *Analysis and Communication At Alverno: An Approach to Critical Thinking* (Loacker et al., 1984).

REFERENCES

Adams, K. H. (1993). *A history of professional writing instruction in American colleges: Years of acceptance, growth, and doubt.* Dallas: Southern Methodist University Press.

Alverno College Faculty. (1994). *Student assessment-as-learning at Alverno College*, (3rd ed.). Milwaukee, WI: Alverno College Institute.

Blanchard, R. O., & Christ, W. G. (1993). *Media education and the liberal arts: A blueprint for the new professionalism.* Hillsdale, NJ: Lawrence Erlbaum Associates.

Camp, R. (1993). Changing the model for the direct assessment of writing. In M. M. Williamson, & B. A. Huot (Eds.), *Validating holistic scoring for writing assessment: Theoretical and empirical foundations* (pp. 45-78). Cresskill, NJ: Hampton Press.

Clark, R. P. (1988, November). Coaching writers: The human side of editing. *Washington Journalism Review*, pp. 34-36.

Diederich, P. B. (1974). *Measuring growth in English.* Urbana, IL: National Council of Teachers of English.

Elbow, P., & Belanoff, P. (1986). Portfolios as a substitute for proficiency examinations. *College Composition and Communication, 37*(3), 336-339.

Elliot, N., Kilduff, M., & Lynch, R. (1994). The assessment of technical writing: A case study. *Journal of Technical Writing and Communication, 24*(1), 19-36.

Ewens, T. (1979). Transforming a liberal arts curriculum: Alverno College. In G. Grant, P. Elben, T. Ewens, Z. Gamson, W. Kohli, W. Newman, V. Olesen, & D. Riesmans (Eds.), *On competence: A critical analysis of competence-based reforms in higher education* (pp. 259-298). San Francisco: Jossey-Bass.

Faigley, L., Cherry, R. D., Jolliffe, D. A., Skinner, A. M. (1985). *Assessing writers' knowledge and processes of composing.* Norwood, NJ: Ablex.

Finn, S. (1991). *Broadcast writing as a liberal art.* Englewood Cliffs, NJ: Prentice-Hall.

Frederiksen, J. R., & Collins, A. (1989). *A systems approach to educational testing. Educational Researcher, 18*(9), 27-32.

Fry, D. (1988) *Writing coaching: A primer.* St. Petersburg, FL: Poynter Institute for Media Studies.

Gipps, C. V. (1994). *Beyond testing: Towards a theory of educational assessment.* London: Falmer.

Greenberg, K. L., Wiener, H. S., & Donovan, R. A. (1986). *Writing assessment: Issues and strategies.* New York: Longman.

Hake, R. L., & Williams, J. M. (1981). Style and its consequences: Do as I do, not as I say. *College English, 43*, 433-451.

Huot, B. (1990). The literature of direct writing measurement: Major concerns and prevailing trends. *Review of Educational Research, 60*(2), 237-263.

Loacker, G., Cromwell, L., Fey, J., & Rutherford, D. (1984). *Analysis and communication at Alverno College: An approach to critical thinking.* Milwaukee, WI: Alverno Publications.

Magner, D. K. (1989, February 1). Milwaukee's Alverno College: For 16 years, a pioneer in weaning students from dependence on teachers. *Chronicle of Higher Education*, pp. A10-A13.

Rogers, E. M., & Kincaid, D. L. (1981). *Communication networks: Toward a new paradigm for research.* New York: The Free Press.

Shannon, C. E. (1949). The mathematical theory of communication. In C. E. Shannon & W. Weaver (Eds.), *The mathematical theory of communication* (pp. 29-125). Urbana: University of Illinois Press.

Spandel, V., & Stiggins, R. J. (1990). *Creating writers: Linking assessment and writing instruction.* New York: Longman.

Tucker, D. E. (1994). Course evaluation. In W. G. Christ (Ed.), *Assessing communication education: A handbook for media, speech, and theatre educators* (pp. 113-130). Hillsdale, NJ: Lawrence Erlbaum Associates.

White, E. M. (1993). Holistic scoring: Past triumphs, future challenges. In M. M. Williamson & B. A. Huot (Eds.), *Validating holistic scoring for writing assessment: Theoretical and empirical foundations* (pp. 79-108). Cresskill, NJ: Hampton Press.

White, E. M. (1994). *Teaching and assessing writing: Recent advances in understanding, evaluating, and improving student performance.* San Francisco: Jossey-Bass.

Williamson, M. M., & Huot, B. A. (Eds.). (1993). *Validating holistic scoring for writing assessment: Theoretical and empirical foundations.* Cresskill, NJ: Hampton Press.

9

Information Gathering

Alan M. Rubin and Rebecca B. Rubin
Kent State University

In this chapter we identify the knowledge, skills, and attitudes that communication students should have for gathering information. We also describe print and electronic sources that students need to access. Students should know what types of sources exist, what sources are most useful, and how to use these sources. They should know the organization and terminology of research reports and principles of research methods. Students should be able to use effective search procedures, to evaluate information they find, and to extract and synthesize what is relevant from those sources. Class experiences can help produce feelings of comfort, appreciation, and internal motivation to approach information gathering as a valued activity. Information-gathering competence can best be assessed within three courses: *Communication Inquiry*, focusing on sources of information for communication research; *Research Methods*, focusing on the conduct of communication research; and *Interviewing*, focusing on gathering information from personal sources.

INTRODUCTION

Information gathering is an essential skill for all students of communication. Students need to be able to identify, to locate, and to use print and electronic sources of information in their class, professional, and research projects. These sources are extremely valuable and are accessible in libraries and via computer. In this chapter, we discuss these information sources and suggest how we might assess students' skills, knowledge, and attitudes about using the sources.

Because we know of few assessment methods in this area, we will concentrate on the essential skills and important attitudes, and recommend a body of knowledge that we feel all mass communication students should have. In so doing, we lay the groundwork for assessment. We also recommend some methods of assessment within a student's program of study.

Communication students also need to ask questions of people who have the information they need. Interviewing skills are essential for conducting some research projects. We address the means of using print and electronic resources to identify and to locate people to interview. However, the actual means of conducting an interview and assessing interviewing skills is beyond our scope in this chapter.

SEARCH STRATEGIES

Communication researchers need to find information by consulting published and electronic sources, interviewing those who know, or by conducting original investigations. When we mention *research* in this chapter, we are referring to an objective and systematic process of inquiry that helps us understand. Mass communication students need research skills for a multitude of class assignments that range from scriptwriting to media programming to audience assessments.

Research begins when we encounter obstacles to our understanding. When that happens, we need to focus our inquiry with precise statements that identify, develop, and narrow our search for information. To do this, we need to attend to what researchers have already learned about the area of our inquiry and to develop a plan of attack, or *search strategy*.

In developing this plan of attack, researchers can use different strategies for searching the literature. A *general-to-specific* strategy is beneficial when we know little about the topic or when compiling a comprehensive overview of the literature. Under these conditions, the search begins with general sources such as textbooks and handbooks. We then turn to primary sources such as journals and information compilations. We use specific finding tools, such as indexes and abstracts, to help locate these primary sources. With this strategy, we narrow our research focus as the search proceeds.

At other times, a *specific-to-general* strategy may be more useful. If we locate one or more key primary sources, or if the topic of inquiry is precise, the search begins with fact finding and then broadens by using finding tools such as citation indexes. We also may concentrate on specific facts if we are reporting new data, providing factual information, or seeking statistical data. The choice of the search strategy relies on what is already known and what information is yet to be uncovered.

Several sources, such as Beasley (1988), Mann (1987), Rubin, Rubin, and Piele (1996), and Ward and Hansen (1993), are useful for additional information on search strategies and conducting library research.

INFORMATION-GATHERING COMPETENCE

Information-literate students are independent learners; they know what information they need and what literature is relevant (Colorado Educational Media Association, 1994, p. 1). They have the ability to manage technological tools to access information, to solve problems confidently, to operate comfortably in confusing situations, to adapt to change, and to create quality products.

Students who are competent in information gathering act in effective and appropriate ways. They have a well-developed knowledge base, refined search skills, and are motivated to find what they need. They not only know how to locate needed information for their research, but they do it well and are enthusiastic about it. Competence requires knowledge, skill, and motivation.

Knowledge

When conducting literature searches, students first need to familiarize themselves with the organization and services of the libraries they will be using. These services include catalogs, document collections, periodicals, reference services, and CD-ROMs. They also need to learn the electronic links to useful databases such as periodical indexes, abstracts, and information resources. Electronic databases have become very important in information gathering. Thus, students need a knowledge of what types of sources exist *(source knowledge)*, what specific sources are most useful *(experiential knowledge)*, and how to put these sources to use *(application knowledge)*. This knowledge can be taught and assessed in communication inquiry and interviewing courses.

When researchers locate useful primary materials–such as journal articles, information compilations, and government documents–they need to read, understand, summarize, and synthesize them. Students need *research-domain knowledge* of the organizational schemes and communication terminology used in empirical research reports. For example, original empirical research reports follow a pattern of organization that begins with an introduction to the problem, and then presents a review of the literature, a description of the methodology, a summary of the results, and a discussion of what the results mean and of future research directions. Research terminology and elements of research reports can be taught and assessed in communication inquiry and research methods courses.

A major goal of research methods courses is for students to increase their understanding of original materials that they read. Another important goal is for students to acquire basic *research-methodology knowledge* and statistical skills. This knowledge is necessary for achieving a degree of research literacy and is taught and assessed in research methods courses.

General or secondary sources provide background about a topic of inquiry and can help researchers locate primary materials from the printed literature or electronic databases. General sources, such as encyclopedias and dictionaries, provide definitions and summarize what is known about the research subject. Students also need to use finding tools, such as indexes and abstracts, to access these primary sources efficiently and to help locate needed information. Indexes and abstracts can identify relevant original research reports. In addition, if students need to find information that is not contained in published materials, directories can identify communication professionals to seek out for interviews.

Thus, for class, professional, and research projects, communication students need to acquire (a) *source knowledge* of what the research sources are, (b) *experiential knowledge* of which are the most useful sources, (c) *application knowledge* of how to access and use the sources, (d) *research-domain knowledge* of how information is organized and what it means, and (e) *research-methodology knowledge* of how the original studies were conducted. These five knowledge bases impact directly on skills.

Skills

Beyond the knowledge of information sources, students need the skills to use sources efficiently and effectively. Skill is the behavioral component of competence. When knowledge precedes skill, behavior or actions demonstrate that knowledge exists. Besides acquiring the knowledge of communication sources and research methods, then, students need to develop three main types of effective information-gathering skills: searching, evaluation, and note-taking skills. By *effective* we mean that information gathering should be an efficient, organized, and systematic process.

First, students need to use effective search procedures or *searching skills*. They need to have in their behavioral repertoires the experience of using sources correctly. They need to do so, not only so that they can draw on these skills and repeat their actions, but also to use similar research strategies when they encounter a new source for the first time.

According to Mischo and Lee (1987), library experts have identified search skills that lead to effective online computer searching: (a) preplanning a search with a search strategy; (b) using a thesaurus to identify precise search terms; (c) typing skill and nonavoidance; (d) a good memory for database search commands; and (e) trying one's own search, no matter how difficult. Mischo and Lee reviewed the literature on search effectiveness and found that students who conducted the most effective and successful searches started with good search strategies, understood Boolean logic and could combine terms successfully, understood print options, could use the thesaurus to broaden or narrow a search, and knew how to truncate search terms. The Library Skills Test for Psychology Majors, for instance, assesses students' knowledge of CD-ROM systems, what is contained in PsychLIT, and basics of searching, such as Boolean logic (Cameron & Hart, 1992).

Reference librarians can often provide instruction in the basic searching skills needed for source retrieval. Sometimes units on library and database searching can be integrated into classes such as Communication Inquiry or Research Methods, and skills assessed in these classes.

Beyond searching skills, students also need to be able to evaluate the information they find and to extract what is relevant from the sources located. Students, then, need effective *evaluation skills* to be able to evaluate the worth or contributions of the different sources such as books, chapters, and journal articles. Using sound research and writing standards, students must develop, throughout their course of study, the ability to be critical of the published literature that they locate.

Students also need effective *note-taking skills* and writing skills so that they can extract, outline, organize, and synthesize the information found in the search. These skills are often taught in university orientation, writing, and argumentation courses, but developed and refined throughout the course of study.

Internet skills, which will be discussed more fully later in the chapter, include the basic skills of being able to log onto one's account, telnet to other systems, transfer files, send and receive mail, join LISTSERVs, use Gopher, and explore the World Wide Web. These skills are technology-focused and require knowledge of the workings of the Internet system as well as basic computer protocols.

Motivation

Motivation is the third component of competence. Motivation results from positive attitudes and success. Success, likewise, serves as positive rein-forcement for acquired knowledge and skill. Because of positive attitudinal and behavioral outcomes, success enhances one's motivation to use the efficient, organized, and systematic procedures again.

Communication classes can produce three types of attitudinal outcomes or motivation. First, the experiences gained from classes and other activities can produce feelings of anxiety or comfort. Recalling our first experiences when searching a CD-ROM database can conjure up old feelings of anxiety with computers. So, too, can wiping out on the Internet increase anxiety to the point where students may avoid these methods for seeking information. Bostick (1993) found five main dimensions of library anxiety: barriers with the staff, comfort with the library, knowledge of the library, mechanical barriers, and affective barriers. Instructors should seek to structure classroom and library experiences to reinforce positive information-seeking attitudes for students.

Second, finding these search methods useful can result in appreciation or valuing these methods. Just as some mass communication students find asking people questions to be an efficient and effective method of gathering information, students need to appreciate the utility of searching databases and finding facts themselves. Again, classroom search exercises can be structured to produce satisfying results.

Third, *internal motivation* to approach information gathering is a value that develops throughout a course of study. It involves enjoying and looking forward to seeking unknown or lesser known facts, asking questions, finding new sources of information, using databases, clarifying discrepancies in the located information, and ironing out intricacies of database searching. Positive attitudes result in motivation to search sources and find information.

Success

The attitudes, affect, and values developed throughout the course of a student's education will determine future searching success. Littlejohn (1987) reported that students with training in searching were more willing to ask for help, when needed. This willingness corresponded positively with the relevance of retrieved references, one element of successful information retrieval. Su (1992) categorized over 20 measures of performance success and found three main elements: relevance (search-strategy precision and recall), utility (time, effort, and cost), and user satisfaction (with search results and how they were obtained).

Regrettably, Su (1992) noted that previous research found high student satisfaction to be linked to low precision; students found searches resulting in fewer references more helpful than those resulting in more references. This confirmed Littlejohn's (1987) finding: "As long as they retrieve satisfactory results, they are not concerned that other databases or systems available at other times can provide material more pertinent to their needs" (p. 464).

By itself, then, user satisfaction is not the best determinant of effective information gathering. Students who rely on one method of information gathering or one database will miss important data that can be uncovered more efficiently and effectively by other means. Enjoying and looking forward to exhausting all relevant information sources is at the root of good reporting, researching, and writing. This attitude must be developed in all coursework.

INFORMATION SOURCES

Earlier in this chapter, we outlined some basic elements of search strategies and developing competence in information gathering. Now we turn our attention to the types of sources that students should know about, be able to use, and feel comfortable with. Much of the information in this section is synthesized and abbreviated from Rubin et al.'s (1996) *Communication Research: Strategies and Sources*. We discuss important general/secondary sources, specific/primary sources, and print/electronic finding tools for information gathering. Important sources from each section are listed in Appendix A for use in assessing students' knowledge and skill.

General/Secondary Sources

General or secondary sources summarize or synthesize generally accepted findings and explanations about various topics. They help identify possible research areas when little is known about the topic. They are often the starting place when using a general-to-specific search strategy. They also help to narrow the topic to a manageable size or to choose the most relevant search terms. General or secondary sources include: handbooks, textbooks, encyclopedias, dictionaries, and annual reviews and series.

Handbooks and Textbooks. Scholarly or subject handbooks help familiarize students with current topics. They provide summaries of past research, themes, and issues. Handbooks, such as Berger and Chaffee's (1987) *Handbook of Communication Science*, are often rather broad in their orientation. Although handbooks are soon dated, they provide important knowledge about the development of many relevant topics.

Textbooks survey a field and present easy-to-understand fundamentals and descriptions of a subject. Basic textbooks present brief summaries of existing knowledge and the author's conclusions about this information. The bibliographies at the ends of chapters are useful for locating other writings about the subject. However, bibliographies in introductory texts are often limited in scope.

Several edited handbooks, though, also serve as advanced-level textbooks. Some, such as Bryant and Zillmann's (1994) *Media Effects: Advances in Theory and Research* and Swanson and Nimmo's (1990) *New Directions in Political Communication,* provide broad coverage of subfields of the communication discipline. Others, such as Alexander, Owers, and Carveth's (1993) *Media Economics: Theory and Practice,* focus on specific aspects of media study. These advanced-level texts typically provide useful summaries and syntheses of research, as well as excellent bibliographies.

Encyclopedias and Dictionaries. Encyclopedias present multifaceted information on a subject. Their essays generally have bibliographies to help locate other general and specific sources that can give background for narrower aspects of the topic.

Subject encyclopedias contain overview articles that summarize what is known about a discipline. One subject encyclopedia in communication, Barnouw's (1989) *International Encyclopedia of Communications,* has over 500 essays on communication subjects and offers broad treatment of topics. More specialized encyclopedias in mass communication include Reed and Reed's (1992) *The Encyclopedia of Television, Cable, and Video* and Hixson's (1989) *Mass Media and the Constitution: An Encyclopedia of Supreme Court Decisions.*

Subject dictionaries list and define terms used in a field. They also provide meanings for abbreviations, jargon, and slang. Some dictionaries, such as Diamant's (1992) *Dictionary of Broadcast Communications* and Weiner's (1990) *Webster's New World Dictionary of Media and Communications,* are particularly relevant to mass communication. Subject dictionaries sometimes resemble encyclopedias by giving descriptions of and bibliographic references for terms. An example of one such source in communication is DeVito's (1986) *The Communication Handbook: A Dictionary.*

Annual Reviews and Series. Two other types of useful general sources are annual reviews and series. Annual reviews provide yearly summaries of current research activities. Some are very similar to edited collections of essays that are found in handbooks. One such annual review, *Communication Yearbook,* has been produced by the International Communication Association since 1977. Currently, this annual source publishes literature reviews of bodies of research in all areas of communication.

Series also appear regularly. They are publications on specific themes or similar topics within a discipline. Two such series have appeared in communication since the 1970s: *Sage Annual Reviews of Communication Research* (1972) and Ablex's *Progress in Communication Sciences* (1979-present). Annual reviews and series are useful for selecting and refining research topics, for locating sources, and for updating bibliographies. One source with which students should be familiar, *Books in Series* (1989-present), identifies series in all disciplines.

These general sources, then, provide a general understanding of interests, concerns, and methodologies of communication researchers. They help to identify a specific research area within communication for class assignments or research projects. General sources in other fields are also important for professional projects such as news stories. In many instances, handbooks, yearbooks, and annual reviews can also serve as vehicles for widening a search strategy and locating other recent sources about a chosen communication topic.

Specific/Primary Sources

Specific or primary sources contain original information and precise data. They help refine research questions and provide important data to develop research projects. Such sources are often the starting place when using a specific-to-general search strategy. They also may be the product of a narrowed search that seeks precise information. Specific or primary sources include: scholarly journals, professional magazines, collections and archives, statistical sources, government documents, yearbooks and directories, and manuals and guides.

Journals and Magazines. Scholarly journals contain the original research in a discipline. This research typically focuses on questions that are current and significant to the discipline. Consequently, journals are important primary sources of information for communication students. Students' abilities to be effective consumers of the scholarly research, though, need to be cultivated in several classes including those in communication inquiry and research methods. These investigations include jargon that is specific to a field, standardized stylistic and organizational structures, and scientific or humanistic methods that may be peculiar to the investigator and to the research question at hand.

Editors of the most respected journals select the research for inclusion in their journals after a careful process of refereed review. Some of the more respected journals that primarily publish research in mass communication include: *Communication Research, Critical Studies in Mass Communication, Journal of Broadcasting & Electronic Media, Journal of Communication,* and *Journalism & Mass Communication Quarterly.*

Professional or trade magazines usually do not publish original research, although they may report about the results of research studies. They do print stories about current issues, professional trends, practical applications, and industry personnel. Awareness of the contents of some trade magazines is important to mass communication students so that they keep abreast of developments in the profession. Some notable professional magazines pertinent to areas of mass media study include: *Advertising Age, Broadcasting & Cable, Columbia Journalism Review,* and *Public Relations Journal.*

Collections and Archives. Original information, whether it be a speech, or document, is useful for many class projects ranging from news stories to legal briefs. Students may need to locate speeches, media transcripts, historical or policy documents, or statistical data. Such information is not always easy to find, but is often accessible in collections and archives.

Published collections allow students to examine primary documents. Ash and Miller's (1993) *Subject Collections* can help locate various collections and archives. Of particular relevance are speech, media, statistical, and legal collections.

Speech collections, such as *Vital Speeches of the Day* (1934-present), provide access to original speeches by society and industry leaders. Such collections of speeches and other documents make it easier to locate and to consult the original text of these documents. In addition, speeches of the President of the United States are published in the *Weekly Compilation of Presidential Documents* (1965-present). Presidential speeches are also available via online computer sources such as the White House home page on the Internet and CRTNet (see later). Past presidential speeches and artifacts, which may need to be consulted when conducting historical research or for media projects such as a script or news story, can be found on-site at presidential libraries.

The content of newspapers is often compiled in one type of media collection. Newspaper collections are useful when students want to learn what journalists have said about a topic. *Editorials on File* (1970-present), for example, collects newspaper editorials from over 100 newspapers. *Viewpoint* (1976-present) contains the work of newspaper and radio columnists and political cartoonists.

Media students also may consult electronic collections when preparing news programs or documentaries, or studying news content. These collections, such as *CBS News Television Broadcasts in Microform* (1975-present), contain printed transcripts in microformat. The National Archives and 13 regional archives will lend the CBS videotapes.

Typically, electronic-media program collections are available on-site in a few archives in the United States, such as the Museum of Television and Radio in New York City and the Museum of Broadcast Communications in Chicago. The Vanderbilt (University) Television News Archive and the Public Affairs Video Archives at Purdue University rent audiotapes and videotapes. Vanderbilt's collection is indexed in the *Television News Index and Abstracts* (1968-present). A more recent archive is the Television Script Archive, which houses over 24,000 television scripts at the University of Pennsylvania.

Two other types of collections are useful for communication students. Measurement collections, such as Rubin, Palmgreen, and Sypher's (1994) *Communication Research Measures: A Sourcebook*, compile original research measures of communication attitudes and behavior. Such collections typically include discussions of the utility, validity, and reliability of the research measures, and are useful for those who want to conduct original research investigations. Legal collections, such as *Pike & Fischer Radio Regulation* (1946-present) and *Media Law Reporter* (1977-present), are particularly useful for students of media policy and freedom of expression. These legal collections compile and make accessible legislative and administrative acts and court decisions.

Statistical Sources. Many government agencies and industries collect statistical data. Because these data provide useful profiles about the society and its media for many research and professional writing projects, students need to know how to access them. *The American Statistics Index* (*ASI*; 1973-present) indexes statistical publications of the U.S. government, including the Federal

Communications Commission (FCC) and the Census Bureau. The *ASI* is also available on CD-ROM as part of *Statistical Masterfile*. The U.S. Department of Commerce's (1879-present) *Statistical Abstract of the United States* is an annual summary of social, economic, and political statistics; it is also available on CD-ROM.

Trade and professional associations, as well as ratings and polling organizations such as Arbitron, A. C. Nielsen, Standard Rate and Data, Gallup, Harris, and Roper, also produce statistical data that are useful for mass communication students.

Government Documents. Publications of the U.S. government inform media students and professionals about what is happening in Congress, the Supreme Court, and federal agencies such as the FCC. The U.S. government publishes an overwhelming number of federal statutes and regulations, Congressional and agency reports, census documents, periodicals, directories, handbooks, and bibliographies.

For example, the laws of the United States are found in the U.S. Congress's (1994) *United States Code*. The U. S. General Services Administration's (1936-present) *Federal Register* publishes executive and federal agency regulations and legal notices, which are codified or indexed in its *Code of Federal Regulations* (1938-present) and *Code of Federal Regulations: CFR Index and Finding Aids* (1963-present). The FCC publishes a weekly *Federal Communications Commission Reports* (1934/1935-present) and a yearly *Annual Report of the Federal Communications Commission* (1935-present). *CIS/Index to Publications of the United States Congress* (1970-present) indexes and abstracts Congressional publications, legislation, and committee hearings.

Yearbooks and Directories. Yearbooks provide current information about a field's structure and development. They also contain statistical data and other relevant information about professional services and personnel in the industry. Two useful yearbooks for mass media students are *Broadcasting & Cable Yearbook* (1935-present) and *Editor & Publisher International Year Book* (1959-present).

Directories, such as the *Gale Directory of Publications and Broadcast Media* (1869-present), identify names, addresses, and factual information about media organizations such as newspapers and periodicals. Similar to yearbooks, they provide facts about the industry, and can also lead students to professionals and trade organizations that may be able to provide current information not contained in other information sources. Other directories, such as Brooks and Marsh's (1992) *The Complete Directory to Prime Time Network TV Shows*, contain useful information about specific media entities that would be useful for projects in media history, programming, and research.

Finding Tools

Some sources are intended to help locate primary and secondary materials that are pertinent to research topics. Indexes and abstracts, for example, help to narrow a general research topic to more specific research questions. They classify or categorize databases by authors, subjects, and/or titles. This sometimes helps to identify subtopics. Indexes and abstracts list both older and more contemporary writings in these areas. Bibliographies and guides to the literature can also be used for this purpose. Finding tools are the most central and important of all resources for students.

Bibliographies and Guides. Many student projects require a list of references about a topic. Sometimes such topical bibliographies appear in book or periodical form, such as Sterling's *Communication Booknotes* (1969-present). More often, selective topical bibliographies are appended to journal articles, books, or chapters. Occasionally, bibliographies, such as Blum and Wilhoit's (1990) *Mass Media Bibliography*, are annotated, that is, they summarize the sources. Bibliographies, then, identify useful primary and secondary sources. Inspecting these sources can expand a student's information search for a variety of class projects.

Guides to the literature are broad bibliographies that identify and organize periodicals, reference works, and other information sources in a field. They also specify search strategies and information for accessing and using these sources. One useful guide to research sources about the electronic media is Bracken and Sterling's (1995) *Telecommunications Research Resources.*

Students who are interested in communication policy and history, in particular, often need to consult the legal literature. Legal decisions affect public policy, freedom of expression, and the conduct of industry. Courses in media law or policy should inform students about primary (e.g., statutes, court decisions, agency rules) and secondary (e.g., encyclopedias, commentaries, textbooks) legal sources and how to access them with appropriate finding tools such as citators (i.e., citation indexes for legal cases), computerized search services such as LEXIS, and legal research guides. Legal guides to the literature also serve as manuals for conducting legal research. They provide access to primary sources, describe legal-research procedures, and identify legal citation forms and abbreviations. Students should be familiar with one especially useful legal research guide, Jacobstein, Mersky, and Dunn's (1994) *Fundamentals of Legal Research.*

Indexes. Researchers use periodical indexes to find scholarly magazine articles. The articles are arranged by subject heading, sometimes also by author, and occasionally by publication. Most students are familiar with the *Readers' Guide to Periodical Literature* (1905-present). Listed by their subject, this index identifies articles found in popular magazines such as *Newsweek.* This may be a useful index for investigating current-events topics, as well as giving historical perspective to a topic. Many libraries now make available CD-ROM indexes such as *General Periodicals Index* and *General Periodicals Ondisc.*

Specialized indexes are published within academic fields. They are more useful than periodical indexes for locating original research. These indexes, such as Matlon's (1992) *Index to Journals in Communication Studies*, list the articles published in the scholarly journals in the discipline. *ComIndex*, which is produced by Comserve and available on computer disk, indexes over 50 journals related to communication. *CommSearch*, a recent CD-ROM index produced by the Speech Communication Association, intends to index and abstract the more than 20 journals included in Matlon's index. The *Index to Journals in Mass Communication* (1988-present) focuses on selected periodicals pertinent to the mass media. These sources will be used most often for locating original information contained in communication periodicals. Several indexes that are published for journal articles in other fields, such as *Business Periodicals Index* (1958-present), can also be useful for communication students.

Another valuable but different format is the citation index, which lists references to selected journals and books by the cited author. The index creates lists of works that have been cited in journal articles by an author. When researchers need to know the name of an author, article, or book on a specific topic, they can use a citation index to find more recently published writings in the area. Citation indexes, then, help locate other relevant sources and update bibliographies. *Social Sciences Citation Index* (1972-present) and *Arts and Humanities Citation Index* (1976-present) index much of the scholarly communication literature.

Another type of index is the media index, which helps find original media writings and programs. Media indexes include indexes of newspaper articles and editorials, videotaped television programs, and films and their reviews. Media indexes are very specialized and focus only on newspaper, video, or film sources.

A newspaper index helps locate news stories, editorials, and media reviews that can be useful for class and research projects. In printed format, these indexes usually reference only one newspaper. For example, the *New York Times*, a comprehensive source of news, publishes the *New York Times Index* (1851-present).

Many university libraries subscribe to CD-ROM indexes that cover several major U.S. newspapers. *Newspaper Abstracts Ondisc* indexes and abstracts eight newspapers: the *New York Times, Wall Street Journal, Christian Science Monitor, Washington Post, Los Angeles Times, Chicago Tribune, Atlanta Constitution/Journal*, and *Boston Globe*. The *National Newspaper Index* covers the first five papers listed above. In addition, the *Newsbank Electronic Information System* provides CD-ROM access to newspapers in 450 U.S. cities. Some CD-ROMs also now provide remote searching of databases for many smaller-community newspapers. More and more, newspapers are becoming available electronically in full-text format.

Another type of media index lists television programs, especially public affairs programming. For example, the *CBS News Index* (1975-1991) identifies, on microfiche, the text of CBS News productions through 1991. There are similar services for ABC News and public television. These indexes provide perspective on current events for many class projects. They are also useful for conducting content analyses of news programs. The *Transcript/Video Index* (1991-present) accesses over 60 television news and public affairs programs that date back to 1968. These programs include CNN News, but exclude NBC programs and *The MacNeil/Lehrer NewsHour*. Another useful source for television news programming is Vanderbilt University Archive's *Television News Index and Abstracts* (1968-present).

A third type of media index references book reviews. Such reviews are useful for summarizing the content and assessing the value of books. *Social Sciences Index* (1974-present) and *Humanities Index* (1974-present) have special sections for academic book reviews. Students can locate general-interest or popular book reviews by using indexes such as *Book Review Digest* (1905-present), as well as CD-ROM indexes such as *General Periodicals Ondisc* and *General Periodicals Index*. Many university libraries have printed guides to book reviews at the reference desk. A quiz based on using such library reference guides could help assess students' evaluation skills.

Abstracts. Abstracts are collections of brief summaries of primary sources. They provide an idea of what the book chapter or journal article is about. Students should never rely on the abstract as a substitute for reading the original source in its entirety. Abstracts, though, are very useful for learning whether an original source is relevant to a research project.

Several abstracts are particularly pertinent to communication students. *Communication Abstracts* (1977-present) is the most widely used abstracting source in communication. The major communication journals, periodicals of allied fields, and books are summarized in this source, which selectively surveys over 200 periodicals. Another useful source for locating theses and dissertations in mass communication is *Journalism & Mass Communication Abstracts* (1963-present).

Abstracts in related disciplines are also useful for communication students. For example, researchers in psychology and sociology often publish communication-related articles, so knowing how to use these abstracts is essential. Such abstracts include *Psychological Abstracts* (1927-present), *Sociological Abstracts* (1952-present), and *Current Index to Journals in Education* (1969-present), as well as their electronic equivalents, *PsychINFO*, *Sociofile*, and *ERIC*.

Computer Access to Indexes and Abstracts. Many periodical indexes and abstracts are now available on CD-ROMs for users to retrieve via a computer terminal or a microcomputer. The database may be available locally on CD-ROM in the library, or may be stored elsewhere in the state or region and accessed by microcomputer protocols from a distance. Many of these databases are relevant to communication students. Some useful databases for mass communication students are presented in Table 9.1.

Searching Computerized Databases. Although they may frighten the novice, computerized databases are fairly easy to search. Most include online tutorials and help screens. Libraries often distribute summary sheets to help the user search the database effectively. Effective searching involves precise, efficient, and utility search skills (Su, 1992).

First, students need to use precise and relevant search terms based on the research subject. For example, most databases allow users to search by typing in an everyday word or phrase. The system then retrieves those citations whose records contain the words or phrases in almost any part of the record: the title, journal title, publisher, abstract, or subject headings.

Using this natural language or *free-text searching* is often effective in locating citations on a topic. However, it does have drawbacks. Because everyday language is imprecise, some of the records retrieved will match the words entered but will not actually fit the intended topic. At the same time, students may miss a number of citations on a topic because a title may have contained a synonym instead of the term entered. So, most databases have a *controlled vocabulary* that is used to describe the subject of articles and books. Students need to learn to use the online thesauri that make searching more precise and relevant.

TABLE 9.1
Selected Computerized Databases

Database	Contents
ABI/INFORM	1,400 business journals
ASI	*American Statistics Index*
CENDATA	U.S. Census data
CIS	Index to U.S. Congress publications
ComIndex	55 communication journals
ERIC	*Current Index to Journals in Education, Resources in Education*
GPO Monthly Catalog	U.S. Government publications
Legal Resources Index	850 law journals
LEXIS	Court decisions, statutes, regulations
National Newspaper Index	*Wall Street Journal, Christian Science Monitor, New York Times, Los Angeles Times*
Newspaper & Periodical Indexes	Major newspapers and periodicals
Newswire ASAP	Full-text articles on most wire services
NEXIS	News articles, government publications, and periodicals
PAIS International	Public Affairs Information Service

Second, a well-designed search strategy is efficient. When conducting a search, students should begin with the controlled vocabulary to choose the most specific descriptor available, enter it as a search statement, and review the result. If they retrieve too few articles, they will need to broaden their search. If they locate too many articles, they will want to narrow their search or develop a more precise research question. By examining the records and the assigned descriptors, students can determine whether to add or drop search terms to achieve more precise or more complete results. Having a good search plan will save search-session time.

Students also need to use *Boolean logic* when developing this efficient search plan. Boolean logic allows the combination of terms to broaden or to limit a search. For example, students can *AND* terms together to narrow a search that has retrieved too many records. Using *AND* requires that all records retrieved include both terms (e.g., "children" *AND* "television"). They can also narrow a search by using *NOT* to exclude a specific domain in which they are not interested (e.g., "video" *NOT* "instruction"). If, on the other hand, the search has produced too few records, they can *OR* terms to expand the search. Using *OR* allows the records retrieved to include one or the other term (e.g., "news" *OR* "journalism"). Boolean logic is important for efficient and effective database searching.

Third, *utility* refers to the overall worth of a search. Worth can be determined on several criteria: dollars spent (on systems where intermediaries do the searching for you), time expended, physical and mental effort expended, and the value of the search results. Students can keep records of their search procedures and efforts for skill evaluation. Students can also be tested on the relevance, efficiency, and utility of their search by giving them all the same term to search. Students could print their search screens and produce the downloaded results for evaluation.

INFORMATION IN CYBERSPACE

The Internet

The Internet connects computer networks. It allows users to communicate with others and to locate and retrieve information from remote databases. It enables access to professional and scholarly associations, electronic periodicals, electronic indexes and abstracts, government data and publications, electronic archives of political speeches and documents, and LISTSERVs and hot lines in different areas of the communication discipline. It is also a vehicle to be researched and studied.

Students need to acquire basic Internet skills to correspond with others, to log-in or telnet to remote computer sites, and to transfer files to their computers from a remote computer via file transfer protocol (FTP). For example, students could:

1. Telnet to the Library of Congress (telnet locis.loc.gov) to find out the author of a particular book.
2. Access radio and television transcripts on the Journal Graphics database via CARL, the Colorado Alliance of Research Libraries (telnet pac.carl.org) to find an important quote.
3. Access WorldCat with its over 30 million sources via FirstSearch (telnet fscat.oclc.org) to find names of books on a particular subject or by a particular author.

Also, students may want to FTP information resources such as electronic text or journals using an anonymous FTP and Internet finding tools such as *Archie*.

The development of *Gopher* and of World Wide Web browsers such as *Mosaic* have largely automated the FTP process. Many universities and organizations have set up Gopher *servers* making information available to users. For example, RiceInfo's listings under "Film & Television" and "News & Journalism" include Gophers for C-Span, PBS, BBC TV and radio, the Voice of America, and the Vanderbilt Television News Archive (gopher riceinfo.rice.edu). A tool known as Veronica allows keyword searching of remote gophers.

World Wide Web

Similar to Gopher, the World Wide Web (WWW) links information resources on servers around the world. Client programs, called *browsers* (e.g., Mosaic, Netscape), are used to access the Web and to provide sound, video, and graphic capabilities. Each WWW browser and server opens with a *home page*, which functions much like a Gopher main menu. To transport users between servers, WWW developers devised standardized Universal Resource Locators (URLs) to address documents, media, and network services. Many government and business organizations have joined the Internet and provide useful information resources. Table 9.2 provides some relevant addresses for media students:

TABLE 9.2
Sample Internet Addresses

ABC Radio Network	http://www.abcradionet.com
CNN News	http://www.cnn.com
C-SPAN	http://www.c-span.org
National Archives	http://www.nara.gov
National Public Radio	http://www.npr.org
Public Broadcasting Service	http://www.pbs.org
RealAudio (ABC, NPR, others)	http://www.realaudio.com
U.S. Census Bureau	http://www.census.gov
White House	http://www.whitehouse.gov

LISTSERVs

LISTSERVs, or newsgroups, are ways to share information. They are set up as mailing lists on an Internet server. *CRTNet* is one such LISTSERV in communication (crtnet@psuvm.psu.edu). It provides discussions of issues relevant to all aspects of communication, and announcements from the national office of the Speech Communication Association, job listings, and texts of recent political speeches.

Comserve and a WWW site at Indiana University devoted to communication and education are two other Internet resources that have been developed to access information in communication. Comserve provides access to information about new books, jobs, syllabi, research articles, news of the discipline, and numerous hotlines in different areas of communication including mass communication *(comserve@cios.llc.rpi.edu)*. Universities that associate with Comserve provide their students and faculty with the ability to conduct searches of *Comserve Journals' Index*.

Indiana University has a comprehensive Web site that provides links to Internet resources in communication covering several media and information sources such as bibliographies: http://alnilam.ucs.indiana.edu:1027/sources/comm.html. This site also provides links to other Web servers such as the National Association of Broadcasters' Library and Information Center and the Vanderbilt Television News Archive. It also includes links to other communication-related resources on the WWW.

RECOMMENDATIONS

The knowledge, skill, and motivation required for information-gathering competence can best be assessed within courses. Because these elements of competence are so basic, we recommend they occur within the first 2 years of college. Three specific courses should help increase students' knowledge base, develop and refine skills, and enhance students' attitudes and motivation to seek information systematically: Communication Inquiry, Research Methods, and Interviewing. Course descriptions are as follows:

Communication Inquiry is an introduction to print and electronic sources of information for communication research. The emphasis is on: (a) building knowledge of primary, secondary, and finding-tool sources in communication; (b) enhancing effective search strategies; and (c) developing basic Internet skills. Students will learn how to use the sources and identify which are useful for specific purposes. The course should help improve source, experiential, application, and research-domain knowledge. It should help decrease library and Internet anxiety, increase appreciation of and motivation to seek appropriate information sources, and improve searching, evaluation, and note-taking skills.

Research Methods is an introduction to the conduct of communication research. The focus is on research literacy and skill. Students will learn research terminology, methodology, and applications. Students will read and evaluate research studies, learn how to conduct their own studies, and appreciate the systematic efforts that underlie the knowledge of the field. The course should help improve research-domain and research-methodology knowledge. It should help decrease research and statistics anxiety, increase appreciation of and motivation to conduct original research, and improve evaluation and analytic skills.

Interviewing focuses on the means of gathering information from other than published sources. Students will learn how to ask the right questions, take field notes, and write accounts of what they are told. Information on identifying and scheduling those to interview will prepare students for information gathering from knowledgeable people. The course should help improve source, experiential, and application knowledge. It should help reduce the anxiety interviewers sometimes experience, increase appreciation of gathering information from personal sources, and improve abilities to formulate questions, evaluate sources, and synthesize information.

Knowledge Assessment

Knowledge is best assessed within structured classes. An integral part of any communication student's course of study should be a Communication Inquiry class in information gathering, which contains knowledge about search strategies, sources, and the Internet. This class should be complemented by courses in Research Methods and in Interviewing. Together, these courses should increase students' knowledge of:

- What sources exist (source knowledge).
- Which sources are most useful (experiential knowledge).
- How to use these sources (application knowledge).
- How research reports are organized and what terms mean (research-domain knowledge).
- How to conduct research studies (research-methodology knowledge).

Traditional examination methods are useful for assessing knowledge. Recall, essay, and recognition tests can identify those who understand basic concepts, principles, and sources. In addition, information gathering, interview, and research applications and exercises can help assess basic knowledge and understanding.

Skill Assessment

We have identified four main skills: searching, evaluation, note-taking, and Internet skills. The Communication Inquiry course can hone searching, note-taking, evaluation, and Internet skills. The Research Methods course could focus on evaluation skills. An Interviewing course could also help sharpen note-taking skills. All three courses would assist proficiency in analyzing and synthesizing information. Precision, utility, efficiency, and effectiveness would be important criteria for assessing skills.

Attitude Assessment

Attitudes are best measured by asking students to self-report feelings. Library anxiety can be assessed at entry into the major and again periodically throughout the program of study. A measure of successful program outcomes (Christ, 1994) might be to show a decline in library and research anxiety. Appreciation and internal motivation, likewise can be assessed throughout the student's academic career. Likert-type scales can be developed to ascertain students' attitudes about and motivation to gather information efficiently and effectively.

SUMMARY

Knowledge, skills, and positive attitudes are essential components of information-gathering competence. In this chapter we have identified (a) the knowledge, skills, and attitudes that can help assure mass communication students of research success; and (b) the classes that can enhance competence.

First, students need to know what pertinent reference sources exist. They also need to understand which sources are most useful for different purposes, and how to choose the right source for the purpose at hand. Knowledge of how to use the print and electronic sources, including the Internet, is also essential in today's online world. A Communication Inquiry class can provide this type of information and help increase students' positive regard for the process.

Second, students need to know how to read the research literature. They need to know about the language and structure of research reports, and how research is conducted. Therefore, a Research Methods class is important in the curriculum. Class experiences can help students appreciate the research process and motivate them to seek answers fully.

Third, when the published sources have not yet answered their questions, students need to know how to seek answers. A Research Methods class can help students develop their own research to seek these answers. In addition, an Interviewing class can hone students' questioning and listening skills so that they can seek answers from others. These classes should reduce apprehension for doing research and for asking knowledgeable others for the information they need. The knowledge and reinforcement that students receive in their communication courses can help them develop the information-seeking competence to assure success in their academic and professional careers.

APPENDIX A: SELECTED RESOURCES
FOR MASS COMMUNICATION STUDENTS

SOURCES	Demonstrates KNOWLEDGE Yes/No	Demonstrates SKILL Yes/No
GENERAL/SECONDARY SOURCES		
Media Effects: Advances in Theory and Research		
International Encyclopedia of Communications		
Webster's New World Dictionary of Media and Communications		
Communication Yearbook		
Sage Annual Reviews of Communication Research		
SPECIFIC/PRIMARY SOURCES		
Communication Research		
Journal of Communication		
Journal of Broadcasting and Electronic Media		
Critical Studies in Mass Communication		
Journalism and Mass Communication Quarterly		
Editorials on File		
Federal Registrar		
Broadcasting and Cable Yearbook		
Gale Directory of Publications and Broadcast Media		
FINDING TOOLS		
Mass Media Bibliography		
Telecommunications Research Resources		
ComIndex		
CommSearch		
Newspaper Abstracts Ondisc		
CIS/Index to Publications of the U.S. Congress		
American Statistics Index–Statistical Masterfile		
Statistical Abstract of the United States		
Television News Index and Abstracts		
Psychological Abstracts–PsychINFO		
Social Sciences Citation Index–Social SciSearch		
Sociological Abstracts–Sociofile		
WorldCat		
Current Index to Journals in Education–ERIC		

REFERENCES

Alexander, A., Owers, J., & Carveth, R. (Eds.). (1993). *Media economics: Theory and practice*. Hillsdale, NJ: Lawrence Erlbaum Associates.

American Statistics Index: A Comprehensive Guide and Index to the Statistical Publications of the U.S. Government. (1973-). Bethesda, MD: Congressional Information Service.

Arts and Humanities Citation Index. (1976-). Philadelphia: Institute for Scientific Information.

Ash, L., & Miller, W. G. (Comps.). (1993). *Subject collections* (7th ed., rev. & enl., 2 vols.). New Providence, NJ: Bowker.

Barnouw, E. (Ed.). (1989). *International encyclopedia of communications* (4 vols.). New York: Oxford University Press.

Beasley, D. (1988). *How to use a research library*. New York: Oxford University Press.

Berger, C. R., & Chaffee, S. H. (Eds.). (1987). *Handbook of communication science*. Newbury Park, CA: Sage.

Blum, E., & Wilhoit, F. (1990). *Mass media bibliography: An annotated, selected list of books and journals for reference and research* (3rd ed.). Urbana: University of Illinois Press.

Book review digest. (1905-). New York: Wilson.

Books in series (5th ed.). (1989). New York: Bowker.

Bostick, S. L. (1993). The development and validation of the library anxiety scale. In M. E. Murfin & J. B. Whitlatch (Eds.), *American Library Association, RASD Occasional Papers, No. 16: Research in reference effectiveness* (pp. 1-7). Chicago: American Library Association.

Bracken, J. K., & Sterling, C. H. (1995). *Telecommunications research resources*. Hillsdale, NJ: Lawrence Erlbaum Associates.

Broadcasting & cable yearbook (2 vols). (1935-). New Providence, NJ: Bowker.

Brooks, T., & Marsh, E. (1992). *The complete directory to prime time network TV shows 1946-present* (5th ed.). New York: Ballantine.

Bryant, J., & Zillmann, D. (Eds.). (1994). *Media effects: Advances in theory and research*. Hillsdale, NJ: Lawrence Erlbaum Associates.

Business Periodicals Index. (1958-). New York: Wilson.

Cameron, L., & Hart, J. (1992). Assessment of PsychLit competence, attitudes, and instructional methods. *Teaching of Psychology, 19*, 239-242.

CBS News Index. (1975-1991). Ann Arbor, MI: University Microfilms International.

CBS News Television Broadcasts in Microform. (1975). Ann Arbor, MI: University Microfilms International.

Christ, W. G. (Ed.). (1994). *Assessing communication education: A handbook for media, speech, and theatre educators*. Hillsdale, NJ: Lawrence Erlbaum Associates.

CIS/Index to Publications of the United States Congress. (1970-). Washington, DC: Congressional Information Service.

Colorado Educational Media Association. (1994). *Information literacy guidelines*. Denver: Colorado State Department of Education. (ERIC Document Reproduction Service No. ED 381 163).

Communication Abstracts. (1978-). Thousand Oaks, CA: Sage.

Communication Yearbook. (1977-). Thousand Oaks, CA: Sage.

Current Index to Journals in Education. (1969-). Phoenix, AZ: Oryx Press.

DeVito, J. A. (1986). *The communication handbook: A dictionary*. New York: Harper & Row.

Diamant, L. (Ed.). (1992). *Dictionary of broadcast communications* (new 3rd rev. ed.). Lincolnwood, IL: National Textbook.

Editor & Publisher International Year Book. (1959-). New York: Editor & Publisher.

Editorials on File. (1970-). New York: Facts on File.

Federal Communications Commission. (1934/1935-). *Federal Communications Commission Reports.* Washington, DC: U.S. Government Printing Office.

Federal Communications Commission. (1935-). *Annual Report of the Federal Communications Commission.* Washington, DC: U. S. Government Printing Office.

Gale Directory of Publications and Broadcast Media (3 vols.). (1869-). Detroit: Gale Research.

Hixson, R. F. (1989). *Mass media and the Constitution: An encyclopedia of Supreme Court decisions.* New York: Garland.

Humanities Index. (1974-). New York: Wilson.

Index to Journals in Mass Communication. (1988-). Riverside, CA: Carpelan.

Jacobstein, J. M., Mersky, R. M., & Dunn, D. J. (1994). *Fundamentals of legal research* (6th ed.). Westbury, NY: Foundation Press.

Journalism & Mass communicationAbstracts: MA, MS, PhD Theses in Journalism and Mass Communication. (1963-). Columbia, SC: Association for Education in Journalism and Mass Communication.

Littlejohn, A. C. (1987). End-user searching in an academic library–The student view. *RQ, 26,* 460-466.

Mann, T. (1987). *A guide to library research methods.* New York: Oxford University Press.

Matlon, R. J. (Ed.). (1992). *Index to journals in communication studies through 1990* (2 vols.). Annandale, VA: Speech Communication Association.

Media Law Reporter. (1977-). Washington, DC: Bureau of National Affairs.

Mischo, W. H., & Lee, J. (1987). End-user searching of bibliographic databases. *Annual review of information science and technology, 22,* 227-263.

New York Times Index. (1851-). New York: New York Times.

Pike & Fischer Radio Regulation. (1946-). Bethesda, MD: Pike & Fischer.

Progress in Communication Sciences. (1979-). Norwood, NJ: Ablex.

Psychological Abstracts. (1927-). Arlington, VA: American Psychological Association.

Readers' Guide to Periodical Literature. (1905-). New York: Wilson.

Reed, R. M., & Reed, M. K. (1992). *The encyclopedia of television, cable, and video.* New York: Van Nostrand Reinhold.

Rubin, R. B., Palmgreen, P., & Sypher, H. E. (1994). *Communication research measures: A sourcebook.* New York: Guilford.

Rubin, R. B., Rubin, A. M., & Piele, L. J. (1996). *Communication research: Strategies and sources* (4th ed.). Belmont, CA: Wadsworth.

Sage Annual Reviews of Communication Research. (1972). Thousand Oaks, CA: Sage.

Social Sciences Citation Index. (1972-). Philadelphia: Institute for Scientific Information.

Social Sciences Index. (1974-). New York: Wilson.

Sociological Abstracts. (1952-). San Diego, CA: Sociological Abstracts.

Sterling, C. H. (Ed.). (1969-). *Communication Booknotes.* Annandale, VA: Author.

Su, L. T. (1992). Evaluation measures for interactive information retrieval. *Information Processing & Management, 28,* 503-516.

Swanson, D. L., & Nimmo, D. D. (Eds.). (1990). *New directions in political communication: A resource book.* Newbury Park, CA: Sage.

Television News Index and Abstracts: Annual Index. (1968-). Nashville, TN: Vanderbilt Television News Archive.

Transcript/Video Index: A Comprehensive Guide to Television News Public Affairs Programming. (1991-). New York: Journal Graphics.

U.S. Congress, House of Representatives. (1994). *United States code* (1988 ed.). Washington, DC: U.S. Government Printing Office.

U.S. Department of Commerce, Bureau of the Census. (1879-). *Statistical Abstract of the United States.* Washington, DC: U. S. Government Printing Office.

U.S. General Services Administration, Office of the Federal Register. (1936-). *Federal register.* Washington, DC: U. S. Government Printing Office.

U.S. General Services Administration, Office of the Federal Register. (1938-). *Code of federal Regulations.* Washington, DC: U. S. Government Printing Office.

U.S. General Services Administration, Office of the Federal Register. (1963-). *Code of Federal Regulations: CFR Index and Finding Aids.* Washington, DC: U.S. Government Printing Office.

Viewpoint. (1976-). Glen Rock, NJ: Microfilming Corporation of America.

Vital Speeches of the Day. (1934-). New York: City News.

Ward, J., & Hansen, K. A. (1993). *Search strategies in mass communication* (2nd ed.). White Plains, NY: Longman.

Weekly Compilation of Presidential Documents. (1965). Washington, DC: U.S. Government Printing Office.

Weiner, R. (1990). *Webster's new world dictionary of media and communications.* New York: Webster's New World.

10

Ethics

Margaret J. Haefner
Illinois State University

Media ethics education needs to be defined and goals for media ethics courses need to be established before assessment can begin. Using Christians and Covert's (1980) study of journalism ethics and a review of media ethics textbooks, the author defines criteria for sound media ethics instruction. Following that, the Hastings Center's (1980) goals for ethics education are explained and adapted for media ethics courses. Astin's (1991) I-E-O model is recommended for formative assessment. Moral development, and learning and teaching styles are presented as important variables affecting students' achievement of stated goals. Finally, possible methods for assessing goals and related variables are presented, with student portfolios being recommended as the primary, overarching method.

INTRODUCTION

"The best moral teaching inspires students by making them keenly aware that their own character is at stake" (Sommers, 1993, p. 18). Those who teach media ethics have the opportunity to help students realize that they are not simply learning to "do a job." Indeed, as people preparing for careers in some of the most culturally influential professions, students must be encouraged to develop moral character based on intertwining personal and professional values. Students are required to get to the soul of the professions they are pursuing, the center at which questions of right and wrong are asked and answered and from which ethical behavior emanates. Christ and McCall (1994, p. 483) suggested that not only should students understand the ethics of the profession, but they should "see if and how they are applied and [understand] and grapple with the relationship between personal and professional ethics." Should some students choose not to pursue media careers, the study of media ethics will stand them in good stead throughout their lives in their roles as media consumers.

During the 1980s and 1990s, journalism and mass communication curricula increasingly have included courses in ethics. Not only is there a crisis of confidence in media among the public (Day, 1991; Jaksa & Pritchard, 1994), but there is strong sentiment that higher education is turning out graduates who are ill-prepared intellectually, technically, and morally. Universities have developed assessment programs to document their effectiveness in many disciplines, but little has been written on assessment of media ethics education. Thus, there has been little discussion within the discipline about such questions as what comprises "good teaching" of media ethics. How do instructors know that their students understand, accept, and apply professional ethics and struggle to integrate personal and professional values? What is reasonable to expect students to know and do as a result of ethics instruction? How do instructors know whether their instruction is effective in achieving those ends? Answers to these questions require explicating goals for instruction and then implementing appropriate methods of assessment. In the pages that follow, several important components of media ethics instruction and goals and objectives for such instruction are recommended. Variables for assessment in addition to those that arise from the goals are proposed. Finally, methods for effective assessment are suggested. Although media ethics assessment can and should take place at the program level, the focus of this chapter is on individual student and course assessment. At the program level, ethics must be integrated with the assessment of a complex array of goals and competencies for mass communication students, many of which are addressed in other chapters of this volume. Before the proper means of assessing media ethics can be addressed at the program level, effective ethics education and the means of assessing it must be defined at more "micro" levels–individuals and courses. We must know what we are looking for before we can determine where it fits in mass communication programs and assessment.

MEDIA ETHICS EDUCATION

Assessment is a somewhat circular process whereby assessment of student learning becomes the groundwork for program and curriculum improvement in order to improve student learning. Instruction must precede assessment, yet little is known about what constitutes sound media ethics education. In order to determine criteria for media ethics education, an early study of journalism ethics instruction and a review of current media ethics textbooks were used.

Criteria for Media Ethics Instruction

Christians and Covert (1980) made six observations about journalism ethics instruction as a result of their survey of over 200 programs. Their first observation was that theoretical frameworks for organizing course material were underdeveloped. Rather than specifying moral decision-making models and general moral theories, most courses were "collectivities–a potpourri of journalistic practices and problems, a series of scattered ethical snippets–rather than theoretically sophisticated approaches" (p. 19). Second, some courses only reinforced certain journalistic conventions and taught students to appeal to "buzz words" or catchy phrases, such as "public's right to know" and "First Amendment freedom." The authors raised several questions about the outcomes of such instruction such as, "Does reinforcement of conventions teach that the press has no room for improvement?" and despite students' familiarity with vocabulary, "Will they be able to explain why they make certain choices over others?" Third, the authors suggest that the content of these courses focused more on press performance rather than serious critical inquiry. Instead of ethics instruction expanding students' abilities to reason morally, it may reduce content to discussion of different sides of media dilemmas, without adequate critical analysis. The authors asked whether such instruction accomplishes anything more than would reading thoughtful reviews of media dilemmas in such publications as *Quill* or *The Columbia Journalism Review*. Fourth, the authors noted the continuing debate about the proper locus of journalism ethics instruction, whether in specific courses, or threaded throughout the media curriculum. They concluded that the complexity of ethical dilemmas seemed to call for specific courses. Short of that, curricula in which ethics is taught across the media curriculum should be examined to ascertain whether ethics is truly being treated, "who covers the issues and how, what normative framework is presented, and are students forced to explain why they hold particular points of view" (p. 22). Fifth, the authors discussed whether media ethics should be taught inside the media curriculum or outside of it, in a philosophy department. A danger of courses within media curricula is reducing ethics to professional correctness, rather than creating awareness of problems of ethics as those of society in general, not just media specifically. Finally, the authors noted the tendency to combine ethics and law into the same course, thereby blurring the distinction between them as two different frames of reference. Although there was no evidence to suggest that instructors equated the moral with the legal, the combination of the two in a single course tilted the emphasis toward the legal as the dominant decision-making criterion.

In view of Christians' and Covert's observations then, what are some criteria that should characterize media ethics instruction?

1. Instruction should be based in clear, sophisticated theoretical frameworks that emphasize values and ethical principles.
2. Instruction should require students to critically analyze media practices and problems and require them to explain why certain choices are better than others.
3. Instruction within media curricula should occur in specific media ethics courses. If that is not practical, careful attention should be paid to the rigor and scope of ethics instruction across the media curriculum.
4. Instruction, when done in a media ethics class rather than a philosophy class, should enlarge the students' understanding of ethics beyond the specifics of the professions to that of society in general.
5. Instruction should carefully distinguish ethics from law.

Media Ethics Texts. A review of media ethics texts suggests that media ethics instruction, not only journalistic content, but persuasive and entertainment content as well, has matured along the lines of Christians and Covert's (1980) observations. The review suggested several areas of instruction that media ethics educators seem to agree are essential parts of instruction.

A serious flaw that Christians and Covert (1980) noted in their analysis of journalism ethics education was the lack of theoretical frameworks to organize the material. However, textbooks in the 1980s and 1990s have emphasized clear decision-making models that require defining ethical dilemmas, analyzing values and applying ethical principles. For instance, Rivers and Mathews (1988), *Ethics for the Media*, used a four-part decision-making model involving (a) stating the *problem;* (b) clarifying one's *beliefs*; (c) examination of loyalty and effects of actions on those to whom one is loyal, termed *result*; and (d) making a decision after weighing right and wrong, termed *justified final decision.* Day (1991), used the SAD model: (a) situation definition; (b) analysis and application of moral theories, and (c) decision. Two texts use the Potter Box; Christians, Fackler, and Rotzoll (1995), *Media Ethics: Cases and Moral Reasoning* and Matelski (1991), *TV News Ethics.* The Potter Box is a four-part decision-making model that requires problem *definition*, identification of *values*, consideration of ethical *principles*, and consideration of *loyalties*, that is, those to whom moral duty is owed. Patterson and Wilkins (1994), *Media Ethics: Issues and Cases*, used Bok's three-part model, which is based on two premises; that we must have empathy for the people involved in ethical decisions and that maintaining social trust is a fundamental goal. Bok's model is: (a) consult your own conscience about the rightness of an action. How do you feel about the action?; (b) ask experts for advice about other possible courses of action that might avoid the ethical problem. Is there another way to achieve the same goal that will not raise ethical issues?; and (c) conduct a discussion with the parties involved in the dispute, with the goal being, How will my action affect others? The implication of these models is that media ethics instruction should be "a vigorous and disciplined effort to analyze and solve vexing moral dilemmas" (Christians & Covert, 1980, p. 21), guided by structured guidelines for critical thought.

A second area of instruction emphasized by media ethics texts is attention to moral philosophers. This seems to address two criteria for ethics instruction; first, that students be required to critically analyze media practices and problems and require them to explain why certain choices are better than others and; second, that instruction enlarge the students' understanding of ethics beyond the specifics of the professions to that of society in general. The moral guidelines being taught provide bases for justifying decisions and students can come to appreciate them as applicable throughout their personal lives and in society. Each of the texts mentioned earlier present at least three philosophers' guidelines or principles to help govern how ethical choices are made. Aristotle's Golden Mean, Mill's Utilitarianism, Immanuel Kant's Categorical Imperative, and John Rawls' Veil of Ignorance are those presented most often. Two recent books, Merrill's (1994) *Legacy of Wisdom* and Knowlton and Parsons' (1994) *The Journalist's Moral Compass* are devoted solely to delineating the philosophical roots on which ethical inquiry is based. Merrill provided short summaries of many major philosophers and frames them in terms of their relevance to media ethics. Knowlton and Parsons' book is an anthology of readings by key philosophers that are particularly relevant to media ethics.

As important as expanding students' appreciation for the scope of ethical considerations beyond media is, these are, in fact, professional ethics courses and so must be expected to address issues and concerns specific to the media professions. A review of the texts mentioned previously and others (Belsey & Chadwick, 1992; Elliott, 1986; Fink, 1988; Goodwin & Smith, 1994; Klaidman & Beauchamp, 1987; Lambeth, 1992; Limburg, 1994; Meyer, 1987; Pippert, 1989; Swain, 1978), suggested the following topics, although few texts cover them all: objectivity, privacy, photojournalism, confidential sources, advertising, public relations, undercover reporting, deception, hidden cameras, business pressures, ownership issues, conflict of interest, coverage of tragedy, professional codes, organizational pressures, antisocial behavior, morally offensive content, stereotypes, juvenile audience, aesthetic tastes and morality, obscenity, censorship, terror and violence, and free press-fair trial.

To the extent that media ethics texts reflect actual media ethics instruction, this review indicates that instruction has matured along the lines of Christians and Covert's observations in 1980. Several texts do organize course material with foundations in moral theory and clear guidelines for disciplined moral reasoning. In so doing, they directly address three of Christians and Covert's observations about: (a) underdeveloped theoretical frameworks; (b) overemphasis on "buzz words" at the expense of understanding why decisions are made; and (c) inadequate critical analysis. Additionally, the emphasis on moral theory and decision making should also help students' understanding of ethics beyond the profession to society in general, despite the focus on media topics and media-related dilemmas, as is expected in any applied ethics instruction. It is also clear from the last decade's proliferation of texts that are solely focused on media ethics that it is viewed by many as a frame of reference separate from law, worthy of study on its own. The review of media texts does not allow for conclusions about where the proper locus of media ethics instruction should be. Most of the texts could be used independently in a course specific to media ethics, whether taught in philosophy or media curricula, or as supplementary texts in curricula wherein media ethics is threaded throughout. In sum, those who do teach or want to teach media ethics have more than adequate textbook resources to help them guide students with sound media instruction.

Goals for Media Ethics Instruction

In 1980, the Hastings Center specified five goals for ethics instruction (Callahan, 1980) that some authors have found appropriate for communication and media ethics instruction. Although some of these goals may be difficult to implement in journalism curricula (see Christians & Covert, 1980), they do direct media ethics instruction away from a preoccupation with professional performance toward a liberal arts perspective rooted in critical inquiry. The following is based on the original goals, as stated by Callahan and others who have adapted them for communication and media ethics instruction (Christians & Covert; Day, 1991; Jaksa & Pritchard, 1994).

Stimulating the Moral Imagination. The first two goals are opposite sides of the same coin. Before anything, ethics instruction should engage the emotions and imagination of students, allowing them to feel their reactions to ethically salient issues and situations. Although the intellect is a necessary balance that should be included soon, students' affect should be awakened first. Journalism students may wrestle to reconcile notions of objectivity and fairness, with their emotional responses arising from conflicts with personal values. Yet, whether they like it or not, ethical choices are inevitable and difficult. By stimulating students to feel their responses, media education is more true to the actual way students will work in the profession. Careers in journalism, advertising, and entertainment are not value-neutral. As Blumefield said, "You have to be dead to be value-neutral" (as cited in Sommers, 1993, p. 14). Media ethics education is more honest when it encourages students to feel their human responses that result from their value-laden humanness.

Media students should recognize the web of moral relationships they live in and the effects of their actions on those relationships. Christians, et al. (1995) described those to whom students must consider being loyal, including themselves, their clients/subscribers/supporters, their organization or firm, their professional colleagues, and society (p. 20). Moral dimensions of situations are often hidden or, for the journalist, arise too quickly for consideration under publishing or broadcast deadlines (Christians & Covert, 1980). Therefore, students should be able to anticipate moral dilemmas and work through possible responses to them, a concept Jaksa & Pritchard (1994) referred to as *preventive ethics.*

Recognizing Ethical Issues. Visceral responses should quickly be subjected to the other side of the coin, the "conscious, rational attempt to sort out those elements in emotional responses that represent appraisal and judgment" (Callahan, 1980, p. 65) After the moral imagination has been stimulated, students should evaluate their immediate response, identify unstated assumptions, and assess whether ethical analysis is called for. Although emotional responses can sometimes signal true moral messages, students must know that what they feel is right may not actually be right. In addition, "ethics takes us out of the world of 'this is the way I do it' and 'this is the way it's always been done' to 'this is what I should do' and 'this is the action that can be rationally justified'" (Patterson & Wilkins, 1994, p. 2).

Eliciting a Sense of Moral Obligation. The major point of ethics instruction is to guide conduct. It is possible that ethical dilemmas can be recognized, discussed, and analyzed without any impact on behavior. Students should recognize an essential requirement of ethical thinking; "that it calls us to act in light of what we perceive to be right and good" (Callahan, 1980, p. 66). How can judgments be made about students' senses of moral obligation without seeming to prescribe moral conduct? According to Callahan (1980) and Day (1991), this is accomplished by making clear the centrality of personal freedom and personal responsibility. Journalists may feel constrained because of time and deadline pressures, as well as their operation within a larger corporate, profit-driven framework (Christians & Covert, 1980). Nevertheless, "the individual is the true moral agent. . . . These individuals alone can be praised or blamed" (Christians et al., 1995, p. 22). As moral agents, we are all liable for our actions and should not blame others for our ethical shortcomings or failures.

Developing Analytical Skills. Students must cultivate the ability to use the tools of rationality in ethics. They must be put through the rigors of defining concepts, analyzing the import and effects of moral rules, and exploring the meaning and scope of ethical principles (Callahan, 1980, p. 67). "Ethics is less about the conflict of right and wrong than it is about the conflict between equally compelling or equally unattractive values and the choices that must be made between them. Rationality is the key . . . modern philosophers should be able to explain their ethical decisions to others" (Patterson & Wilkins, 1994, p. 3). Reaching adequate conclusions can be an exacting process, in which the decision-making process takes center stage. The review of textbooks earlier indicates that this is the case for several of them, with the process of situation definition, values explication, and reasoning using ethical principles being central. In addition, for media ethics students, this involves defining such concepts as justice, moral duty, moral rights, respect for others, dignity, and autonomy (Day, 1991; Jaksa & Pritchard, 1994), as well as traditional media concepts such as press freedom, objectivity, public's right to know, confidentiality, and advertising puffery, among others.

Tolerating–and Reducing–Disagreement and Ambiguity. Reasonable people will disagree. Students should be able to clarify facts and lay out meticulous arguments, but that is not always sufficient to bring agreement. In that event, students should be discouraged from viewing those with whom they disagree as immoral. Instead of trying to prove the correct or true answers, the arguments of those with whom students disagree can be evaluated for their internal consistency and coherence, their breadth, clarity, reasoning, and so forth. Media students in particular should be good listeners and be willing to thoughtfully discuss matters with those with whom they disagree (Jaksa & Pritchard, 1994).

What Should Be Assessed in Media Ethics Education?

Although each of these goals could be measured at the end of students' formal exposure to ethics instruction, the processes students go through to achieve these goals is perhaps the most interesting component of ethics education. Assessing the processes allows for adjustments by both students and instructors. In many people's minds, assessment *is* summative, focusing on final outcomes or effects of instruction. But formative assessment provides feedback to faculty and students for the purposes of improvement. It is diagnostic and its purpose is to improve student learning by providing them with continual feedback about their performances. It helps faculty both to identify students' strengths and weaknesses, and to monitor and refine courses. Thus, formative assessment seems most appropriate for media ethics instruction.

Assessment of the processes of achieving goals for ethics education should not be limited to those areas strictly associated with ethics instruction. Perhaps no other part of the media curriculum is as personal or reflective. Thus, for a professor to understand how far a student has come as a result of instruction, he or she must know where the student came from, what values were brought with the student to the class, and the sources of competing or conflicting values the student confronts on- and off-campus.

Astin's (1991) model for program assessment includes assessment of variables that certainly contribute to students' moral education, although they are not under the control of an ethics instructor. Although it is intended for program assessment, this model can easily be adapted for course assessment and media ethics, in particular.

Astin strongly urged accounting for a variety of variables in assessment programs. His I-E-O model presents a simple framework for considering the appropriate components of an assessment program. By measuring and evaluating inputs (I), environment (E), and outcomes (O), faculty can assess the effectiveness of courses and improvements made by students as a result of their educational experiences. The model is based on three premises: (a) The output of any course does not accurately reflect its educational impact or effectiveness in developing talent; (b) Any output measure is not determined solely by a single input measure; and (c) Even if good longitudinal input and output data are available, our understanding of educational processes and impacts cannot be complete without accounting for students' environment while in college.

In Astin's model, *inputs* are those personal qualities that students bring to the educational program. *Environment* refers to students' experiences while in the program. *Outcomes* refer to the "talents" that the program is intended to develop. Astin's general questions with respect to each of the three components can be adapted for those assessing media ethics education. As input variables, media educators would ask, "Is it reasonable to suppose that an instructor should want to know something about his or her students before formal ethics instruction begins? For instance, an instructor might want to know some general things about students such as, what are their plans and aspirations? What do they want out of college? What are their academic strengths and weaknesses? What is their socioeconomic background? What were their achievements and activities in high school? With respect to media ethics, what do they want out of a course in media ethics? What is each student's level of moral development? What are their current personal and professional values? What sources have significantly affected the values students bring to the class, sources such as family, church, youth organizations, primary and secondary education, and other ethics education in college? How aware are students of the ethical dimensions of media? How well do they think critically? How aware are they of media theory and effects? Although hardly an exhaustive list, it is evident that such an ethical profile at the start of a media ethics regimen will allow for statements of change and improvement as a result, in part, of the program.

Not only do students bring complex set of variables with them that will affect their personal processes of goal achievement, but their environment in college during the ethics program will also influence their goal achievement.

Astin asks whether it is reasonable to expect that we should know what concurrent educational experiences our students are having while in this course. Beyond the courses they are now taking, what kind of extracurricular activities do different students participate in? How are they supporting themselves? How many of them work and what kinds of jobs do they hold? What goes on in their residence halls? Are they participating in special educational programs? With respect to media ethics, are they currently working, for pay or in unpaid internships, at media outlets, either on- or off-campus? How active are they in other values-oriented groups, such as family, peers, church, or media organizations? How much time do they spend with the media?

Finally, Astin asked whether it is reasonable to expect that we should know something about the educational progress of each student, during college and after graduation? How long is it taking them to complete their programs of study? What are students actually learning in this class and others? How do they perceive their educational experiences? How do they rate the quality of instruction they get in this course and others? Are they getting what they want out of college? What happens to students when they leave? What kinds of jobs do they hold? Do they feel we have prepared them adequately for work, for marriage, for parenthood, and so forth? For media students and alumni, how well were they prepared for ethical dilemmas they face as media professionals? How critical of media are they as citizens and consumers? (Astin, 1991).

This description of Astin's model suggests a variety of variables that could be assessed at the beginning, throughout, and at the end of media ethics education. Ethics instructors would do well to recognize at least three other variables that are particularly relevant to media ethics instruction: (a) students' moral and cognitive development; (b) instructors' teaching styles; and (c) students' learning styles. In Astin's (1991) I-E-O model, moral and cognitive development and learning styles could be considered both input and outcome variables; whereas instructors' teaching styles is an environmental variable. Each is important in assessing ethics education because, in many ways, the extent of individual students' achievement of the goals of stimulating the moral imagination, recognizing ethical issues, and developing analytical skills, depends on these very factors. In fact, it can be argued that students who achieve these goals have made, by some definitions, significant moral advancements, so moral development becomes an overarching goal of ethics education.

Moral and Cognitive Development

Kohlberg and others proposed that moral development, both vertical and horizontal, should be the central aim of all education (see Lickona, 1980, p. 110). Vertical development refers to achieving more complete, consonant, and integrated stages of moral reasoning, and horizontal development refers to the application of one's highest stage to wider realms of experience. Lickona pointed out that changes in moral stages are small over the course of a semester or year and that changes may be slow and not appear at all until well after instruction has occurred. These observations should not prevent moral development from becoming a goal of ethics instruction. Rather, it simply means that assessments may need to be sensitive to modest change and may need to occur over a period of time, even after graduation.

Moral development. Kohlberg's (1984) and Gilligan's (1982) theories of moral development are two of the most dominant in ethics education. Kohlberg's model divides development into three levels with two stages each. The key variable in determining stage is how one reasons to a conclusion, not the conclusion itself. To have achieved the goals set up for instruction in media ethics is for students to have reached the third level of Kohlberg's model, called postconventional. The two stages of moral reasoning at this level are characterized by self-reflective thinking, independence of mind in moral thought, and embracing a more comprehensive and impartial point of view (Jaksa & Pritchard, 1994, p. 97).

One problem with using Kohlberg's stage theory is its focus on the male moral voice, an *ethic of justice,* that is characterized by logically derived absolute principles that equate morality with justice (Gilligan, 1982). The characteristics of the female moral voice, an *ethic of care,* are not as valued. Female accentuation of relationships, compassion, and nurturance of others is considered to be only at Stage 3 in Kohlberg's model. Gilligan argued that the female voice is equally as valuable as the male voice, and may be complementary to it. The male and female voices, although typically characteristic of men and women, respectively, may be found in either men or women. And, although the female moral voice may develop along a different track than the male voice, it is not less morally mature. "It is important for both women and men to know and admit that the Female System exists and is good–not necessarily better, but good" (Schaef, as cited in Johannesen, 1990, p. 131). Thus, in considering moral development as variables affecting media ethics education, instructors must be sensitive to different kinds of moral maturity and give equal value to male and female moral voices (Johannesen, 1990).

Cognitive Development. Katz and Henry (1988), McBeath (1992), and Yingling (1994) agreed that improvement in learning can only be understood when students' cognitive maturity is accounted for. One theory of cognitive development that is particularly pertinent for ethics education because it also includes ethical development is Perry's (as cited in McBeath, 1992) stages of learning. Perry identified nine growth steps, which he grouped into four major stages of intellectual and ethical development. "The Perry outline shows how students move from the need for certainties and a dependence on authority, to being able to accept ambiguity as they create meaning and order in their world. . . . As in the other stage theories of development (e.g., Piaget), each stage is more complex and comprehensive than the previous one, as the student perceives increased complexities in the world and uncertainties in knowledge" (McBeath, 1992, pp. viii, x). The four major stages in Perry's model are:

1. *Dualism.* The dualistic student sees the world in polar terms of right and wrong, good and bad, not better or worse. Right answers exist for each problem and are known by an authority, usually the teacher. The dualistic student wants

directions in black and white, and will do as told by the authority without critical evaluation of the directions.

2. *Multiplicity*. At this stage the dualistic, authority structure is modified. Ambiguity is unwillingly acknowledged, but it is seen as a temporary thing because the final truth has yet to be determined. Everyone is seen as having a right to his or her own opinion, but the resulting uncertainty will be resolved by the authority. Students at this stage have no pattern to their thinking and the quantity of information held has more significance than the quality.

3. *Relativism*. Rather than accumulating quantities of information to prove right and wrong, students see all knowledge and values as contextual and relativistic. Ambiguity is accepted, and knowledge is seen as a blend of fact and opinion. Knowledge is now qualitative and some opinions are seen as important; others as not important, depending on the context.

4. *Commitment*. Students at the stage of commitment are accepting responsibility for their own ideas and actions. They hold convictions and acceptance of their own doubts; they can see their potential and their limitations. A strong sense of identity is developed as the students learn to explore and develop a sense of confidence in a relativistic world where reasonable people can disagree, where there are no pat answers and where new challenges continue to appear (McBeath, 1992, pp. viii-x).

Teaching Styles

An associated variable that seems important for assessing students' achievement of goals for media ethics education is instructor's teaching style. McBeath (1992) argued that teaching styles can have a serious effect on students' progress through Perry's stages of learning. The four stages of teaching are closely correlated to those four stages of learning. These are:

1. *Teacher dominated*. This stage is associated with the dualistic learning stage. Its characteristics are "teaching is telling," one-way communication; questions and answers; subject matter acquisition is basic; and tests on recall.

2. *Subject centered*. This stage is associated with the multiplicity learning stage. Its characteristics are "teaching is telling," plus media; one way communication with some ambiguity; cites multiple authorities; students are expected to be active learners; evaluation on recall and applications.

3. *Learning task oriented*. This stage is associated with the relativism learning stage. Its characteristics are teaching includes group and individual work; assessment using alternative methods; different authorities and ambiguity is accepted; two-way communication for mastery; evaluation on recall, applications, implications.

4. *Inquiry centered*. This stage is associated with the commitment learning stage. Its characteristics are courses based on readiness level; critical inquiry encouraged; creativity supported; collaborative problem

solving; evaluation based on mastery of criteria.   (McBeath, 1992, pp. ix-xii)

Student Learning Styles

Given differences in students' cognitive and moral development, it is not surprising that they would differ in their expectations for education, as well. These differences in expectations, or learning styles, have important implications for media ethics instruction because they reflect the diversity of the students in a typical classroom. And, although one might presume that all mass communication students have at least some interest in the content area, they likely have very different expectations for faculty, assignments, exams, projects, and their own work habits (Potter, 1994).

Potter (1994) identified five broad categories of learning styles from which 16 specific styles stem. The five broad style categories are (a) *Dependent*–students want direction from instructors or texts, they want to follow the rules and get the most content out of a course for the least amount of effort; (b) *Independent*–students take pride in setting and achieving their own goals, following their own course, and developing their own strategies for success; (c) *Competitive*–students see the course as a game to be won. The best instructors make the game interesting and reward the best players; (d) *Participant*–students like being part of the class because of their contact with others. The best instructors have a lot class activities that involve students; and (e) *Avoidant*–students dislike their courses and want to be left alone by instructors. They want to have to do as little as possible to get through the course.

The discussion of Astin's I-E-O model, and the emphasis on students' cognitive and moral maturity, their learning styles, and instructors' teaching styles as crucial input and environmental variables indicates the complexity of assessing student outcomes. Their measurement is not always easy, but they ought to be considered if the goal of assessment is improved teaching and learning. In the section that follows, methods for assessing several variables that are essential to media ethics instruction are presented.

HOW TO ASSESS MEDIA ETHICS

This section addresses the methods available for assessing students' achievement of the five course goals laid out earlier. Throughout the literature, a debate continues as to the appropriateness of quantitative versus qualitative measures of assessment. Although quantitative measures that yield statistics about student performance and program quality are the most important means of providing information to external constituencies, many of those who advocate assessment primarily as a means of improving student learning lean toward qualitative measures. Qualitative measures provide the rich feedback that is essential to improving teaching and learning. Nevertheless, some of the additional variables mentioned already are best measured by the quantitative instruments designed specifically for them.   After a very brief review of quantitative measures appropriate for moral development and values, the use of student portfolios as a

TABLE 10.1
Measurement of Variables Relevant to Media Ethics Instruction

Variable	What Is Assessed	How to Assess
Moral Development		
Kohlberg's Stages of Moral Development	Level of moral judgment, not moral worth or likely moral conduct.	Rest's Defining Issues Test (DIT) (See Caplan, 1980).
Ethic of Justice versus Ethic of Care	Whether students tend to have male moral voice (justice) or female moral voice (nurturance, compassion, relationships).	Gilligan and Attanucci's Real-life Dilemma Test (1988).
Perry's Stages of Cognitive and Intellectual Growth	Comprehensiveness with which students perceive complexities of the world and uncertainties of knowledge.	McBeath (1992).
Teaching Styles	Extent of teacher domination vs. student collaboration; one-way vs. two-way communication; single vs. multiple means of assessing student learning, etc.	McBeath (1992).
Learning Styles	Students' expectations for faculty, assignments, projects, own work habits.	Potter & Emanuel's Student Learning Style Instrument (1990).
Values	Several types: Altruism, masculine/feminine; work/professional, instrumental vs. terminal, etc.	See Grandy (1989).

comprehensive means of assessment is recommended. In addition, a variety of methods for assessing each of the five goals for a course in media ethics are suggested.

Some of the input and environment variables are appropriately measured using standardized instruments (see Table 10.1). For instance, Rest's Defining Issues Test (DIT) is a measure of moral development that is correlated with Kohlberg's stages of moral development. According to Rest, the DIT is only intended to measure moral judgment, not moral worth or likely moral conduct (as cited in Caplan, 1980, p. 142). Gilligan and Attanucci (1988) developed a Real-Life Dilemma test to measure whether students primarily hold an ethic of justice or an ethic of care. Perry's stages of cognitive and intellectual growth can be assessed by administering his instruments, as can McBeath's (1987) teaching styles measures that correlate with Perry's stages. Students' learning styles can be measured using Potter and Emanuel's (1990) Student Learning Style Instrument. Grandy (1989) listed and critiqued several instruments suitable for measuring values, including Sawyer's Altruism Scale, Bode and Page's Ethical Reasoning Inventory, Steinmann and Fox's Maferr Inventory of Masculine-Feminine Values, Super's Work Values Inventory, and Rokeach's Value Survey (all are cited in Grandy, 1989). These instruments can be useful for establishing personal values as input or environment variables, and give students a base from which to integrate professional values throughout the course.

Student Portfolios as a Comprehensive Assessment Method. In view of the complex goals for a course in ethics, student portfolios can be used as one overarching means of assessment; that is, they give students the opportunity to reflect on their own progress and evaluate their own learning (metathinking). Portfolio assessment is the most appropriate method for formative assessment in a course because students collect work over time and portfolios are evaluated at several points throughout the semester. Black (1993) described portfolios as folders into which students put products of learning. The folders are kept for a specified period of time and are intended to document improvements in student performance over that time.

Student portfolios are ideal means of assessing student performance in a media ethics course for several reasons. First, they provide evidence of "doing" in the course through the collection of student materials, and evidence of student "learning" in the course through self-reflection on experiences in the course (Orlik, 1994). Portfolios allow instructors to "get inside students' learning" (Romano, 1994, p. 73). Second, portfolios are "historical" documents in that they can show changes over time and the chronological development of students' mastery of course goals (Aitken, 1993; Arneson, 1994). Third, portfolios lend themselves well to a course format that implements formative assessment using Astin's I-E-O model, by allowing students to include input information, and collect environment information that can be used to interpret final outcomes. As Romano (1994) observed, portfolios, "measure success not simply by where learners end their journey, but also where they began, how and where they traveled, what they encountered along the way, and what they did in the face of it" (p. 73). Fourth, portfolios can help improve students' self-esteem as they compile information about their growth and accomplishments (Aitken, 1993, p. 10).

Lenning (1988) suggested two principles that should guide the use of portfolios. First, they should be just one of multiple assessment methods employed and, second, "they should include the *smallest* number of class products that provide adequate information about the goals being measured" (p. 142). Almost anything having to do with the media ethics class can be included as an artifact in student portfolios, as long as it truly represents progress students have made. One of the beauties of portfolio assessment is their flexibility to meet the individual needs of students. Throughout the semester, students complete assignments, exams, and other measures designed to assess their progress toward the goals for the course. Rather than a portfolio becoming a "catch all," only those items that reflect progress should be included. Additionally, students' self-reflections on those artifacts and their own progress should be included.

What Evidence Should a Portfolio Contain? Artifacts should be selected that will allow students to reflect on their progress toward achieving the five goals for a media ethics course. Examples of artifacts that lend themselves to reflective analysis include:

Rough drafts, final copies, self-awareness journals, study skills inventories, observations, interviews, individual learning contracts, anecdotal files, videotapes, communication logs, dialogue journals, tape recordings, narrative accounts, written responses to content area text-books, standardized tests, nonstandardized tests, peer critiques, group assessment, and cumulative folders. Students' personal reflections and analyses should accompany all artifacts. These are not intended to 'show and tell,' but thoughtful, reflective comments. (Arneson, 1994, p. 116)

Although students may be reticent at first to engage in this exercise that is, for many, the first time they've been asked about their own learning, Perry (as cited in Waluconis, 1993) found that as students progress in their studies, they look forward to the opportunity to evaluate themselves. Also, Bard (as cited in Lenning, 1988) found that students are relatively honest even when dealing with sensitive questions.

Arneson (1994), Astin (1991), Black (1993), Courts and McInerny (1993), and Lenning (1988) are among many who lauded portfolios for the rich information they provide for improving academic programs, and the opportunities for ongoing review and improvement of student work. Nevertheless, Lenning noted some drawbacks in portfolio assessment. Many practical questions can be difficult to resolve, such as what is to be collected, by whom, when, and how will the information be evaluated? Also, because there are no real prescriptions for what a portfolio should look like, instructors may take a long time to develop portfolio requirements that are useful and meaningful to students and the instructor. Even with a small number of student portfolios, evaluation can be very time consuming, especially if the plan requires intermittent evaluation at several points in the program. With respect to evaluation, Arneson noted that criteria for evaluation need to be clarified at the outset and be clearly linked to learning goals. Criteria may include "evidence of improvement, student effort, quality of self-evaluation, range of projects, presentation, and future goals" (Tierney, Canter, & Desai, as cited in Arneson, 1994). Lenning also noted concern for student privacy and protection of instructors' exams and assignments for future use as considerations. One additional challenge addressed by Arneson is authenticity. She suggested that to ensure the authenticity of student work, students should be required to demonstrate how each artifact was prepared and how it fits into the progressive growth toward course goals.

Despite these challenges, the student portfolio is an excellent overarching method of assessment. However, assignments and assessments must be made throughout the semester so that students can have artifacts from which to choose for inclusion in their portfolios. Following are a few suggestions about appropriate methods of assessment for each of the goals. Any of the artifacts, then, can be selected for inclusion in the portfolio (see Table 10.2).

For the first goal, stimulating the moral imagination, instructors may consider not only having practicing media professionals speak to classes about their own experiences, but people who have been affected by the media (Christians & Covert, 1980). Films, novels, and plays can also be effective in eliciting emotions (Callahan, 1980; Christians & Covert, 1980). Students' moral imagination can be assessed through in-class observations, both by instructors and peers, role-playing, students' own self-reflective written essays or one-on-one interviews with the instructor. Lenning (1988) suggested the Behavioral Events Analysis, which is a 2 1/2 hour, one-on-one interview, that may be adapted for assessing the first goal. "Successful as well as unsuccessful students are asked to identify and describe, in concrete and generic behavioral terms, events . . . and to tell all they know about these episodes, including their own feelings before, during , and after the events" (p. 44).

For the second goal, recognizing ethical issues, current events journals that are analyzed for ethical dimensions are useful. Students can be asked to keep media-use diaries that focus on looking for ethical components of media performance and their own relationships to media. Cases are among the most frequently used means of helping students to expand their conceptions of where and how ethical issues arise. Students should also be encouraged to look for ethical issues that arise in other classes, especially seeking out components having to do with media.

For the third goal, eliciting a sense of moral obligation that results in changed behavior is exceedingly difficult to do. Although moral behavior may be the ultimate goal of ethics teaching, observing changes in moral behavior and attributing them to a course in ethics is dubious. Even if input and environmental variables are considered as part of the behavior change, behavior is a complex phenomenon that may have no relation at all to one's level of moral development or ability to reason morally. (See Lickona's [1980] discussion of social psychology in the teaching of ethics.) "With respect to behavior, however, the most important goal would be that of providing the student with those

TABLE 10.2
Assessment of Goals for Media Ethics Education

Goal	What Is Assessed	How To Assess (All may be artifacts for the student portfolio)
Stimulate the Moral Imagination	Students' emotional responses to ethically salient issues and situations. May be elicited by guest speakers, novels, plays, films, current media events.	(1) Instructor and peer in-class observations; (2) Self-reflective essays; (3) Personal interviews; (4) Lenning's (1988) Behavioral Events Analysis.
Recognizing Ethical Issues	Students' unstated assumptions and abilities to assess whether ethical analysis is called for.	(1) Current events journal; (2) Media-use diary; (3) Case analyses; (4) Reports of ethical issues that arise in other media classes.
Eliciting a Sense of Moral Obligation	Changes in moral behavior or the *will* to behave ethically.	(1) Written or oral self-evaluations; (2) Reports from other instructors about students' willingness to raise ethical issues outside of class (with students' permission); (3) Reports (personal or from others) about students' actions in media-related settings (jobs, internships, student newspaper, radio station, etc.).
Developing Analytical Skills	Students' proper use of ethical decision-making models.	(1) Written or oral presentations of cases or current media events; (2) Issues brief (Warnick & Inch, 1993); (3) Games and simulations.
Tolerating and Reducing Disagreement and Ambiguity	Students' respect for others, listening skills, and their abilities to evaluate others' arguments.	(1) In-class observations of small group or class discussions; (2) Students' essays about discussions they've had with people with whom they disagree.

229

ingredients of ethical analysis and self-criticism, such that he would, if the analysis seemed to require it, both recognize the importance of changing behavior, and be prepared to change it" (Callahan, 1980, p. 70). Students' sense of the importance of changing behavior and their willingness to do so can be assessed through their own written or oral self-evaluations, instructors' observations of students in class, and students' willingness to raise issues concerning media ethics problems outside the ethics classroom in other classes (as observed by other instructors), such as "hands-on" media classes (e.g., reporting, TV or radio production).

For the fourth goal, developing analytical skill, students' proper use of ethical decision-making models, such as those mentioned in the review of ethics textbooks, and their proper application of moral principles can be assessed through written or oral presentations of cases or ethical issues that arise in the course of daily life. The issues brief (Warnick & Inch, 1993) allows students to become familiar with multiple views on an issue, so as to improve their own arguments, as well as their abilities to anticipate and respond to the opinions and arguments of others. Caplan (1980) noted that games and simulations can also help to indicate students' abilities to analyze hypothetical moral problems. They can help determine the extent to which students can take sides, and articulate the reasoning underlying different points of view. They can help students put themselves in the shoes of others to see problems from something other than a personal standpoint.

For the fifth goal, assessing students' abilities to tolerate and reduce disagreement, group discussions, in which students can be observed to clarify facts and to listen carefully and nonjudgmentally, can be audiotaped or videotaped. Observations of students performance in class can be with attention to their willingness to discuss, challenge and listen to classmates and the instructor's points of view. Students can write about assigned audiotaped conversations they have with people they know will disagree with them. The instructor can listen to the tape and determine, by comparing the student's writing with the conversation, how well the student listened, clarified facts and misunderstandings, and how the student reacted to that person once the pair agreed to disagree.

CONCLUSION

The purpose of this chapter has been to articulate criteria and goals for media ethics instruction and suggest means of assessing students' achievement of those goals. The Hastings Center's five goals assume that the criteria for media ethics instruction are well established in the classroom. However, Astin's (1991) I-E-O directs attention away from these goals as the only important variables in ethics assessment. Perhaps nowhere else in the media curriculum are moral and cognitive development and learning and teaching styles more salient than in the media ethics course, for they have the potential to affect the achievement of goals in tangible ways. The methods recommended, although far from comprehensive, are reasonable for true assessment of teaching and learning. Qualitative methods, especially student portfolios, are time consuming and, often, difficult.

However, they yield the kinds of information that get to the heart of a media ethics class–emotions and moral imagination, analytical skills, moral will (if not behavior)–in ways that quantitative methods cannot. Courses in media ethics give instructors a unique opportunity to help students develop moral character that will carry them through personal and professional ethical dilemmas. Careful assessment can help instructors be sure that they are making the most of the opportunity, for their students' sake.

REFERENCES

Aitken, J. E. (1993, April). *Empowering students and faculty through portfolio assessment.* Paper presented at the annual meeting of the Central States Communication Association, Lexington, KY.

Arneson, P. (1994). Assessing communication competence through portfolios, scoring rubrics, and personal interviews. In S. Morreale, M. Brooks, R. Berko, & C. Cooke (Eds.), *1994 summer conference proceedings and prepared remarks* (pp. 113-123). Annandale, VA: The Speech Communication Association.

Astin, A. W. (1991). *Assessment for excellence.* New York: Macmillan.

Belsey, A., & Chadwick, R. (1992). *Ethical issues in journalism and the media.* New York: Routledge.

Black, L. C. (1993). Portfolio assessment. In T. W. Banta and Associates, *Making a difference: Outcomes of a decade of higher education* (pp. 139-150). San Francisco: Jossey-Bass.

Callahan, D. (1980). Goals in the teaching of ethics. In D. Callahan & S. Bok (Eds.), *Ethics teaching in higher education* (pp. 61-74). New York: The Hastings Center.

Caplan, A. L. (1980). Evaluation and the teaching of ethics. In D. Callahan & S. Bok (Eds.), *Ethics teaching in higher education* (pp. 133-150). New York: The Hastings Center.

Christ, W. G., & McCall, J. M. (1994). Assessing the "what" of media education. In S. Morreale, M Brooks, R. Berko, & C. Cooke (Eds.), *1994 Summer Conference Proceedings and Prepared Remarks* (pp. 476-493). Annandale, VA: Speech Communication Association.

Christians, C. G., & Covert, C. L. (1980). *Teaching ethics in journalism education.* New York: The Hastings Center.

Christians, C. G., Fackler, M., & Rotzoll, K. B. (1995). *Media ethics: Cases and moral reasoning.* White Plains, NY: Longman.

Courts, P. L., & McInerny, K. H. (1993). *Assessment in higher education: Politics, pedagogy, and portfolios.* Westport, CT: Praeger.

Day, L. A. (1991). *Ethics in media communications: Cases and controversies.* Belmont, CA: Wadsworth.

Elliott, D. (Ed.). (1986). *Responsible journalism.* Beverly Hills, CA: Sage.

Fink, C. C. (1988). *Media ethics: In the newsroom and beyond.* New York: McGraw-Hill.

Gilligan, C. (1982). *In a different voice.* Cambridge, MA: Harvard University Press.

Gilligan, C., & Attanucci, J. (1988). Two moral orientations: Gender differences and similarities. *Merrill-Palmer Quarterly, 34*(3), 223-237.

Goodwin, G., & Smith, R. F. (1994). *Groping for ethics in journalism* (3rd ed.). Ames: University of Iowa.

Grandy, J. (1989). Assessing changes in student values. In C. Adelman (Ed.), *Performance and judgment: Essays on principles and practice in the assessment of college student learning* (pp. 139-161). Washington, DC: U.S. Department of Education.

Jaksa, J. A., & Pritchard, M. S. (1994). *Communication ethics: Methods of analysis* (2nd ed.). Belmont, CA: Wadsworth.

Johannesen, R. L. (1990). *Ethics in human communication* (3rd ed.). Prospect Heights, IL: Waveland.

Katz, J., & Henry, M. (1988). *Turning professors into teachers*. New York: American Council on Education/MacMillan.

Klaidman, S., & Beauchamp, T. L. (1987). *The virtuous journalist*. New York: Oxford University Press.

Knowlton, S. R., & Parsons, P. R. (Eds.). (1994). *The journalist's moral compass*. New York: Praeger.

Kohlberg, L. (1984). *The psychology of moral development: The nature and validity of moral stages*. San Francisco: Harper & Row.

Lambeth, E. B. (1992). *Committed journalism* (2nd ed.). Bloomington: Indiana University Press.

Lenning, O. T. (1988). Use of noncognitive measures in assessment. In T. W. Banta (Ed.), *Implementing outcomes assessment: Promise and perils* (pp. 41-52). San Francisco: Jossey-Bass.

Lickona, T. (1980). What does moral psychology have to say to the teacher of ethics? In D. Callahan & S. Bok (Eds.), *Ethics teaching in higher education* (pp. 103-132). New York: The Hastings Center.

Limburg, V. E. (1994). *Electronic media ethics*. Newton, MA: Butterworth-Heinemann.

Matelski, M. J. (1991). *TV news ethics*. Stoneham, MA: Butterworth-Heinemann.

McBeath, R. J. (1987). Stages in learning, teaching, and media support services. *Educational Technology, 27*(10), 50-54.

McBeath, R. J. (1992). *Instructing and evaluating in higher education: A guidebook for planning learning outcomes*. Englewood Cliffs, NJ: Education Technology Publications.

Merrill, J. C. (1994). *Legacy of wisdom: Great thinkers and journalism*. Ames: University of Iowa.

Meyer, P. (1987). *Ethical journalism*. White Plains, NY: Longman.

Orlik, P. B. (1994). Student portfolios. In W. G. Christ (Ed.), *Assessing communication education: A handbook for media, speech, and theatre educators* (pp. 131-154). Hillsdale, NJ: Lawrence Erlbaum Associates.

Patterson, P., & Wilkins, L. (1994). *Media ethics: Issues and cases* (2nd ed.). Madison, WI: Brown & Benchmark.

Pippert, W. G. (1989). *An ethics of news: A reporter's search for truth*. Washington, DC: Georgetown University.

Potter, W. J. (1994). Teaching evaluation. In W. G. Christ (Ed.), *Assessing communication education: A handbook for media, speech, and theatre educators* (pp. 89-112). Hillsdale, NJ: Lawrence Erlbaum Associates.

Potter, W. J., & Emanuel, R. (1990). Students' preferences for communication styles and their relationship to achievement. *Communication Education, 39*(3), 234-249.

Rivers, W. L., & Mathews, C. (1988). *Ethics for the media*. Englewood Cliffs, NJ: Prentice-Hall.

Romano, T. (1994). Removing the blindfold: Portfolios in fiction writing classes. In L. Black, D. Daiker, J. Sommers, & G. Stygall (Eds.), *New directions in portfolio assessment* (pp. 73-82). Portsmouth, NH: Boynton/Cook.

Sommers, C. H. (1993, September 12). Teaching the virtues: A blueprint for moral education. *Chicago Tribune Magazine, 255,*14, 16, 18.

Swain, B. M. (1978). *Reporters' ethics.* Ames: University of Iowa

Waluconis, C. J. (1993). Student self-evaluation. In T. W. Banta and Associates *Making a difference: Outcomes of a decade of higher education* (pp. 244-255). San Francisco: Jossey-Bass.

Warnick, B., & Inch, E. S. (1993). *Critical thinking and communication: The use of reason in argument.* New York: MacMillan.

Yingling, J. (1994). Development as a context of student assessment. In S. Morreale, M Brooks, R. Berko, & C. Cooke (Eds.), *1994 Summer Conference Proceedings and Prepared Remarks* (pp. 167-178). Annandale, VA: Speech Communication Association.

11

Production

Suzanne H. Williams
Trinity University
Norman J. Medoff
Northern Arizona University

Much of the criticism that purports to assess production in media education calls for greater technical proficiency in order to prepare students for entry-level jobs. Such criticism ignores the three revolutions occurring in media education: the campus revolution which calls for a greater integration of professional and liberal studies, the industry revolution characterized by accelerating change in and integration of technologies and industry structures, and the communication revolution in which communication forms are increasingly becoming interrelated (see Blanchard & Christ, 1990). Production should actively move beyond technical instruction toward being the glue that binds disparate elements of the communication and liberal arts curriculum together. It should provide a laboratory in which theory and innovation is put to the test. Rather than just being technical or peripheral, production is central to (a) knowledge, (b) skills, and (c) attitudes, affect, and values identified by Christ and McCall (1994) as "the What" of media education.

INTRODUCTION

Since the establishment of the first college course in radio broadcasting in 1929 (Niven, 1961), production has been an integral part of media curricula. Most early radio courses were offered through departments of speech, drama, or journalism and included production elements such as performance and writing (Smith, 1964). By the 1939-1940 school year, production or production-related offerings comprised three of the top five course categories and included radio speech, radio scriptwriting, and program planning and production (Brand, 1942). By the time that television became a commercial reality, both undergraduate and graduate degrees were being offered in radio broadcasting. With the introduction of the smaller, less expensive vidicon camera in the late 1950s, colleges were able to afford to offer television production to their students, and television courses within media curricula expanded (Smith, 1964).

Production continues to be central to or a major part of most media curricula. Porter and Griffith (1986) and Eastman (1987) reported that a majority of communication programs offered television and/or audio production courses. Eastman and Adams (1986) and Warner and Liu (1990) found that production was one of the top three sequences offered in communication programs. The ubiquitous nature of production in media curricula is evident in the view expressed by Porter and Griffith (1986): "It seems difficult to call yourself a mass media program if you cannot even offer the 'basic' [production] courses within this field of studies" (p. 18).

However, production has also been at the center of much of the debate surrounding the development of media curricula. One of the major controversies was an outgrowth of the curriculum trends that began in the 1940s but did not surface until the late 1950s. The issue was whether the broadcasting major should be part of a liberal arts curriculum or whether it should be a professional program (Smith, 1964). Niven (1961) reported that by 1960 most schools had adopted a liberal-professional philosophy, "a broad liberal arts background plus professional training for 'first job skills' and a basic knowledge of the industry" (p. 248). Some educators felt that narrow, specific, industry-oriented training might make a student less flexible on the job (Willis, 1962) and that the liberal arts background would guard against the "danger of broadcast professional people being dominated, consciously or unconsciously, by the internal problems of the industry and not being concerned with problems of the society which they are supposed to serve" (Kucera, 1963, p. 132). Even those who championed basic performance, writing, and production skills were often not seeking a purely vocational program (Robbins, 1962).

Despite the fact that many educators recognize the importance of a liberal arts approach, the curriculum debate often focuses on technical and vocational insufficiencies of media programs–including inadequate equipment, too few courses, and the lack of practical experience of instructors (Riley, 1938)–rather than how best to integrate production into a liberal arts approach. Researchers continue to report that according to their surveys of broadcast professionals the curricula do not adequately prepare students for entry-level positions. One of the reported deficiencies is in production training (Abel & Jacobs, 1975; Oliver & Haynes, 1978; Parcells & Hadwiger, 1984; Parcells, Hamilton, & Bradd, 1992; Renz, 1987; Steinke, 1993). Educators view "hands-on" experience with communication equipment in "real-world" situations as important in learning to deal with time and audience pressures (Conover, 1984), in developing personal qualities such as responsibility, dependability, initiative, and dedication (Parcells & Hadwiger, 1984; Taylor, 1987), and in learning to develop good, interpersonal, working relationships with other crew members and clients (Pesha, 1993). Students also report the need for hands-on learning and instructors with professional experience (McCluskey, 1993). These criticisms suggest that there should be a stronger emphasis on the professional/technical side of the curriculum.

Further, each new technology, such as teletext (Reilly, 1986), and each new production/distribution opportunity, such as corporate/professional video, brings with it calls for special skills (Carrington, 1993). Programs become fragmented and courses proliferate during a period when communication technologies and industries are becoming increasingly integrated.

There are a growing number of educators, however, who suggest that training that focuses on entry-level skills is shortsighted (Blanchard, 1988; Gullifor, 1991; Perkins, 1988; Rubin, 1988; Williams, 1992). They predict that in the near future current entry-level equipment operation may become more automated, reducing the need for human operators (Rogers & Chaffee, 1983) or that computers will spell the end of production as it is currently practiced or at least will force a rethinking of production instruction (Ferraro & Olson, 1993; Miller, 1992). Even if equipment operators are still required, Dugas (1984) noted: "It is easier to teach production skills to a nonbroadcasting [liberal arts] student than to teach a technically trained broadcasting student how to read and write . . . for an entry level position, a trade school approach is fine. But students should understand for advancement, a broad cultural background is essential" (p. 23).

Does production have a part to play in the media curriculum of the future? If the mission of the program is purely vocational, then previous calls for technical expertise to fulfill industry, entry-level expectations are on target. However, even if a vocational emphasis is important or central, few schools are able to supply state-of-the-art equipment or keep up with the proliferation of communication technologies. Also, such programs do not address the three revolutions, which Blanchard and Christ (1990) suggested are currently occurring in media education.

First, by focusing on technical instruction as primary with only a nod toward a liberal arts education, vocational programs ignore the campus revolution in which there is a call for greater integration of professional and liberal studies. This call has been echoed by Eastman (1987) who suggested that liberal arts goals such as understanding aesthetics, disciplining the creative imagination, thinking critically and analytically, and applying evaluative methods should be part of media curricula. Dates (1990) affirmed: "We must prepare students to participate in the world as people of intellectual competence and conscience . . . higher education must assume responsibility to help students learn to think critically and rationally, seeing the larger picture and articulating where elements fit within the context of historical and intellectual surroundings" (p. 10). To address this revolution, the assessment process should illuminate and evaluate the connections students make in the production process or through their productions to liberal arts themes or goals.

The second revolution noted by Blanchard and Christ (1990) is an industry revolution characterized by accelerating change in and integration of technologies and industry structures. Some production curricula have responded to such changes by generating additional sequences or courses rather than focusing on integration; however, as Porter and Griffith (1986) noted, "it is very possible to have a well-defined area of emphasis in 'professional video', without offering specific courses in this area" (p. 18). Further, Ferraro (1993) called for the development of and a focus on concepts to cover new, integrative processes, which combine tools such as the video camera and the computer. Production courses should begin to focus less on the techniques that are applicable to one type of delivery system or industry structure and more on ways in which techniques are applicable across media. As Eastman (1993) noted, "Effective message design is not medium-specific" (p. 7). The assessment process should be designed to allow the student to evaluate disparate elements of production processes to help illuminate their interconnections, similarities, and differences.

The third revolution is one in which communication forms are increasingly becoming interrelated. The focus on creating a technically superior product often diverts attention from and leaves little time for an examination of the levels of communication within the process. The assessment process should provide an opportunity for students to examine and evaluate additional levels of communication beyond that of the production itself (O'Connor & Kamalipour, 1994; Turner, 1989).

However, if students make liberal arts connections, develop structures or concepts to illuminate interrelated production structures, and/or identify connections among communication levels, the next important question becomes: Against what standard are these connections and conceptualizations to be measured? Is the student's work acceptable if it meets professionally established, industry standards or is there some other criterion? Kucera (1963) warned against media education being "'dominated' by the internal problems of the industry" (p. 132). One of the innovative recommendations to come from the work of Blanchard and Christ (1993) is the call for the establishment of a media laboratory:

> Whereas the workshop strives to create an enlightened practitioner ethos so that students can experience some of the trials, tribulations, and challenges facing media practitioners, the media laboratory directly challenges the practitioner ethos as it is practiced at many industrial sites. . . . [M]edia laboratories reflect the entrepreneurial, democratic, liberal ethos of the university classroom at its best. . . . [T]his direct challenge of the occupational and [an] enlightened professional ethos will serve students well as they become practitioners and are asked to develop creative solutions to intransigent problems. (pp. 109-110)

Students should be encouraged to do more within their production experience than produce a technically superior product by industry standards; they should be challenged to experiment and should be able to explain the innovative qualities within their work.

What is being suggested is that production actively move beyond technical instruction (which many students are being provided as early as high school) toward being the glue that binds disparate elements of the media and liberal arts curricula together. It should also provide a laboratory in which theory and innovation are put to the test. Christ and McCall (1994) identified (a) knowledge, (b) skills, and (c) attitudes, affect, and values, which they suggest are "the What" of media education assessment. Production rather than being technical and peripheral to these areas should be central to most of them.

KNOWLEDGE

Of the knowledge areas identified by Christ and McCall as central to media education, aural and visual literacy, philosophy and ethics, legal and regulatory knowledge, communication theory, media effects knowledge, uses and gratifications, and cultural understanding are all important to the production student. For purposes of our discussion, we include media effects knowledge, uses and gratifications, and cultural understanding under communication theory.

Aural and Visual Literacy

Aural and visual literacy is important in the understanding of all types of mediated messages, including computerized texts such as teletext (Reilly, 1986). Although it takes no special decoding skills to understand a visual or aural message at a rudimentary level, going beyond a surface level understanding requires analytical skills provided through aural and visual literacy. Aural and visual literacy is based in semiotics and recognizes that just as written texts are formed from letters that are combined into words (signifiers) associated with concepts (meaning), there are elements or signifiers within audio and video productions that have conceptual significance and when joined with other signifiers form more complex messages. In order to construct complex aural and visual messages, the producer must be able to get beyond the use of iconic signs (the direct, literal connections between the images or sounds and their meanings) which are illustrations of what is happening at a particular place and time. Depth and complexity come from the ability of the producer to use more abstract signs, symbols, and sign systems (or codes) in a deliberate manner (Peirce in Fiske, 1991).

Further, the producer must also understand that the structural elements of the medium are not neutral; that is, they can and do add to meaning. For example, the use of a particular typeface provides an immediate visual impression before any words are read, the camera angle from which a subject is photographed may alter the viewer's perception of the subject, and the use of different types of microphones affects the sound and, therefore, audience interpretation of the sounds. Also, the choice of representation medium—that is, photograph versus line drawing versus painting—affects the interpretation of the original signifier.

The producer must take into account that visual and aural signs are often culturally and temporally relevant. Different cultures provide their members with different experiences from which to form connections between signifiers and that which is signified. Thus, a specific signifier may have different significance for different cultures and/or for people who grew up in different time periods.

The trend toward the integration of images, sounds, and written texts is producing increasingly complex, multimedia messages. The modern communicator must be able to control and incorporate each of these communicative avenues in the final message. The assessment process should then involve a component that would allow the student to demonstrate his or her understanding of how these disparate elements work together to create the meaning the student envisions.

Philosophy, Ethics, and Legal and Regulatory Concerns

Media programs have a particular interest in educating their students beyond technical competence in production. Although technology has no inherent moral properties, its use is the result of a series of ethical decisions, most of which are unarticulated. An Electronic Newsgathering (ENG) photographer constantly acts as a gatekeeper by deciding which visual elements of a scene will be included and which will be excluded. Without the appropriate context, a scene can be shot to give an entirely misleading story. This underlying ethical dilemma becomes even more important as the competition to get the story first with the most revealing video is heightened by shows that blur the line between electronic journalism and simple gossip (e.g., *Hard Copy* and *A Current Affair*). In addition, the technical equipment has become smaller and lighter, allowing for unobtrusive videotaping by photographers who may not even appear to be holding cameras (Medoff & Tanquary, 1992).

In news, we expect our students not only to provide an accurate context for the audio and video information that they gather, but also to be able to balance the public's right to know with an individual's right to privacy. Students should know about trespassing laws, the rights of public figures, and when personal information like a name or other personal data (e.g., phone number or address) of subjects in the video can be revealed, if ever.

Legal and ethical considerations extend to nonnews productions as well. Students should know about copyright law and the appropriate permission to be secured and the acknowledgment to be given when using other people's materials. Because issues of privacy may also involve nonnews productions, students should be familiar with requirements for and methods of obtaining permission when including unsuspecting people in addition to paid actors in their audio or video work. Further, production students should also be cognizant of ethical issues surrounding the inaccurate or stereotypical portrayal of characters, which could lead to unnecessarily negative or distorted perceptions of the people in the society they represent.

New technologies also introduce new problems. Should a student use an unauthorized copy of a software program to create special effects or edit their audio track on a project? Students should have an awareness of the letter and the spirit of laws regarding privacy, copyright, and related issues. Although such knowledge can be tested, it may be best (as noted by Watson, 1985) to give students an opportunity to demonstrate ethical behavior in their production work before they leave the program.

Communication Theory

In many programs in the past, theory has been sharply distinguished from production or application with theory being the abstract domain of research and media studies courses and production focusing on technical and aesthetic practicalities. What is being suggested here is that theory is integral to the production process. Although it is possible for a child to pick up a camcorder and/or microphone and record images and sounds without understanding theory, the liberally educated communicator must be able to do much more. In addition to producing a product that demonstrates technical expertise, the student must be able to achieve intellectual distance from the production in order to assess the content, the creative process, how the production might fit into the continually expanding communication environment (both in terms of the industry and the regulatory organizations that affect it), and how the production might be received and perceived by the audience and its various subcultures. Communication theory is imminently practical for the producer and should be incorporated into production classes, and production opportunities should be included in media studies and theory classes.

There are a number of different theories, which address message content, that are applicable to production. As already noted, a prerequisite for production is an understanding of the aural and visual elements involved in creating a message and the way they are structured. This understanding moves the focus of the production away from technical expertise and toward the message and its interpretation. Without this type of analytical ability the student may become a proficient technician but will not grow into a creative communicator. Thus, a basic understanding of aural and visual literacy and semiotics (discussed earlier) and other structural theories including those developed in literature (such as narrative and audience-oriented theories) is important for the communication student. Genre theory gives the production student an appreciation of the impact of the communication industry on the structure of media content. Innovative educators such as Chism (1986) have also incorporated theories developed from film studies (such as realism) into their production courses.

With the possible exception of some video artists, the producer is not creating messages in a vacuum. There is the anticipation that an audience will see the message and often there is some information to be conveyed, emotion to be tapped, or behavior to be elicited. The production student should also have an understanding of the audience itself and the way it approaches the mass media. Theories, which address the audience and the effect of media messages on it, have evolved from critical, psychological, and sociological research.

There are message-based, qualitative theories that examine issues of cultural significance, such as feminist, gender and psychoanalytic theories (examining the depiction of males and females), ideological theory (analyzing the economic and class issues), and postmodern or cultural theories (focusing on the fragmentation of modern life). All of these message-based theories provide ways of illuminating the possible interpretations of the media message which allows the student to understand more thoroughly its meaning for the audience.

There are also quantitative theories based in psychology and sociology, which focus on the effects of media messages on the audience and the uses and gratifications derived by the audience from these messages. Media effects research attempts to determine through a number of scientific means, including controlled laboratory experiments, surveys, and so forth, how members of the audience react to the messages they are receiving. This research involves not only interpretative, but also cognitive, behavioral, attitudinal, and emotional responses. Media effects research has also incorporated marketing and advertising theories, which provide insight into how messages persuade audiences to believe or act in a particular manner. Other theories examine how the audience uses the mass media and what sorts of gratifications they receive from it.

Although most major productions are collaborative efforts, the student must also be able to take a step backward and examine the production process. Organizational and interpersonal theories are important here, because they assist the student in dealing with problems that may arise during production but also alert the student to other communication issues of which she or he may not be aware (such as ways to make the process more efficient, to maximize creative input from the crew, to enhance collaboration, etc.).

Having the ability to analyze content, understand the audience, and examine the production process is essential in order for the producer to be able to make informed choices in order to create a production that will communicate both the information and emotion of the message and that will increase the likelihood that the audience will attend to, understand, and/or act on the message. However, a communication researcher who does not know anything about production may also be missing important elements of the research question. For example, changes in shot sizes may be affected by moving the camera or changing the camera lens by zooming into or out from the subject. However, changing the camera lens could affect distance perception and depth of field. A scholar who is examining mediated images or a researcher who is preparing mediated material to be used in laboratory experiments must take into account all of these effects. Therefore, production experience can be important for the communication scholar, whether he or she is a qualitative or quantitative researcher.

Assessing all of these connections within even two or three production classes or a portfolio is impossible. What is required is a new way of thinking about production. Production is not the antithesis of theory but part of the process of understanding and developing theories. Thus, where possible, production should be incorporated into classes that focus on theory so that students can test for themselves how changes within the production change the interpretation or the effect that the production has on the audience. Being able to use theory to gain greater understanding of possible interpretations, the audience, and the production process is also essential to the producer and should be an integral part of production classes and a part of a student's final portfolio.

SKILLS

Normally skills in the production curriculum are defined as technical, operational competencies; however, in the broader definition of skills offered by Christ and McCall (1994), production competency is only one of the skills necessary for the media student. Others include aural and visual literacy, critical thinking, information gathering and research, computer literacy, media writing capability, and adaptive competency. The discussion of skills begins with production competency, but as aural and visual literacy has been discussed under Knowledge, the discussion of skills then moves to critical thinking.

Production Competency

Although it is our recommendation that all communication students have a working knowledge of the production process, specifically students who complete a degree in media with an emphasis in production are expected to be knowledgeable about the process of designing and creating messages. This would mean that production students understand that the creation of mediated messages is a purposeful and deliberate process that progresses in several stages: preproduction (assessing the communication problem and planning the message, which also involves research), production (creating the message), postproduction (editing and audio/video sweetening), and in some cases exhibition and testing the effectiveness of the message. Students are expected to understand how these stages flow from one to another and the tasks that must be accomplished at each stage.

Students are also expected to be able to demonstrate technical competencies in the procedures and equipment involved. This often necessitates knowledge of a wide range of technologies including audio, video, and text-producing equipment (such as microphones, cameras, lights, computers, etc.); video, sound, and print-shaping technologies (such as computerized image and paint systems, sound equalization and reverberation equipment, print editing software, etc.); audio and video/graphics mixers; recorders; postproduction editing equipment; and multimedia workstations.

More importantly, whether it is a video, audio, or multimedia production, a successful production student must have the ability to understand the aesthetic results of technical changes and how changing one variable will affect other variables within the production. Students must be able to understand simple relationships such as the different ways to change the amount of light on a subject and how changing the amount of light requires a change in the f/stop on the camera. They must know the inverse square law and be able to anticipate the relationship between subject to light-source distance and the resulting amount of light that reaches the subject or between subject and microphone distance and the resulting sound volume. However, it is also important for the student to know how changing one variable affects other variables within the production, which is another level of complexity. Therefore, the student should know that increasing the amount of light falling on a subject also affects depth of field. Finally, whenever multimedia production is attempted, students must understand the capabilities of both the hardware and the software (and sometimes have the patience to call the manufacturer on the 800 number to ask for assistance).

The difficult task, then, for production students is not only to have some knowledge in other fields (such as aesthetics, computer software, and elementary physics) but more importantly to know when to apply that knowledge to the production situation and how the concepts translate into the practical use of equipment.

Preproduction. Whether a production is done within a studio, in the field, or on a multimedia workstation, most of the important conceptualization is done in preproduction planning. This preproduction conceptualization is documented by production materials, such as production treatments, set designs, lighting plots, audio plans, storyboards, camera shot sheets, and graphic insert plans. A studio situation, whether it is audio, video, film or still photography, inherently provides a great amount of control over many production variables; however, this control suggests that greater attention to preproduction detail may be necessary in some areas. For example, because a studio generally has no existing architecture, natural lighting, or environmental sound, all of the sets, props, lighting, and sound must be added and coordinated by the producer. This may even involve the construction of necessary sets. A field production situation affords the production student less control over most production variables. Therefore, preproduction planning must include location scouting, sound and lighting assessments, and an analysis of necessary props and set pieces. Also, because the audio and/or video will be recorded in pieces to be edited together later, preproduction planning should also include a shooting or recording schedule to insure that all of the necessary footage is obtained. Although set designs, lighting and audio plots, and so forth, are not required for multimedia workstation production, the need for extensive storyboarding still remains in order to control the numerous elements within the message. Thus, although the requirements and adaptations may differ depending on the type of production, all forms of production require extensive preplanning, which can be used as an assessment tool within the student's portfolio.

Production. No matter what type of equipment is being used or what facility the university has, the end result of the production process is a message. Thus, an important competence for the production student is the execution of preproduction plans to create a message. The first step is the creation of the raw material from which the message is formed. This could include input into a computer in order to create a multimedia message, the gathering of audio (including microphone selection and placement and/or selection of appropriate sound from a library) for an aural or aural-visual message, and the creation of appropriate lighting (including making the best use of existing lighting or augmenting it with lighting instruments and reflectors), images (including setting up the camera, demonstrating proper framing and composition for a variety of shots, and performing camera actions like tilts, pans, and zooms), and graphics or written text for visual messages.

Although the multimedia workstation, still photography, audio, and some video productions may not require extensive assistance by a production crew for this phase in the process, many audio and video production situations involve more than one person. Because interaction between crew members during recording in a field production would require some type of interpersonal communication system usually found only in the studio or in larger budget field productions, the director or producer must convey to the crew exactly what must be accomplished before the recording begins. This requires that the producer clearly explain his or her creative vision as well as the primary actions of each crew member. A multicamera television production or complex audio production could involve from 5 to 10 individuals. A large crew changes the requirements for successful work, because the student producer must develop the ability to communicate effectively under time constraints. Verbal feedback must be succinct, informative, and timely. Students who take the role of director must be decisive and have the ability to communicate their ideas and commands quickly and clearly in order to control the disparate areas of the production. Crew members are expected to take direction and give appropriate responses. This small group communication situation is one where slight miscommunications may lead to production errors and discord among crew members.

Postproduction Work. Whether the production is created at a multimedia workstation, in an audio or video studio, or in the field, the creation of the final message often requires postproduction work in the form of editing or sweetening (augmentation) of the raw material. These are important skills for production students, because they provide greater control over the production process (i.e., the producer is not limited by the raw material he or she has available). It is expected that students know a number of different editing strategies, include among their production materials an edit decision list or plan, and be able to execute these plans on the equipment that is available to them.

Computers are now supplanting other pieces of equipment in the production process. Audio editing for sound tracks or radio can now be easily accomplished with one of many digital editing programs. Graphic material can be generated by computer and added to video without elaborate art facilities. Video editing programs are readily available and are low enough in cost and flexible enough in capabilities that they may be incorporated into media programs. And multimedia workstations will soon make all of the stand-alone, single-purpose editing equipment obsolete. Computer literacy is no longer an option; it is becoming a necessity for the production student. Media students should be exposed to these changes and urged to take advantage of the many opportunities both inside and outside of the media program to use and experiment with these systems.

Critical Thinking

Brown (1991) developed two criteria for critical thinking skills:

> Projects should train participants in the process of selective discrimination, analytical observation, and reasoned assessment based on factual data judged according to meaningful criteria. . . . The process should begin with analysis and end with synthesis, merging learned factual data with receivers' experience of TV and their own value-system; it should stress inductive (heuristic, a posteriori) exploration from which principles are drawn out, along with the deductive (a priori) process. (p. 52)

In many respects, the process described previously as critical thinking is the production process. It is more than picking up a camera or a microphone and pointing it in the correct direction and maintaining the proper recording levels. Production involves information gathering in which the producer gathers factual data for news, documentary, and/or corporate subjects and for authentic fictional productions and production data such as possible production sites, characters, available technical equipment, and so forth. The next step is the discrimination among the data to extract the salient communication elements for the production that allows the student to make reasoned choices between many alternative elements and synthesize the chosen elements into a production product. Although many other areas of the media curriculum provide opportunities for information gathering, discrimination, and analysis, production provides the opportunity to complete the process through synthesis. However, in order to bring the components of critical thinking to light, it is important for the assessment of the production to include not only the finished product but to incorporate the preproduction plans such as treatments, research, scripts, set designs, and so forth. This is the inductive process during which important production elements are identified and chosen, and it is important for students to stop and think about those choices.

A second important element of this process would be an inclusion of the deductive process in which critical theories are applied to the student's production. The object of most criticism courses is the examination of current media offerings after they have been distributed; however, students should be urged to apply the same theories to their own work both during the production process and afterward in a formal critique. The production process should be one in which the student makes reasoned choices and is able to articulate those choices in connection within a theoretical perspective (such as a semiotic, feminist or gender, genre, narrative, audience-oriented, ideological, psychoanalytic, postmodern, or cultural critique). However, the student must also be able to distance him or herself from the final product and the production process to analyze it in a more formal, theoretical critique.

Information Gathering and Research

Production students are called on to create messages involving content that is outside their range of expertise. The assessment process should evaluate the process the student follows in order to gain appropriate fluency in the subject area. In many cases, the technical nature of the material or the nonfamiliar setting for the production will be beyond the scope of the producer or scriptwriter's education and experience. For example, if a student produces a dramatic piece that is set in 14th-century England or in the diamond mines in South Africa, he or she should gather essential, basic information regarding wearing apparel, furniture, vernacular speech and/or accent, and even lifestyle of the characters in the production. Vernacular language and accent are certainly important, but it may be equally as important to use the sounds from instruments that were popular at that place and/or time–a lute may be more appropriate than a six-string guitar. In corporate video, an independent producer may be asked to create a video that explains the use of a new version of a word processing program that will be installed in all of the client's computers. In all of these examples, the producer must gain a fluency with the subject matter to give the production authenticity. This is an extremely important part of the production process, because it is the informational base on which the message is constructed.

Students should be able to complete the following process: (a) assess the research needs for the project, (b) determine the research strategy, (c) gather the information, and (d) apply the necessary information to the current project. The first task then is for students who function as producers to assess the research needs for the project. As the nature of the necessary information becomes known, the producer can select one or more of the following techniques to obtain it: interviews with subject and/or content experts, seeking reference materials from the library, Internet, and so forth, and/or investigating previous materials produced by or for the client. Gathering the information not only requires a definite idea of what information is to be sought and how or where to find it, but also a realistic time plan for its acquisition. The final step in this process is to prepare materials that incorporate the knowledge gained into the script, the set, the costumes, the props, the graphic materials, and soundtrack as needed for the production. Any assessment of a media production should carefully examine the student's ability to gather the necessary ingredients needed to solve the communication problem.

Computer Literacy

In the past, knowledge about computers was thought to be separate and apart from audio and visual production; however, this distinction was never completely correct. Very early in the development of video technologies, computers were added to provide textual capabilities to the video mix (e.g., the character generator that allows textual information to be inserted into a video message) and stability for the video signal (through the time base corrector). However, computers have also been integrated into the internal workings of most types of modern audio-video equipment. Today with the use of the computer for information gathering and the ability to place moving images and sounds into computerized messages, any remaining distinction is being eradicated. It has become important for the textually oriented student to understand audio and video production and similarly for the audio-video producer to understand textual issues.

Further, for the modern video or audio production student, the recorded image or sound, which in the past could only be changed in a few very detectable ways, can now with digital technology be sampled, altered, compressed, and/or expanded by the computer in ways that are not detectable by the audience. Using a nonlinear digital editor, a student can produce numerous variations of a project in about the same time it took to produce one version with linear editing. Therefore, the computer and other forms of digital technology are giving the student even greater ability to control and experiment with the construction of his or her images and sounds but, at the same time, it is raising new production and ethical decisions. The assessment process should incorporate an evaluation of the computer literacy of the student, and where appropriate, a recognition by the student of the ethical dilemmas that this technology poses.

Media Writing Capability

Media writing (even scriptwriting) has traditionally been separated from audio-video production because it is often part of print-oriented courses. However, such distinctions are counterproductive, because scripts are written with the expectation of being produced, and (as noted earlier) computerized text is being integrated with moving images and sound. Thus, media writing capability is central to the production process, and it is important for the production student to experience the entire process from start to finish to understand the contribution of each step to the final product.

Adaptive Competency

The true mark of a competent producer is when that person can produce the desired results regardless of the variables present in the production situation. This requires an ability to change from standard procedures and techniques in order to create the conditions necessary to facilitate the successful attainment of the production goals.

In many production situations, the production team often feels as if better weather, more equipment, more crew members or a more cooperative performer is needed to get the desired result. Most often, the budget, the weather, and the choice of talent are variables that cannot be changed on the day of the shoot. The most effective production personnel are those who can note the deficiencies and adapt to garner the desired effect.

ATTITUDES, AFFECT, AND VALUES

Finally, Christ and McCall (1994) suggested that the assessment of media education should include the evaluation of attitudes, affect, and values, such as aesthetic sensibility, professional identity, professional ethics and legal concerns (discussed under Knowledge), leadership, and motivation to continue learning. These are qualities that move the student beyond being an equipment operator toward becoming a professional, ethical communicator.

Aesthetic Sensibility

What production seeks to do is to develop within the student an aesthetic sensibility. The process of this development may differ from student to student but involves an understanding of sounds and images that goes beyond how to reproduce them technically. Rather, the student becomes sensitive to variations of light, shadow, focus, distance, and image that face all photographers and artists, to differences in key, pitch, timbre, and so forth that face musicians, and to issues of movement that face dancers. It is more than the ability to create productions that are acceptable or even superior by industry standards and conventions, but the ability to recognize the conventions, to use them when appropriate, and more importantly to develop innovative productions and techniques that reach beyond the conventions. It is the ability to go beyond illustration to communication at a number of different levels. And it is the ability to bring a personal quality or style to one's work, which will set it apart from other conventionally limited productions.

Professional Identity

In the past, production students have been encouraged to think of themselves as broadcasters or film producers. In the 1980s, production programs began to embrace the idea that students should be educated for a more general career, that is, one that encompasses a broader application of their talents than just broadcasting. This broadening led to programs in corporate video that took skills and talents generally assumed to be broadcast-oriented and applied them to messages produced for government agencies, hospitals, corporations, and educational institutions. In the 1990s, the explosion of multimedia tools available to production students has further widened the scope of careers for media students. This broadening of application allows media students to look at themselves more as professional communicators who use a variety of talents and tools to solve communication problems rather than button-pushers or "A-V" people–the "techies" that carry out the wishes of the decision makers.

Leadership

A desired outcome of a media education, regardless of emphasis within the major, is leadership. In many different production situations, students must work in groups to complete the production. This, perhaps, is best exemplified in studio television where a crew of 10 people or more must coordinate their efforts to create a program. Although all of the crew members must contribute to reach this goal, the producer and/or director assumes a leadership role by giving direction to other crew members in order to execute the creative vision. However, leadership is more than direction or order-giving behavior. Successful production requires real leadership that utilizes human communication to modify the attitudes and behaviors of others in order to meet group goals and needs (Hackman & Johnson, 1991).

Where management focuses on maintenance and efficiency, leadership focuses on direction, dealing with change, and meeting the needs of the group in the future. This requires more than an understanding of the tools and techniques of production; it also requires skills involving human communication, problem finding and solving, and persuasion. Therefore, a successful production student should not only be able to demonstrate competence in the technical and creative aspects of mediated communication but also in the area of human communication. Hackman and Johnson (1991) asserted that, in order to influence others, leaders should be able to demonstrate the ability to:

1. Develop perceptions of credibility.
2. Develop and use power bases effectively.
3. Make effective use of verbal and nonverbal influence cues.
4. Develop positive expectations for others.

5. Manage change.
6. Gain compliance.
7. Negotiate productive solutions.

Motivation to Continue Learning

If production students drill on particular types of equipment, using only industry standards and techniques, in narrowly defined fields tied to distribution systems or industries, then when new challenges arise utilizing different types of equipment, methods, and content outside of their narrow area of expertise, they will have to start over to learn the new equipment and techniques. However, if they are challenged to innovate with the equipment at hand (no matter how rudimentary), if they are challenged to bring ideas, theories, and skills outside of the production arena into their creative endeavor, if they are challenged to think of ways to use the knowledge and skills in one area to their benefit in another area, and if they can take a step back, evaluate their own production and the production process, and relate both to the broader communication environment and culture, then they will have the basis to easily incorporate change and additional learning.

Our goal should be to provide the students with the knowledge, skills, and attitudes to be able to meet these changes and opportunities. The knowledge will be broader than equipment operation and production techniques but should also introduce the students to aural and visual literacy and communication theory. In addition to basic production competency, students should be able to think critically, gather information, use computers, write clearly, and be adaptable. Finally, they should fit this knowledge and these skills into their own mental framework by developing aesthetic sensibility, professional ethics and identity, leadership qualities, and a motivation to continue learning to help them implement their knowledge and skills now and in the future.

Assessment Strategy

In the past, assessment in production courses has evaluated the proficiency of equipment operation, the quality of the production (often as measured by industry standards), and the development of personal skills such as organization, judgment, dependability, initiative, and adaptability. Although most programs have moved well beyond equipment operations tests, except in very basic, entry-level classes, currently most assessment strategies begin in some way with the production itself. Excellent production assessment forms have been developed for in-class use (e.g., Gross, 1986). Further, as more production experiences are incorporated into media studies or theory classes, the connection between production and theory can be assessed through class assignments and papers. However, as production moves toward an integrating and/or capstone experience, more extensive material is required to develop a complete assessment strategy. To fully assess the integrative and innovative nature of the production experience, one needs a portfolio, which includes the following: a résumé tape and/or disk, preproduction materials, a personal journal, and a self-evaluative essay.

A résumé tape and/or disk including a variety of productions is an important part of the assessment package but no longer the only or the most important part. The productions on the tape or disk should exhibit a basic level of technical mastery; a variety of production experiences; the integration of sound, images, and text into coherent messages with appropriate textual, visual, and aural pacing; and a use of video and audio elements that goes beyond mere illustration of the written text to develop the more abstract and complex overarching meanings and themes within the script or written text.

In addition to the résumé tape or disk, supporting, preproduction materials for one complex program (or a series of shorter messages) should also be incorporated into the portfolio. This would include: research documents, which reflect the student's information gathering skills and the use of the research material in the production; scripts, which indicate media writing skills; and treatments, pre- and postproduction plans, which explain the student's communicative intent and the critical thinking involved in the development of the project.

The portfolio should also include a personal journal to document the thinking behind important production decisions and crew interactions throughout the production process. Often the reasoning behind creative decisions and the linkages between practice and theory are not articulated, so when problems arise or changes must be made there is no established framework to guide the changes. The purpose of the journal would be to encourage students to articulate this reasoning and these ties early in the production process to provide a creative focus for the project and to prepare them for the self-assessment essay. Also, differences of opinion and misunderstandings arise within the crew that are often difficult to focus on when they occur. It is important for the student to take the time to step back from these interactions to understand the organizational and communicative forces that were operating and to pinpoint ways to improve these interactions. The students must also understand the interaction among various levels of communication; that is, how interpersonal interactions affect the final mediated product.

Finally, the portfolio should include a document that is a self-assessment of at least one complex production or a series of productions. This portion of the portfolio may be designed to fit the student's program and experiences but should include an analysis of the content from one of the major theoretical perspectives, an examination of how the production(s) might fit within the current communication environment (including an assessment of industry regulatory and legal issues), and how the production(s) might fit into the discourses within the culture. Some areas of this document may be developed within media-studies course offerings if the student begins early in his or her career to prepare. Audio-visual productions created as part of production courses will most likely be accompanied by the preproduction materials specified above and may only need to be augmented by self-evaluative material. Productions created as part of a media studies class will most likely include the analytical component of the portfolio but may need additional preproduction or production documentation. However, even if elements of the portfolio must be generated in addition to coursework, both the preproduction and analytical components are important to establish the links to other communication experiences, communication theories, and other liberal arts perspectives and theories.

Students should be encouraged to think about the portfolio and to begin compiling the necessary components early within their educational career. This will not only make the final preparation of the portfolio easier but will also make the portfolio an experience that enriches the production curriculum and contextualizes production experiences within other educational experiences. However, the types of materials required for the portfolio can also be generated within production courses.

In summary, if production is ever to move beyond the technical-vocational debate within which it has been mired, production students must be educated as future communication professionals who use both tools and theories to solve communication problems. There must be also a recognition of the reciprocal importance of production to the development of and experimentation with theory. Both of these goals require the linkage of production to communication competencies beyond technical skill, a greater focus on the relationship of production to other levels of communication, and a recognition of the role of production within a liberal arts curriculum. These linkages and roles can only be explicated through a comprehensive portfolio, including not only the production materials but also a final evaluative essay.

REFERENCES

Abel, J. D., & Jacobs, F. N. (1975). Radio station manager attitudes toward broadcasting graduates. *Journal of Broadcasting, 19*(4), 439-452.

Blanchard, R. O. (1988). Put the Roper Survey on the shelf–we have our own agenda. *Feedback, 29*(3), 3-6.

Blanchard, R. O., & Christ, W. G. (1990). Essential outcomes. *Feedback, 31*(3), 8-9.

Blanchard, R. O., & Christ, W. G. (1993). *Media education and the liberal arts: A blueprint for the new professionalism.* Hillsdale, NJ: Lawrence Erlbaum Associates.

Brand, R. C. (1942). The status of college and university instruction in radio training. *Quarterly Journal of Speech, 28*(2), 156-160.

Brown, J. A. (1991). *Television "critical viewing skills" education: Major media literacy projects in the United States and selected countries.* Hillsdale, NJ: Lawrence Erlbaum Associates.

Carrington, M. E. (1993). Corporate television: A viable alternative for broadcast majors. *Feedback, 34*(1), 13-15.

Chism, B. (1986, August) *Applying orthodox film theory to television.* Paper presented at the Annual University Film and Video Association Conference, Athens, OH.

Christ, W. G., & McCall, J. (1994). Assessing "the what" of media education. In S. Morreale & M. Brooks (Eds.), *1994 SCA summer conference proceedings and prepared remarks* (pp. 477-493). Annandale, VA: Speech Communication Association.

Conover, P. D. (1984). Campus cable television: Teaching professionalism and program responsibility. *Feedback, 26*(2), 3-7.

Dates, J. L. (1990). The study of theory should guide the curriculum. *Feedback, 31*(3), 10-11.

Dugas, W. T. (1984). "Educated" vs. "trained" production students. *Feedback, 26*(1), 22-23.

Eastman, S. T. (1993). Theme-based curricula: A response. *Feedback, 34*(2), 4-7.

Eastman, S. T. (1987). A model for telecommunications education. *Feedback, 28*(2), 21-25.

Eastman, S., & Adams, B. (1986). A radio-TV program profile. *Feedback, 27*(5), 10-12.

Ferraro, C. D. (1993). Embracing the changes: Teaching the factors of computer-based image construction and manipulation. *Feedback, 34*(3), 20-25.

Ferraro, C. D., & Olson, B. (1993). Teaching from the desktop: The use of microcomputers in video production at U.S. colleges and universities. *Feedback, 34*(4), 8-11.

Fiske, J. (1991). *Introduction to communication studies* (2nd ed.). London: Methuen.

Gross, L. S. (1986). Grading TV production classes: A performance appraisal form. *Feedback, 27*(4), 10-11.

Gullifor, P. F. (1991). Is state-of-the-art equipment really necessary. *Feedback, 32*(2), 16-17.

Hackman, M. Z., & Johnson, C. E. (1991). *Leadership*. Prospect Heights, IL: Waveland Press.

Kucera, G. Z. (1963). Professional education for broadcasting. *Journal of Broadcasting, 7*(2), 123-133.

McCluskey, J. J. (1993). Outcomes-based educators: A reality check on hiring broadcast educators. *Feedback, 34*(1), 19-20.

Medoff, N. J., & Tanquary, T. (1992). *Portable video: ENG and EFP*. White Plains, NY: Knowledge Industry Publications.

Miller, E. J. (1992). Exploring a new synthesis: Multimedia in video production curriculum. *Feedback, 33*(4), 2-7.

Niven, H. (1961). The development of broadcasting education in institutions of higher education. *Journal of Broadcasting, 5*(3), 241-250.

O'Connor, M. B., & Kamalipour, Y. R. (1994). Documentary television: A successful approach for dual level production courses. *Feedback, 35*(4), 14-17.

Oliver, W. J., & Haynes, R. B. (1978). What radio and TV managers want in the broadcast curriculum. *Communication Education, 27*, 228-234.

Parcells, F. E., & Hadwiger, K. E. (1984). Radio employee competence: A message from managers to educators. *Feedback, 26*(1), 11-13.

Parcells, F. E., Hamilton, M. L., & Bradd, M. G. (1992). Performance expectation-based broadcast education. *Feedback, 33*(4), 15-17.

Perkins, D. J. (1988). The basic skills of television production: A redefinition. *Feedback, 29*(1), 18-21.

Pesha, R. (1993). Freshman video production students serve real world clients. *Feedback, 34*(1), 9-10.

Porter, M. J., & Griffith, B. L. (1986). "Professional video" programs in higher education. *Feedback, 27*(6), 16-18.

Reilly, S. S. (1986). Special skills for teletext writers. *Feedback, 27*(6), 19-20.

Renz, B. B. (1987). Tracking in curriculum: An interdisciplinary approach. *Feedback, 28*(1), 31-35, 48.

Riley, D. W. (1938). The place of radio in the speech curriculum today. *Quarterly Journal of Speech, 24*(4), 622-627.

Robbins, B. (1962). Specific broadcast training for the student. *Journal of Broadcasting, 6*(4), 344-348.

Rogers, E. M., & Chaffee, S. H. (1983). Communication as an academic discipline: A dialogue. *Journal of Communication, 33*(3), 18-30.

Rubin, A. (1988). Bashing academia again: The Roper study. *Feedback, 29*(3), 37-40.

Smith, L. (1964). Education for broadcasting: 1929-1963. *Journal of Broadcasting, 8*(4), 383-398.

Steinke, G. L. (1993). Tennessee broadcasters prefer workers with college communications training. *Feedback, 34*(1), 8-9.

Taylor, J. L. (1987). Crossing boundaries between academia and the television industry. *Feedback, 28*(1), 3-6, 45.

Turner, J. C. (1989). Personality type indicators as a tool in teaching television production. *Feedback, 30*(1), 19-24.

Warner, C., & Liu, Y. (1990). Broadcast curriculum profile. *Feedback, 31*(3), 6-7.

Watson, M. A. (1985). A relic of the sixties? Humanism in broadcast education. *Feedback, 27*(3), 36-37.

Williams, S. H. (1992). Innovative techniques for moving toward conceptually-based television production courses. *Feedback, 33*(4), 18-21, 27.

Willis, E. E. (1962). A general university education for the broadcasting student. *Journal of Broadcasting, 6*(4), 340-344.

12

Management

Barry L. Sherman
The University of Georgia

This chapter provides an overview to the process of assessment as it relates to coursework in media management within the larger curriculum in the liberal arts, communication, journalism, telecommunications, or mass communication. First, the role of the management course (or sequence) is identified, including the general approach of the course; its level (undergraduate or graduate); varying modes of instruction; and the background and approach(es) brought to bear by the particular instructor.

Next, general issues in management education are correlated with the special case of media management. This section includes a brief history of management education; the schism between industry and academic views of the objectives of management education and the debate among practitioners and the professorate about theoretical versus practical training.

The chapter then moves to a discussion of the core content or body of knowledge that constitutes "management education." What are the core constructs, skills, and demonstrated abilities that together comprise "management ability" among our graduates? Once these constructs, skills, and abilities are identified, the chapter concludes with suggestions about modes of assessment in management education involving both university degree programs and the professional media community.

MANAGEMENT IN THE MEDIA CURRICULUM

The first step toward assessment of management within the media curriculum is to identify the role of management coursework within that curriculum. How central is management to media education generally? How do we define the term *management* in relation to the other cognate skills that comprise the objectives of our degree programs? At which instructional level do we teach management—undergraduate, masters, or PhD? How does that impact on our definitions of successful pedagogy? How do we normally administer and teach courses in media management? Who teaches the courses? What background and training do management instructors normally hold? How does that define and limit any discussion of outcome assessment?

COURSEWORK IN MEDIA MANAGEMENT

First, it should be stressed that, at best, skills development in management is generally not within the core of competencies expected of majors in communication, journalism, broadcasting, telecommunications, or mass communication. For example, the most recent directory of education in journalism and mass communication (Association for Education in Journalism and Mass Communication, 1994) listed 398 university-level programs. Of these, just 23 (5.78%) offer majors, emphases, or cognate areas in management. Within the management area, treatment of the topic is diverse, including such concentrations as administration, business, newspaper management, media management, circulation management, even recording-industry management.

A more complete picture emerges from the directory of courses and curricula in media (primarily electronic) published by the Broadcast Education Association (Sapolsky, 1994). All told, 301 colleges and universities surveyed offer programs leading to undergraduate degrees in mass media. Ninety-six (31.89%) offer coursework at the masters level; 23 (7.64%) provided coursework leading to the PhD.

Detailed lists of course offerings were available from 135 schools (44.85%). Undergraduate coursework in "Sales & Management" (combined by the authors of the survey) were listed by 86 of the schools (63.7%). At the graduate level, coursework in management/sales was available in only 22 schools (16.29%). In addition, only half of the PhD programs listing their coursework (6 of 12) boasted at least one course in media management.

Thus, there seems to be something of a pyramid shape to education in media management, at least in the United States. Very few of our undergraduates exit the university with a degree or emphasis in the area of media management. At most, two of three undergraduates can be expected to have taken a course in the topic. At the graduate level, about one in five students may take a management course; at the PhD level, no more than one in two (and, given the research/theory orientation of most PhD programs, the real figure is likely less than that).

APPROACHES TO THE COURSE

A second set of problems related to assessment in media management concerns the approach to the course. Although recent technological developments and corporate mergers may have made such distinctions moot, many university programs perpetuate a dichotomy between print and electronic media management. This schism is revealed by the thrusts of the leading textbooks.

For example, some texts emphasize newspaper management (Fink, 1988; Goulden, 1967; Rankin, 1986; Willis, 1988); others broadcasting and cable (Marcus, 1986; Pringle, Starr, & McCavitt, 1991; Sherman, 1995). Still others make distinctions within electronic media among radio stations (Hunn, 1988; Keith & Krause, 1993; Lange, 1985; O'Donnell & Hausman, 1989); television stations (Hilliard, 1989; Roe, 1964) and cable systems (Baldwin & McVoy, 1983).

The situation is compounded by the amalgam of teaching methods utilized in the management course, regardless of its orientation. McNulty (1969) identified 10 teaching methods common to management education, including lecture, group discussion, the case method, workshops, T-group techniques, simulation, gaming, role-playing, feedback, and the so-called "syndicate" method (a combination of lecture and group projects). Over the years, new technologies have engendered new techniques, including videotaped instruction, teleconferencing, and computer simulation (Keys & Wolfe, 1988). Most recently, media management education has even made its way onto the World Wide Web (Ferguson, 1996; Warner, 1995).

A further difficulty in media-management education concerns the background of those who teach it. In broadcast education, for example, there has been a long tradition of having the management course taught by an industry executive. Many such executives teach only part-time, as they maintain full-time employment as general managers or sales executives. The most common case involves the hiring of a manager from a radio or television station in or near the University community to teach a general management or sales class.

Other management instructors from the industry, particularly those who have retired from full-time jobs or who have been "outplaced" by industry downsizing, may have full-time appointments. However, among this group, few boast the PhD, which tends to restrict the ability of "industry-oriented" faculty to be promoted and tenured. Their creative outputs (consulting, trade publishing, etc.) tend to be outside traditional academic reward systems (refereed journal articles, funded research, etc.) and are given comparatively little weight in issues of retention and advancement. In response to this, a group of newspaper publishers and editors has called for changes in the tenure and promotion policies in our colleges of journalism and mass communication, albeit with little success to date ("Statement on Tenure and Promotion," n.d.).

As a result, it has been argued that media education suffers from an elitist bias, in which training in skills perceived as valuable by industry executives, including management, is supplanted by an emphasis on media criticism or research (Roper, 1988). For their part, members of the professorate have noted among their professional colleagues a general misunderstanding of the goals and purposes of a university education (Rubin, 1988).

Thus, it appears that in the case of media-management education, what we have are a relatively few courses, taught in more than a dozen different ways by a mix of academics and former practitioners, each of whom tends to mistrust the value of the information imparted by the other. This situation does not bode well for reliable and valid assessment. The good news, if indeed there is any, is that this situation is similar to that which exists in management education generally, the subject to which we now turn.

LESSONS FROM MANAGEMENT EDUCATION

It should not be surprising that a review of the literature reveals that the problems that affect assessment in media-management education are very similar to those that plague general education in management in colleges of business in the United States and abroad.

The primary concern has been philosophical. Is management an "art" or a "science?" Should we emphasize the liberal arts approach—including critical thinking, logic, and other qualitative constructs—or do we study the behavior of companies and their managers through the application of mathematical models and other quantitative means? For much of the history of management education, the emphasis has been on the latter. As Bain (1992) pointed out, such an approach is perceived as more "scientific" than a liberal arts approach and is thus "more congenial to the academic mind" (p. 56).

A related question concerns whether the management program should emphasize specific skills (e.g., budgeting, accounting) and provide specialized education in different areas (such as real estate, insurance, or in our case, media writing, media production, etc.), or eschew specialization in favor of generalized learning.

As Locke (1989) argued, the management curriculum should stress general principles because technological, economic, and social change tend to render university-based skills training rather speedily outmoded. Indeed, Porter and McKibben (1988) revealed how the American Assembly of Collegiate Schools of Business (AACSB) has called on university management curricula to increase students' general education and liberal arts training; emphasize rigorous analytical, qualitative and behavioral components; and reduce highly specialized and narrow concentrations and majors in any one area or vocation.

That most colleges and schools of business today follow a scientific, quantitative approach is not in dispute. Nor is the fact that, as is the case in mass media, there is a good deal of criticism from the professional community about it. In fact, the conflict between the industry desire for "skills" training and the academic approach preferred by business schools was the subject of a recent case in the *Harvard Business Review* (Linder & Smith, 1992). Not surprisingly, no consensus was reached among the business and academic communities as to the proper role and function of the universities in the preparation of managers and business leaders.

Thus, it appears that education in media management reflects the situation in management education generally. Our professional consumers—the firms that hire our students—wish us to emphasize basic skills, primarily for nonmanagement, entry-level positions. Our academic reward systems (and our general philosophy of liberal education) promote scientific, analytical, and conceptual approaches, which professional managers often view with skepticism or outright contempt but which may ultimately provide better preparation for a career in management. So what do we teach in media management and how do we assess it? That is the topic of our next section.

MANAGEMENT: THE BODY OF KNOWLEDGE

Torrington and Sutton (1973) captured the essential problem of management education when they suggested, "When considered as a sphere of academic learning, management suffers from there being no single formal body of knowledge"(p. 155). Indeed, the manager must draw his or her expertise from a wide range of disciplines, including economics, psychology, human relations, sociology, law, and mathematics. Given the paucity of coursework in management in the media curriculum (and the extensive attention elsewhere in the curriculum given to media writing, production, and history, among other topics), what are the core management skills we wish to impart to our students?

Various scholars have attempted to codify what it is we might assess in management education. Forrester (in Kakabadse & Mukhi, 1984) identified three broad areas that comprise the body of knowledge in management: (a) the ability to conceptualize work (i.e., to move above menial labor); (b) basic economic literacy–the recognition that the purpose of work is to produce added value; and (c) interpersonal skills, particularly the ability to coordinate and take responsibility for the work of others.

Another useful model is provided by the graduate management program at the Massachusetts Institute of Technology (MIT; outlined in Rohlin, 1982, p. 8). Four areas for management study are identified in the MIT plan: policy formation, human resource development, external environmental factors, and managerial decision making.

Torrington and Sutton (1973) offered a more detailed framework for the body of knowledge which comprises management education. Three sets of management skills are stressed in their typology: technological knowledge, basic background knowledge, and specific training in management. This typo-logy has particular utility to the case of broadcast and cable management in higher education.

The first criterion, technological knowledge, involves managers' familiarity with the basic technology of the work environment of their subordinates. This criterion has direct relevance for media management. One core aspect of our management training should be (and is, in most degree programs) basic skills training in the tools and techniques of modern media production, including newspapers, magazines, radio, television, and cable operations.

The second component of the body of knowledge is background academic knowledge of general principles in economics, the law, general social patterns, politics, and ethics. Again, this set of skills is particularly relevant for teachers and students of media management. General economic principles that our students should understand include such items as the laws of supply and demand; elements of price setting in media; the product life-cycle curve and other macroeconomic principles. In the legal area, media management students should have an understanding of the First Amendment, including landmark cases related to the establishment and maintenance of freedom of speech. An understanding of basic business law, including the formation and legal status of corporations, is also strongly suggested.

Basic knowledge of general social patterns is particularly critical in media management, as such trends directly associate with patterns of media consumption and use. Students prepared for careers in media management should be cognizant of population trends in the United States, including general demographic patterns (age, gender, and socioeconomic trends) and trends in immigration and emigration.

Background knowledge of the political environment has taken on even more importance to the student of media management in recent years. An understanding of the role of the executive, legislative, and judicial branches in print and telecommunications law and policy is of critical importance. The pace of deregulation, matched by the proliferation of new technologies, and concerns with violence and indecency have placed media managers in direct contact, and often conflict, with political forces on both the local and national levels.

The third element of Torrington and Sutton's (1973) typology is specific knowledge in management techniques and skills. What are these? A good starting point is offered by Porter and McKibbin (1988) in a review of curriculum standards set out by the AACSB. Five specific areas are included as basic to the degree program in business administration and management (p. 59):

1. A background of the concepts, processes and institutions in the production and marketing of goods and/or services and the financing of the business enterprise or other forms of organization.

2. A background in the economic and legal environment as it pertains to profit and/or nonprofit organizations along with ethical considerations and social and political influences as they affect such organizations.

3. A basic understanding of the concepts and applications of accounting, of quantitative methods, and management information systems, including computer applications.

4. A study of organization theory, behavior, and interpersonal communications.

5. A study of administrative processes under conditions of uncertainty, including integrating analysis and policy determination at the overall management level.

MAKING THE LEAP: THE BODY OF KNOWLEDGE IN MEDIA MANAGEMENT

Based on these various typologies, what should students of media management know? Sherman (in Mouritsen, 1995) identified 10 major areas in which students may be assessed:

- *Ownership*, including knowledge of specific ownership regulation and contemporary trends (including concentration, consolidation, and duopoly).
- *Finance*, including knowledge of the basic accounting equation, reading and understanding income statements and balance sheets; demonstrating basic knowledge of capitalization, leverage and liquidity of media companies.

- *Organization*, including tables of organization, reporting relationships, and line and staff functions common to media companies.
- *Employment*, including trends and issues in hiring, training, recruitment, advancement and termination of employees in media companies.
- *Sales*, including and understanding of rate setting, marketing, promotion and audience measurement in media organizations.
- *Programming*, including strategies and practices involved in the acquisition and production of original, network, and syndicated programming.
- *Community relations*, including formal and informal methods of identifying community problems, needs and interests; community relations, image and corporate citizenship.
- *Ethics and social responsibility*, including the role of the media organization in relation to competitors, suppliers, and the general public (including such issues as indecency, obscenity, violence, payola, plugola, etc.).
- *Computers/MIS*, including knowledge of and basic competency in hardware and software common to media management (basic word processing, spreadsheet programs, program and audience analysis software, etc.).
- *Planning*, including analysis of new competition, new technology, new markets, and changing patterns of audience consumption and use of media products and services.

Of course, providing adequate instruction on these 10 points is especially ambitious, given that the management track is often no more than a single course within the mass media curriculum. Equally challenging is the development of adequate modes of assessment.

APPROACHING ASSESSMENT IN MEDIA MANAGEMENT

It should come as no surprise that developing reliable means of assessment in management education has been as elusive as defining the discipline and the body of knowledge. In their review of assessment in the field of management development (MD) Rothwell and Kazanas (1993) identified the four main questions to be addressed by any assessment procedure as:

1. What changes resulted from the management instruction?
2. How much change resulted from the instruction?
3. What value can be assigned to those changes?
4. How much value can be assigned to those changes?

Thus, in developing and administering an assessment program, we are interested not only in the direction of change from our students, but also the degree to which their management skills and knowledge have been improved. How do we measure the dimensions of change? Kirkpatrick's hierarchical model (1960, cited in Rothwell & Kazanas, 1993) offers a useful typology. The lowest level of assessment is participant reaction–the overall perception of the instruction held by our students. The most common means of this level of assessment include end of class surveys, informal interviews, and group discussions. Although we place much stock (and faith) in such methods as course evaluations and exit interviews (Hay, 1992), Rothwell and Kazanas rightly pointed out that these modes of assessment are reactive and subjective. They do not measure student learning, on-the-job performance, or results when our students enter the workforce.

Level 2 in the hierarchy of management evaluation is participant learning–the use of cognitive measures of outcomes after management instruction. Paper-and-pencil tests, demonstrations, and role-playing games are the most common means of this type of assessment. This form of assessment is the basis for, for example, the Telecommunications Management Game, designed by Sherman (1987; revised in Mouritsen, 1995). The mode of assessment involves dividing the management class into competitive teams of broadcast and cable managers, in which students role-play major management positions, from General Manager to Program and Sales Director, to Chief Engineer and Research Director. The various managerial positions role-played by students and the outcomes expected of these students are presented as Appendix A.

The Telecommunications Management Game permits three forms of student assessment. First, the students themselves can provide Level-1 feedback on their feelings about the simulation and the performance of their peers in the group setting (Appendix B). Second, faculty, fellow students, and guest evaluators (including panels of management professionals) can provide written feedback on oral presentations made by the role-players, in the form of the simulated presentation of a business plan or FCC license renewal proceeding. A sample instrument utilized in the group evaluations is included as Appendix C. In addition, the faculty member can provide a written assessment of the reports (papers) prepared by each student participant in the simulation. Lastly, if time permits, traditional midterm and final examinations can be given on lecture, text material, and other course content in the media-management seminar.

The third and fourth levels of management assessment have generally gone beyond the scope of our curriculum. These are on-the-job performance of the students who have received management training and the corporate performance of the organizations managed by our former students. Arguably, this degree of assessment can and should be the goal of our curriculum in media management.

TOWARD "LEVEL 3 AND LEVEL 4" ASSESSMENT

Levels 3 and 4 of Rothwell and Kazanas' (1993) model are participant performance and organizational/corporate results. Reaching this degree of assessment requires stronger connections with the media industries. Although the relationship between mass media curricula and the professional community has been strained (Sherman, 1988), of all the emphases in mass media curricula, management would seem to be the area that can best engage and impact on the professional community.

Assessing the performance of our graduates in the professional setting could utilize a range of evaluative mechanisms. The most common means of such assessment is the employer survey, already in use by about one in six communications departments as part of its general education evaluation (Hay, 1992). A well-drafted survey of those who take our students on as interns and who employ them following graduation can help assess their management potential.

We can and should seek comparative analysis among interns and employees from competitive academic programs. For example, we can ask industry professionals to rate our graduates against other university programs on such items as students' knowledge of general management principles, sales, programming, audience research, ethics and the like. The management assessment inventory included as Appendix C could be modified and form the basis for such a real-world assessment.

Extending this notion, although necessarily subjective and prone to wide variation, it is at least feasible to regularly survey groups of media professionals to evaluate and rank the various programs for the degree of managerial preparation and competency encountered of their graduates in the workforce. One possible mechanism for this level of assessment might involve the participation of a leading trade publication (such as *Broadcasting & Cable*, *Radio & Records*, or *CableVision*). Similar programmatic evaluations in the business community have provided useful feedback to the academy on the perceived value and impact of the degree program in business management, particularly the Masters in Business Administration (MBA; Byrne, 1994). However, except for a few sporadic and highly idiosyncratic reports, such evaluations have not normally been a part of the professional discourse in media management.

Moreover, the increasingly public scrutiny attending to the management behavior of media companies and the heightened visibility of professional managers in both the popular and trade press enables programmatic assessment in the real world. One useful stream of research would track the academic preparation of media managers. From which schools and degree programs do our leading media managers boast degrees? What were their majors? Who were their professors? Which schools and colleges are associated with successful media managers (whether such success is defined by profit and loss, employment diversity or equity, community service, or ratings)? Are media managers better prepared by business schools? Colleges of Arts and Sciences? Schools of Journalism and Mass Communication? Departments of Speech Communication?

MEDIA MANAGEMENT ASSESSMENT: A FINAL WORD

In the final analysis, the move to assessment in media-management education faces a difficult road. As we have seen, media management is more often than not an elective, a single course, or a narrow interest area in the typical degree program in journalism, mass communication, broadcasting, and related fields. Those of us who teach the course are often at odds with the credentialing and reward systems that pervade university environments. Our professional constituency has demonstrated low regard over the years for what it is we teach regarding the ethics and business practices of media corporations. For their part, unlike the situation in the general business community, there has traditionally been little interest in our curriculum and capital needs among our professional colleagues in the broadcast and cable industries (Sherman, 1988).

Lest this chapter close on an entirely negative note, the fact is that we have been educating at least some students in media management for more than a generation. Our alumni are now in leading management positions in industry, government, and academe. All three groups seem to be in agreement that the unprecedented technological, political, and social changes that characterize contemporary mass communication require more and better education in media management. By improving our modes of assessment on campus and among the various media industries, we might have lasting impact on the form and character of the media industries of the next millennium.

APPENDIX A: THE TELECOMMUNICATIONS MANAGEMENT GAME. DIVISION OF RESPONSIBILITY AMONG STUDENT MEMBERS OF ROLE-PLAYING TEAMS

Station Representative	Responsibility
General Manager	Ownership and financial report; Station organizational chart; ownership profiles; station expenses and revenues for the first year of operation; short and long term objectives; prospects for growth and expansion
Station Manager (radio or TV) or Operations Manager (cable)	Station policy book; staff size; employee qualifications; procedures for recruitment, training, evaluation, termination; union agreements, salaries; vacations; employee benefits; equal opportunity and affirmative action policies
Sales Manager	Market report: population characteristics; market data; retail and consumer trends; major employers in the area; retailers; advertisers; rate schedules, including special plans; sales promotions and premiums
Program Director (radio or TV)	Programming report: Program audience and daypart breakdown of radio and TV competitors; analysis of competitor's schedules, program types, and formats; program and promotion strategies; detailed weekday and weekend schedules; programming sources used; affiliation agreements; regional and special networks; playlist for radio stations; prime and fringe program and counterprogram strategies for TV
Program Director (cable)	Channel capacity and usage, must-carry stipulations, basic, pay and multipay offerings; provision for local loops, interconnects, and/or community-access channels; interactive and teletext plans; analysis of competing systems, subscribers, and services; prospects for competition

APPENDIX A (Continued)

Station Representative	*Responsibility*
Program Director (cable)	Channel capacity and usage, must-carry stipulations, basic, pay and multipay offerings; provision for local loops, interconnects, and/or community-access channels; interactive and teletext plans; analysis of competing systems, subscribers, and services; prospects for competition.
Community-Affairs Director	Community report: political and social profile of community; names and positions of significant leaders, groups, and institutions; community self-perceptions, image, and lifestyle characteristics; role of mass media in the community; ascertain community problems, needs and interests; public and press relations plan.

(The following management positions are optional, depending on group size and student interest.)

Chief engineer or technician	Physical plant and/or equipment report: Schematic layout of buildings and grounds; specifications and cost of major equipment, including transmitter or head-end facilities, cameras, audio and video boards, and lighting; initial equipment list and outlay; maintenance and operation budget.
Research director (radio or TV)	Research report: Station and competitor performance in recent Nielsen and/or Arbitron reports; plans for in-house research; ratings projections.
Research director (cable)	Research report: Analysis of performance on basic and premium programming; analysis of penetration and churn rates; converter usage; access viewing; pay-per-view.

©Copyright, 1996. Telecommunications Management Game, designed by Sherman (1987; revised in Mouritsen, 1995). Appendixes A, B, and C are reproduced with permission of The McGraw-Hill Companies.

APPENDIX B: THE TELECOMMUNICATIONS MANAGEMENT GAME: LEVEL 1 EVALUATION INSTRUMENT FOR STUDENT PARTICIPANTS IN ROLE-PLAY

GROUP EVALUATION SHEET

Use a tally sheet like the sample below to give all members of your group–except yourself–a 1, 2, 3, or 4 rating on the performance factors listed at the top of the table. A "1" means that the person's performance in a given area was unsatisfactory; a "4" means the person's performance was outstanding.

PERFORMANCE FACTOR

Member's title and name	General Manager	Station Manager	Program Director	Sales Manager	Direrctor of Public Affairs	Chief Engineer	Research Director
Attendance at meetings							
Time, energy devoted to project							
Quality of work							
Quantity of work							
Attitude toward group							
Attitude toward task							
Data-gathering effort							
Work on final report							
Depend-ability							
Total							
Rank							

Signed _____

APPENDIX C: THE TELECOMMUNICATIONS MANAGEMENT GAME. ASSESSMENT INSTRUMENT FOR GROUP ROLE-PLAY EXERCISE

Group Calls or Name

Evaluator

TELECOMMUNICATIONS MANAGEMENT EVALUATION SHEET

Circle the number that best reflects the group's performance.

	Disagree	Neutral	Agree	Strongly Agree
1. *Ownership*: Station or system ownership is consistent with industry trends and complies with FCC regulations.	1	2	3	4
2. *Finance*: Station or system is on firm financial ground; sound projections for future.	1	2	3	4
3. *Organization*: Station or system organizational structure and hierarchy of reporting relationships are clear and functional.	1	2	3	4
4. *Employment*: Hiring, training, recruiting, and advancement plans comply with government regulations and are consistent with industry needs.	1	2	3	4
5. *Market analysis*: Group has thorough knowledge or retail, economic, and business outlook of market.	1	2	3	4
6. *Sales:* Rates and sales policies are competitive, enable group meet projections.	1	2	3	4
7. *Analysis or competition*: Group has thorough knowledge of policies and rates of competitors in market.	1	2	3	4
8. *Programming*: Original and syndicated programming are competitive and are within the financial reach of the group.	1	2	3	4
9. *Community*: Group demonstrates knowledge of and commitment problems, needs, and interests of community.	1	2	3	4

APPENDIX C (Continued)

Circle the number that best reflects the group's performance.	Disagree	Neutral	Agree	Strongly Agree
10. *Promotional campaigns, public relations*: Promotional, publicity, and public relations plans are creative and serve needs of community.	1	2	3	4
11. *Miscellaneous*: The group showed extra effort in the preparation of this report (handouts, premiums, media, etc.).	1	2	3	4
12. *Overall grade for group*: (4=A, 3=B, 2=C, 1=D).	1	2	3	4
General Comments (continue on back if necessary)				

REFERENCES

Association for Education in Journalism and Mass Communication. (1994). *Journalism and mass communication directory*. Columbia, SC: AEJMC.

Bain, G. S. (1992). The future of management education. *Journal of the Operational Research Society, 43*(6), 557-561.

Baldwin, T. F., & McVoy, D. S. (1983). *Cable communications*. Englewood Cliffs, NJ: Prentice-Hall.

Byrne, J. A. (1994, October 24). The best B schools. *Business Week*, (3395), 62-69.

Fink, C. C. (1988). *Strategic newspaper management*. New York: Random House.

Ferguson, D. (1996) *Home page for the BEA Management Sales and Sales Division* (http://www.bgsu.edu/~dfergus/index.html).

Goulden, J. F. (1967). *Newspaper management*. London: Heinemann.

Hay, E. A. (1992). A national survey of assessment trends in communication departments. *Communication Education, 41*(3), 247-257.

Hilliard, R. L. (1989). *Television station operations and management*. Boston: Focal Press.

Hunn, P. (1988). *Starting and operating your own FM radio station: From license application to program management*. Blue Ridge Summit, PA: Tab Books.

Kakabadse, A., & Mukhi, S. (Eds.). (1984). *The future of management education*. New York: Nichols.

Keith M. C., & Krause, J. M. (1993). *The radio station*. Boston: Focal Press.

Keys, B., & Wolfe, J. (1988). Management education and development: Current issues and emerging trends. *Journal of Management, 14*(2), 205-229.

Lange, M. R. (1985). *Radio station operations*. Vincennes, IN: The Original Co.

Linder, J. C., & Smith, H. J. (1992, September-October). The complex case of media management education. *Harvard Business Review, 70*(5), 16-33.

Locke, R. L. (1989). *Management and higher education since 1940: The influence of America and Japan on West Germany, Great Britain, and France*. New York: Cambridge University Press.

Marcus, N. (1986). *Broadcast and cable management.* Englewood Cliffs, NJ: Prentice-Hall.

McNulty, N. G. (1969). *Training managers: The international guide.* New York: Harper & Row.

Mouritsen, R. H. (1995). *Instructor's case manual to accompany Sherman: Telecommunications management.* New York: McGraw-Hill.

O'Donnell, L. B., & Hausman, C. P. (1989). *Radio station operations: Management and employee perspectives.* Belmont, CA: Wadsworth.

Porter, L. W., & McKibben, L. E. (1988). *Management education and development: Drift or thrust into the 21st century?* New York: McGraw-Hill.

Pringle, P. K., Starr, M. F., & McCavitt, W. E. (1991). *Electronic media management* (2nd ed.). Boston: Focal Press.

Rankin, W. P. (1986). *The practice of newspaper management.* New York: Praeger.

Roe, Y. (Ed.). (1964). *Television station management; the business of broadcasting.* New York: Hastings House.

Rohlin, L. (1982). *U. S. trends in management and management development.* Lund, Sweden: Studentlitteratur.

The Roper Organization, Inc. (1988). *Electronic media career preparation study.* New York: International Radio & Television Society.

Rothwell, W. J., & Kazanas, H. C. (1993). *The complete AMA guide to management development training.* New York: American Management Association.

Rubin, A. (1988). Bashing academia, again: The Roper study. *Feedback, 29*(3), 37-40.

Sapolsky, B. S. (Ed.). (1994). *Directory of media programs in North American universities and colleges.* Washington, DC: Broadcast Education Association.

Sherman, B. L. (1988). The industry's role in broadcast education: A response to the "Roper Study". *Feedback, 29*(3), 21-24.

Sherman, B. L. (1995). *Telecommunications management: Broadcasting/cable and the new technologies.* New York: McGraw-Hill.

Torrington, D. P., & Sutton, D. F. (Eds.). (1973). *Handbook of management development.* Epping Essex, England: Gower Press.

Warner, C. (1995). The Goldenson program home page at Missouri (http://www.missouri.edu/~jourcw/goldensn.html).

Willis, W. J. (1988). *Surviving the newspaper business.* New York: Praeger.

13

Reporting and Editing

Thomas Dickson
Southwest Missouri State University

The strategy for assessment outlined in this chapter includes a three-stage process: planning, implementation, and system feedback. The planning stage includes construction of course goals; preparation of informational, procedural, conceptual, and attitudinal objectives as well as assessment criteria for each objective; and development of pertinent course content, including discussion topics and course activities designed to help students achieve the course objectives. The implementation stage involves using the assessment criteria and instruments selected in the planning stage to determine the success of the teaching and learning process. The system feedback stage involves making changes to instructional objectives, assessment criteria, and course content based on course assessment. A sample assessment plan for media reporting and editing is included.

INTRODUCTION

A number of institutions of higher education have begun to embrace an "outcomes" approach to education in recent years by attempting to document how much their students have learned during their college experience. Those institutions that have not carried out assessment most likely will need to do so in the near future, however, because assessment is being demanded by students, the states, and the general public. The Educational Commission of the States (1994), for example, stated: "Neither individuals nor the broader society can afford to be indifferent to concerns about the quality of our higher education institutions. . . . Nor can they allow quality to be defined solely in terms of academic studies that are isolated from the rapidly changing world in which knowledge and skills must be applied" (p. 1).

Although the importance of course and program assessment has been noted for several years, media units have been somewhat slow to assess individual courses and program components in regard to how they address desired student outcomes. The 1984 Oregon Report, prepared by the Project on the Future of Journalism and Mass Communication Education, proposed that each skills-oriented course have "specific goals and expected outcomes for students," but it noted that "(f)ew if any faculties have carefully defined their goals with regard to the specific skills and knowledge a competent graduate should have" and that "fewer still have related such 'desired educational outcomes' to particular courses" (Project, 1987, p. 50). It also called for testing media students in their senior year to determine whether they had synthesized their coursework and reached a satisfactory level of understanding and competence.

The Oregon Report's call for assessment apparently was largely ignored by media educators, however. Several years later, for example, Farrar (1988) noted that "remarkably few specific statements of objectives appear to exist" in media education (p. 2). In addition, in her study of the 276 institutions belonging to the Broadcast Education Association, Eastman (1993) found that only 14 (6%) of the 226 units responding used an exit test for media majors. Ten of the 14 gave written examinations that students did not have to pass and sometimes did not have to take. Also, Ervin (1988) found that outcomes assessment was not well understood by media educators. Although 39% of 181 media units responding to a survey stated that they were using outcomes assessment, Ervin reported that most respondents who reported that their unit had assessment measures were referring to course tests, writing assignments, or student evaluations of faculty or course content instead of tested instruments for outcomes assessment.

In addition to the lack of assessment taking place and the misunderstanding of assessment that apparently exists among media educators, studies show that many of the instruments used are thought to be inadequate by educators using them. Among units that apparently had put in place true outcomes assessment, Ervin (1988), for example, found that administrators often noted that the instrument was not adequate and did not measure such important skills as writing or critical thinking. Caudill, Ashdown, and Caudill (1990) stated that most locally developed assessment tests are seen as "either too vocational or too academically arcane" (p. 14).

Ervin (1988) noted that the existing standardized assessment instruments were not designed for media education and were not adequate to meet media educators' needs. He also called for educators to create standardized instruments that would meet their needs. Critics of standardized tests, however, charge that such tests do not measure important outcomes–such as analytical ability and creativity, which defy quantitative analysis (Eastman, 1987; Nielsen & Polishook, 1990). Critics also charge that quantitative tests used as exit exams often are a compilation of questions from several program areas and do not appear to be driven by outcome objectives (Caudill, Ashdown, & Caudill, 1990). Eshelman (1991) suggested that such tests are basically meaningless, that they stifle creativity, that they lead to test buying and cheating by students, that faculty tend to "teach to the test," and that they are easy to manipulate by units wanting to raise average scores to please administrators and state higher education coordinating boards. In addition, critics of such assessment practices charge that quantitative assessment tests tend to confuse rather than inform.

Benjamin (1990) warned that a discipline's place in the liberal arts could be jeopardized by quantitative tests because they "would encourage students' tendency toward excessive specialization and vocationalism and diminish the opportunity the major provides for independent and analytical inquiry" (p. B1). Eastman (1993) also noted that development of specialty tests in media tracks would result in an emphasis on entry-level job skills training and devalue the liberal arts aspects of the field (p. 89).

The assessment plan outlined in this chapter allows a unit to assess while avoiding the problems of quantitative tests. The plan can be used for evaluating individual units within a course, entire reporting or editing courses, a block of courses within a particular program, or the program itself. Also, effective overall assessment of a media unit (division, department, college, or school) requires that evaluation of program components be integrated into the unit's overall review. The plan is presented with the hope that it will be useful both to faculty members who are new to assessment and those who are more experienced in assessment but who would like additional perspectives. This chapter is designed with the hope of providing an assessment plan that can be enacted without a heavy burden of time or resources and that stresses objectives that are neither too vocational nor arcane but which will be helpful for educators to fine-tune courses to enable students to meet the desired curricular objectives.

THE "WHY" OF ASSESSING REPORTING AND EDITING

Banta (1994) defined assessment as "a process of providing credible evidence of the outcomes of higher education that is undertaken for the purpose of improving programs and services within an institution" (Doyle, Eckert, Kemmerer, & Wohlrabe, 1994, p. 1). Likewise, Angelo (1994) defined it as "a means for focusing our collective attention, examining assumptions and creating a shared culture dedicated to understanding and continuously improving the quality of higher learning" (Doyle et al., 1994, p. 2). Similarly, the purpose of assessment used in this chapter is: to refine course objectives, modify course content, and improve instruction for the purpose of increasing student learning and retention of course information.

Results from the assessment of editing and reporting courses, then, could be used in a variety of ways: to increase student achievement of course objectives; to improve course design and instruction; to evaluate a particular program, such as a news/editorial or magazine program; or to augment the evaluation of an entire media unit. Beyond that, educators have a responsibility to improve higher education, and that starts at the level of basic competencies. The alternative to assessment is trying to educate students in a vacuum.

The importance of assessing reporting and editing in a media unit can hardly be overstated. The courses included among the reporting-editing component of the curriculum are the "nuts and bolts" courses for news/editorial students and often are required for other majors as well. Yet journalism education has been under attack for years by editors and news directors for producing graduates who do not measure up to their expectations. For example, when editors compared recent hires who were journalism school graduates to other hires on competencies related to reporting and editing, they rated nonjournalism school graduates better in some competencies and no worse than journalism school graduates in several others (ASNE, 1990). The importance of assessing reporting and editing was addressed by Beasley (1990, p. B2), who wrote: "(I)t is imperative that even those students not at all interested in newspapers should have a good grounding in basic writing and news-gathering skills so that they will have the tools to succeed in whatever field they pursue. Otherwise, what value is there in a journalism degree?"

THE "WHERE" AND "WHO" OF ASSESSING
REPORTING AND EDITING

The "where" and "who" of assessing reporting and writing involve where assessment should take place and who does the assessing as well as who is assessed. Assessment activities take place in faculty and administrative offices, in the classroom, and at the offices of media-related enterprises. Faculty and administrators must plan for assessment, and faculty members normally will implement it and use feedback from assessment to improve their courses. However, graduates and media employers also have a role in assessment. Students are the basic "target" of assessment, but graduates also should be assessed. Not only are students assessed concerning their progress in accomplishing competencies established by the media unit, but their progress is the basis for much of the assessment of individual courses and course components.

Haley and Jackson (1995, p. 27) proposed a hierarchy of assessment for mass communication courses. Their hierarchy was based on what they saw as levels at which assessment information should be gathered; however, it essentially involves the "where" and "who" of assessment. At the lowest level of mass communication evaluation, according to Haley and Jackson, are individual program components. Assessment at that level is mainly formative. At the second level is assessment of graduating seniors. Assessment at that level is summative. The third level is evaluation of important internal and external constituents. Assessment at that level goes beyond the student and includes input from persons outside the environment of specific program components: other faculty, administrators, and potential employers. The fourth is overall program evaluation, which involves analysis of the inputs from the previous three levels.

Possibly a better way of visualizing assessment than a hierarchy is a series of concentric circles. The innermost ring is component assessment. For the purposes of this assessment model, program components are defined as "individual curriculum or learning units designed to impart particular competencies to students." The second ring represents the particular program, which normally is a degree or degree option: for example, news/editorial, visual communication, advertising, public relations, speech/rhetoric, or media studies. The basic organizational unit (e.g., department or school) comprises the third ring. Component and course assessment are central at all three places. The fourth ring is the broader organizational unit (school or college), and the fifth ring is the academic institution itself. This chapter deals mainly with assessment activities involving the first two rings (program components and entire programs), although results from that assessment are important to evaluation concerning the third ring (the organizational unit) as well.

A variety of inputs are received at all five rings of this concentric model of assessment, and outputs should come from all levels. They comprise the "who" in assessment. Inputs are received from internal constituencies (students, faculty, and administrators) and external constituencies (graduates and potential employers). Internal inputs come from faculty members and administrators as they adjust course content in response to assessment results. External inputs come both from graduates and their opinions of the utility of their education after they have had some experience in the work world and from employers' opinions of the competencies of their new hires. Outputs consist of student competencies, curricular adjustments, and changes in teaching methods. They are discussed in the sections dealing with the "when" and "how" of assessment.

THE "WHEN" AND "HOW" OF ASSESSING REPORTING AND EDITING

Ideally, assessment is always taking place, either informally or formally. Informal assessment is taking place when the instructor obtains feedback from students orally or through assignments and makes adjustments to the course content and structure. Formal assessment in a media unit also might be ongoing, possibly on a 5-year cycle with a fifth of the courses being evaluated each year. An alternative plan would be to have formal assessment of one fifth of the learning units in a course each year or one tenth of the learning units each semester for courses offered that often. During formal assessment, some evaluation would take place at the end of individual curriculum units (formative evaluation) and some at the end of the semester (summative). Moreover, the media unit's assessment of program components should be based not only on students' activities in the classroom (formative evaluation), but also during a formal assessment activity before graduation (summative) as well as after students are in the workforce.

How assessment is done should be tied closely to when it is done as well as where it is done. The overall approach to assessment used in the chapter ties assessment to curriculum development because, as Heywood (1989) noted, "the processes of curriculum, lecture design and assessment are the same" (p. 23). The plan is grounded in the systems approach to curriculum design developed by Banathy (1968) and draws from the competency-based, goal-centered approach to curriculum proposed by Tyler (1950) and the approach to developing instructional objectives suggested by Mager (1962). The systems approach to curriculum design has six steps:

1. Formulate specific learning objectives.
2. Develop a test to determine learner attainment of objectives.
3. Analyze the learning tasks.

4. Consider alternatives and design the system based upon the learning content, learning experiences, curriculum components, and resources needed to achieve the stated objectives.
5. Implement the system, collect information on performance, and evaluate the system.
6. Change the system and improve learning through a feedback mechanism.

The first four steps can be called the *planning* process, the fifth step is the *implementation* process, and the sixth step is the system evaluation or *feedback* process.

Thus, assessment requires planning, implementation, and feedback and must be tied to curriculum design throughout the process. That means (a) developing course and program goals and objectives through a planning process that includes devising learning experiences to meet those objectives; (b) implementing methods for measuring how well course material is being learned in order to determine how well course and program goals and objectives are being met; and (c) using the results of assessment for modifying both courses and programs and improving instruction. What binds the three aspects of assessment together is the need to devise course content that best helps to achieve student learning. In any successful assessment plan, as Heywood (1989) wrote, the evaluator must design an appropriate method of testing for each objective and must devise specific learning strategies for students to meet the course objectives.

THE "WHAT" OF ASSESSING REPORTING AND EDITING

The "what" of assessment is the competencies that are the basis for devising goals and instructional objectives. A number of journalistic skills are needed for reporting and editing. They include such things as being able to write concisely and precisely and to use correct grammar, punctuation and spelling; being able to conduct interviews, edit copy, and write headlines; being able to use cameras, computers and other equipment; and being able to design a publication page or prepare a newscast. Even such skills-based competencies, however, require higher level abilities that are associated with the liberal arts and sciences, such as critical thinking and reasoning.

Farmer (1988) devised a list of eight "transferrable skills of liberal learning," the top three of which were critical thinking, creative thinking and problem-solving strategies, and effective writing. Media educators such as Blanchard (1988), Blanchard and Christ (1988, 1993), and Parsigian (1992) have suggested media educators should do more to improve students' higher order cognitive skills. Grow (1989) noted that the newspaper editors he studied saw higher order skills as being of considerably more importance than media educators did. Moreover, the Associated Press Managing Editors (APME) put critical thinking at the top of its Agenda for Journalism Education (Ceppos, 1994).

Grow (1991) noted educators' lack of emphasis not only on critical thinking skills but also on affective competencies such as developing self-esteem and self-direction in their courses. Other educators also have called for more emphasis on the affective side, particularly in developing values. Lambeth (1986) and Bugeja

(1996), for example, stressed the need for developing professional values. Other educators have emphasized the need for professional judgment, which includes both domains. Hausman (1990), for example, noted the need for young journalists to understand journalistic decision-making processes, and the AEJMC Curriculum Task Force (AEJMC, 1996) called on media educators to put more emphasis not only on what professional practices are but also on what they should be. It also called for higher level skills to be integrated into the media curriculum at all levels.

Putting competencies into categories or taxonomies for assessment purposes allows educators to determine the extent to which courses or course components include various cognitive and affective competencies. Chickering (1969) devised seven affective competencies or *vectors,* and Gable (1986) named four affective characteristics. Cognitive categories usually are devised hierarchically. The best known of them were developed by Bloom and others (1956). Bloom developed a taxonomy with six cognitive and five affective categories. Heywood (1989) criticized Bloom's taxonomies for separating the cognitive and affective domains and for paying too little attention to values as well as for developing categories that were not mutually exclusive and for not having a category for originality and creativity.

Several educators have suggested three or four categories of student competencies that include both cognitive and affective domains. Zais (1976) stated that the effective curriculum consists of *knowledge, skills, processes,* and *values.* Similarly, the Carnegie Foundation (1979) proposed the categories of *knowledge, skills, principles,* and *values.* Heywood (1989) identified three types of instructional objectives: *knowledge, learning skills,* and *values.* Christ and McCall (1994) discussed *skills; attitudes, affect, and values;* and *knowledge.*

In this chapter, four categories of instructional objectives are used: *informational, procedural, conceptual,* and *attitudinal.* Informational competencies relate to knowledge recall and comprehension, and procedural competencies involve application of information. Both are basically cognitive and are lower level abilities. Conceptual competencies have to do with creativity and with analysis, synthesis, and evaluation of material; attitudinal competencies relate to values, principles, and self-direction. Conceptual and attitudinal competencies involve both the cognitive and the affective domain and are both higher level abilities.

Different verbs are used in constructing instructional objectives in each of the four categories. The following is a list of verbs that could be used in writing objectives in each of the categories:

• *Informational*: To define, to recognize, to name, to translate, to restate, to explain, to understand, to comprehend.
• *Procedural*: To apply, to relate, to organize, to perform, to present, to write, to create, to conduct, to identify, to correct, to improve, to make, to find, to gather, to accomplish, to devise, to design, to undertake, to construct, to choose (a course of action), to select (a proper procedure), to determine (a proper procedure).

• *Conceptual*: To analyze (break down), to distinguish, to synthesize (combine), to evaluate (the merits of), to rate (the benefits of), to challenge (the accuracy of).
• *Attitudinal*: To value, to appreciate, to prefer, to accept, to reject, to challenge (an attitude or value position), to question (a position).

After categories of instructional objectives have been devised and appropriate verbs selected, instructional objectives can be written. Heywood (1989) noted that the big advantage of the movement toward use of instructional objectives has been that "it has forced teachers in higher education to define what they mean when they speak of concepts as 'problem-solving', 'creativity', and 'critical thinking'" (p. 124). As Mager (1962) noted early in the objectives movement, objectives must be measurable. Erwin (1991) noted that instructional objectives should be "comprehensive and specific and should state expected changes if possible" (p. 45). For a balanced curriculum, objectives should be devised to measure student achievement in each category. Whereas upper level courses might put more emphasis on higher level skills than lower level ones, higher level skills should be integrated into courses at all levels of the curriculum.

Sources of objectives are faculty themselves as well as the curriculum resources used in the course, such as texts, lectures, workbooks, and assigned readings, or a useful activity or assignment. Another source of objectives for a course is outside experts. In reporting and editing, sources include media professionals and educators from other institutions. Input also can be obtained through such techniques as interviews or surveys. The objectives become the essential ingredient in the course syllabus and must relate to overall course goals. To determine broad competencies required of reporters and editors as the basis for writing instructional objectives, this author referred to numerous reporting and editing texts as well as several major studies by educators and media organizations.

Reporting texts consulted were: Harriss, Leiter, and Johnson (1992); Brooks, Kennedy, Moen, and Ranley (1992); Garrison (1992); Hausman (1992); White (1993); Itule and Anderson (1994), Izard, Culbertson, and Lambert (1994); Mencher (1994); and Lorenz and Vivian (1996). Editing texts consulted were: Bowles, Borden, and Rivers (1993); Harrington (1993); and Stovall, Self, and Mullins (1994).

Major studies consulted were by the Roper Organization (Roper, 1987), the Project on the Future of Journalism and Mass Communication (Project, 1987), the Task Force on the Future of Journalism and Mass Communication Education (Task Force, 1989), the American Society of Newspaper Editors Committee on Education for Journalism (ASNE, 1990), the Associated Press Managing Editors Association (Ceppos, 1994), and the Association for Education in Journalism and Mass Communication Curriculum Task Force (AEJMC, 1996). Lists of competencies for writing, reporting and editing also were devised by: Jones (1978); Mills, Harvey, and Warnick (1980); Hudson (1981); Thayer (1990); and Olson and Dickson (1995).

DEVELOPING AN ASSESSMENT PLAN FOR REPORTING AND EDITING

The development of an assessment plan for reporting and editing involves the three stages of assessment mentioned earlier: planning, implementation and feedback. The following section outlines how such an assessment plan could be devised.

I.   The Planning Stage

This stage has 4 steps taken from Banathy's systems approach: (a) formulating learning goals and instructional objectives; (b) developing assessment criteria to determine if the objectives have been met; (c) determining what course content is needed to achieve the desired objectives; and (d) preparing the appropriate discussion topics and learning activities.

Step 1: Formulating Learning Goals and Instructional Objectives. The first step in the planning stage is to state the overall mission or purpose of the course or group of courses. Whether planning for assessment takes place before or after the course is instituted, activities at the planning stage must involve designing appropriate goals and objectives. Planning requires collaboration among faculty members and input from a variety of outside sources. The faculty must determine goals in relation to the course's stated purpose and the purpose of the program or overall administrative unit. Goals are broad aims or outcomes for a particular major, department, or larger academic unit as well as for a course or a particular subunit of the course. They must be concrete, however. Mager (1962) noted that if goals are not clear and focused on by both the evaluator and the person being evaluated then tests are misleading at best and "irrelevant, unfair, or useless at worst" (p. 4). Each goal is related to at least one course objective. The learner must be provided a copy of the expected outcomes at the start of the course, most likely in the syllabus.

An example of a mission statement that might be devised for reporting and editing is: The purpose of the program's reporting and editing components is to provide the student with reporting abilities, newswriting skills, editing ability, and an understanding of the legal and professional responsibilities of journalists. A unit goal might be: The student should be able to demonstrate an ability to make necessary revisions and improvements to a story to make it ready for dissemination. Similar goals would be developed for each of the course components identified.

Next, actual instructional objectives students are expected to reach at the end of the course or program are devised. A well-written objective must state the expected outcome, and the verb used in the objective must relate to an observable and measurable behavior. It is important that instructional objectives be prepared before assessment criteria are devised. As Erwin (1991) noted, "The program objectives must drive the assessment methods and instruments, not the other way around" (p. 37). An example of an objective to go with the unit goal is: By the end of the unit, the student should be able to analyze the content of stories, to identify problems with content, clarity and mechanics, and to make necessary changes.

Tucker (1994) noted the importance of dividing courses into units "with conceptually consistent content" (p. 116). After such units are devised, the goals and objectives can be grouped into the appropriate learning units. Reporting and editing texts provide a number of suggestions for learning units. Four broad unit themes that seem to encompass the competencies needed in reporting and editing are: (a) conceptualizing and gathering the news, (b) constructing the story, (c) preparing the story for presentation, and (d) upholding professional standards.

Step 2: Developing Assessment Criteria to Determine if the Objectives Have Been Met. According to Mager (1962), assessment criteria include any conditions under which the behavior will occur and a level of acceptable performance. The conditions state what will be provided or denied in carrying out the objective. The level of acceptable performance might be a time limit for a competency to be exhibited, a minimum number of correct responses, a certain percentage of correct responses, a range of accuracy, or some other standard. Criteria for the objective above might be: The objective will be met when the student, within the hour, (a) identifies problem areas with a story or areas needing changes and (b) makes changes to the story so that it is ready for publication or broadcast to the satisfaction of the evaluator.

Multiple assessment measures are needed to provide a more accurate picture of how well the course or courses are meeting their overall goals. The need is met by having multiple objectives and a variety of criteria rather than a pretest and posttest on one or two aspects of the course. (An example of various objectives and assessment criteria is given in Appendix A.) Assessment criteria for individual courses and multicourse units are of two types: *formative* (conducted during a learning experience) and *summative* (following a learning experience or course). Both can be used in evaluating performance of individual students or the success of individual courses in meeting objectives. Formative evaluation is being used whenever the instructor seeks to find out whether the course is accomplishing what it is designed to accomplish, whether assessment takes place following a lecture or following a unit (or module). Summative evaluation is being used when the instructor or evaluator is seeking the same information at the end of the course or at the end of a particular program or degree (Tucker, 1994). Erwin (1991) explained the purpose of formative evaluation as measuring improvement and the purpose of summative evaluation as measuring account-ability.

Step 3: Determining What Course Content Is Needed to Achieve the Desired Objectives. After learning units and objectives have been devised, it is relatively easy for the instructor to assemble the necessary course material. Course content must be determined by the goals and objectives of the course and program. The purpose of assessment is to determine if the course content selected is adequate in assisting students in achieving the course objectives. If not, the content and instructional methods must be modified. The content of individual courses and components is largely determined by the text or texts used; therefore, the selection of texts is a major factor in what students will learn. It also is important that the content of various courses in a particular program is coordinated and that appropriate prerequisites are required so that students can work toward overall program objectives in an orderly and efficient fashion.

Step 4: Preparing the Appropriate Discussion Topics and Learning Activities. Course discussion and activities are the instructor's main tools to ensure that students achieve the competencies they are expected to acquire. The syllabus is vital in making students aware of what is expected of them. Heywood (1989) stated that "the syllabus is the sum of the activities designed to meet the objectives thought to be essential" (p. 21).

Possible discussion topics for the learning unit under discussion in this section are: the story revision process; newsroom procedure and copy flow; responsibilities of an editor; copy editing and proofreading procedures; editing for meaning; mechanics of style, grammar, spelling, and punctuation; editing for accuracy, conciseness, and precision; and video and sound editing though splicing, dubbing, and electronic editing. A possible learning activity for the unit being discussed is: Students will analyze stories for content, clarity, and conciseness and make improvements as necessary.

The following is a sample assessment plan for one concept (The full plan is available from the author.):

Unit 1: Conceptualizing and Gathering the News
Unit Content:
This unit focuses on how the reporter defines and identifies news and obtains
  information for presentation.
Unit Instructional Goals and Objectives:
Unit Concept No. 1: Journalists must be able to generate story ideas by
  determining what is newsworthy.
Unit Goal No.1: At the end of the unit, the student should be able to demonstrate an ability to answer the question, "What is news?"
Objectives: When presented with story ideas with varying news value, the
  student will be able (1) *to explain (informational)* the purpose of news; (2)
  to identify (procedural) the possible news values in the stories; (3) *to
  evaluate (conceptual)* the stories based upon their newsworthiness for a
  specific audience; (4) *to prefer (attitudinal)* stories that would be most
  appropriate for the stated audience; and (5) *to select (procedural)* stories
  ideas that have the most potential.
Criterion: The objectives are achieved when the student selects story ideas
  that the evaluator finds to be sufficiently newsworthy for a particular
  audience.
Learning Plan:
Discussion Topics: Criteria of news value and writing for an audience.
Activity: Students will look for news values present in a variety of articles
  and analyze the articles' newsworthiness for different audiences.

II. The Implementation Stage

The second stage of the assessment is implementation of the assessment plan just devised. It involves using the assessment criteria and instruments selected in the planning stage to determine if the course content and instructional methods led to a satisfactory number of students achieving course or program objectives. Assessment should be continual. That is, changes to both curriculum and instruction should be implemented often. However, as noted earlier, it is not necessary to have a formal assessment of each course unit every semester or year. A 5-year assessment plan might be devised, for example, in which one fifth of the units in a course or program are assessed each year.

Students' assistance in assessment is vital to its implementation. Erwin (1991) listed several ways of obtaining students' cooperation for assessment. He suggested, for example, that faculty (a) not surprise students with assessment; (b) explain the purpose and expectations of assessment; (c) include students on assessment planning committees; (d) use existing student groups for publicity about the process; and (e) explain to them how it will benefit them.

The implementation stage of the plan consists of the actual activities of instruction and assessment using the concepts incorporated in the assessment plan. Evaluators determine what percentage of students have learned what they were supposed to learn and if that is an acceptable level of achievement. As Erwin (1991, p. 128) noted, the basis for a "program-centered" approach to assessment is that the same people involved in planning are involved in the entire process. And they should be the people most involved in the program–the course faculty.

Oetting and Cole (1978) listed 10 questions to ask at this stage of assessment:

1. Is the educational program doing what was planned?
2. Is the educational program under study achieving its objectives effectively?
3. Are program parts equally effective?
4. Does the educational program maintain its effectiveness?
5. Are students responding as planned?
6. Are some students reached more effectively than others?
7. Is the program meeting goals other than those expected?
8. Is the assessment plan being followed?"
9. Is anything happening that might distort the data?"
10.What are the real costs of the educational program? (quoted in Erwin, 1991, pp. 129-130).

Erwin's (1991) three essentials for reporting and using assessment data are (a) accuracy, (b) quality, and (c) confidentiality.

III. The System Evaluation Stage

The third stage of the process of course or program assessment is system evaluation or feedback, which involves making changes to the instructional objectives, assessment criteria, and course content based on course assessment. It is summative in that it is conducted at the end of the course, but it is also a formative process in that it is ongoing and results in continual change in course content. It involves ensuring that the selected procedures, content, and teaching methods used in courses indeed are appropriate in helping students learn the important course material as set forth in the course objectives.

The system evaluation stage might be called a "feedback loop" (Tucker, 1994, p. 115). The process of system evaluation involves ensuring (a) that the content of the course relates directly to the objectives established during the planning process; (b) that the methods needed to ensure that the material necessary for students to achieve the objectives was presented using appropriate teaching and learning methods; and (c) that the assessment measures themselves were the best measures for evaluating student learning.

The activities of the planning and feedback stages are quite similar. In fact, after the initial assessment plan is devised, planning and feedback are merged, and the process begins again. In evaluating the course or program assessment plan, faculty would analyze the curriculum (based on unit goals and objectives), instruction (based on the learning plan as implemented by individual faculty), and assessment instruments (based on the assessment criteria in the plan) in relation to the mission statement and the assessment statement.

Faculty would determine whether the content of the course actually does relate directly to the goals and objectives established during the planning process. They would ask several questions at this stage: (a) Do the units devised adequately cover the breadth of information desired for the course or program (i.e., is any essential content omitted)? (b) Do the units devised cover material not desired (i.e., is extraneous material included)? (c) Do individual units have goals that are not appropriate to that unit (i.e., can better unit concepts be devised)? (d) Are course and program objectives appropriate and measurable?

An important ingredient at the feedback stage of assessment is information gleaned from multiple assessment measures. As noted earlier, assessment involves more than faculty members evaluating student classroom performance. Input is needed from other faculty, administrators, media employers, current students, and recent graduates. Several of the studies noted earlier provide types of questions that might be used for an assessment survey. Such assessment should be tied to the goals and objectives of the program. However, graduates' and employers' feedback can be useful in modifying those goals and objectives, as well. Surveys might consist of Likert-type scales, as used by the ASNE (1990) and Olson and Dickson (1995); a semantic differential, as employed by Thayer (1990); rankings, as done by the Associated Press Managing Editors (Ceppos, 1994); or ratings, as used by the AEJMC (1996).

Some of the competencies that might be included in the survey are:

1. Problem-solving ability.
2. Information-gathering ability.
3. Ability to write concisely, precisely, and clearly.
4. Understanding of media law.
5. Ability to use standard grammar and correct spelling.
6. Ability to punctuate correctly.
7. Ability to use computers, cameras, and other media technology.
8. Ability to identify news.
9. Ability to research stories.
10. Accuracy of stories.
11. Fairness and balance of stories.
12. Ability to do layout and design or video/audio editing.
13. Interviewing skill.
14. Ability to cover a beat.
15. Professional ethics and standards.
16. Judgment.
17. Understanding of professional practices.
18. Sensitivity to multiethnic, multiracial issues.
19. Sensitivity to bias based on age, race, gender, or disability.
20. Adaptability.

SUMMARY

Key questions about the assessment of program components are listed in Appendix B. Assessing courses for higher level competencies as well as professional skills helps assure that media education is not on the periphery of higher education but central to producing educated graduates. An assessment plan as outlined in this chapter should overcome the objections to assessment by critics who argue that quantitative assessment tests stifle creativity and are easy for students and faculty to manipulate. The process outlined here provides qualitative as well as quantitative means for evaluating students. Thus, it provides results that are useful for media faculty and administrators who need quantitative data to please college or university administrators and also provides results that are useful for faculty in improving their courses. Assessment of student competence as outlined here is based on abilities acquired instead of memorization. It also allows faculty to report the percentage of students who have achieved course objectives and also the ratings obtained from graduates and media professionals who have hired recent graduates. And, because improvement of curriculum and instruction is built into assessment, student achievement should continue to improve without faculty having to "teach to the test."

Viewing assessment from a systems perspective means that assessment is never divorced from what it is that educators are doing continuously: devising and improving curriculum. Moreover, assessment that is done not because it is mandated from above but because it is essential to what educators do allows assessment to be more than an academic exercise. It becomes something that is done as a matter of course and that is implemented by those who have most at stake in students' performance: the faculty members themselves. Results of assessment of components like reporting and editing, moreover, become inputs into the larger system of program and unit review and can lead to broader improvements to curriculum and student outcomes. Assessment, then, becomes not just something that educators are expected or required to do. It becomes something they want to do.

APPENDIX A: SAMPLE ASSESSMENT PLAN FOR A LEARNING UNIT

The following section is a portion of an assessment plan for a learning unit based on the strategy outlined in this chapter. The full plan is available from the author. It consists of the (a) *mission statement*, (b) *assessment statement*, (c) *unit themes*, (d) *curricular objectives*, and (e) *unit evaluation procedures (assessment criteria)*.

Mission Statement: The purpose of the reporting and editing components is to provide the student with reporting abilities, newswriting skills, editing ability, and an understanding of the legal and professional responsibilities of journalists.

Assessment Statement: The purpose of the assessment procedure is to determine whether the course or courses are adequately preparing students to be able to gather information, prepare stories, and edit them for presentation for both print and broadcast media using acceptable professional practices.

Unit Themes: The competencies required for media reporting and editing are divided into four units, whose themes are: (a) Conceptualizing and Gathering the News; (b) Constructing the Story; (c) Preparing the Story for Presentation; and (d) Upholding Professional Standards.

Curricular Objectives and Evaluation Procedures for Unit 3 (Preparing the Story for Presentation):

Objective 1: At the end of the unit, the student should be able to *analyze (Conceptual)* the content of stories, *to identify (Informational)* problems with content, clarity and mechanics, and *to make (Procedural)* necessary changes.

Assessment Criteria: The objective will be met when the student (1) identifies problems with a story or changes needed and (2) makes changes to the story so that it is ready for publication or broadcast to the satisfaction of the evaluator.

Objective 2: At the end of the unit, the student will be able *to evaluate (Conceptual)* visuals and sound for a story, *to select (Procedural)* the best visuals and/or sound and *to determine (Procedural)* the best way to present them.

Assessment Criteria: The objectives will be met when the student, when presented a choice of visuals and/or sound, makes a selection and prepares a story presentation that the evaluator finds satisfactory.

Objective 3: At the end of the unit, the student will be able *to comprehend* (*Informational*) the main idea of story and *to write* (*Procedural*) headlines or story lead-ins to the satisfaction of the evaluator.

Assessment Criterion: The objectives will be met when the student presents headlines or lead-ins that the evaluator finds to be satisfactory for both content and length.

Objective 4: At the end of the unit, students will be able *to evaluate* (*Conceptual*) the news values of available stories, *to select* (*Procedural*) the best stories and visuals and *to design* (*Procedural*) a newspaper page or *to organize* (*Procedural*) a newscast.

Assessment Criteria: In order to meet the unit objectives, the student will be able to design a page or to prepare a newscast to the satisfaction of the evaluator.

APPENDIX B: KEY QUESTIONS ABOUT ASSESSMENT OF PROGRAM COMPONENTS

1. Why Should Course and Component Assessment Take Place?

Results from the assessment can be used (a) to increase student achievement of course objectives, (b) to improve course design and instruction, (c) to evaluate a particular program, and (d) to augment the evaluation of an entire media unit.

2. Where Should the Assessment Take Place?

Aspects of assessment should take place in faculty and administrative offices, in the classroom, and at organizations that hire media graduates.

3. Who Should Carry Out the Assessment, and Whom Should They Assess?

The assessment should be done not only by course instructors, but also by other faculty members, administrators, graduates, and media employers. The media unit should gather assessment information on both current students and graduates.

4.   When Should the Assessment Take Place?

Informal assessment is ongoing. It takes place when the instructor obtains feedback from students orally or through assignments and makes adjustments to the course content and structure. During formal assessment, evaluation should take place at the end of individual curriculum units and at the end of the semester. Assessment of program components should take place both while the student is taking courses to be assessed, shortly before graduation, and after students are in the workforce.

5. How Should the Assessment Be Done?

The development of an course or component assessment plan involves the three stages of assessment: planning, implementation, and feedback. All must be tied to curriculum design. Assessment is done by (a) developing course and program goals and objectives through a planning process that includes devising learning experiences to meet those objectives; (b) implementing methods for measuring how well course material is being learned in order to determine how well course and program goals and objectives are being met; and (c) using the results of assessment for modifying both courses and programs and improving instruction.

6. What Should Be Assessed?

The "what" of assessment is the desired student competencies that are the basis for devising goals and instructional objectives. Four categories of instructional objectives are used in this chapter: (a) *informational competencies,* which relate to knowledge recall and comprehension; (b) *procedural competencies,* which involve application of information; (c) *conceptual competencies,* which concern creativity and analysis, synthesis and evaluation of information; and (d) *attitudinal competencies,* which relate to values, principles, and self-direction. Conceptual and attitudinal competencies involve both the cognitive and the affective domain and are both higher level abilities.

7. What Comprises the Assessment Plan?

The assessment plan consists of the (a) *mission statement,* (b) *assessment statement,* (c) *unit themes,* (d) *curricular objectives,* and (e) *unit evaluation procedures (assessment criteria).*

REFERENCES

Association for Education in Journalism and Mass Communication Curriculum Task Force (AEJMC). (1996). Responding to the challenge of change. *Journalism and Mass Communication Educator, 50*(4), 101-119.

American Society of Newspaper Editors (ASNE). (1990, April). *Journalism education: Facing up to the challenge of change.* Washington, DC: ASNE Foundation.

Angelo, T. A. (1994, July-August). Classroom assessment: Involving faculty and students where it matters most. *Assessment update: Progress, trends, and practices in higher education,* 1-2, 5, 10.

Banathy, B. H. (1968). *Instructional systems.* Belmont, CA: Fearon.

Banta, T. (1994, July). *Are we making a difference? Outcomes of the U.S. experience in quality assessment.* Paper presented at the meeting of the International Conference on Assessing Quality in Higher Education, Hong Kong.

Beasley, M. (1990, May 23). Journalism schools are not preparing their students for economic reality. *Chronicle of Higher Education*, B1-B2.

Benjamin, E. (1990, July 5). The movement to assess students' learning will institutionalize mediocrity in colleges. *Chronicle of Higher Education*, B1-B2.

Blanchard, R. O. (1988). Our emerging role in liberal and media studies. *Journalism Educator, 43*(3), 28-31.

Blanchard, R. O., & Christ, W. G. (1988, August). *Beyond the generic curriculum: The enriched major for journalism and mass communication.* Paper presented at the annual convention of the Association for Education in Journalism and Mass Communication, Portland, OR.

Blanchard, R. O., & Christ, W. G. (1993). *Media education & the liberal arts: A blueprint for the new professionalism.* Hillsdale, NJ: Lawrence Erlbaum Associates.

Bloom, B. (Ed). (1956). *Taxonomy of educational objectives: Vol. 1. Cognitive domain.* New York: McKay.

Bowles, D. A., Borden, D. L., & Rivers, W. (1993). *Creative editing for print media.* Belmont, CA: Wadsworth.

Brooks, B. S., Kennedy, G., Moen, D. R., & Ranley, D. (1992). *News reporting & writing* (4th ed.). New York: St. Martin's.

Bugeja, M. J. (1996). *Living ethics: Developing values in mass communication.* Boston: Allyn & Bacon.

Carnegie Foundation for the Advancement of Teaching. (1979). *Missions of the college curriculum: A contemporary review with suggestions.* San Francisco: Jossey-Bass.

Caudill, E., Ashdown, P., & Caudill, S. (1990). Assessing learning in news, public relations curricula. *Journalism Educator, 45*(2), 13-20.

Ceppos, J. (1994, January-February). Teach students to think analytically, APME members tell journalism educators. *APME News*, 3-6.

Chickering, A. W. (1969). *Education and identity.* San Francisco: Jossey-Bass.

Christ, W. G. (Ed.) (1994). *Assessing communication education: A handbook for media, speech & theatre educators.* Hillsdale, NJ: Lawrence Erlbaum Associates.

Christ, W. G., & McCall, J. (1994). Assessing "the what" of media education. In S. Morreale & M. Brooks (Eds.), *1994 SCA Summer Conference Proceedings and Prepared Remarks* (pp. 477-493). Annandale, VA: Speech Communication Association.

Doyle, K., Eckert, C., Kemmerer, B., & Wohlrabe, M. D. (1994). *Academic assessment resource manual: A series of questions.* Charleston: Eastern Illinois University, The College Academic Assessment Resource Faculty.

Eastman, S. T. (1987). A model for telecommunications education. *Feedback, 28*(2), 21-25.

Eastman, S. T. (1993, May). *Assessment in mass communication.* Paper presented at the annual meeting of the International Communication Association, Washington, DC.

Educational Commission of the States. (1994). *Quality counts: Setting expectations for higher education . . . and making them count.* Washington, DC: Author.

Ervin, R. F. (1988, July). *Outcomes assessment: The rationale and the implementation.* Paper presented at the annual meeting of the Association for Education in Journalism and Mass Communication, Portland, OR.

Erwin, T. D. (1991). *Assessing student learning and development: A guide to the principles, goals, and methods of determining college outcomes.* San Francisco: Jossey-Bass.

Eshelman, D. (1991, April). *Outcomes assessment strategies: Implications for broadcast education.* Paper presented at Broadcast Education Association meeting, Las Vegas, NV.

Farmer, D. W. (1988). *Enhancing student learning: Emphasizing essential competencies in academic programs.* Wilkes-Barre, PA: King's College.

Farrar, R. T. (1988, July). *Competencies for outcomes assessment in mass communications graduate education: The South Carolina Experiment.* Paper presented at the ASJMC Administrators Conference, Portland, OR.

Gable, R. K. (1986). *Instrumental development in the affective domain.* Boston: Kluwer-Nijhoff.

Garrison, B. (1992). *Professional news reporting.* Hillsdale, NJ: Lawrence Erlbaum Associates.

Grow, G. (1989, August). *Self-directed, lifelong education and journalism education.* Paper presented at the AEJMC convention, Washington, DC.

Grow, G. (1991). Higher order skills for professional practice and self-direction. *Journalism Educator, 45*(4), 56-65.

Haley, E., & Jackson, D. (1995). A conceptualization of assessment for mass communication programs. *Journalism and Mass Communication Educator, 50*(1), 26-34.

Harrington, J. T. (1993). *The editorial eye.* New York: St. Martin's.

Harriss, J., Leiter, K., & Johnson, S. (1992). *The complete reporter: Fundamentals of newsgathering, writing, and editing* (6th ed.). New York: Macmillan.

Hausman, C. (1990). *The decision-making process in journalism.* Chicago: Nelson-Hall.

Hausman, C. (1992). *Crafting the news for electronic media: Writing, reporting and producing.* Belmont, CA: Wadsworth.

Heywood, J. (1989). *Assessment in education* (2nd ed.). New York: Wiley.

Hudson, J. C. (1981). Radio-TV news staff employers prefer broadcasting degree, strong liberal arts foundation. *Journalism Educator, 36*(2), 27-28, 46.

Itule, B. D., & Anderson, D. A. (1994). *News writing and reporting for today's media* (3rd ed.). New York: McGraw-Hill.

Izard, R. S., Culbertson, H. M., & Lambert, D. A. (1994). *Fundamentals of news reporting* (6th ed.). Dubuque, IA: Kendall/Hunt.

Jones, D. M. (1978). Editors, educators are close on what "makes" a newsman. *Journalism Educator, 33*(2), 17-18.

Lambeth, E.B. (1986). *Committed journalism: An ethic for the profession.* Bloomington: Indiana University Press.

Lorenz, A. L., & Vivian, J. (1996). *News reporting and writing.* Boston: Allyn & Bacon.

Mager, R. (1962). *Preparing instructional objectives.* Belmont, CA: Fearon.

Mencher, M. (1994). *News writing and reporting* (6th ed.). Dubuque, IA: Brown.

Mills, G., Harvey, K., & Warnick, L. B. (1980). Newspaper editors point to j-grad deficiencies. *Journalism Educator, 35*(2), 12-19.

Nielsen, R. M., & Polishook, I. H. (1990, April 11). Taking a measure of assessment. *Chronicle of Higher Education*, p. A14.

Oetting, E. R., & Cole, C. W. (1978). Method, design, and implementation in evaluation. In G. R. Hanson (Ed.), *New directions for student services, No. 1: Evaluating program effectiveness* (pp. 44-46). San Francisco: Jossey-Bass.

Olson, L. D., & Dickson, T. (1995). English composition courses as preparation for news writing. *Journalism and Mass Communication Educator, 50*(2), 47-54.

Parsigian, E. K. (1992). *Mass media writing.* Hillsdale, NJ: Lawrence Erlbaum Associates.

Project on the Future of Journalism and Mass Communication Education (Project). (1987). *Planning for curricular change in journalism education* (2nd. ed.). Eugene: School of Journalism, University of Oregon.

Roper Organization (Roper). (1987, December). *Electronic media career preparation study*. Storrs, CT: Roper Center for Public Opinion Research.

Stovall, J. G., Self, C. C., & Mullins, E. (1994). *On-line editing*. Northport, AL: Vision Press.

Task Force on the Future of Journalism and Mass Communication Education (Task Force). (1989). Challenges & opportunities in journalism & mass communication education. *Journalism Educator, 44*(1), A1-A24.

Thayer, F. D. (1990). Using semantic differential to evaluate courses. *Journalism Educator, 45*(2), 20-24.

Tucker, D. E. (1994). Course evaluation. In W. G. Christ (Ed.), *Assessing communication education: A handbook for media, speech, and theatre educators* (pp. 113-130). Hillsdale, NJ: Lawrence Erlbaum Associates.

Tyler, R. W. (1950). *Basic principles of curriculum and instruction*. Chicago: The University of Chicago Press.

White, T. (1993). *Broadcast news writing and reporting*. New York: St. Martin's.

Zais, R. (1976). *Curriculum: Principles and foundations*. New York: Harper & Row.

14

Public Relations

Dean Kruckeberg
University of Northern Iowa

Although early college education in this nation was "classical," and some public relations professionals today argue a "liberal arts" baccalaureate in its contemporary form remains the best preparation for future practitioners, colleges and universities in the 19th century began offering majors and electives for a wide range of specialized education. Also, the emerging "research universities" began emulating German higher education that emphasized research and graduate instruction. Contemporary public relations education is consistent with this pattern. There is much dissatisfaction with today's colleges and universities, and student outcomes assessment has been mandated to monitor student learning as well as to improve higher education.

Calls for "outcomes assessment" are particularly problematic for public relations educators who represent an ill-defined, quasi-professional field that is taught in a range of departments by faculty having diverse academic and professional backgrounds as well as differing pedagogical perspectives. However, although public relations education may first appear to be an academic "demilitarized zone," in fact it is not so anarchic. This chapter gives recommendations for developing a student outcomes assessment program for public relations education.

INTRODUCTION

It is unlikely that Harvard had considered outcomes assessment for its first class of nine students in 1640, and nowhere is it recorded that this oldest U.S. institution of higher education ever offered a public relations curriculum. However, for many of today's 3,300 U.S. colleges and universities–with their 14 million students in what has become a $100 billion industry (Kerr, Gade, & Kawaoka, 1994)–formalized outcomes assessment has become an overriding concern. Moreover, hundreds of educators at scores of these institutions are now deliberating how to assess educational outcomes to evaluate their students who are studying public relations.

A BRIEF HISTORY OF U.S. HIGHER EDUCATION

To best understand how outcomes assessment can be applied to public relations education, as well as to better appreciate the arguments of those proffering opposing perspectives on such education, a brief history is helpful, outlining the evolution of higher education in the United States.

Colonial American colleges followed the British tradition, which prescribed a 3- to 4-year baccalaureate curriculum (Shore, 1992). Most of their graduates became ministers, teachers, lawyers, and statesmen (Douglas, 1992)–with perhaps a few relegating themselves to the more leisurely occupation of "gentleman." Students were exposed to a classical education. This uniform curriculum began with Latin and Greek (to impose rigor as well as to teach logic, grammar, and rhetoric), followed by mathematics, natural philosophy, geology, biology, and astronomy. Such preliminary coursework led to studies in philosophy and culminated in a course in moral philosophy–the latter often taught by the college president (Anderson, 1993).

Today, few U.S. students receive such classical education; nevertheless, some public relations professionals argue that a liberal arts baccalaureate in its contemporary form–as opposed to a journalism degree or a major in public relations–remains the best preparation for future practitioners. (For example, see the arguments presented in *O'Dwyer's PR Services*, 1993, pp. 1, 5-9, 15.) Requisite professional education would either be learned on the job or in graduate school.

Whether such practitioners indeed want to invest the time and money to train such promising graduates for public relations careers always remains suspect, as opposed to hiring students who can "hit the ground running" because of specific undergraduate education in public relations. However, there is some precedent in other developed countries for generalized liberal arts education as a foundation for postbaccalaureate professional training. Walshok (1995) reminded us:

> . . . (N)ations such as England and Japan regard the function of a university education primarily to be the screening, selection, and general preparation of talented youth. The "real" training and job skills development is the responsibility of the employer. In fact, Japanese employers do not want recruits with specialized and applied skills. Broadly educated new employees allow the company maximum flexibility to assign, reassign, and even retrain people. This practice contributes not only to company flexibility but to the ability of companies to assure more job security in the face of uncertain and changing economic conditions for their employees. It does, however, require companies to make a major and continuous investment in people development well after college completion. (p. 42)

During the 19th Century, U.S. institutions of higher learning deviated dramatically from their tradition of highly prescribed classical education. A rising patriotism in the United States prompted the accusation that a classical education ignored indigenous history and culture (Jacoby, 1994). In the early 1800s, students already were clamoring for more courses in the physical sciences; however, when these classes were adopted, they were often relegated to separate schools (Simpson & Frost, 1993).

Nevertheless, elective courses were added to permit students some discretion in their subject matter; by 1900, most students were allowed to choose a major (Simpson & Frost, 1993). This concept of a range of course offerings, which had diffused from Harvard to other U.S. colleges and universities during the last decades of the 19th century, fostered the belief that larger society could help define a college curriculum (Shore, 1992).

"Electives" connoted cessation of the implicit relationship among courses and suggested denial of prescribed course progression (Anderson, 1993). To illustrate this emerging diversification of baccalaureate instruction, Jacoby (1994) described the impact of the Land-Grant Act to broaden the scope of higher education:

After the Civil War the pressures intensified to reform curriculum and to open wider the college gates. The Morrill Act, or Land-Grant Act, passed in the midst of the Civil War, accelerated the collapse of the classical curriculum. Inasmuch as it provided federal support for colleges that included agricultural and mechanical arts, it spurred the shifting of resources from classical studies to sciences and modern languages. It also facilitated the democratization of higher education. (p. 98)

Colleges and universities' curricular offerings during this era provided students with educational preparation for a wide range of production-oriented occupations that were needed in an increasingly industrialized nation; furthermore, scientific method was becoming accepted, and the United States was becoming increasingly heterogeneous (Kerr et al., 1994). U.S. higher education was experiencing its greatest growth, with classical education yielding to the newly defined mission of land-grant schools and other "research universities" (Kerr et al.). Specialization of occupation required specialization of education, which had sociological as well as economic ramifications. Kruckeberg and Starck (1988) noted: "The specialized needs of a culminating urban-industrial economic and social system gave people an identity through their professions and occupations. Such identification gave them the deference of their neighbors, while the increasingly formal entry requirements protected their occupations' prestige" (p. 40).

These formal entry requirements usually included a specified and highly specialized college curriculum, which directly affected collegiate administration. Damrosch (1995) further explained:

The shape of the modern American university was forged during roughly twenty years, from the early 1870s through the mid-1890s. Not only did many of our current disciplines arise or achieve their characteristic shape during this time, but many of the basic bureaucratic mechanisms of modern academic life were instituted as well: the division of academic work into departments, headed by a chair and responsible to a dean; the standardization of course requirements and grading policies; the division of undergraduate work into "majors," "minors," and electives; the institution of the Ph.D. degree and the doctoral dissertation. (p. 24)

The first organized curriculum in journalism was offered at the University of Pennsylvania in 1893, and the first school of journalism opened in 1908 at the University of Missouri (Emery & Emery, 1988). Today, most public relations major programs and sequences within broader degree programs (such as journalism) in the United States are a legacy of these efforts in demarcation of education toward the desired end of graduates' specialized occupational roles within industry and commerce.

Also at this time, the emerging research universities began emulating German higher education. Before the Civil War, the term *university* referred to a college having an affiliated professional school (Douglas, 1992). However, U.S. universities of the 1870s had a markedly revised identity in which the priority of undergraduate education was being superseded by a research role and graduate instruction.

In the German tradition, scholarship became the organized production of knowledge—the antithesis of the United States' norm in education, that is, classical education (Anderson, 1993). Yale awarded the first earned PhD in 1861, and presentation of like research degrees was quickly replicated by other universities. A PhD degree rapidly became associated with the holder's very competence to teach at the university level (Shore, 1992). In 1900, research universities formed the Association of American Universities to help standardize PhD requirements (Simpson & Frost, 1993).

This commonly accepted prerequisite of a terminal *research degree*, (i.e., a PhD), together with the corollary assumption of a *research agenda*, likewise is found today among public relations educators who accept this professionalized occupation as an applied social and behavioral science for which theory can and should be built. (Probably the first scholar to overtly declare public relations as an applied social and behavioral science was Edward J. Robinson [1966]. However, some earlier authors, especially Edward J. Bernays [1923, 1961], strongly connoted and practiced public relations as such.)

Following World War II, the research role of U.S. higher education continued to mushroom; since 1950, more new knowledge has been amassed than in all the preceding generations of civilization (Simpson & Frost, 1993). Additional impetus (and accompanying anxiety) to this preoccupation with research and the accumulation of new knowledge was prompted by a singular incident in 1957: the Soviet Union's launch of Sputnik that merged the computer to the satellite—essentially allowing for the telecommunications industry, among other technological innovations. The launch of that Soviet satellite did much to shake U.S. complacency and especially its sense of global scientific superiority; indeed, it took only a year after Sputnik began its orbit around the earth for the

U.S. Congress to pass the National Defense Education Act–massively funding education in science, mathematics, and languages (Jacoby, 1994).

Such interest in research, especially in science and technology (and likewise evidenced within the ranks of contemporary public relations educators), continues among U.S. colleges and universities as this nation recognizes the exorbitant demands for knowledge required by an increasingly technological society. Gilley (1991) observed: "By 1970, the growing power of science and technology had begun to supplant the old industrial economy with a new information-driven economy. (By coincidence, the industrial economy began dominating the agricultural economy nearly a century before–about 1870)" (p. 1).

Millard (1991) opined that this information-technology revolution has become to the last half of the 20th and 21st centuries as was the Industrial Revolution to the 19th and first half of the 20th centuries.

He is undoubtedly correct. By and large underappreciated, if at all recognized, are the social ramifications of such information technology that promise to have direct impact on contemporary and future public relations practice and thereby its education. Sclove (1995) explained:

The phrase "social structure" refers to the background features that help define or regulate patterns of human interaction. Familiar examples include laws, dominant political and economic institutions, and systems of cultural belief. Technologies qualify as social structures because they function politically and culturally in a manner comparable to these other, more commonly recognized kinds of social structures. (p. 11)

Through their research agendas, faculty at U.S. colleges and universities are supporting this information-technology revolution with the same characteristic fervor in which they have supported the nation's economic growth and development since the Civil War (Walshok, 1995).

Obviously, the advent and geometrically increasing sophistication of such information technology have particular import to public relations educators. Practitioners, by the very nature of their organizational role as professional communicators, are virtually certain to influence their organizations' application of emerging information technology because of organizational assumptions about practitioners' responsibilities in presenting communication content; of course, present and future generations of practitioners will have to be sufficiently educated about this information technology to assume this critical role.

U.S. HIGHER EDUCATION TODAY

Despite this emphasis on research, and based wholly on the numbers of students served, it must be readily conceded that U.S. colleges and universities have also maintained a commendable–if not stellar–record of serving their students. Numbers can allude to colleges and universities' service to this primary constituency. Percentages of enrollment among the 18- to 21-year-old U.S. population throughout the years attest to colleges and universities' progressively greater record in providing higher education to this traditional market:

- 3% in 1890 of the 18- to 21-year-old population
- 16% in 1940
- 30% in 1950
- 40% in 1990 (50% attend at some point in their lives) (Kerr et al, 1994, pp. 5-6)

Simpson and Frost (1993) reported that, from World War II to the 1970s, the traditionally aged college student population dramatically increased, although the numbers were declining by the 1980s. Nevertheless, data from the 1990 census suggest that the pool of traditionally aged college students will once again increase in the later 1990s and into the next century. It is estimated that more than 16 million students will attend U.S. colleges and universities in the year 2002.

The United States remains the undisputed global leader in higher education of its own citizens (Kerr et al., 1994). Furthermore, Kerr et al. noted that the United States also is recognized as the world's center of higher learning. Such distinction has shifted throughout history from Greece in the classical age; to the Muslim world in the Middle Ages; then successively to Italy, England, France, Germany, and the United States. Kerr observed that the pattern since 1540 has been for leadership to last an average of 80 years.

SOME CRITICISMS OF U.S. HIGHER EDUCATION

Thus, it can be convincingly argued that U.S. institutions of higher learning–at least at face value–have excelled, both in research and in education. But do they enjoy the accolades of a grateful government and citizenry; do taxpayers cheerfully encourage legislators to allot more funding to expand university programs; are students and their parents appreciative of the efforts of the large cadre of professors dedicated to teaching?

The answer is a resounding no. U.S. higher education's proud legacy is not universally lauded, and for a plethora of probably valid reasons. Particularly in the 1990s, complaints from many quarters have been forthcoming in manifold books and articles raucously attacking the academy and the professorate. (For a sampling of such literature, see the references at the end of this chapter.)

Increased public skepticism has seemed especially focused on research universities. Walshok (1995) speculated this criticism comes in large part from constituents' concern about the willingness and ability of research universities to diffuse their new knowledge to wider communities and in forms amenable to resolving contemporary social and economic problems.

But critics have identified a still more fundamental problem in higher education. A range of constituents, especially during the past 3 decades, has vociferously questioned the pedagogical methods and the very role of higher education in the United States, that is, *who* is being taught *what* and *how* in the nation's colleges and universities.

Most notably, stakeholders have been dissatisfied with educational institutions' alleged failure to adequately and sufficiently teach their students. To many (including the students, themselves), there is questionable "value added" by the time graduates are awarded their baccalaureate degrees. And it has been relatively easy for everyone to pass the buck–blaming those educators preceding them in students' progression toward educational attainment. Sadovnik (1994) observed:

> During the 1960s and 1970s, a growing literature on the problem of the underprepared student emerged as significant numbers of this population entered the open access institutions. Moreover, as it became clear that underpreparation was not a small problem localized to the new minorities in the system, but was instead endemic to significant numbers of majority students as well, colleges began to direct serious efforts at the amelioration of these deficits. (p. 28)

If not a panacea to directly resolve such problems, at least a better means to monitor students' achievements (and hopefully to invalidate or at least counter stakeholders' complaints) has been some type of outcomes assessment that extends far beyond normal course grading procedures and other traditional (and arguably fragmented) measurements.

During the past decade in particular, demands from several quarters for "accountability" (as well as defense of the "centrality" of educational programs' mission to their specific institutions) have resulted in the mandate for such outcomes assessment to better determine what students are learning. There has been a general feeling that higher education's traditional assessment methods have been both inadequate and unidimensional, thereby lacking credibility (Erwin, 1991).

The National Governors' Association was a major proponent for outcomes assessment, with the gubernatorial leaders declaring such measurement would be a catalyst for improved educational quality. Furthermore, they reasoned, such assessment would help define the mission of each institution and would encourage the use of assessment information for program improvement. (For an excellent history of the evolution of outcomes assessment see Rosenbaum, 1994.)

Today, outcomes assessment is mandated or is about to be mandated in a majority of states (Erwin, 1991). Millard (1991) warned with a pragmatism that must be appreciated by public relations educators: "Regardless of what initially may have led to the 'new assessment' movement, it has become a fact of academic and institutional life and one that rather clearly links the academic and political communities" (p. 165).

CALLS FOR OUTCOMES ASSESSMENT ARE PROBLEMATIC

Given the reality of outcomes assessment, it behooves educators to learn means to measure student outcomes for their particular areas of instruction. However, such efforts are fraught with danger; albeit clearly more comprehensive, purported assessment instruments and methodologies to evaluate student outcomes often have been questionable in their validity and reliability as well as vague in their purpose.

Furthermore, the task is daunting to college and university faculty and administrators already besieged with excessive demands on their human and other resources. Finally, at graduation time, would a failure to show a sufficiently high level of outcomes among students in fact prevent or delay the awarding of degrees? Why have extended and comprehensive evaluation if no sanctions are associated with it? At best, such assessment without sanctions would show embarrassing empirical evidence of overall baccalaureate education's failure without any appropriate recourse to rectify inadequacies among the students thus evaluated.

However, calls for outcomes assessment are particularly problematic for public relations educators who represent an ill-defined, quasi-professional field that is taught in a range of departments by faculty having diverse academic and professional backgrounds as well as differing pedagogical perspectives.

Grunig and Hunt (1984) identified four models of public relations, which they consider evolutionary, but each of which is predominantly practiced by a portion of contemporary professionals; furthermore, any of the models may be emphasized, at least in derivative form, among the range of public relations faculty in the nation's colleges and universities.

First, the *press agentry/publicity* model that evolved from about 1850 to 1900 is promotional in its orientation and grew out of historic "public relations-like" activities. Second, *public-information* was the major model from about 1900 to the 1920s, with its practitioners likened to newspeople-in-residence; third, it was followed by a *two-way asymmetric* model, persuasive in intent and based on scientific behaviorism.

During the 1960s and 1970s emerged the fourth model, the *two-way symmetric* practice stressing balanced and mutually beneficial communication between an organization and its publics. Although the latter model, or its primary use in a "mixed-motive" model (Grunig & White, 1992), is considered superlative by many educators and practitioners, realistically all the models and their strategies, tactics and techniques should be taught; certainly, the *two-way symmetric* model is by no means being universally advocated or primarily taught by contemporary public relations educators.

Furthermore, public relations education programs still differ somewhat according to the disciplinary orientation of the academic units in which they are housed as well as the scholarly backgrounds of the faculty teaching the public relations courses. Journalism schools were historically the almost exclusive bastion of public relations education, where the latter was frequently unappreciated and denigrated; however, communication departments in the 1970s and 1980s began offering public relations education programs when some units began losing their service role within their institutions and as they recognized their students' employment potential in public relations.

Whereas early journalism sequences were often accused of being excessively vocational, that is, in overemphasizing journalistic skills and (especially print) media production courses, the speech-oriented communication departments were frequently charged with attempting to redefine public relations and making their curricula overly theoretical–failing to appreciate and thereby omitting sufficient journalistic skills training that was highly valued by potential employers. (Of course, public relations coursework also has been taught in academic units other than in journalism and speech communication, e.g., in business administration programs.) Still another issue being discussed in recent years has been the blending of the public relations, advertising, and marketing functions into "integrated marketing communications." (A description of this movement and its rationale are in Duncan, Caywood, & Newsom's *Task Force on Integrated Communications*, 1993).

Compounding such complexities and vagaries about public relations education and the assessment of its students are issues that have emerged within journalism education during recent years that likely will impact public relations education–as may fundamental issues being deliberated throughout the academy-at-large. Blanchard and Christ (1993) vehemently and credibly called for a "new professionalism" in media education, that is, a cross-media, liberal, integrative program consistent with broader undergraduate reform efforts. These scholars said such reform will reduce present "excessive structure and overprescription of training in currently fashionable technique, ephemeral information and obsolescent technology" (pp. 70-71).

The Curriculum Task Force of the Association for Education in Journalism and Mass Communication (AEJMC, 1996) recommended demotion of the association's media-specific (including public relations) divisions to the level of interest groups and has called for "creativity and experimentation" in journalism/mass communication curricula. Furthermore, there appears to be increasing dissatisfaction with and specific plans to revise the *Design for Undergraduate Public Relations Education* (1993) of the Commission on Undergraduate Public Relations Education that was established by the AEJMC Public Relations Division and the Public Relations Society of America (PRSA) Educators Section. In addition, public relations is being taught in an academic environment in which faculty representing many disciplines are arguing the relative merits of postmodernism, critical theory, and related topics and issues that will likely impact all collegiate and university curricula. Tierney (1993) said these debates have been primarily within the humanities and liberal arts and, to a lesser extent, within the social sciences.

All of these factors and considerations may be enough to clinically depress the strongest of public relations educators who may wonder if they can adequately determine *what* to measure before they can resolve *how* to measure it, that is, can they define what is public relations so they can determine how to measure their success in educating students to prepare for such a career?

Although public relations education may first appear to be an academic "demilitarized zone," in fact it is not so anarchic. Good public relations education is being provided in a large number of colleges and universities throughout this country by many highly competent public relations educators, and this excellence can be measured through valid and reliable student outcomes assessment. Furthermore, in reality, there is considerable consensus among educators and practitioners about what constitutes good public relations education.

Right or wrong, good or bad, specific curricular parameters are dictated or recommended by such bodies as the Accrediting Council on Education in Journalism and Mass Communications (ACEJMC; for an excellent reference see *Accredited Journalism and Mass Communications Education: 1994-95*); the by-and-large compatible "Certified in Education for Public Relations" (CEPR) program of PRSA, which certification may be attainable by academic units that are not eligible for accreditation by ACEJMC. (For information about the CEPR program, contact the PRSA, 33 Irving Place, New York, NY 10003-2376.) Criteria also exist to charter college and university chapters of the Public Relations Student Society of America (PRSSA–at the PRSA headquarters); and the International Association of Business Communicators (IABC; for information about student chapters, contact IABC, One Hallidie Plaza, Suite 600, San Francisco, CA 94102). There also is a codified body of knowledge and a substantial bibliography of public relations literature (see *Bibliography for Public Relations Professionals* published each year by the PRSA).

Furthermore, there is considerable consistency in the selection and adoption of textbooks by public relations educators, despite these educators' varying unit affiliation within their colleges and universities.

Much progress also has been made in reconciling programmatic differences, in great part because of the active involvement by a large number of public relations educators in a range of scholarly associations representing both journalism and speech communication as well as in practitioner-based organizations. It is common for public relations educators to be active in most, if not all, of such organizations as the AEJMC, Speech Communication Association, International Communication Association, PRSA, IABC, International Public Relations Association, and various interdisciplinary associations. Furthermore, discussion has been initiated to consider establishing an unofficial Council for Public Relations Education that may help facilitate communication and policymaking related to public relations education among these organizations.

Finally, as a generalization, journalism faculty have become far more accepting and appreciative of speech communication faculty's contributions to public relations education and scholarship, and communication faculty are more cognizant (or at least more pragmatic) about the continued need for skills courses in mass communication.

Special Considerations Determine Outcomes

In considering appropriate outcomes assessment measurements and methodologies, some special considerations must be made for public relations education. First, the responsibility of public relations educators is to prepare students for careers in professional public relations practice.

Students wanting to use the degree as a preparation for other professional education or occupations, ranging from law school to real estate brokerage to retail management or–for that matter–for careers as journalists, may have found a comprehensive major that is helpful to those pursuing different career goals; however, it is not the responsibility of public relations educators to prepare students for such careers lest public relations becomes a watered-down, generic, "general studies" degree.

Although public relations educators should applaud and strongly support contemporary efforts to enrich students' education in the liberal arts, this support should be primarily because such liberal arts education ensures higher quality public relations graduates. Public relations educators have primary responsibility for, and thus should maintain primary allegiance to, the best possible education preparing students to become public relations practitioners. These educators have a vested interest in assuring that their students are exposed to the widest and best possible liberal arts education as well as the greatest infusion of the liberal arts into the professional components of public relations education.

It also is important that public relations education is not seen as analogous to specialized education in journalism sequences such as newspaper journalism, magazine journalism, photo-journalism, broadcast/electronic media journalism or related media specializations serving specific "media" industries; there is not a public relations "industry" in the sense that there is a newspaper industry, magazine industry, broadcast industry, and so forth, which hire graduates as "line" employees.

Rather, public relations is a "staff" function in a range of virtually all businesses and industries. Granted, public relations agencies hire graduates as line employees within their firms, but such agencies' personnel serve as external staff to other organizations that are their clients. Thus, public relations must be recognized as a staff function within a range of all types of organizations, rather than as a line function within a specific media industry. This distinction suggests a functional approach to public relations education, that is, practitioners should be able to know and to do many career tasks and not be prepared for only one specific job. Given this distinction, outcomes assessment that may be appropriate for students preparing for careers within specific media industries–taught typically in the same academic units where public relations instruction is based–most often will be misapplied in public relations education. Blanchard and Christ (1993), in their book, *Media Education and the Liberal Arts: A Blueprint for the New Professionalism,* made a telling remark about business schools: "Business schools long ago eliminated industry-specific approaches, replacing them with generic cross-industry subjects such as accounting, management, finance, and marketing" (p. 70).

Public relations education is more appropriately grouped with business schools' "generic cross-industry subjects" cited by the authors, for example, accounting, management, finance and marketing, than according to "lines" in media-specific industries.

Therefore, public relations educators should applaud contemporary efforts to defocus media-centric education. Those of us who had earned our print journalism-oriented baccalaureate degrees a quarter of a century ago or longer recall entry-level public relations responsibilities performing media relations for all types of media, including writing broadcast media releases, writing scripts for slide shows, writing speeches and supervising filmstrip production, as well as performing the print-oriented public relations tasks for which we were educated; today's graduates, of course, will be working with video news releases and a range of media applications requiring far more than the traditional print journalism knowledge and skills.

Case Study: Early Outcomes Assessment Effort

The University of Northern Iowa is a comprehensive university that has a "normal school" tradition. Its Department of Communication Studies has a tradition in speech communication–although it is a comprehensive department that offers baccalaureate degrees in a range of communication majors, as well as electronic media and public relations and a minor in print journalism. It also has several "model programs"–including public relations–for students earning their master of arts degrees in communication. The department is not ACEJMC-accredited, nor is the public relations degree program CEPR-certified, although the latter is under strong consideration. However, the program fulfills the criteria for and has a chapter of the PRSSA.

The department's communication/public relations major was approved during the academic year 1977-1978, and the major began with 12 students in the following fall of 1978. It is by far the largest undergraduate major in the department, and the number of the program's baccalaureate degree holders now exceeds well over 1,000 graduates. These former students work in a wide range of career positions throughout the United States and elsewhere in the world.

The public relations curriculum, although historically quite stable, has been refined throughout the years during the university's 2-year curriculum cycles. This interdisciplinary major includes business courses (economics, marketing, consumer behavior, organizational management, and accounting); journalism courses (mass communication and society, reporting methodologies and sources, newswriting for print media, editing and design); communication courses (interpersonal, organizational, business and professional oral, communication theories, and communication research methods); and public relations (principles, public relations writing including electronic media writing, public relations methods, integrated communications, public relations cases and studies). (Global public relations will be an alternative option to integrated communications beginning fall 1996.)

Alumni of the public relations degree program report that entry-level job success has often been contingent on the *range* of knowledge and skills they possess. For example, journalism schools and many communication departments do not require business courses in their curricula; such a foundation in business, coupled with journalism courses and an applied and theoretical background in communication, in addition to a comprehensive range of public relations courses, makes these graduates highly versatile in their preparation for many different types of public relations-related positions in a wide variety of industries.

As with all the department's majors and minors, the public relations major is under an enrollment management policy. Students are prospective majors until they complete 24 hours of university coursework with at least a 2.5 grade point average (GPA), complete college writing and oral communication courses with a combined GPA of at least 2.5, complete with at least a combined 2.5 GPA the mass communication and society and the principles of public relations courses, and pass a spelling/punctuation/grammar test.

Although such admission criteria may seem elitist, failure to meet such standards that assure students' basic preparation and potential success before acceptance into the program can be viewed as exploitative of students who must face a rigorous curriculum to adequately prepare for the highly competitive public relations job market.

When asked to design a student outcomes assessment program for the communication/public relations major, faculty reacted with bemused puzzlement, followed by consternation and finally by apprehension–appreciating the truth of what Erwin (1991) had warned:

> To ignore calls for evaluation is to allow other groups to choose methods of assessment, which are sure to influence educational goals. Besides the new accrediting requirements regarding assessment, both public and private institutions should pay heed to discussions about a proposed national standardized testing program. If a nationwide program is implemented, it is unlikely that the diversities in our institutions will be retained. . . . (I)f professionals refrain from contributing, then non-professionals will go about evaluation unaided. (p. 7)

Other warnings prompted equal alarm, such as Christ and Blanchard's (1994) admonition that, if communication education programs appear to university committees to be fragmented, peripheral, or nonessential to a university's overall mission, they are more susceptible to being downsized or eliminated.

Liberal arts education is required or recommended by all bodies germane to public relations education (see Accrediting Council on Education in Journalism and Mass Communications, 1994; AEJMC Curriculum Task Force, 1996; International Public Relations Association, 1990, September). The International Public Relations Association uses concentric circles to illustrate a recommended public relations curriculum; the "largest circle represents the general liberal arts and humanities background that is essential preparation for a successful professional" (p. 2).

The *Design for Undergraduate Public Relations Education* (Commission on Undergraduate Public Relations Education, 1993) uses stacked squares to illustrate a proposed curriculum. The largest and outside-parameter, "first, main square represents the minimum credit hours required for a bachelor's degree" and the majority of the area of that square that is not covered "represents courses in liberal arts (minimum of 65 credit hours) and general education (maximum of 25 credit hours, including a minor area of concentrated study, e.g., business)–a total of 75% or 90% of the 120 credit hours requirred for graduation" (p. 28).

Such overall emphasis on liberal arts education is hardly misplaced. Public relations practitioners are expected to know a wide breadth of general knowledge, have in-depth knowledge of their professional specialization and subspecializations and be highly knowledgeable about the particular industries in which they work.

Anecdotal evidence supports a powerful correlation between successful, high-ranking public relations practitioners and their extensive knowledge that ranges from current events and history to economics and government policies.

Despite liberal arts' importance to students' undergraduate education, faculty in the program were at a loss as how to measure it for student outcomes assessment. In addition to a 47-hour general education curriculum, students also take a range of minors and second majors. Furthermore, there is a strong liberal arts component to students' required courses within the public relations curriculum. Likewise, in this multidisciplinary major, it would be difficult to determine how to overtly measure coursework in business–save for such knowledge evident from students' preparation of campaign proposals, and so forth. That is, at a rudimentary level, accounting expertise would be evident in a budget proposal, for example, as would be a basic understanding of management theory and practice. (However, certainly at the collegiate level, it was recognized that such assessment would be possible–as it is through GRE, GMAT, and LSAT testing as examples.)

Also, successful students not only obtain an extensive breadth of general knowledge through their liberal arts education and general electives, but usually through their second major, minor, or area of concentration. In addition, they may use such education to learn intensive knowledge about a specific industry or other business. Such esoteric knowledge would be difficult to measure through student outcomes assessment because of its individualized nature among the students.

Thus, somewhat by default, student outcomes assessment procedures were focused primarily on the professional component of the public relations major. Taken into account was the spirit, if not the specific criteria, of accrediting and certifying agencies. However, as noted earlier, the program is neither ACEJMC-accredited, nor is it presently CEPR-certified, although the program has a PRSSA chapter and is accountable under the "five-course" ruling to maintain such a chapter.

Particular attention was paid to the mission statements of the program, department, college, and university. And certainly, the resultant outcomes assessments reflected the professional biases of the faculty as well as consideration of alumni's experiences and students' self-perceived needs.

This has become truly a "living" document that was developed by public relations/mass communication faculty of the time and that has been subject to continual, albeit primarily minor editorial, revisions by department faculty. The first document identified eight outcomes (see Appendix A, B, and C), each with specific "competencies" students should have achieved by their time of graduation. Also, taken into primary consideration were the missions and ongoing strategic plans at the university, department and the communication/public relations undergraduate major levels; the latter mission is:

(a) to prepare students, within a liberal arts context, for positions in public relations within organizations and professional agencies; and (b) to prepare students for graduate study by providing them with foundations in mass communication theory, methodology, and related skills and knowledge. (Department of Communication Studies, undated, no page number given)

ASSESSMENT PLAN–COMMUNICATION/PUBLIC RELATIONS (Department of Communication, 1991)

Outcomes and Competencies

Outcome 1

Students will have a thorough understanding of: communication, including mass communication; such communication's role in society and in mass culture–both past and present, with insights into the future; and the role and uses of the mass media–both print and broadcast; as well as the uses of a range of specialized communication applications, including advertising, marketing and related areas. This understanding will include international and intercultural perspectives.

Competency 1.1. Students will be familiar with and articulate in: the nature of communication within mass society and mass culture; the past and present of print and electronic media, advertising, marketing and related areas, and international/multicultural communication.

Competency 1.2. Students will be familiar with and articulate in: public relations principles; public relations' historical development; the concept and dynamics of publics and public opinion; persuasion strategies, tactics, and techniques as they relate to the various models of public relations; and public relations ethics.

Competency 1.3. Students will be familiar with and articulate in: a range of appropriate historical and contemporary mass communication and public relations theoretical models.

Competency 1.4. Students will be familiar with and articulate in: the relationship between communication and public relations, particularly as this relationship is impacted by the nature, potential uses, and range of communication forms used in public relations. Students will be able to critically understand the relationship between the mass media and public relations.

Outcome 2

Students will have a thorough understanding of: professionally accepted public relations fundamentals; the vocabulary of public relations and related areas and public relations perspectives as these perspectives impact society; and the role of public relations in contemporary world society.

Competency 2.1. Students will be familiar with and articulate in: contemporary public relations literature and scholarship; contemporary issues of public relations, particularly those impacting the welfare of society; and projections and forecasts of public relations practice, particularly those impacting society. All of these competencies will be based on a thorough understanding of and appreciation for the history of public relations.

Competency 2.2. Students will be familiar with and articulate in: the nature, potential uses, and range of communication forms used in public relations.

Competency 2.3. Students will be familiar with and articulate in: public relations as a communication management function through which organizations adapt to, alter, or maintain their environments to achieve organizational goals.

Competency 2.4. Students will be familiar with and articulate in: how public relations is used to improve productivity for business, associations, government and not-for-profit organizations; how organizations can more effectively respond to regulatory initiatives and changing social trends; and how communication management can better assist in organizational strategic planning.

Outcome 3

Students will have a thorough understanding of: communication methods used by public relations practitioners and of public opinion formation and change as viewed by contemporary public relations literature and scholarship.

Competency 3.1. Students will be familiar with and articulate in: public relations formative and evaluative research methodologies; the rationale for research in public relations; and the ethical considerations related to public relations issues.

Competency 3.2. Students will be familiar with and articulate in: public relations programming, planning, decision making and executing, being able to bring to bear an analysis of research findings and an understanding of public opinion formation and change to make informed public relations management decisions. Students will be skilled in appropriate public relations and related strategy formulation.

Outcome 4

Students will have a thorough understanding of: professional mass communication and interpersonal communication skills.

Competency 4.1. Students will be familiar with and articulate in: writing and oral presentation of public relations messages as appropriate for a range of media, including those in both print and broadcast. They will be able to both write and speak at an entry-level professional proficiency.

Competency 4.2. Students will be familiar with and articulate in: identifying communication channels to send messages to specific audiences and will be able to understand and appreciate the unique characteristics of the various media.

Competency 4.3. Students will be familiar with and articulate in: the ability to explore social and cultural environments impinging on organizations, including multicultural perspectives.

Competency 4.4. Students will be familiar with and articulate in: the complexities of programming accountable objectives for themselves and for other organizational managers.

Competency 4.5. Students will be familiar with and articulate in: recognizing trends affecting channels of communication in society.

Competency 4.6. Students will be familiar with and articulate in: exploring the organizational as well as the professional responsibilities of public relations practitioners.

Outcome 5

Students will have a thorough understanding of: the overall synthesis of public relations concepts; ethical considerations and the appropriate resolution of ethical dilemmas; and public relations problem resolution.

Competency 5.1. Students will be familiar with and articulate in: general management theories and literature, including financial management; and will be able to communicate with and work together in managerial problem resolution with other managers within their organizations.

Competency 5.2. Students will be familiar with and articulate in: general management theories and the management literature's particular application to public relations problems and cases; working as a management team member, together with other organizational executives, to resolve public relations and other management problems; and formulating overall management strategies. Students will be prepared to be organizational management officers, fulfilling a critical staff role–that of public relations officers and executives–within their organizations.

Outcome 6

Students will have a thorough understanding of: the various theories of mass communication and interpersonal communication and of their applications for public relations.

Competency 6.1. Students will be familiar with and articulate in: flexible theoretical thinking as it relates to communication, being able to comprehend, select, and convincingly argue theoretical positions.

Competency 6.2. Students will be familiar with and articulate in: their own theoretical disposition and will be able to compare and contrast the many applicable communication theories relevant to public relations.

Outcome 7

Students will have a thorough understanding of: appropriate communication research principles, concepts, and procedures, particularly as they can be applied in public relations planning, but also in the broader societal context.

Competency 7.1. Students will be familiar with and articulate in: their critical and analytical abilities in research design and data analysis.

Competency 7.2. Students will be familiar with and articulate in: their marketable knowledge for professional public relations practice and for future graduate study.

Outcome 8

Students will have a thorough understanding of: the exigencies of the professional public relations working environment.
    Competency 8.1. Students will be familiar with and articulate in: professional office protocol and regimen.
    Competency 8.2. Students will be familiar with and articulate in: portfolio and résumé construction and evaluation.
    Competency 8.3. Students will be familiar with and articulate in: professional evaluation and review techniques and self-evaluation.

OPERATIONALIZING MEASUREMENTS IS THE CHALLENGE

Of course, operationalizing, that is, providing measurements for, these outcomes and competencies has been the real challenge. Obviously, a longitudinal study is called for, as well as constant monitoring of students throughout their undergraduate careers. Assessment remains ongoing and on a virtual continuum, with the continuum beginning when students enter the major, proceeding throughout their undergraduate careers up to the time of graduation and then periodically throughout their professional careers.

The student outcomes assessment plan relies heavily on students' portfolios. Students are formally counseled in the Principles of Public Relations class about how to begin building their portfolios. Students are encouraged throughout their careers to continue to build their portfolios, with evidence of work from internships and cooperative education experiences, relevant summer and part-time employment as well as work in PRSSA and the student-run public relations firm.

Immediately preceding graduation, students in the program historically have been assessed by professional public relations practitioners in the capstone class, Public Relations: Cases and Studies.

Historically, an orally presented final case study is evaluated by professional public relations practitioners as well as by peers and instructors, and professionals and students attending these final presentations also examine and evaluate students' résumés and portfolios. Although students keep their portfolios (and are encouraged to keep them updated throughout their professional careers), evaluation forms of their work provide an "audit trail."

Traditionally, careers of the program's graduates have been assessed during the 5-year department program review; during interim periods through surveys; and, as well as informally, through content analysis of graduates' correspondence and conversations with faculty.

Changes undoubtedly will occur in this student outcomes assessment program as public relations faculty become more sophisticated in the usage of student outcomes assessment and as accrediting body and university requirements change. However, our research has shown substantive agreement with the final product among all responsible parties; we have achieved overall consensus and have developed an outcomes assessment plan based on this consensus.

Student outcomes assessment is a mandate, but such evaluation also has proven to be an opportunity to better measure the educational accomplishments of students as well as a means for program improvement.

What outcomes assessment will do for public relations education is what it undoubtedly was intended to do for educational institutions and programs in general. Within a professional community of public relations educators and practitioners, immediate deliberation must continue to better determine what public relations is, what are appropriate definitional parameters, what knowledge and skills practitioners must have and what are suitable (i.e., valid and reliable) measurements to determine whether a student is learning such knowledge and skills.

Public relations educators collectively and together with public relations practitioners should continue a dialogue about outcomes for public relations students and how to assess such outcomes. It is certainly true that, if we do not do this collectively and with solidarity, others may do it for us.

APPENDIX A: ASSESSMENT PLAN–COMMUNICATION/PUBLIC RELATIONS

Outcomes and Commission and IPRA Criteria Include:

Outcome 1–Students will have a thorough understanding of: communication, including mass communication; such communication's role in society and in mass culture–both past and present, with insights into the future; and the role and uses of the mass media–both print and broadcast; as well as the uses of a range of specialized communication applications, including advertising, marketing and related areas. This understanding will include international and intercultural perspectives.

Satisfies
Commission: A. 2.   **Historical/Institutional**
                          A. 3.   **Communication Process/Structure**

Satisfies IPRA: A. 1.   **Theory and Process of**
                                   Communication
                          A. 2.   **Advertising**

Outcome 2–Students will have a thorough understanding of: professionally accepted public relations fundamentals; the vocabulary of public relations and related areas and public relations perspectives as these perspectives impact upon society; and the role of public relations in contemporary world society.

Satisfies
Commission: B. 1.   **Principles, Practices and Theory**
                                   of Public Relations

APPENDIX A   (Continued)

Satisfies IPRA: B. 1. Origins and Principles of Public
                              Relations
                      B. 2. The Public Relations Field
                      B. 3. Public Relations Specializations

Outcome 3–Students will have a thorough understanding of: communication methods used by public relations practitioners and of public opinion formation and change as viewed by contemporary public relations literature and scholarship.

Satisfies
Commission: B. 4. Public Relations Strategy and
                              Implementation

Satisfies IPRA: B. 5   Public Relations Planning
                      B. 7   Public Relations
                              Action/Implementation
                      B. 8   Public Relations Communication

Outcome 4–Students will have a thorough understanding of: professional mass communication and interpersonal communication skills.

Satisfies
Commission: A. 1   Technical Production
                      B. 2   Public Relations Techniques:
                              Writing, Message Dissemination,
                              and Media Networks
                      B. 4. Public Relations Strategy and
                              Implementation

Satisfies IPRA: A. 6   Graphics of Communication
                      A. 7   Editing
                      A. 8   Writing for Mass Media

Outcome 5–Students will have a thorough understanding of: the overall synthesis of public relations concepts; ethical considerations and the appropriate resolution of ethical dilemmas; and public relations problem resolution.

Satisfies
Commission: B. 1   Principles, Practices and Theory
                              of Public Relations

Satisfies IPRA: A. 3   Media Law and Ethics
                      B. 6   Public Relations Ethics and Law

APPENDIX A (Continued)

Outcome 6–Students will have a thorough understanding of: the various theories of mass communication and interpersonal communication and of their applications for public relations.

Satisfies
Commission: **A. 3**   **Communication Process/Structure**

Satisfies IPRA: **A. 1**   **Theory and Process of Communication**

Outcome 7–Students will have a thorough understanding of: appropriate communication research principles, concepts, and procedures, particularly as they can be applied in public relations planning, but also in the broader societal context.

Satisfies
Commission: **B. 3**   **Public Relations Research for Planning and Evaluation**

Satisfies IPRA: **A. 4**   **Research**
                     A. 5.   **Media Analysis**
                     B. 4   **Public Relations Research**
                     B. 9   **Public Relations Performance Evaluation/Measurement**

Outcome 8–Students will have a thorough understanding of: the exigencies of the professional public relations working environment.

Satisfies
Commission: **B. 5**   **Supervised Public Relations Experience**
                     B. 6   **Specialized Advanced Study**

Satisfies IPRA: **B. 2**   **The Public Relations Field**

NOTE: The outcomes in toto cover all criteria of the Commission and of IPRA, i.e.:

Satisfies Commission: **A. 1-3; B. 1-6.**

Satisfies IPRA: **A. 1-8; B. 1-9**

PRSA requirements for a PRSSA Charter and ACEJMC requirements can be collapsed into the criteria of the Commission and IPRA.

APPENDIX A (Continued)

Note. A Public Relations Student Society of America charter requires at least five courses in public relations supplemented by courses allied to this field of study, i.e., public relations. The parent body, the Public Relations Society of America, subscribes to the subject areas and credit hours identified by the 1987 Commission on Undergraduate Public Relations Education. Areas of study for this charter specifically includes B. 1-5, omitting 6. Specialized Advance Study.

Note. Accrediting Council on Eduation in Journalism and Mass Communications (1994, pp. 19-20).

(Theoretical instruction and practical laboratory experiences should be provided in the basic skills and writing, reporting, editing, visual communication, layout and design, and other fundamental techniques appropriate for such specialties as advertising, public relations, and broadcasting. Whatever the specialization, the skills work should be offered in a context of philosophical instruction in such areas as history, law, ethics, and mass communications theory.)

APPENDIX B: ASSESSMENT PLAN–
COMMUNICATION/PUBLIC RELATIONS

Commission Criteria and Outcomes that Require These Criteria:

The Design for Undergraduate Public Relations Education (1993, pp. 21-27).

II.   Professional Education

A.   Studies in Communication
   1.   Technical/Production
      a.   Copy Preparation and Editing
      b.   Graphic Arts and Typography
      c.   Still Photography
      d.   Production for Electronic Media
      e.   Public Speaking and Oral Presentation

Outcome 4–Students will have a thorough understanding of: professional mass communication and interpersonal communication skills.

   2.   Historical/Institutional

Outcome 1–Students will have a thorough understanding of: communication, including mass communication; such communication's role in society and in mass culture–both past and present, with insights into the future; and the role and uses of the mass media–both print and broadcast; as well as the uses of a range of specialized communication applications, including advertising, marketing and related areas. This understanding will include international and

APPENDIX B (Continued)

intercultural perspectives.

3. Communication Process/Structure

Outcome 1–Students will have a thorough understanding of: communication, including mass communication; such communication's role in society and in mass culture–both past and present, with insights into the future; and the role and uses of the mass media–both print and broadcast; as well as the uses of a range of specialized communication applications, including advertising, marketing and related areas. This understanding will include international and intercultural perspectives.

Outcome 6–Students will have a thorough understanding of: the various theories of mass communication and interpersonal communication and of their applications for public relations.

B. Studies in Public Relations

1. Principles, Practices and Theory of Public Relations

Outcome 2–Students will have a thorough understanding of: professionally accepted public relations fundamentals; the vocabulary of public relations and related areas and public relations perspectives as these perspectives impact upon society; and the role of public relations in contemporary world society.

Outcome 5–Students will have a thorough understanding of: the overall synthesis of public relations concepts; ethical considerations and the appropriate resolution of ethical dilemmas; and public relations problem resolution.

2. Public Relations Techniques: Writing, Message Dissemination and Media Networks

Outcome 4–Students will have a thorough understanding of: professional mass communication and interpersonal communication skills.

3. Public Relations Research for Planning and Evaluation

Outcome 7–Students will have a thorough understanding of: appropriate communication research principles, concepts, and procedures, particularly as they can be applied in public relations planning, but also in the broader societal context.

APPENDIX B (Continued)

4. Public Relations Strategy and Implementation

Outcome 3–Students will have a thorough understanding of: communication methods used by public relations practitioners and of public opinion formation and change as viewed by contemporary public relations literature and scholarship.

5. Supervised Public Relations Experience

Outcome 8–Students will have a thorough understanding of: the exigencies of the professional public relations working environment.

6. Specialized Advance Study

Outcome 8–Students will have a thorough understanding of: the exigencies of the professional public relations working environment.

APPENDIX C: ASSESSMENT PLAN– COMMUNICATION/PUBLIC RELATIONS

IPRA Criteria and Outcomes that Require These Criteria:

Public Relations Education–Recommendations and Standards, IPRA Gold Paper No. 7, September 1990, pp. 2 and 28-30.

II. General Field of Communication

A. Theory and Process of Communication

Outcome 1–Students will have a thorough understanding of: communication, including mass communication; such communication's role in society and in mass culture–both past and present, with insights into the future; and the role and uses of the mass media–both print and broadcast; as well as the uses of a range of specialized communication applications, including advertising, marketing and related areas. This understanding will include international and intercultural perspectives.

Outcome 6–Students will have a thorough understanding of: the various theories of mass communication and interpersonal communication and of their applications for public relations.

B. Advertising

Outcome 1–Students will have a thorough understanding of: communication, including mass communication; such communication's role in society and in mass culture–both past and present, with insights into the future; and the role

APPENDIX C (Continued)

and uses of the mass media–both print and broadcast; as well as the uses of a range of specialized communication applications, including advertising, marketing and related areas. This understanding will include international and intercultural perspectives.

C. Media Law and Ethics

Outcome 5–Students will have a thorough understanding of: the overall synthesis of public relations concepts; ethical considerations and the appropriate resolution of ethical dilemmas; and public relations problem resolution.

D. Research

Outcome 7–Students will have a thorough understanding of: appropriate communication research principles, concepts, and procedures, particularly as they can be applied in public relations planning, but also in the broader societal context.

E. Media Analysis

Outcome 7–Students will have a thorough understanding of: appropriate communication research principles, concepts, and procedures, particularly as they can be applied in public relations planning, but also in the broader societal context.

F. Graphics of Communication

Outcome 4–Students will have a thorough understanding of: professional mass communication and interpersonal communication skills.

G. Editing

Outcome 4–Students will have a thorough understanding of: professional mass communication and interpersonal communication skills.

H. Writing for Mass Media

Outcome 4–Students will have a thorough understanding of: professional mass communication and interpersonal communication skills.

APPENDIX C (Continued)

III.   Theory and Practice of Public Relations

A.   Origins and Principles of Public Relations

Outcome 2–Students will have a thorough understanding of: professionally accepted public relations fundamentals; the vocabulary of public relations and related areas and public relations perspectives as these perspectives impact upon society; and the role of public relations in contemporary world society.

B.   The Public Relations Field

Outcome 2–Students will have a thorough understanding of: professionally accepted public relations fundamentals; the vocabulary of public relations and related areas and public relations perspectives as these perspectives impact upon society; and the role of public relations in contemporary world society.

Outcome 8–Students will have a thorough understanding of: the exigencies of the professional public relations working environment.

C.   Public Relations Specializations

Outcome 2–Students will have a thorough understanding of: professionally accepted public relations fundamentals; the vocabulary of public relations and related areas and public relations perspectives as these perspectives impact upon society; and the role of public relations in contemporary world society.

D.   Public Relations Research

Outcome 7–Students will have a thorough understanding of: appropriate communication research principles, concepts, and procedures, particularly as they can be applied in public relations planning, but also in the broader societal context.

E.   Public Relations Planning

Outcome 3–Students will have a thorough understanding of: communication methods used by public relations practitioners and of public opinion formation and change as viewed by contemporary public relations literature and scholarship.

F.   Public Relations Ethics and Law

Outcome 5–Students will have a thorough understanding of: the overall synthesis of public relations concepts; ethical considerations and the appropriate resolution of ethical dilemmas; and public relations problem resolution.

APPENDIX C (Continued)

G. Public Relations Action/Implementation

Outcome 3–Students will have a thorough understanding of: communication methods used by public relations practitioners and of public opinion formation and change as viewed by contemporary public relations literature and scholarship.

H. Public Relations Communication

Outcome 3–Students will have a thorough understanding of: communication methods used by public relations practitioners and of public opinion formation and change as viewed by contemporary public relations literature and scholarship.

I. Public Relations Performance Evaluation/Measurement

Outcome 7–Students will have a thorough understanding of: appropriate communication research principles, concepts, and procedures, particularly as they can be applied in public relations planning, but also in the broader societal context.

REFERENCES

Accrediting Council on Education in Journalism and Mass Communications. (1994). *Accredited journalism and mass communications education: 1994-95.* Columbia, SC: Author.

Anderson, C. W. (1993). *Prescribing the life of the mind: An essay on the purpose of the university, the aims of liberal education, the competence of citizens, and the cultivation of practical reason.* Madison: The University of Wisconsin Press.

AEJMC Curriculum Task Force (AEJMC). (1996). Responding to the challenge of change. *Journalism and Mass Communication Educator, 50*(4), 101-119.

Bernays, E. L. (1923). *Crystallizing public opinion.* New York: Boni-Liveright.

Bernays, E. L. (1961). *Crystallizing public opinion.* New York: Liveright Publishing.

Blanchard, R. O., & Christ, W. G. (1993). *Media education and the liberal arts: A blueprint for the new professionalism.* Hillsdale, NJ: Lawrence Erlbaum Associates.

Christ, W. G., & Blanchard, R. O. (1994). Mission statements, outcomes, and the new liberal arts. In W. G. Christ (Ed.), *Assessing communication education: A handbook for media, speech, and theatre educators* (pp. 31-55). Hillsdale, NJ: Lawrence Erlbaum Associates.

Commission on Undergraduate Public Relations Education. (1993). *Design for undergraduate public relations education.* (reissued) New York: Public Relations Society of America.

Damrosch, D. (1995). *We scholars: Changing the culture of the university.* Cambridge, MA: Harvard University Press.

Department of Communication Studies. (Undated). *Mission statement. Undergraduate major in communication/public relations.* Cedar Falls: University of Northern Iowa, Department of Communication Studies.

Department of Communication Studies. (1991). *Assessment plan–communi-cation/public relations.* Cedar Falls: University of Northern Iowa Department of Communication Studies.

Douglas, G. H. (1992). *Education without impact: How our universities fail the young.* New York: Birch Lane Press.

Duncan, T., Caywood, C., & Newsom, D. (1993). *Preparing advertising and public relations students for the communications industry in the 21st century.* A report of the Task Force on Integrated Communications. Columbia, SC: AEJMC.

Emery, M., & Emery, E. (1988). *The press and America: An interpretive history of the mass media.* Englewood Cliffs, NJ: Prentice-Hall.

Erwin, T. D. (1991). *Assessing student learning and development: A guide to the principles, goals, and methods of determining college outcomes.* San Francisco: Jossey-Bass.

Gilley, J. W. (1991). *Thinking about higher education: The 1990s and beyond.* New York: Macmillan Publishing.

Grunig, J. E., & Hunt, T. (1984). *Managing public relations.* New York: Holt, Rinehart & Winston.

Grunig, J. E., & White, R. (1992). The effect of worldviews on public relations theory and practice. In J. E. Grunig (Ed.), *Excellence in public relations and communication management* (pp. 31-64). Hillsdale, NJ: Lawrence Erlbaum Associates.

International Public Relations Association. (1990, September). *Public relations education–recommendations and standards: Gold paper no. 7.* Geneva, Switzerland: Author.

Jacoby, R. (1994). *Dogmatic wisdom: How the culture wars divert education and distract America.* Garden City, NY: Doubleday.

Kerr, C., Gade, M. L., & Kawaoka, M. (1994). *Troubled times for American higher education: The 1990s and beyond.* Albany: State University of New York Press.

Kruckeberg, D., & Starck, K. (1988). *Public relations and community: A reconstructed theory.* New York: Praeger.

Millard, R. M. (1991). *Today's myths and tomorrow's realities: Overcoming obstacles to academic leadership in the 21st century.* San Francisco: Jossey-Bass.

O'Dwyer, J. (1993, July). *O'Dwyer's PR Services,* 7(7), pp. 1, 5-9, 15.

Robinson, E. J. (1966). *Communication and public relations.* Columbus, OH: Merrill.

Rosenbaum, J. (1994). Assessment: An overview. In W. G. Christ (Ed.), *Assessing communication education: A handbook for media, speech & theatre educators* (pp. 3-29). Hillsdale, NJ: Lawrence Erlbaum Associates.

Sadovnik, A. R. (1994). *Equity and excellence in higher education: The decline of a liberal educational reform.* New York: Peter Lang.

Sclove, R. E. (1995). *Democracy and technology.* New York: Guilford.

Shore, P. (1992). *The myth of the university: Ideal and reality in higher education.* Lanham, MD: University Press of America.

Simpson, R. D., & Frost, S. H. (1993). *Inside college: Undergraduate education for the future.* New York: Plenum.

Tierney, W. G. (1993). *Building communities of difference: Higher education in the twenty-first century.* Westport, CT: Bergin & Garvey.

Walshok, M. L. (1995). *Knowledge without boundaries: What America's research universities can do for the economy, the workplace, and the community.* San Francisco: Jossey-Bass.

15

Advertising

Edd Applegate
Middle Tennessee State University

Undergraduate advertising education has changed over the years, since the first course that included information about advertising was offered more than 100 years ago, and it will continue to change.

Change for all areas of journalism and mass communications was called for in *Planning for Curricular Change in Journalism Education: Project on the Future of Journalism and Mass Communication Education* (Oregon Report), which was published in 1984. Change for advertising and public relations education specifically was called for in *Preparing Advertising and Public Relations Students for the Communications Industry in the 21st Century: A Report of the Task Force on Integrated Communication* (Duncan, Clarke, & Newsom, 1993). Assessing the undergraduate advertising curriculum will be difficult in this climate of change. However, by examining (a) advertising education's history, (b) the development of its curriculum, and (c) the latter report mentioned earlier, this chapter proposes specific curricula in advertising education, then concludes with a description of assessment criteria appropriate for the proposed curricula.

HISTORY OF ADVERTISING EDUCATION

Proposals for the Creation of Journalism Programs

The early programs in journalism were based on one of several proposals. The proposal by General Robert E. Lee, who had been the leader of the Confederate Army during the Civil War, was for the first academic program in journalism. In 1869 Lee, who had become president of Washington College (Washington and Lee University) in Virginia, proposed to the college's board of trustees to allow the institution to offer 50 scholarships to young men who desired to become journalists. Lee's proposal would allow young men the opportunity to study the technical aspects of printing. Although the proposal was adopted, the curriculum was not put into effect (*The Training of Journalists: A World-Wide Survey on the Training of Personnel for the Mass Media*, 1958).

Another proposal was by Joseph Pulitzer (1904). Pulitzer, who had become an extremely successful publisher and editor, had desired to endow a school of journalism. He expressed his position on education for journalism in an article that appeared in the *North American Review*. Pulitzer described a program that focused on style, law tailored for the journalist, ethics, literature, truth and accuracy, history tailored for the journalist, sociology, economics, "the enemies of the republic," arbitration in its broad sense, statistics, modern languages, especially French and German, science, the study of newspapers, the power of ideas, principles of journalism, and the news (pp. 641-680). In short, Pulitzer recommended a program that "emphasized editorial training in the collection and dissemination of news, with major stress placed on the social sciences. Courses dealing with the business aspect of newspaper publishing were to be carefully avoided" (Sutton, 1945, p. 13).

Another proposal was made by Dr. Charles W. Eliot, president of Harvard University, in 1903. Eliot, who had learned of Pulitzer's interest in funding a school of journalism, designed a curriculum that stressed the business side of journalism, as the following courses illustrate: Newspaper Administration (the organization of a newspaper office and functions of various departments and services); Newspaper Administration (study of printing presses and other mechanical devices used in publishing); The Law of Journalism; Ethics of Journalism; History of Journalism; The Literary Form of Newspapers (approved usage in punctuation, spelling, abbreviations, typography, etc.); Reinforcement of Existing Departments of Instruction for Benefit of Students in Journalism (background courses coordinated with journalism) (Lee, 1918, p. 13).

Because of Eliot's emphasis on the business aspects of journalism, Harvard University did not receive Pulitzer's endowment. Columbia University was honored instead. Nonetheless, Eliot's plan, which had emphasized a "practical" education but which was not enacted at Harvard, was adopted at other universities (see Table 15.1).

Today, the curriculum of journalism at most schools of journalism and/or mass communications has combined the two philosophies. Even programs in advertising have embraced these concepts in the kinds of courses offered.

Journalism Programs That Included Advertising

Advertising education has been connected with business, specifically marketing, and journalism from its beginning in 1893, when Joseph Johnson of the Wharton School of Business, University of Pennsylvania, developed one of the earliest curricula in journalism in the country, primarily to train individuals who desired to work as reporters for newspapers. This curriculum contained five courses in journalism, and one of these courses–Journalism-Law of Libel, Business Management, Typographical Union, Cost and Revenue, Advertising, Method of Criticism, an so on–contained information about advertising (O'Dell, 1935).

TABLE 15.1
Proposals For The Creation Of Journalism Programs

Date	Who	Proposal
1869	Robert E. Lee Washington College (Washington & Lee U.)	Proposed a program in printing. (Did not include advertising.) Aborted.
1875	Andrew Dickson White Cornell University	Proposed a program in journalism. (Did not include advertising.) Aborted.
1895	Bessie Tift College	Proposed a program in journalism. (Did not include advertising.) Program offered years later.
1903	Joseph Pulitzer	Proposed a program in journalism. (Did not include advertising.)
1903	Charles W. Eliot Harvard University	Proposed a program in journalism. (Included advertising.) Aborted.

In 1898 the University of Missouri, which had been offering courses in journalism for at least 2 decades, offered a course in journalism–Newspaper Making–that provided information about advertising (O'Dell, 1935, p. 89).

Four years later, the Department of Rhetoric and Oratory offered the first course in journalism at the University of Illinois. Part of the course focused on advertising (O'Dell, 1935).

In 1908 Walter Williams was named dean of the country's first school of journalism at the University of Missouri. Williams mentioned advertising in *The Journalists' Creed*, "I believe that advertising, news, editorial columns should alike serve the best interests of the readers; that a single standard of helpful truth and cleanness should prevail for all; that the supreme test of good journalism is the measure of its public service" (*University of Missouri Bulletin*, 1930, p. 2).

Needless to say, advertising became part of the school's curriculum, with Advertising and Publishing, which was offered in 1908, as the school's first course in advertising (Williams, 1929).

Courses in advertising continued to flourish in journalism schools. For instance, in 1927, 18 of the 20 schools of journalism offered courses in advertising. Ten years later, 30 of the 32 schools of journalism offered courses in advertising (Ford, 1947; see Table 15.2).

Business Programs That Included Marketing/Advertising

Although several schools of business existed before 1900, courses in marketing were not offered until 1902. According to Maynard (1941, p. 382), the first

TABLE 15.2
Programs That Included Advertising

Date	Who	Proposal
1893	Joseph Johnson Wharton School U. of Pennsylvania	Advertising as one part of one course in a five course proposal.
1838	U. of Missouri	Advertising as one part of one course in a three course proposal.
1902	U. of Illinois	Advertising as one part of one course in a one course proposal.
1908	School of Journalism U. of Missouri	Advertising as one course in a ten course proposal.

course, The Distributive and Regulative Industries of the United States, was offered by the Economics Department of the University of Michigan in 1902. The description of the course appeared in the university's catalog:

> This course which alternates with Course 34, will include a description of the various ways of marketing goods, of the classification grades, brands, employed, and of the wholesale and retail trade. Attention will also be given to those private organizations, not connected with money and banking, which guide and control the industrial process, such as trade associations, boards of trade, and chambers of commerce. (Maynard, 1941, p. 383)

Litman (1950, p. 220), on the other hand, claimed that the course, The Technique of Trade and Commerce, which he taught in 1902 at the University of California, was one of the first courses in marketing. Litman also claimed that a similar course was offered the same year at the University of Illinois. One of the first courses with marketing in its title was The Marketing of Products, which was offered at the Wharton School of Business, University of Pennsylvania, in 1904. The course emphasized advertising and publicity, as the following description from the university's catalog illustrates: "The methods now practiced in the organization and conduct of the selling branch of industrial and mercantile business. The principal subjects in the field are publicity, agency, advertising, forms and correspondence, credit and collections, and terms of sale" (Maynard, 1941, p. 383).

The Ohio State University offered courses in marketing as early as 1904; in 1907 it offered Mercantile Institutions, a course that included advertising, as the description from the specific bulletin on Business Administration and Social Science illustrates:

This course considers mercantile organization from two points of view:
(1) The evolution of mercantile organizations in the United States and
their relation to each other; the origin and development of the various
mercantile institutions with special reference to the economic conditions
which brought them into existence and perpetuated them. The various
methods of marketing goods, and the functions of the various distributors,
manufacturers, manufacturers' agents, brokers, jobbers, travelling
salesmen, etc. Advertising, its psychological laws, its economic importance and the changes it has introduced in selling goods. The work of
stock and produce exchanges. (2) The internal or administrative
organization of mercantile concerns. A study of the divisions and subdivisions of mercantile concerns and the relation of the various
departments to each other and to the whole. The systems in use of
recording and preserving data. (Hagerty, 1936, p. 21)

In 1909 the Harvard School of Business Administration offered the course
Commercial Organization and Methods, which included advertising (Hagerty,
1936).

As more schools of business opened, more courses in marketing were offered.
These courses included advertising as part of their subject matter. The first
course devoted exclusively to advertising was offered by New York University in
1905 (Maynard, 1941).

In 1908 Advertising and Salesmanship was offered by Northwestern
University. A year later, Psychology of Business, Advertising and Salesmanship
was offered and was taught by Walter Dill Scott, the president of the university
(Maynard, 1941).

Courses in advertising were offered by other universities in the years
following. The first program in advertising was developed by the School of
Journalism at the University of Missouri in 1908 (*University of Missouri
Bulletin*, 1959). The first department to include advertising in its title was the
Department of Advertising and Marketing at New York University (*Advertising
Age*, 1963). This department was started in 1915 (see Table 15.3).

Before 1959, the year Frank C. Pierson's *The Education of American
Business* was published, courses as well as programs in advertising were found
in schools of business and schools of journalism. Pierson's study, which had
been sponsored by the Carnegie Foundation, examined the various disciplines,
including marketing, offered by schools of business and recommended that
courses in advertising be excluded from the undergraduate curriculum. After the
study had been read by academicians, action regarding the curriculum was taken
at several schools of business. For instance, by 1963 at least 13 schools of
business had discontinued their programs in advertising. By 1964, other schools
of business that had programs in advertising had discontinued more than 60
courses in advertising. Some of these courses included: Advertising Plans and
Campaigns; Buying, Selling Printed Advertising Media; Creative Advertising;
Media Methods; Social Responsibility of Advertising; Radio-TV Advertising
(Ross, 1965).

TABLE 15.3
Programs That Included Marketing/Advertising

Date	Who	Proposal
1881	U. of Pennsylvania	Wharton School of Finance & Economics
1898	U. of California	School of Business founded
1898	U. of Chicago	School of Business founded
1902	U. of Michigan	Marketing as one part of one course in economics
1902	U. of California	Marketing as one part of one course in economics
1902	U. of Illinois	Marketing as one part of one course in economics
1904	U. of Pennsylvania	Marketing as one course in the Wharton School
1904	Ohio State U.	Marketing as one course in the College of Commerce and Administration
1905	New York U.	Advertising as one course
1908	Northwestern U.	Advertising as one course
1908	U. of Missouri	Program in advertising founded
1909	Harvard U.	Advertising as one part of one course in marketing in the Graduate School of Business Administration
1915	New York U.	Department of Advertising & Marketing founded

Subsequently, some of these programs in advertising were adopted by schools of journalism and/or mass communications.

In 1965 Ross found that 77 institutions had programs in advertising. Of this figure, 36 were in schools of journalism and/or mass communications, and 27 were in schools of business. Fourteen were administered jointly between the two schools.

In 1990 Ross claimed that among the 111 institutions with programs in advertising, 98 were located in schools of journalism and/or mass communications, and 11 were in schools of business; two were administered jointly between the two schools (Ross, 1991).

This trend continues. Of the more than 120 institutions with programs in advertising, only a few of the programs are located in schools of business (Ross & Johnson, 1993).

THE DEVELOPMENT OF THE ADVERTISING CURRICULUM

Accreditation guidelines in journalism and business emphasize two very distinct philosophies of advertising education. According to the Accrediting Council on Education in Journalism and Mass Communications (ACEJMC), in order for a program in journalism education, including advertising, to receive accreditation, "students in units on the semester system must take a minimum of 90 semester hours in courses outside the major area of journalism and mass communications, with no fewer than 65 semester hours in the basic liberal arts and sciences" (*Accredited Journalism and Mass Communication Education: 1993-94*, 1993, p. 15). The Accrediting Council does not accredit specific sequences; rather, it accredits colleges, schools, or departments. The American Assembly of Collegiate Schools of Business (AACSB) is similar in that it accredits schools of business, not specific programs such as advertising. However, the AACSB allows students to earn more credit in their major discipline, including advertising, than does the ACEJMC. In short, an emphasis in liberal arts and sciences is not as important to the AACSB as it is to the ACEJMC (*1990-92 Accreditation Council Policies, Procedures, and Standards*, 1990).

After courses in advertising had been offered for several years, members of several professional organizations investigated the curriculum. In 1912, for instance, the Associated Advertising Clubs of America created a Committee on Standard Qualifications of an Advertising Man. Among the Committee's recommendations was that every student who desired to work in advertising should study psychology as it controlled advertising. Although members of committees of certain professional organizations recommended from time to time specifics about the curriculum in advertising, few academicians voiced any concern until the 1950s.

In 1955 C. H. Sandage, former professor of advertising at the University of Illinois, expressed his views about the advertising curriculum. Sandage believed that too many courses in advertising focused on skills, not "on the 'why' of advertising in its business and social environment" (1955, p. 209). He claimed that a university would be wise to offer few specific courses in advertising. He wrote, "Schools that have an advertising curriculum might limit specific advertising courses to a range of 10 to 12% of the student's total university program" (1955, p. 210). Sandage claimed that these courses should be a mixture of "why" and "how," and that they should be offered during the student's junior and senior years. He also advised that the student should be required to take electives in the humanities, sciences (social and natural), and business.

In 1959 Vernon Fryburger, who chaired the Advertising Department at Northwestern University, told members of the Central Region of the American Association of Advertising Agencies, "The young man going into advertising should be broadly educated in the arts, the sciences, and the humanities" (1959,

p. 14). Fryburger then presented Northwestern's curriculum for students majoring in advertising (see Table 15.4).

TABLE 15.4
A Liberal Education for Advertising

32% Professional:	12% Advertising
	10% Journalism and Mass Communication
	10% Marketing and Business Administration
68% Liberal Arts:	10% Natural Sciences and Mathematics
	14% Literature and Composition
	18% History, Philosophy, Art
	26% Social Sciences

Northwestern's curriculum emphasized the liberal arts primarily because the advertising program was in the School of Journalism, which was accredited, and the accrediting body placed an emphasis on the liberal arts.

The same year one of the first studies concerned with the advertising curriculum was conducted by Link and Dykes (1959), who examined various institutional catalogs as well as surveyed various programs. Based on their observations and returns they presented A Typical Advertising Curriculum, which totaled 15 hours (see Table 15.5).

TABLE 15.5
A Typical Advertising Curriculum

Course	Hours
Advertising (survey course)	3
Copy and/or Layout	3
Newspaper Advertising or Retail Advertising	3
Radio and Television Advertising	3
National Advertising or Advertising Campaigns	3

The same year Richard McGarrity asked 426 advertising professionals in Milwaukee to rate based on value certain courses offered by advertising programs. McGarrity (1959, p. 51) learned the following (see Table 15.6).

In 1960 Allen conducted a study for the American Academy of Advertising and found the following courses to be the most often offered (listed in descending order of appearance): Principles (survey course), Copy and Layout, Campaigns, Media, Problems, Radio and/or TV, and Retail Advertising (1960, pp. 2-7.)

Two years later Allen (1962) surveyed 35 programs of advertising and learned that the average program required 13.5 semester hours in advertising, 13.3 in journalism, and 6.2 in marketing. Allen also learned that professors of advertising desired a curriculum of 15.5 semester hours in advertising, 10.8 in journalism, and 7.3 in marketing.

TABLE 15.6
Rated Value in Relative Percentage

Course	Important	Desirable	Unimportant	Total
Principles of Advertising	83	13	4	100
Copy Writing	71	26	3	100
Advertising Campaigns	57	34	9	100
Advertising Media	52	38	10	100
Advertising Research	50	43	7	100
Layout	49	40	11	100
Typography	30	50	20	100

These early studies' findings, especially the hours in advertising, seem to respect the wishes of Sandage and other academicians.

In 1965 Ross surveyed every university that had a program in advertising and learned which courses were offered by 90 programs, as shown in Table 15.7.

TABLE 15.7
Frequency of Course Titles

Course	Frequency
Principles (survey course)	83
Copy and/or Layout	75
Radio and/or TV Advertising	44
Newspaper Advertising	33
Advertising Campaigns	26
Retail Advertising	24
Advertising Media and Markets	24
Advertising Problems	22
Advertising Production	19
Advanced Advertising	16
Advertising Management	12
Advertising Research	8
Advertising Practice and Procedures	8
Advertising Agencies	8
Creative Advertising	5
Industrial Advertising	5
Psychology of Advertising	5
Advertising Selling	5

Several of these courses were comparable to the courses listed in previous studies, including McGarrity's, and illustrate that the typical curriculum in advertising, like other aspects of journalism and/or mass communications, was based on the proposals by Pulitzer and Eliot. That is, certain courses emphasized theory, and other courses emphasized skills. The few programs that existed in schools of business were similar; however, fewer courses in the creative area of advertising were offered. The reason for few, if any, courses in the creative area of advertising was as a result of the Pierson study as well as the AACSB accreditation guidelines, which deterred such courses.

In 1973, Moore and Leckenby surveyed 200 professors of advertising, 200 advertising agency practitioners, and 40 advertising majors about to graduate to determine their view toward advertising education. Eighty-seven professors, 71 executives, and 40 students responded. Although the groups differed slightly on several aspects, they differed greatly on whether one needed to study advertising to have a successful career in the field (1973, p. 7). The authors also had each group rate various courses in advertising that had been separated into three categories: Institutional Concepts, Process, and Related Areas. Institutional Concepts included Advertising History, Advertising and Society, and Advertising and the Economy. Process included Advertising Organization, Advertising Research, Art and Layout, Copywriting, Legal Aspects of Advertising, Mechanical Production, Media Planning, Radio-TV Advertising, and Retail Advertising. Related Areas included Consumer Behavior, Communications Theory, Computer Technology, Magazine Article Writing, Marketing Concepts, Photography, and Public Relations.

The authors mentioned that when the group means were compared, the rankings by the students and by the practitioners were similar. "In descending order of importance these are: the process, related areas, and the institutional concepts. The educators ranked the institutional concepts above the related areas in importance" (Moore & Leckenby, 1973, p. 9). Students and practitioners agreed that skills courses were more important than theory courses, but the educators thought the theory courses were more important. In individual areas of content there were significant differences between evaluations of educators and students. These included Advertising and Society, Art and Layout, Copywriting, Mechanical Production, and Photography. Differences between educators and students occurred in these individual areas of content because of their attitudes toward the subject's importance in the advertising curriculum. Significant differences between practitioners and educators and between practitioners and educators and between practitioners and students occurred in four categories: Art and Layout, Mechanical Production, Retail Advertising, and Magazine Article Writing. Significant differences between practitioners and students occurred in two categories: Advertising and the Economy and Communications Theory.

Two years later Gifford and Maggard (1975, p. 13) surveyed chief executives of 526 advertising agencies to learn their attitudes toward advertising education. The response rate was 49.2%. In addition to learning about their preferred academic degrees for anyone pursuing a career in advertising, the authors asked those surveyed to design an "ideal" curriculum of 15 courses (out of 45 provided) for students pursuing a career in advertising. Table 15.8 not only lists their final choices but ranks the courses' importance as well:

TABLE 15.8
The "Ideal" Curriculum

FIRST:	Marketing
	English
	Introduction to Advertising
SECOND:	Journalism
	Psychology
	Creative Strategy
THIRD:	Speech/Communication
	Sociology
	Copywriting
FOURTH:	Economics/Commercial Art
	Humanities
	Media Strategy/Advertising
	Design and Layout
FIFTH:	Management
	Theatre
	Advertising Campaigns

In 1980 Marquez surveyed presidents of 118 advertising agencies in Pennsylvania and New York. The response rate was 43.2%, and Marquez learned that the majority believed an education in advertising was useful in preparing one for a career in advertising. He also learned that the respondents believed the following courses, which have been listed in descending order of importance, should be included in an advertising curriculum: Principles of Advertising; Advertising Management; Advertising Research; Advertising Copywriting; Advertising Psychology; Advertising Law and Ethics (p. 46).

Johenning and Mazey (1984) of the New York Institute of Technology surveyed presidents and managers of advertising agencies across the nation to determine the ideal curriculum for an undergraduate advertising program. Of the 3,040 questionnaires mailed, 445 (15%) were returned. The ideal curriculum in advertising included the following in descending order of importance: Marketing, Advertising Principles, Advertising Copywriting, Advertising Media, and Marketing Research. Other courses were mentioned as least important. These included: Advertising Print Production, Merchandising, Business-to-business Advertising, Television Commercial Production, and Advertising's Role in Society (p. 39).

In 1984 Doerner reported on the University of Missouri's School of Journalism's Future Committee's *Communications 1990*, a report that attempted to identify changes in mass communications by the end of the 1980s. In response to the report, the Department of Advertising revamped its curriculum. The course Ad Sales was replaced with Introduction to Selling for the Mass Media, and Retail was dropped altogether. Five new courses were added: Promotional Writing, Introduction to Selling for the Mass Media, Research in Advertising, Creative Strategy and Tactics, and Sales Promotion. The curriculum for advertising majors included the following required courses: Advertising Principles and Practices (3 hours), Graphics (2 hours), Ad Copy, Layout and Production (3 hours), Introduction to Selling (3 hours), and 9 hours of advertising electives from Retail Advertising (2 hours), Advertising Sales (3 hours), Research in Advertising (2 hours), Creative Strategy/Tactics (2 hours), Sales Promotion (2 hours), Advertising Psychology (2 hours), Advertising Campaigns (2 hours), Broadcast Advertising (3 hours), Direct and Mail Order Advertising (2 hours), Markets and Media (2 hours), Advertising Management (2 hours), International Advertising (2 hours), and Public Relations (3 hours) (pp. 19-20.)

The same year Kim Rotzoll (former chair, Department of Advertising, now dean, College of Communication, University of Illinois) and Arnold Barban (chair, Department of Advertising-Public Relations, University of Alabama) discussed the changes of advertising education from its earliest beginnings to the early 1980s and claimed that practitioners believed "that advertising is a business best learned 'on the job.' Yet those championing advertising education, at least those polled, seem to be questing for the corpus. To oversimplify, they seem to be saying send us young men and women who have a foundation in advertising, but are broadly educated. We'll provide the specialized training" (1984, p. 16). However, Rotzoll and Barban (1984) claimed that such a core existed primarily as a result of changes in the curriculum. The core's content consisted of the following: "The nature and organization of the advertising business. The research function. The creative function. The media function. Synthesis" (p. 16).

In 1985, Rotzoll discussed the future of advertising education and claimed that two premises had occurred. He wrote:

> *Advertising education will continue to reflect existing advertising practice* . . . . The more inductive approaches will follow the business trends toward specialization, with a growing number of course offerings in direct marketing, new communications technologies, and the like . . . . In general, advertising education will continue to take on the configurations of the business itself.
> *Advertising education may mature, by concentrating on a deductive, principles-first approach built around a corpus of knowledge in advertising's enduring areas of concern.* (pp. 40-41)

Rotzoll preferred the second premise, which was not based on skill or practical hands-on knowledge, on which to build a curriculum in advertising. The University of Missouri's Department of Advertising had adopted the first premise, however, as illustrated by the kinds of courses it offered, and many advertising programs copied Missouri's.

In 1988 Kent Lancaster, Helen Katz, and Jungsik Cho (1990) surveyed 692 members of the American Academy of Advertising "to examine the perceptions and activities of teachers concerning the gap between advertising education and the industry" (1990, p. 13). Although 349 members responded, only 283 (41%) indicated that they taught a course in advertising. Consequently, these were used to calculate the results. In addition to providing demographic information about the respondents, the authors learned that the following courses were taught on a regular basis: Introduction to Advertising (56%), Advertising Management (42%), Advertising Campaigns (36%), Copywriting (24%), Advertising Media Planning (22%), Advertising Research Methods (19%), Social and Ethical Issues (12%), Advanced Copywriting (10%), Marketing (7%), Advanced Research Methods (7%), Promotion (7%), Consumer Behavior (6%), Direct Marketing (5%), Layout and Design (5%) (p. 15).

As the authors mentioned, the courses comprising the core of most advertising programs came out on top: Introduction to Advertising, Advertising Management, Advertising Campaigns, Copywriting, Advertising Media Planning, and Advertising Research Methods.

In 1989, members of the Advertising Task Force of the Task Force on the Future of Journalism and Mass Communication Education surveyed advertising educators and advertising practitioners to determine their perceptions of what makes a strong advertising program. There were 523 usable responses for an 80% response rate. Among the findings, the members learned the following:

RATINGS OF IMPORTANCE OF SPECIALIZED COURSES

Professors' and practitioners' average ratings of the importance of 14 specialized courses offered in typical communications- or journalism-centered advertising programs. Average ratings are based on a 5-point "very important-not important" scale, with 1 = very important (see Table 15.9).

For the most part, professors and practitioners agreed about a specialization in advertising, and ranked most courses similarly. The major discrepancy was in the importance of an Advertising Internship, which the professors placed eighth and the practitioners placed first.

In 1990 Dennis Ganahl and Richard Ganahl III (1992) surveyed chairs or sequence heads of 97 advertising programs to determine the status of advertising education. Sixty-five (67%) responded. The authors learned that 88% of the respondents offered Advertising Campaigns. Other courses offered by at least 80% of the respondents were: Public Relations (85%), Copywriting (85%), and Media Strategy Planning (83%). Print Advertising Design was offered by 70% of the respondents while Television Advertising Production was offered by 63%. Six other courses were offered by at least 50% of the respondents: Advertising Management (59%), Creative Strategy and Tactics (57%), Advertising Ethics and Law (54%), Advertising Research (54%), Radio Advertising Production (54%), and Media Sales (52%). The remaining courses were offered by less than 40% of the respondents. These included: Retail Advertising (39%), Sales Promotion

(35%), Direct and Mail Order Advertising (28%), and History of Advertising (26%) (pp. 13-14).

TABLE 15.9
Average Ratings

Specialization	Professors	Practitioners
Principles of Advertising	1.16 (1)	1.44 (2)
Advertising Copywriting	1.21 (2)	1.48 (4)
Advertising Strategy	1.28 (3)	1.46 (3)
Advertising Media/Planning	1.34 (4)	1.51 (6)
Advertising Research	1.50 (5)	1.50 (5)
Consumer Behavior	1.53 (6)	1.54 (7)
Creative Design/Layout	1.58 (7)	1.72 (8)
Advertising Internship	1.59 (8)	1.41 (1)
Communication Ethics/Law	1.81 (9)	1.94 (12)
Advertising Sales	2.25 (10)	1.80 (9)
Promotions	2.27 (11)	1.87 (10)
Retail Advertising	2.40 (12)	1.89 (11)
Advertising History	2.69 (13)	2.59 (13)
International Advertising	2.83 (14)	2.60 (14)

Based on these studies, the curriculum in advertising programs, much like the curriculum in other aspects of journalism and/or mass communications, has changed in the sense that more courses in advertising have been developed and added. Whether this increase has been a response to practitioner criticism or a response to the changes within the profession or a response to faculty desire is anyone's guess. This writer believes that all three have been responsible–at least, indirectly if not directly–for the number of courses that have been added to the advertising curriculum. Although certain courses such as Principles of Advertising, Advertising Copywriting and/or Layout, Advertising Campaigns, Advertising Media, and Advertising Problems or Advertising Research have been around a long time and comprise the core of many programs, courses such as Advertising Management, Television Advertising Production, Radio Advertising Production, Advertising Law and Ethics, among others, have been added to the curriculum. However, the philosophies on which many advertising programs are based have not been replaced. Indeed, certain academicians believe that more advertising programs today have a practical or skills-oriented curriculum, which is based on Lee's and Eliot's proposals, than a principles-oriented one. Rotzoll and Barban (1984), for instance, claimed that the curriculum of most advertising programs contained skills courses. They reminded readers that a *curriculum* was "a *systematic* progression through a recognized body of knowledge" (p. 16). According to them, programs in advertising needed to change from a skills orientation to a principles orientation in order to gain credibility among advertising professionals. Of course, it should be mentioned that another change has occurred as a result of certain accreditation bodies revising their accrediting guidelines. As mentioned, the ACEJMC and the AACSB limit the number of hours (courses) one may earn in the major, and both associations emphasize more hours (courses) in liberal arts and sciences.

THE CURRICULUM IN THE 21ST CENTURY

The Task Force on Integrated Communications (Duncan, Caywood, & Newsom, 1993) report, *Preparing Advertising and Public Relations Students for the Communications Industry in the 21st Century*, uses the Oregon Report, *Planning for Curricular Change* (1984), and Blanchard and Christ's (1993) book, *Media Education and the Liberal Arts: A Blueprint for the New Professionalism*, to stress integration. A debate concerning advertising and public relations curriculum ensued. The idea of merging public relations with an area of marketing in the professional environment had been discussed as early as 1969 by Kotler and Levy. Kotler continued the discussion in 1972, and he and Mindak discussed the issue further in 1978. They even discussed the educational gap between the two disciplines:

> The counseling potential of the public relations director depends on his being 'a thorough going professional, seasoned and skilled.' This begs the question of what training a fully effective public relations director should have. The present arrangements for training public relations people leave a great deal to be desired. Public relations people receive their training for the most part in schools of journalism, which equip them to spell but hardly to understand economics and take a management point of view. Business schools still refuse to offer majors or even courses in public relations. Thus there is a serious educational gap. (1978, p. 20)

Perhaps in response to Kotler and other academicians advocating change as well as the major strides made in technology and productivity that occurred in the 1980s, Northwestern University, which had offered separate graduate programs in corporate public relations, advertising, and direct marketing, fused the programs into an integrated marketing communications program. Although Northwestern's program actually came after a similar graduate program was launched by the College of St. Thomas in Minneapolis, it was Northwestern's that received considerable recognition. Similar graduate programs have started at the University of Colorado at Boulder and the University of Alabama, Tuscaloosa. However, the first university to integrate public relations and advertising at the undergraduate level was Texas Christian University, which recognized in 1974 that the roles of public relations and advertising practitioners were similar; consequently, these professionals' educational needs were similar. According to Rose and Miller (1993), there were at least 12 undergraduate pro-grams with integrated marketing communications emphases in 1993 (p. 22). The public relations/advertising sequence at Texas Christian University required 33 hours.

The required courses included Communication in Society, Media Writing and Editing I and II, Advertising Principles, Public Relations Principles, Copy, Layout and Production, Writing for Public Relations and Advertising, and Media Analysis and Research. Elective courses included Reporting, Broadcast News, Public Relations and Advertising Cases and Problems, Internship, Campaigns, International and InterCultural Communications, and Public Opinion and Persuasion (*Preparing Advertising and Public Relations Students for the Communications Industry in the 21st Century*, 1993, p. 21).

What incited certain academicians to either initiate or contemplate changes in advertising programs? According to the Task Force on Integrated Communications, they realized that (a) industry was moving toward integrated marketing communications; (b) customers were integrating more information into their purchasing decisions; (c) the integration concept was being used more in management; (d) communication agencies were moving away from traditional practices and were offering more services; and (e) integrated marketing communications was being used outside the United States (*Preparing Advertising and Public Relations Students for the Communications Industry in the 21st Century*, 1993, pp. Appendix 13-17). In essence, if certain programs in advertising had as their primary function to teach students the necessary skills and principles required for employment, then these programs had to offer a curriculum that reflected the profession. In the late 1980s and early 1990s, advertising agencies either merged with public relations firms or started public relations departments. Chairs and heads of certain advertising departments and sequences realized that their curriculum needed overhauling. Others, however, had a "wait and see" attitude; to this day, they have refused to revamp their program's curriculum. Certain administrators and faculty who are in public relations, for instance, have not seen the need to create an integrated marketing communications curriculum. And the Educational Affairs Committee (EAC) of the Public Relations Society of America issued a statement opposing the recommendations of the report by the Task Force on Integrated Communications. The EAC claimed that the functions of advertising, marketing, and public relations fulfilled different purposes (Miller & Rose, 1994). Nonetheless, it is this writer's belief that more programs in public relations will cooperate with programs in advertising and together offer what could be considered an integrated marketing communications curriculum.

MODEL CURRICULA FOR THE FUTURE

For small, liberal arts colleges and universities that have few faculty and resources, the ideal curriculum in advertising for the present and the future should include courses in public relations. For instance, the following curriculum combines the two areas: *Core Courses* = 9 hours (three courses): Journalism and/or Mass Communications; *Required Courses* = 18 hours (six courses): Principles of Advertising and Public Relations, Advertising and Public Relations Creative Strategy (Design), Advertising and Public Relations Campaigns, Advertising and Public Relations Communications (Copy), Public Relations Publications, Advertising and Public Relations Management; *Elective Courses* =

9 hours (three courses): Internship, Advertising Research, Advertising Media, Public Relations Case Studies, Advertising and Public Relations Law.

For large colleges and universities that have many faculty and resources, the ideal curriculum in advertising for the present and the future should include courses in public relations. For instance, the following curriculum includes courses from the two areas: *Core Courses* = 6 hours (two courses): Journalism and/or Mass Communications; *Required Courses* = 21 hours (seven courses): Principles of Advertising, Advertising Creative Strategy (Design and Copy), Advertising Campaigns, Advertising Media, Advertising Management, Principles of Public Relations, Public Relations Communications; *Elective Courses* = 9 hours (three courses): Internship, Advertising Research, Issues in Advertising, Public Relations Publications, Public Relations Case Studies, Public Relations Campaigns, Advertising, and Public Relations Law.

Of course, certain titles could be changed to better reflect the content. Furthermore, instead of having separate courses that discuss certain aspects of advertising and public relations, one course may be designed to cover both areas. These curricula certainly have possibilities and are, in the writer's opinion, in the right direction. However, this writer suggests that administrators and faculty consider the following before they change or design a curriculum: (a) course content–what needs to be taught based on goals/purpose of the program; (b) course requirements–what kinds of assignments and how many based on goals/purpose of the course; (c) instructional strategy–what method of instruction based on goals/purpose of the course; (d) student outcomes; and (e) accreditation guidelines concerning the curriculum.

Assessing the Ideal Curriculum in Advertising

Advertising curricula must be assessed by several criteria (see Banta and Associates, 1993).

1. Accreditation. The first is the accrediting body. As mentioned, the ACEJMC and the AACSB have accreditation guidelines that stipulate certain requirements such as number of hours permitted in the major discipline. Of course, these accrediting bodies' guidelines differ, as Table 15.10 illustrates.

If an advertising program is located in an ACEJMC accredited school of journalism and/or mass communications, it will offer a curriculum that is different in focus from that of a program found in an AACSB accredited school of business.

2. Professional Community/Industry. The second is the needs of the professional community that the program and university serves. The chair or head of the program or sequence must keep abreast of the changes occurring in the professional community, as well as understand the professional community's needs. This information can be obtained by attending professional meetings such as those sponsored by the local chapter affiliated with the American Advertising Federation or the local chapter affiliated with the Public Relations Society of America. Also, members from the professional community may

TABLE 15.10
Course Requirements of ACEJMC and AACSB

ACEJMC	Semester System:	90 hours outside major; 65 hours in the liberal arts and sciences; 6 hours can be applied from major toward liberal arts and sciences section.
	Quarter System:	131 hours outside major; 94 hours in liberal arts and sciences.
AACSB	Semester/Quarter System:	50% of coursework outside business major.

serve on panels to review the curriculum and the overall program to determine whether the courses meet their expectations. Feedback from professionals should be valued by administrators and faculty.

3. Faculty. The third is faculty expertise. Faculty should be qualified academically and professionally in the areas they teach.

4. Students. The fourth is students and their academic needs. If the courses selected by students match the professionals' expectations, students should benefit by obtaining entry-level positions in the careers of their choice upon graduation. This should be the primary purpose of the curriculum. Of course, student evaluations may provide insight about course content and their instructors.

5. Internship. The fifth is the internship. Internships benefit students by allowing them the opportunity to experience the field they have chosen. Internships benefit faculty and administrators by the feedback from the students' supervisors. Strengths and weaknesses of students provided by supervisors may imply that certain courses need to be deleted from or added to the curriculum.

6. Evaluation. The sixth is the senior survey. Before students graduate they should be given a questionnaire about the curriculum. Each course and the overall program may be evaluated in-depth by students. This information may be extremely valuable, especially if students feel free to express what is right as well as what is wrong with the curriculum and the program.

7. Budgeting. The seventh is the budget. Certain courses, especially those in the creative aspects of advertising and public relations, require more in goods and services than other kinds of courses. If these courses are required, more money must be allocated for supplies and equipment. Even courses such as Advertising Media and Advertising Campaigns may require computers, which may be expensive to purchase and maintain. Also, some courses may require certain qualified faculty. A program may have to hire at a greater expense to the institution a person with a particular expertise.

Other criteria may exist, but the ones mentioned earlier will be helpful to anyone responsible for designing or assessing the curriculum, which may or may not be easy, depending on what resources and faculty are available. For instance, each course that is added, deleted, or merged with another may effect faculty workloads, scheduling, and probably the budget. Thus, designing or assessing the curriculum should be performed by a committee, not just one person such as the dean of the college or chair of the department, and the committee must weigh all the variables, not just a few. For instance, what impact will a change have on the faculty, curriculum, department, college, and/or university? Such questions have to be answered before one change can be implemented. However, change may be seen as a positive step, but change should not occur just for the sake of change. In order for change to be effective, it must benefit everyone involved, especially the students.

REFERENCES

Accredited journalism and mass communication education: 1993-94 (1993). Accrediting Council on Education in Journalism and Mass Communications. Lawrence: University of Kansas.

Allen, C. L. (1960). *Survey of advertising courses and census of advertising teachers.* Research study for the American Academy of Advertising. Stillwater: Oklahoma State University.

Allen, C. L. (1962). *Advertising majors in American colleges and universities 1962.* A report prepared for the American Academy of Advertising. Stillwater: Oklahoma State University.

Banta, T. W., & Associates (1993). *Making a difference: Outcomes of a decade of assessment in higher education.* San Francisco: Jossey-Bass.

Blanchard, R. O., & Christ, W. G. (1993). *Media education and the liberal arts: A blueprint for the new professionalism.* Hillsdale, NJ: Lawrence Erlbaum Associates.

Challenges and opportunities in journalism and mass communication education (1989). A report of the task force on the future of journalism and mass communication education. Columbia, MO: Association for Education in Journalism and Mass Communication.

Doerner, R. C. (1984). Advertising program revised to prepare for needs of 1990s. *Journalism Educator, 39*(1), 18-20..

Duncan, T., Caywood, C., & Newsom, D. (1993). *Preparing advertising and public relations students for the communications industry in the 21st Century .* A Report of the Task Force on Integrated Communications. Columbia, SC: AEJMC.

Ford, J. L. C. (1947). *A study of the pre-war curricula of selected schools of journalism.* Unpublished doctoral dissertation, University of Minnesota, Minneapolis.

Fryburger, V. (1959). Better education for advertising. *Proceedings from American association of advertising agencies.* Paper presented at the 1959 Regional Conference, Chicago.

Ganahl, D. J., & Ganahl, R. J., III. (1992). *Assessing baccalaureate advertising education outcome utilizing marketing education curriculum development strategies.* Paper presented at the Annual Meeting of the Association for Education in Journalism and Mass Communication, Montreal, Canada.

Gifford, J. B., & Maggard, J. P. (1975). Top agency executives' attitudes toward academic preparation for careers in the advertising profession in 1975. *Journal of Advertising, 4*(4), 9-14.

Hagerty, J. E. (1936). Experiences of an early marketing teacher. *Journal of Marketing, 1*(1), 20-27.

How colleges and universities educate future practitioners in advertising (1963, January 15), *Advertising Age* , p. 224.

Johenning, J., & Mazey, J. (1984). Professionals rate ideal curriculum for ad majors. *Journalism Educator, 39*(3), 38-40.

The journalists' creed. (1930, July). *University of Missouri Bulletin,* (p. 2). Columbia, MO: The University of Missouri.

Kotler, P. (1972). A generic concept of marketing. *Journal of Marketing, 35*(2), 46-54.

Kotler, P., & Levy, S. J. (1969). Broadening the concept of marketing. *Journal of Marketing, 32*(1), 10-15.

Kotler, P., & Mindak, W. (1978). Marketing and public relations: Should they be partners or rivals? *Journal of Marketing, 42*(4), 13-20.

Lancaster, K. M., Katz, H. E., & Cho, J. (1990). Advertising faculty describes theory v. practice debate. *Journalism Educator, 45*(1), 9-21.

Lee, J. M. (1918). *Instruction in journalism in institutions of higher education.* Washington: U. S. Bulletin No. 21, Department of Interior, Bureau of Education.

Link, G., Jr., & Dykes, J. E. (1959). Advertising course offerings of accredited schools. *Journalism Quarterly, 36*(1), 64-65.

Litman, S. (1950). The beginnings of teaching marketing in American universities. *Journal of Marketing, 15*(2), 220-223.

Maynard, H. H. (1941). Marketing courses prior to 1910. *Journal of Marketing, 5*(4), 382-384.

Marquez, F. T. (1980). Agency presidents rank ad courses, job opportunities. *Journalism Educator, 35*(2), 46-47.

McGarrity, R. A. (1959). *A survey of Milwaukee's advertising men and women to determine their background and opinion on modern education for advertising.* A Report Prepared for Robert A. Johnson College of Business Administration, Marquette University. Milwaukee, WI: Bureau of Business and Economic Research.

Miller, D. A., & Rose, P. B. (1994). Integrated communications: A look at reality instead of theory. *Public Relations Quarterly, 39*(1), 13-16.

Moore, F., & Leckenby, J. (1973). The quality of advertising education today. *Journal of Advertising, 2*(2), 6-10.

1990-92 accreditation council policies, procedures, and standards. (1990). St. Louis, MO: American Assembly of Collegiate Schools of Business.

O'Dell, D. (1935). *The history of journalism education in the United States.* New York: Teachers College Press: Columbia University.

Planning for curricular change in journalism education: Project on the future of journalism and mass communication (Oregon Report). (1984). Eugene: School of Journalism, University of Oregon.

Pulitzer, J. (1904). The college of journalism. *North American Review, 178*(5), 641-680.

Rose, P. B., & Miller, D. A. (1993). Integrated communications and practitioners' perceived needs. *Journalism Educator, 48*(1), 20-27.

Ross, B. I. (1991). *The status of advertising education.* Lubbock, TX: Advertising Education Publications.

Ross, B. I. (1965). *Advertising education: Programs in four-year American colleges and universities.* Lubbock: Texas Tech Press.

Ross, B. I., & Johnson, K. F. (1993). *Where shall I go to study advertising and public relations?.* Baton Rouge, LA: Advertising Education Publications.

Rotzoll, K. B. (1985). Future advertising education: Ideas on a tentative discipline. *Journalism Educator, 40*(3), 37-41.

Rotzoll, K. B., & Barban, A. M. (1984). Advertising education. *Current Issues and Research in Advertising, Vol. 2,* 1-18.

Sandage, C. H. (1955). A philosophy of advertising education. *Journalism Quarterly, 32*(2), 209-211.

Standards for business and accounting accreditation. (1991). St. Louis, MO: American Assembly of Collegiate Schools of Business.

Sutton, A. A. (1945). *Education for journalism in the United States from its beginning to 1940.* Evanston, IL: Northwestern University Press.

The training of journalists: A world-wide survey on the training of personnel for the mass media. (1958). Paris: UNESCO.

University of Missouri bulletin (1959, October 15). Columbia: University of Missouri.

Williams, S. L. (1929). *Twenty years of education for journalism.* Columbia, MO: Stephens Publishing.

AUTHOR INDEX

SUBJECT INDEX

Criteria for the Assessment of
Oral Communication

Speech Communication Association

A National Context

Assessment has received increasing attention throughout the 1970s and into the 1990s. Initially appearing in the standards developed by state departments of education, by 1980 over half of the states had adopted statewide student-testing programs. In *Educational Standards in the 50 States: 1990,* the Educational Testing Service reported that by 1985, over 40 states had adopted such programs, and between 1985 and 1990, an additional five states initiated statewide student-testing programs, bringing the number of such program to 47.

During the 1970s and 1980s, the number of different subjects and skills tested has also consistently increased, with additional attention devoted to how assessments are executed. Moreover, during this period, organizations, such as the National Assessment of Educational Progress, intensified and expanded the scope of their assessment procedures as well as extensively publi-

cized the results of their findings nationally and annually.

By the end of 1989, the public recognized the significance of national educational assessments. In the *Phi Delta Kappan*-Gallup poll reported in the September 1989 issue of Phi Delta Kappan, 77 percent of the respondents favored "requiring the public schools in this community to use standardized national testing programs to measure academic achievement of students" and 70 percent favored "requiring the public schools in this community to conform to national achievement standards and goals."

Likewise, towards the end of the 1980s, colleges and universities began to realize that formal assessment issues were to affect them. For example, in its 1989-1990 *Criteria for Accreditation,* the Southern Association of Colleges and Schools—which provides institutional certification for over 800 colleges and universities in the South—held that "complete requirements for an associate or baccalaureate degree must include competence in reading, writing, oral communications and fundamental mathematical skills." They also held that the general education core of colleges and universities "must provide components designed to ensure competence in reading, writing, oral communication and fundamental mathematical skills."

In 1990, a series of reports appeared which suggested that systematic and comprehensive assessment should become a national educational objective. In February 1990, for example, the National Governors' Association, in the context of President Bush's set of six educational goals, argued that, "National educa tion goals will be meaningless unless progress toward meeting them is measured accurately and adequately, and reported to the American people." The nation's Governors argued that "doing a good job of assessment" requires that "what students need to know must be defined," "it must be determined whether they know it," and "measurements must be accurate, comparable, appropriate, and constructive." In July 1990, President Bush reinforced this line of reasoning in *The National Education Goals: A Report to the Nation's Governors.* And, in September 1990, the National Governors' Association extended and elaborated its commitment to assessment in *Educating America: State Strategies for Achieving the National Education Goals: Report of the Task Force on Education.*

Additionally, in 1990, in their report *From Gatekeeper to Gateway: Transforming Testing in America,* the National Commission on Testing and Public Policy recommended eight standards for assessment, arguing for more humane and multicultural assessment systems. Among other considerations, they particularly maintained that "testing policies and practices must be reoriented to promote the development of all human talent," that "test scores should be used only when they differentiate on the basis of characteristics relevant to the opportunities being allocated," and that "the more test scores disproportionately deny opportunities to minorities, the greater the need to show that the tests measure characteristics relevant to the opportunities being allocated."

SCA's Assessment Activities

The evaluation and assessment of public address has been of central concern to the discipline of communication since its inception and to the Speech Communication Association when it was organized in 1914. In 1970, SCA formalized its commitment to assessment when it created the Committee on Assessment and Testing (now known by the acronym CAT) for "SCA members interested in gathering, analyzing and disseminating information about the testing of speech communication skills." CAT has been one of the most active, consistent, and productive of SCA's various committees and task forces.

Under the guidance of CAT, SCA has published several volumes exploring formal methods for assessing oral communication. These publications began to appear in the 1970s and have continued into the 1990s. In 1978, for example, the Speech Communication Association published *Assessing Functional Communication,* which was followed in 1984 by two other major publications, *Large Scale Assessment of Oral Communication Skills: Kindergarten through Grade 12* and *Oral Communication Assessment Procedures and Instrument Development in Higher Education.*

In 1979, in *Standards for Effective Oral Communication Programs,* SCA adopted its first set of "standards" for "assessment and evaluation." The first standards called for "school-wide assessment of speaking and listening needs of students," "qualified personnel" to "utilize appropriate evaluation tools," a "variety of data" and "instruments" which "encourage" "students' desire to communicate."

In 1986, in *Criteria for Evaluating Instruments and Procedures for Assessing Speaking and Listening,* SCA adopted an additional 15 "content" and "technical considerations" dealing "primarily with the substance of speaking and listening instruments" and "matters such as reliability, validity and information on administration." These criteria included the importance of focusing on "demonstrated" speaking skills rather than "reading and writing ability," adopting "assessment instruments and procedures" which are "free of sexual, cultural, racial, and ethnic content and/or stereotyping," employing "familiar situations" which are "important for various communication settings" in test questions, using instruments which "permit a range of acceptable responses" and generate "reliable" outcomes, employing assessments which are consistent with other "results" and have "content validity," and employing "standardized" procedures which "approximate the recognized stress level of oral communication" which are also "practical in terms of cost and time" and "suitable for the developmental level of the individual being tested."

In 1987, at the SCA Wingspread Conference, "conference participants recommended that the chosen instrument conform to SCA guidelines for assessment instruments," and they specifically suggested that "strategies for assessing speaking skills" should be directly linked to the content of oral communication performances and student speaking competencies. Prescribed communication practices were to determine the choice of assessment strategies, with the following content standards guiding formal evaluations: "determine the purpose of oral discourse;" "choose a topic and restrict it according to the purpose and the audience;" "fulfill the purpose" by "formulating a thesis statement," "providing adequate support material," "selecting a suitable organization," "demonstrating careful choice of words," "providing effective transitions," "demonstrating suitable interpersonal skills;" employing "vocal variety in rate, pitch, and intensity;" "articulate clearly;" "employ the level of American English appropriate to the designated audience;" and "demonstrate nonverbal behavior that supports the verbal message." Additionally, the Wingspread Conference participants considered strategies for assessing listening and for training assessors (see: *Communication Is Life: Essential College Sophomore Speaking and Listening Competencies,* Annandale, Va.: Speech Communication Association, 1990, pp. 51–74).

In 1988, the SCA Flagstaff Conference generated a series of resolutions calling for a "national conference" and "task force on assessment" because "previous experience in developing standardized assessment has met with problems of validity, reliability, feasibility, ethics, and cultural bias" (in *The Future of Speech Communication Education: Proceedings of the 1988 Speech Communication Association Flagstaff Conference,* ed. by Pamela J. Cooper and Kathleen M. Galvin, Annandale VA: Speech Communication Association, 1989, p. 80).

In July 1990, a National Conference on Assessment was sponsored by SCA, the SCA Committee on Assessment and Testing or CAT, and the SCA Educational Policies Board (EPB). The Conference generated several resolutions regarding assessment. Some of these resolutions reaffirmed existing SCA oral communication assessment policies. Others provided criteria for resolving new issues in assessment. Still others sought to integrate and establish a more coherent relationship among the criteria governing oral communication assessment. The recommended assessment criteria are detailed immediately below .

General Criteria

1. Assessment of oral communication should view competence in oral communication as a gestalt of several interacting dimensions. At a minimum, all assessments of oral communication should include an assessment of knowledge (understanding communication process, comprehension of the elements, rules, and dynamics of a communication event, awareness of what is appropriate in a communication situation), an assessment of skills (the possession of a repertoire of skills and the actual performance of skills), and an evaluation of the individual's attitude toward communication (e.g., value placed on oral communication, apprehension, reticence, willingness to communicate, readiness to communicate).

2. Because oral communication is an interactive and social process, assessment should consider the judgment of a trained assessor as well as the impressions of others involved in the communication act (audience, interviewer, other group members, conversant), and may include the self report of the individual being assessed.

3. Assessment of oral communication should clearly distinguish speaking and listening from reading and writing. While some parts of the assessment process may include reading and writing, a major portion of the assessment of oral communication should require speaking and listening. Directions from the assessor and responses by the individual being assessed should be in the oral/aural mode.

4. Assessment of oral communication should be sensitive to the effects of relevant physical and psychological disabilities on the assessment of competence. (e.g., with appropriate aids in signal reception, a hearing impaired person can be a competent empathic listener.)

5. Assessment of oral communication should be based in part on atomistic/analytic data collected and on a holistic impression.

5. Criteria for the Content of Assessment

1. Assessment of oral communication for all students should include assessment of both verbal and nonverbal aspects of communication and should consider competence in more than one communication setting. As a minimum assessment should occur in the one-to-many setting (e.g. public speaking, practical small group discussion) and in the one-to-one setting (e.g., interviews, interpersonal relations).

2. Assessment of speech majors and other oral communication specialists could include in addition assessment in specialized fields appropriate to the course of study followed or the specialty of the person being assessed.

2. Criteria for Assessment Instruments

1. The method of assessment should be consistent with the dimension of oral communication being assessed. While knowledge and attitude may be assessed in part through paper and pencil instruments, speaking and listening skills must be assessed through actual performance in social settings (speaking before an audience, undergoing an interview, participating in a group discussion, etc.) appropriate to the skill(s) being assessed.

2. Instruments for assessing oral communication should describe degrees of competence. Either/or descriptions such as "competent" or "incompetent" should be avoided as should attempts to diagnose reasons why individuals demonstrate or fail to demonstrate particular degrees of competence.

3. Instruments for assessing each dimension of oral communication competence should clearly identify the range of responses which constitute various degrees of competence. Examples of such responses should be provided as anchors.

4. Assessment instruments should have an acceptable level of reliability, e.g. test/retest reliability, split-half reliability, alternative forms reliability, inter-rater reliability, and internal consistency.

5. Assessment instruments should have appropriate validity: content validity, predictive validity, and concurrent validity.

6. Assessment instruments must meet acceptable standards for freedom from cultural, sexual, ethical, racial, age, and developmental bias.

7. Assessment instruments should be suitable for the developmental level of the individual being assessed.

8. Assessment instruments should be standardized and detailed enough so that individual responses will not be affected by an administrator's skill in administering the procedures.

8. Criteria for Assessment Procedures and Administration

1. Assessment procedures should protect the rights of those being assessed in the following ways: administration of assessment instruments and assessment and the uses of assessment results should be kept confidential and be released only to an appropriate institutional office, to the individual assessed, or if a minor, to his or her parent or legal guardian.

2. Use of competence assessment as a basis for procedural decisions con-

cerning an individual should, when feasible, be based on multiple sources of information, including especially a) direct evidence of actual communication performance in school and/or other contexts, b) results of formal competence assessment, and c) measures of individual attitudes toward communication (e.g., value placed on oral communication, apprehension, reticence, willingness to communicate, and readiness to communicate).

3. Individuals administering assessment procedures for oral communication should have received sufficient training by speech communication professionals to make their assessment reliable. Scoring of some standardized assessment instruments in speaking and listening may require specialized training in oral communication on the part of the assessor.

3. Criteria for Assessment Frequency

Periodic assessment of oral communication competency should occur annually during the educational careers of students. An effective systematic assessment program minimally should Occur at educational levels K, 4, 8, 12, 14, and 16.

Criteria for the Use of Assessment Results

The results of student oral communication competency assessment should be used in an ethical, non-discriminatory manner for such purposes as:

1. Diagnosing student strengths and weaknesses;

2. Planning instructional strategies to address student strengths and weaknesses;

3. Certification of student readiness for entry into and exit from programs and institutions;

4. Evaluating and describing overall student achievement;

5. Screening students for programs designed for special populations;

6. Counseling students for academic and career options; and

7. Evaluating the effectiveness of instructional programs.

No single assessment instrument is likely to support all these purposes. Moreover, instruments appropriate to various or multiple purposes typically vary in length, breadth/depth of content, technical rigor, and format.

The criteria contained in this document were originally adopted as resolutions at the SCA Conference on Assessment in Denver, Colorado, in July of 1990. Several of the criteria were authored by the Committee on Assessment and Testing Subcommittee on Criteria for Content. Procedures, and Guidelines for Oral Communication Competencies composed of Jim Crocker-Lakness (Subcommittee Chair), Sandra Manheimer, and Tom Scott. The introductory sections entitled. "A National Context" and "SCA's Assessment Activities," were authored by James W. Chesebro, SCA Director of Education Services.

For further information on the assessment of communication, contact the Speech Communication Association, 5105 Backlick Rd. #F, Annandale   VA   22003;   703-750-0533; http://www.scassn.org